UNDERSTANDING ACCOUNTING STANDARDS

Understanding Accounting Standards

BY

Emile Woolf, FCA
Kingston Smith

and

Suresh Tanna, FCA
Emile Woolf and Associates

The Institute of Chartered Accountants
in England and Wales
in association with
McGraw-Hill Book Company

In publishing this book the Council of The Institute of Chartered Accountants in England and Wales considers that it is a worthwhile contribution to discussion, without necessarily sharing the views expressed, which are those of the authors.

No responsibility for loss occasioned to any person acting or refraining from action as a result of any material in this publication can be accepted by the authors or publisher.

© 1988 E. Woolf

ISBN 0 85291 945 X

First published in Great Britain in 1988 by
The Institute of Chartered Accountants in England and Wales,
Chartered Accountants Hall, Moorgate Place, London, EC2P 2EJ
in association with
McGraw-Hill Book Co. (UK) Ltd, Maidenhead, Berks.

All rights reserved. No part of this publication may be reproduced, stored in a retrieval system, or transmitted, in any form or by any means, electronic, mechanical, photocopying, recording or otherwise, without the prior permission of the publisher.

Printed and bound in Great Britain by
Biddles Ltd, Guildford and King's Lynn

Preface

Accounting standards have become an integral feature in the life of accountants, whether they are in professional practice or working in commerce and industry. However, this is not a local phenomenon. International committees have extended the acceptance of standards in financial reporting to countries all over the world. It is almost impossible for those entering the profession now to conceive of a financial accounting framework devoid of SSAPs or their local equivalent. It is just as difficult for those of us whose professional careers spanned the point of inception of SSAPs in 1970 to recall 'how things were'.

The reason for such difficulty is that the SSAP framework did not in fact alter, update or even supersede a previous order, acceptable at the time. There simply *was* no such order or framework. Subject to the minimal and liberally interpreted requirements of the Companies Acts of 1948 and 1967, accounting was a veritable 'free-for-all'.

One of the authors of this text recalls a pre-Standards assignment for the BBC Money Programme, involving an analysis of the financial statements of a major UK listed company for successive years. The task was rendered doubly difficult by the fact that each year's set of accounts adopted its own brand of sub-headings freshly invented, and its own method of classifying items into particular sub-headings. As a result the disclosed comparatives bore no relationship to the published accounts of the previous year which they purported to represent!

Why the early seventies proved to be the watershed for this momentous initiative is not our immediate concern and has, in any case, been fully documented elsewhere. The purpose of this text is to provide practitioners, accountants in industry and commerce, teachers and students of accounting, and all others in related professions and occupations whose work requires an understanding of accounts, with an intelligible and straightforward guide to understanding the body of current UK SSAPs.

There is no shortage of textual material on SSAPs – indeed the ICAEW Accountants' Digest Series is an authoritative source for unravelling many complex issues raised in SSAPs. But there is, to our knowledge, no single text devoted to explaining both the rationale and the mechanics of each SSAP, together with illustrations wherever appropriate.

In facing this task, daunting in the case of certain SSAPs whose ramifications appear in places to defy all laws of reason and logic, we have not shunned the complexities. We have set as our objective the need to expound and explain the principal issues involved; the alternative approaches to resolving the problems raised by those issues; the solutions preferred and adopted by the standard in question; and any subsidiary difficulties entailed. Standards of the more numerate variety are further illustrated so that those who require a 'nuts and bolts' approach to applying SSAPs to the circumstances of a particular company will not be disappointed.

In the interests of improving the usefulness of the text to students, we have included additional questions at the end of each chapter, the solutions to which should be evident from careful reading of the relevant chapter.

We are most grateful to the Institute of Chartered Accountants in England and Wales and the Chartered Association of Certified Accountants for permission to reproduce examination questions where relevant to particular standards. We are also indebted to Stephen Cooper, MSc, FCCA for reading several of the more technical chapters and suggesting changes and additions which have undoubtedly improved the material presented here.

Contents

Chapter 1: The regulatory basis of accounting standards

The status of accounting standards
Truth and fairness
Objectives of the accounting standards
Explanatory foreword to Statements of Standard Accounting Practice
Review of the standard-setting process – a report by the ASC published in 1983
Arguments for and against the setting of mandatory accounting standards
Small companies and accounting standards
Questions

Chapter 2: Accounting principles

SSAP 2 – Disclosure of accounting policies
SSAP 17 – Post-balance sheet events
SSAP 18 – Accounting for contingencies
Off-balance sheet finance
Conceptual framework of accounting
Profits available for distribution
Questions

Chapter 3: Extraordinary items and prior year adjustments

Concept of profit
Extraordinary items
Presentation
Exceptional items
Prior year adjustment
Terminated activities
Revaluation and realisation of fixed assets

Reserve movements
Questions

Chapter 4: Accounting for depreciation

Conceptual background
The cost or revaluation of the asset
The residual value
The useful life
The depreciation method
SSAP 12 (as revised in 1987)
Standard accounting practice
SSAP 19 Accounting for investment properties
Question

Chapter 5: SSAP 9 and ED 40: Stocks, work in progress and long-term contracts

Principles
Methods of determining costs
Net realisable value
Disclosures
Long-term contracts
The SSAP 9 approach
Calculating attributable profit
Other ways of calculating attributable profit
Other considerations
Contracts which are expected to make losses
Disclosure
Problems with SSAP 9 approach
The ED 40 approach
Question

Chapter 6: SSAP 13 and ED 41: Accounting for research and development

SSAP 13 Accounting for research and development
Pure and applied research
Development expenditure
ED 41 Accounting for research and development
Question

CONTENTS

Chapter 7: SSAP 8: The treatment of taxation under the imputation system in the accounts of companies

Corporation tax
Dividends
Franked investment income
Advance corporation tax
Rules regarding ACT set off against corporation tax
SSAP 8 – Standard accounting practice
Unfranked income and payments
Taxation in accounts: a detailed example

Chapter 8: SSAP 15: Accounting for deferred taxation

The principles
Methods of computation
SSAP 15 (Revised) approach
Criteria for assessing whether deferred tax liabilities or assets will or will not crystallise
Differences between the original SSAP 15 and revised SSAP 15
Accounting for deferred tax on timing differences
Revaluations not incorporated in the accounts
Deferred tax debit balances
Trading losses
Capital losses
Short-term timing differences
Advance corporation tax
Disclosure of deferred tax in financial statements
Detailed example
Question

Chapter 9: Accounting for investments (1)

Methods of recognising investments
Circumstances under which each method is appropriate
SSAP 1: Accounting for associated companies
Bases of accounting for associated companies
Deficiency of net assets in associated company
Other points
Arguments for and against the use of equity method for associated companies

ix

Absence of consolidated accounts
Questions

Chapter 10: Accounting for Investments (2): SSAP 14 Group Accounts

SSAP 14 Requirements
Consolidated financial statements
Reasons for preparing consolidated accounts
Arguments against preparing consolidated financial statements
Exclusion from consolidation
Reasons for having non-coterminous dates
Changes in the composition of the group
Other considerations (SSAP 14)
Questions

Chapter 11: Accounting for Investments (3): SSAP 22: Accounting for Goodwill

Fixed asset without amortisation
Fixed asset subject to amortisation
Immediate write off to profit and loss account
Carry-forward as a deduction from reserves
SSAP 22: Accounting for goodwill
Measurement of goodwill
Purchased goodwill
Amortisation
Negative goodwill
Purchased goodwill – some current practices
Question

Chapter 12: Accounting for investments (4): Accounting for business combinations

Acquisition accounting
Merger accounting
Mechanics
Background to the merger method
Merger relief
SSAP 23: Accounting for acquisitions and mergers

Conclusion
Questions

Chapter 13: Accounting for Investments (5): SSAP 20: Accounting for foreign currency translations

Accounting procedures
The individual company stage
Forward contracts
Consolidated financial statements
The closing rate method (Net investment method)
The temporal method
Choice of method
Foreign equity investments financed by foreign loans
Associated companies
Foreign branches
SSAP 20 and distributable profits
Disclosures
Detailed example
Question

Chapter 14: Accounting for leases and hire purchase contracts

Finance lease
SSAP 21 definition
Operating lease
Accounting treatment
Hire purchase
Operating leases in lessor's books
Questions

Chapter 15: Earnings per share

Earnings on Net and Nil basis
Equity share capital
Fully diluted earnings per share
A detailed example
Usefulness of the earnings per share figure

UNDERSTANDING ACCOUNTING STANDARDS

Problems that may arise in practice from the interpretation of earnings per share
Questions

Chapter 16: SSAP 10: Statements of source of application of funds

Formats
Detailed example
Solution to detailed example
Question

Appendix 1: The accounting treatment of government grants

Appendix 2: Accounting for value added tax

Appendix 3: Accounting for pension costs

Index

Chapter 1
The regulatory basis of accounting standards

The Status of Accounting Standards

1.1 Perhaps the greatest accolade which can be accorded the Accounting Standards Committee (ASC) of the UK accountancy bodies is that life without Accounting Standards is difficult to imagine. Yet the ASC's existence spans only 18 years and in that time its efforts have resulted in 23 Standards, several of which have been extensively revised in the light of external developments, chiefly economic or legislative.

1.2 Prior to the inception of Standards financial reporting was a hit-and-miss affair with consistency pretty low in the order of priority. Accounting treatments and classifications were determined afresh each year, with the appearance of profitability and stability most in mind. No accounting policies as such were formulated, still less published. Fulfilment of the legal requirement that accounts should give a 'true and fair view' depended on a particularly liberal interpretation of that phrase – and much emphasis on the indefinite article which precedes it!

1.3 Despite the essential simplicity of its founding aim – to narrow and regularise the range of permissible accounting treatments applicable to comparable transactions and situations – the ASC's efforts have always been attended by criticism, itself almost polarised in its inconsistency: on the one hand that particular Standards are excessively rigid and unbending in their adherence to conceptual integrity and suffer a corresponding loss of realism; while, on the other, that Standards are being pragmatically drafted in deference to the interests of particular user groups, representing compromise at best and wholesale abandonment of principle at worst.

1.4 Responses to such a fundamental dilemma require a degree of political subtlety which, for the most part, has eluded the ASC's particular mixture of academic and practical disciplines. As a consequence its history is chequered with instances of embarrassed backtracking and revision of over-ambitious standard-setting targets, as exemplified by the inflation accounting saga. Other Standards are so flexible – some would say wishy-washy – in their prescription of accounting treatments (e.g. SSAPs 22 and 23 on goodwill and mergers/acquisitions) that their original aims of consistency and comparability are all but lost to view.

1.5 Members of the ASC must be deeply envious of their Canadian colleagues, whose pronouncements are given automatic force of law. Canadian legislation requires all public companies to conform with the accounting treatments and disclosure requirements prescribed by the Canadian Institute of Chartered Accountants. Such a stipulation endows those charged with the duty to draft standards with a sense of public responsibility backed by independence of mind.

1.6 Although the UK government has not yet seen fit to elevate the ASC's status in this way (partly because of our EC membership, which prohibits governments from delegating sovereign duties to private sector institutions), each successive Companies Act (CA) draws heavily on extant Accounting Standards in determining the treatments and disclosures to be prescribed with statutory backing.

1.7 Standards are, of course, given additional, if unofficial, force by requirements imposed by the accountancy bodies on their own members. Any unjustified (in the auditors' eyes) departure from an Accounting Standard shall be accompanied by a qualified auditors' report which declares disagreement with the accounts in explicit terms, and quantifies the effect on the accounts of such departure.

1.8 At the time of writing the standard-setting process is about to undergo another of its periodic reviews, as a result of which it is possible that the status of the Accounting Standards Committee (ASC) may become more elevated than at any previous time in its 18 year history. Hitherto it has not been authorised to issue standards in its own name; once passed by the ASC a standard must then be adopted by each individual CCAB body for acceptance by its own members. In the past this has led to considerable delay in the enforcement of standards. It has also resulted in certain standards being flawed by undue compromise in order to accommodate the sometimes opposed views of particular sectors or bodies.

1.9 If the ASC becomes a fully independent standard-setting authority in its own right, and such status is accepted by the accountancy bodies themselves, a new standard will become binding upon them (and hence their members) as soon as it is passed by ASC. This would bring ASC's status, in the public's view, much closer to that enjoyed by the Financial Accounting Standards Board (FASB) in the USA.

THE REGULATORY BASIS OF ACCOUNTING STANDARDS

1.10 It would also represent a move in the direction of sanction-backed Stock Exchange recognition and, perhaps, of full statutory backing in due course. Such official acknowledgement of the importance of enforcing standards must be the ultimate ASC target. Not least of its benefits would be that standards could be formulated on the strength of their economic realism rather than an ability to negotiate the tightrope between conflicting lobbies and the semblance of conceptual integrity. Standards like those on goodwill and mergers and acquisitions are notorious examples of this particular syndrome.

1.11 Accounting regulation in Canada enjoys this supreme advantage. The governing statutes simply declare that accounting treatment and disclosure shall be in accordance with the standards of the Canadian Institute of Chartered Accountants, thus endowing standards with full legal support and also avoiding any of the conflict (whether real, potential or imagined) between standards and statutory requirements which has plagued the UK regulatory scene for many years.

1.12 That is not, of course, to suggest that the UK standards have been devoid of any government backed support; but rather that it has been forthcoming on a piecemeal basis. The accounting concepts described in SSAP 2, for example, have become legally formalised as accounting principles in CA 1985. The principles of current cost accounts, although the subject of the most acrimonious professional argument this century, have achieved some considerable legal recognition in the alternative accounting rules in CA 1985, and are widely applied in practice in the revaluation of property assets – which, after all, are those whose current values are most likely to vary from their book values to a degree capable of distorting the accounts materially.

1.13 While current cost purists may not favour the 'hybrid' version of accounts (whereby assets – even stocks – may be restated at current cost selectively rather than wholly), there is little doubt that in this particular instance the compromise is better than nothing at all – or, should we say, than historic cost accounting which, while being consistent, is dangerously susceptible to producing unrealistic financial statements.

1.14 Our chapters on particular standards will, of course, highlight in more detail the degree to which UK company law has adopted accounting standards, sometimes using phrases taken directly from those standards. This represents an important acknowledgement by government of its own dependence on the standard-setting process as the principal authority on best accounting practice. Yet, despite this affirmation of the generally high quality of its output, the ASC continues to find itself in the frustrating position of having to back-pedal on key accounting issues because of its lack of formal authority. The vociferous disputation which inevitably follows compromised solutions to complex accounting issues causes government, in turn, to withhold its wholehearted support for standards for this very reason! It is a self-perpetuating syndrome, and it is difficult to predict when, and how, the mould will be broken.

1.15 One of the principal adversaries in the accountants' fight to achieve 'substance over form' in financial statements has, perhaps understandably, been the legal profession, in whose eyes any form of quasi-legislation by the ASC is suspect *ab initio*, despite the ASC's purpose being a determination to do justice to the overriding true and fair criterion. Lawyers have seriously questioned the role of accounting standards from their very inception in the early seventies, and believe in a far closer, perhaps literal, approach to legal compliance. They see SSAPs as a form of back door legislation, without parliamentary backing, and imposed by means of threatened audit qualifications. This view fails to recognise that parliamentary legislation on company accounts places great reliance on extant SSAPs, and a surprising proportion of SSAP requirements has in fact been implemented in this way.

1.16 While the legalistic stance merits respect, members of the legal profession do not as such have to contend, as a statutory duty, with a sensitive public interface. In their capacity as financial executives accountants are legally responsible for both the form and content of their companies' accounts; as auditors they give assent to the accounts as a true and fair statement of the financial position and results. These capacities are potentially in conflict: shareholders hardly favour accounting treatments which are seen to be inflexibly restrictive, while creditors and investors at large expect prudence to be the auditor's watchword.

1.17 Some lawyers have been giving effective expression to their feelings by providing 'expert opinions' to boards of directors seeking to know whether their proposed treatments are lawful. This practice of 'opinion shopping' leaves individual auditors in considerable difficulty. They might not like the finished accounting product, but cannot easily give a qualified report on legally-backed interpretations of issues which even the major accountancy bodies have yet to resolve – particularly when the legal opinion adds, gratuitously, that the accountants' 'best practice' treatment is the one that is unlawful!

1.18 In the Courts, by contrast, great weight is attached to official professional announcements of both the ASC and its Auditing Practices

Committee (APC) counterpart. In a notable judgment *Lloyd Cheyham & Co. Ltd* v *Littlejohn & Co* [1985] QBD Mr Justice Woolf declared that if a firm observed accounting standards it could not be found guilty of negligence. Particularly relevant to this case were SSAP 2 on disclosure of accounting policies and SSAP 18 on contingencies. On the subject of standards the judge stated: *'While they are not conclusive, so that a departure from their terms necessarily involves a breach of duty, and they are not clear, rigid rules, they are very strong evidence as to what is the proper standard which should be adopted and unless there is some justification, a departure from this will be regarded as constituting a breach of duty'.*

1.19 The point at issue was whether trailer tyres should have been depreciated separately from the trailers themselves. The plaintiff company (which had just acquired the trailer business) maintained that the extensive tyre wear should have been the subject of a specific provision in the accounts. The defendant auditors successfully held, however, that a correct construction of the matching principle in SSAP 2 requires a clear relationship between the amount of any provison and the costs which it purports to measure: revenue and costs should be matched with one another only 'so far as their relationship can be established or justifiably assumed'. In this particular instance no such correlation could be established with reasonable certainty. It was, furthermore, clear from the audit files that the matter had not been dealt with 'by default': there was ample evidence, including notes taken at meetings with the Institute's Technical Director, that the matter had been carefully considered before reaching a decision not to create a specific provision. The only criticism of the accounts was that the accounting policies note might have been clearer on this question.

Standards and CA 1985

1.20 As already noted, features of particular standards have found their way into the *Companies Act 1985*. These include the disclosure requirements in Schedule 4 on prior year items, extraordinary and exceptional items, the wording having been taken almost verbatim from SSAP 6; similarly, following the SSAP 9 requirement for stocks and work in progress, current assets must be stated, with certain exceptions such as debtors, at the lower of (i) purchase price or production cost, and (ii) net realisable value. The statutory requirements for depreciation of fixed assets closely follow those of SSAP 12, although both this standard and SSAP 6 suffer from the absence of any reference to the consequences of asset revaluations for depreciation charges and the disposal of previously revalued assets. The accounting treatment of revaluations therefore remains variable, pending the findings and recommendations of an ASC working party studying this area.

1.21 Development costs may be carried in the balance sheet only in special circumstances. The Act does not define the special circumstances but the Department of Trade and Industry (DTI) have recently confirmed that the conditions set out in SSAP 13 satisfy the term 'special circumstances'. The Act also requires that research costs must not be treated as assets. The provisions on Goodwill are similar to those in SSAP 22. Goodwill (but not goodwill arising on consolidation) must be depreciated over a period which must not exceed the useful economic life of the goodwill in question. The provisions of the Act apply only to goodwill which is carried forward as an asset in the company balance sheet. If goodwill has been written off to reserves on acquisition the depreciation provisions will not apply. The judgement in the case of *Shearer* v *Bercain* gave a stricter interpretation of the rules for creating share premium accounts contained in S56 of the 1948 Act. Sections 36 to 41 (now S131 to 134, CA 1985) were introduced in the 1981 Act to legitimize the merger method of accounting.

Modified accounts

1.22 The CA 1985 provides that small and medium-sized companies which are not members of a public group may file a modified set of accounts with the Registrar, although a full set of accounts will still be required for submission to the members of the company. A company may qualify as small or medium-sized if it does not exceed at least two of the following limits:

	Small	*Medium*
Turnover	£2 million	£8 million
Gross assets at end of the year	£2.95 million	£10.80 million
Average number of employees	50	250

Truth and fairness

1.23 The degree of probability which financial statements are expected to display is reflected in the familiar phrase 'true and fair'. These words were preceded by 'true and correct' prior to the CA 1947, which was consolidated in the 1948 Act. The change was needed on the grounds that there was no clear distinction between the two adjectives when used in an accounting context. Could accounts be *true* though *incorrect*? *Correct* yet *untrue*? Were both indeed necessary?

1.24 The shift to 'true and fair' in 1947 took place in recognition of the fact, no doubt discovered through harsh experience, that a set of accounts, in themselves beyond criticism in terms of bookkeeping rectitude and detailed computational accuracy, could be grossly misleading to its users, or some of them. This could be due to a variety of reasons, most notable of which are:
 (i) the susceptibility of all judgmental issues to excessively optimistic interpretation;
 (ii) the omission of certain transactions and/or balances, particularly liabilities;
 (iii) the manner in which transactions are categorised, possibly giving rise to set-off;
 (iv) the manner in which balances are grouped, similarly allowing set-off or otherwise facilitating concealment;
 (v) the manner of general presentation in which priority and emphasis is given selectively, depending on the impression intended to be given; and
 (vi) the possibility that supporting narrative will be drafted to serve a particular purpose, once again rendering objective assessment more difficult.

1.25 The pursuit of objectivity in accounting therefore produced a change in the legal formulation of its principal attribute. Paradoxically, this change to incorporate the word 'fair' thus introduced a concept which is itself beyond any objective analysis. As a result, the past 40 years have witnessed a search akin to that for the Holy Grail, in which each step in the right direction is matched by a shift on the part of its desired object, which thus becomes frustratingly more elusive.

1.26 Given that wholly objective accounting can exist, like all absolutes, in the mind alone, we are obliged to settle for relatives. In this sense the search for truth and fairness is inseparable from that for an acceptable conceptual framework, for such a framework will define the particular range of relative values which the various users of accounts may justifiably expect of the financial statements of the entities in which they are interested.

1.27 The work of the Accounting Standards Committee of the UK CCAB (and that of its international counterparts) is dedicated to the development of just such a framework. Although it will never be able to claim to have arrived at the whole solution to the intractable problems implicit in period-based reporting, it can certainly map out the steps which will lead us in the right direction.

1.28 Nevertheless it must be recognised that while 'true and fair' is a legal requirement for published accounts, Accounting Standards, as such, enjoy no official legal support, and members of the legal profession have, ever since the inception of the ASC, held important reservations concerning the status of SSAPs in law and, particularly, the notion that any failure to comply with a SSAP precludes, except in a very small minority of instances, the possibility of a true and fair view being given by the accounts in question. Such concern is, of course, lent additional urgency by the virtual compulsion on auditors to qualify their reports in all cases of departure from SSAPs, except in very rare circumstances where compliance would clearly result in a true and fair view not being given.

1.29 In order to seek clarification on the legal meaning of 'true and fair' with particular reference to SSAPs the ASC sought the written opinion of legal Counsel in 1983. Counsel noted that the true and fair requirement has existed in statute law since 1947, whereas SSAPs emerged much later; and are indeed evolving and being developed continuously. How then, it might be asked, can this later development be reconciled with the statutory requirement of a true and fair view which has been embodied in the law in the same language since 1947? Does the issue of a new Standard render it unlawful to published accounts in a manner which was acceptable to both accountants and the law prior to the issue of the new Standard?

1.30 Counsel noted that the Courts, wisely, have never attempted to define 'true and fair'. It is an abstract concept which does not bear amplification in alternative language. It is always preferable to understand it by reference to particular applications; it may therefore be possible to explain why a specific set of accounts does or does not satisfy the true and fair requirement. In this sense it is similar to other legal abstractions such as 'reasonable care'. Their very abstraction endows them with the dynamic quality needed to endure the substantial ongoing changes in the financial reporting environment to which they apply.

1.31 Counsel observed that attributes of true and fair reporting will include accuracy and comprehensiveness, within 'acceptable' limits. There is therefore bound to be some difference between accountants and businessmen in particular cases regarding both the limits of acceptability and the methods to be adopted in order to give a true and fair view. In such cases there may well be more than one view that satisfies the magic criterion, and the cost-effectiveness of pursuing greater accuracy or comprehensiveness must inevitably play a part in determining the final form and amount of information sufficient to make accounts true and fair.

1.32 In the end only judges can determine whether accounts satisfy the CA's true and fair requirement. In reaching such a decision judges are inevitably influenced by the ordinary practices of professional accountants, and not merely because judges find it difficult to understand the language in which accounts are expressed. More relevant is the fact that accountants are aware of the requirement for accounts to be true and fair and that satisfaction of this requirement demands reporting of such quantity and quality as will meet the needs of a wide range of business interests. In turn these readers of accounts grow accustomed to receiving reports of the standard ordinarily received by them. Thus, cyclically, this in turn depends largely on the practices of accountants.

1.33 For these reasons the Courts will treat compliance with generally accepted accounting principles as *prima facie* evidence that the accounts are true and fair; and, conversely, will treat departures from such principles as *prima facie* evidence that they are not. Indeed, just such issues were confronted by the Court in the *Lloyd Cheyham* v *Littlejohn* case already described earlier in this chapter.

1.34 In the opinion of Counsel, the function of the ASC is simply to formulate what it considers should be generally accepted accounting principles. Having done so, the value of SSAPs to the Courts is twofold: first, it represents an authoritative professional opinion on what readers may reasonably expect from accounts intended to give a true and fair view, at the same time reducing the number of divergent practices hitherto regarded as acceptable. Secondly, the reader's knowledge that all accountants are professionally expected to comply with SSAPs engenders a parallel expectation that accounts may be assumed to conform to SSAPs in all cases.

1.35 A SSAP has no legal effect, but it will have an indirect effect on the substance which the Courts will impute to the 'true and fair' concept. For example, a SSAP may increase the likelihood that accounts which would, previous to its introduction, have been considered true and fair will no longer satisfy the law. The meaning of the 'true and fair' concept remains the same, but the facts and circumstances to which it is applied have changed.

Objectives of the Accounting Standards

1.36 In 1969 the Institute of Chartered Accountants in England and Wales issued a *Statement of Intent on Accounting Standards*. The statement listed five objectives:
  (i) to narrow the areas of difference and variety in accounting;
  (ii) to recommend disclosure of accounting bases;
  (iii) to require disclosure of departure from standards;
  (iv) to introduce a system of wide consultation on standard setting; and
  (v) to seek improvements in existing disclosure requirements of company law and the stock exchange.

1.37 The above document was produced in response to the criticism that the user of accounts could not always tell whether the accounts had been prepared on the basis of a conservative set of principles or on the basis of principles which would give highest (or, in some cases, lowest) profit. The measurement of profit is subjective and a range of profit or loss figures can be produced based on the assumptions that are made. The aim of the Institute had been to narrow the choice of accounting treatment so as to make the financial statements comparable.

1.38 The Accounting Standards Committee (ASC) published a consultative document which stated:
(a) Accounting Standards are necessary and will continue to be necessary. One of their main aims should be to narrow the choice of accounting treatment so as to make financial statements reasonably comparable one with another.
(b) Statements of Standard Accounting Practice (SSAPs) should continue to be used as definitive principles for use in financial statements and not merely as a benchmark against which deviations can be measured.
(c) A material departure from a SSAP should continue to be allowed only in those exceptional circumstances where to adhere would fail to give a 'true and fair view' in a particular case, or because to follow the SSAP would be demonstrably inappropriate.

1.39 The standards that have been produced fall into four main categories. There are many standards which are hybrid and cover more than one category.

Type 1: description of accounting practice

SSAP 2 which falls into this category requires firms to describe the accounting policies which the firm has adopted. This category seeks to make accounts more comparable. Since there are a number of accounting policies which can be used in applying an accounting base it is necessary to disclose which ones have been adopted so that the user of the accounts can make adjustments to those of one company before making comparisons with another.

Type 2: presentation of specific items

EXAMPLE: SSAP 6 gives guidelines on how to identify extraordinary items, exceptional items and prior year adjustments and requires a uniform presentation of information. Information well presented is communicated to, and understood, by the user of the accounts.

Type 3: disclosure of items

EXAMPLE: SSAP 12 requires the depreciation charge for the year, the method of depreciation and the rate (or estimate useful life) used to be disclosed in the accounts. This category of standard has often been in advance of the disclosure requirements of the Companies Acts.

Type 4: Income measurement and asset valuation

EXAMPLE: SSAP 1 requires that the investments in associated companies should be valued by the equity method. SSAP 21 gives guidance on the manner in which a lessor company should recognise its income. Valuation and income measurement are important for determining and understanding dividend policy and measures of efficiency.

1.40   The aims, scope and application of standards are contained in the Explanatory Foreword issued in May 1975 (revised 1986) set out below.

Explanatory foreword

Authority

1   Statements of standard accounting practice ('accounting standards') are developed in the public interest by the Accounting Standards Committee (ASC) as being authoritative statements on accounting practice. Their primary aim is to narrow the areas of difference and variety in the accounting treatment of the matters with which they deal. They are accepted and issued by the Councils of each of The Institute of Chartered Accountants in England and Wales, The Institute of Chartered Accountants of Scotland, The Institute of Chartered Accountants in Ireland, The Chartered Association of Certified Accountants, The Chartered Institute of Management Accountants and The Chartered Institute of Public Finance and Accountancy ('the accountancy bodies').

Scope and application

2 Accounting standards are applicable to all financial statements whose purpose is to give a true and fair view of financial position and of profit or loss for the period, whether prepared on the basis of historical cost or on an alternative accounting convention generally accepted at the time of preparation.

3 Accounting standards are intended to be applied where financial statements of overseas entities are incorporated into United Kingdom and Irish group financial statements. They are not intended to apply to financial statements prepared for local purposes in overseas territories.

4 Accounting standards need not be applied to items whose effect is judged to be immaterial to an understanding of the financial statements.

5 In applying accounting standards, it will be important to have regard to the spirit of and reasoning behind them. They are not intended to be a comprehensive code of rigid rules. They do not supersede the exercise of an informed judgement in determining what constitutes a true and fair view in each circumstance. It would be impracticable to establish a code sufficiently elaborate to cater for all business situations and innovations and for every exceptional or marginal case. A justifiable reason may therefore exist why an accounting standard may not be applicable in a given situation, namely when application would conflict with the giving of a true and fair view. In such cases, modified or alternative treatments will require to be adopted.

6 In applying a modified or alternative treatment it will be important to have regard to the spirit of and the reasoning behind the relevant accounting standard, and to the overriding aim of giving a true and fair view.

7 Where accounting standards prescribe specific information to be contained in financial statements, such requirements do not override exemptions from disclosure given by law to, and utilised by, certain types of entity.

Significant departures

8 Significant departures from accounting standards should be disclosed and explained in the financial statements. The financial effects of

such departures should be estimated and disclosed unless this would be impracticable or misleading in the context of giving a true and fair view. If the financial effects of any such departure are not disclosed, the reasons for such non-disclosure should be stated.

Obligation to observe accounting standards or justify departures

9   The Councils of the accountancy bodies expect members who assume responsibilities in respect of financial statements to observe accounting standards.

10   Where this responsibility is evidenced by the association of their names with such financial statements in the capacity of directors or other officers, the onus will be on them to ensure that the existence and purpose of accounting standards are fully understood by fellow directors and other officers. They should also use their best endeavours to ensure that accounting standards are observed and that significant departures found to be necessary are adequately disclosed and explained in the financial statements.

11   Where members act as auditors or reporting accountants, they should be in a position to justify significant departures to the extent that their concurrence with the departures is stated or implied. They are not, however, required to refer in their report to departures with which they concur, provided that adequate disclosure has been made in the notes to the financial statements.

12   The accountancy bodies, through appropriate committees, may enquire into apparent failures by members to observe accounting standards or to ensure adequate disclosure of significant departures.

Relationship with International Accounting Standards

13   The accountancy bodies attach importance to fostering the harmonisation of accounting standards internationally. To this end, they have collectively undertaken to support the work of the International Accounting Standards Committee.

14   As part of such support, accounting standards contain a section explaining their relationship to any relevant International Accounting Standard. In most cases, compliance with the accounting standard automatically ensures compliance with the International Accounting Standard. If it does not do so, the United Kingdom and Irish accounting standard explains the extent of divergence. If, in rare cases, the two standards were to differ significantly, the United Kingdom and Irish accounting standard would prevail.

Future developments

15 Methods of financial accounting evolve and alter in response to changes in the environment, developments in business and financial practice, and accounting thought. From time to time, therefore, existing accounting standards will be reviewed and, where appropriate, amended, or new accounting standards issued.

Other ASC pronouncements

16 The ASC may also issue other pronouncements, including Statements of Recommended Practice (SORPs) and guidance notes on accounting standards, including guidance notes for certain parts of the public sector. Unlike accounting standards, these are not mandatory on members of the accountancy bodies, but are consistent with accounting standards in that they help define accounting practice in the particular area or sector to which they refer.

The Public Sector*

17 The prescription of accounting requirements in the public sector is statutorily a matter for the Government, and its Accounts Directions for the nationalised industries require the accounts to give a true and fair view. The Government also expects the nationalised industries to have regard to best commercial practice. Consequently, the Government requires the nationalised industries to adhere to the accounting standards, SORPs or guidance notes which are relevant to them.

18 In the case of other Public Sector Bodies, the Government's requirements may or may not refer specifically to the 'true and fair' aspect, but it could be expected that such requirements will normally be in accord with the principles of relevant ASC pronouncements, except where they are clearly inappropriate.

---

*Paragraphs 17 and 18 apply to the United Kingdom. As regards the Republic of Ireland, accounting standards will normally be applicable to enterprises in the public sector. This is so because either (a) such enterprises have been established under companies legislation and their financial statements are required to give a true and fair view of financial position and of profit or loss for the period or (b) although established under special legislation, their financial statements are either required to give a true and fair view or in practice are so as to give a true and fair view.

Review of the Standard-Setting Process – A report by the ASC published in 1983

Introduction

Reasons for the review

1.41   The standard-setting process was reviewed for three reasons:

(a) To develop certain recommendations contained in the Watts Repprt (*Setting Accounting Standards*, 1981), with particular regard to consultations;
(b) To seek ways by which the standard-setting process could be shortened whilst ensuring that the resultant standards commanded general support;
(c) To consider whether there was a need for alternative or new types of pronouncement.

Terms of reference

1.42   The terms of reference of the ASC working party were as follows:

(a) To examine the adequacy of the ASC's existing procedures for identifying topics for consideration, preparing its pronouncements, and the public consultative procedures related thereto;
(b) To consider how the consultative procedures involving the Councils and Technical Committees of the six governing bodies prior to the submission of SSAPs for approval might be improved;
(c) To consider whether and, if so, in what circumstances the ASC should produce discussion drafts, guidance notes, interpretations, recommendations or other documents in addition to SSAPs;
(d) To examine the desirability and feasibility of the 'franking' route for specific industry pronouncements.

Conclusions

1.43   The report was published in 1983. Its principal conclusions are set out below.

General Aspects

Accounting Standards Committee (ASC)

The present structure of ASC, following recent revisions, is:

(a) Currently the ASC has 21 voting members falling into the categories set out overleaf:

In practice	9
In private and public industry and commerce	6
Users	3
Non-trading public sector	2
Academic	1
Total	21

(b) Standing sub-committees – these deal with planning, inflation accounting and international affairs and report to the ASC.
(c) Working parties – these are formed whenever it becomes necessary to consider specific topics under review (e.g. CCA) and also report to the ASC.

Procedure for general consultation and communication
1.44 The ASC seeks to carry out as wide a range of consultations as is possible. This includes meetings involving the ASC chairman and individual members of the ASC. Regular press conferences are held in order to stimulate public interest.

Characteristics and scope of standards
1.45 (a) *Essential characteristics*
  (i) Standards will be prepared by the ASC but issued by and subsequently enforced by the six CCAB bodies;
  (ii) They will deal only with those matters which are of major and fundamental importance and which affect the generality of companies. Consequently, future standards will be few in number;
  (iii) Accounting standards will continue to apply to all accounts which are intended to show a true and fair view of financial position and profit or loss.
 (b) *Cost/benefit test.* The ASC recognises that different users have different information needs and considers the best approach is to consider each case on its individual merits using a cost/benefit test. The view expressed is that there may be cases where an exemption from a particular requirement of a standard is justified on the grounds that the cost of providing the information exceeds the benefits likely to be derived by users.

An alternative pronouncement
1.46 For some subjects tackled by the ASC in the future the issue of an accounting standard may not be appropriate. However, this should not

THE REGULATORY BASIS OF ACCOUNTING STANDARDS

rule out the issue of some other kind of pronouncement which could provide a stimulus to accounting thought and help improve accounting practice. Consequently, Statements of Recommended Practice (SORPs) will be issued. SORPs (by contrast with SSAPs) will *not* be mandatory.

Interpretations
1.47 Interpretations of standards have been issued in the USA for some years. The ASC rejects this practice which it considers can lead to a 'cook-book' of detailed rules. Instead, only the UK practice of issuing standards containing general principles will continue. Particular problems will continue to be solved by amending or supplementing existing standards, if this is required.

Standard-setting Process (SSAPs)

Introduction
1.48 This section considers the new process by which an individual SSAP will be developed. The section concludes with a flowchart (taken from the ASC paper) which summarises the overall situation.

Identification of topics
1.49 Topics are usually placed on the ASC's agenda for a combination of reasons. Individual reasons might include:

(a) A major area of accounting on which current practice is deficient;
(b) Areas where there is a need to narrow down the areas of difference in accounting (e.g. accounting for goodwill);
(c) A request from an interested party such as a specific industry group;
(d) The consequence of a change in law, e.g. *Shearer* v *Bercain* (1980), the Companies Act 1981 and merger accounting;
(e) As a result of an international development, (e.g. International Accounting Standards).

A newly formed planning sub-committee is required to 'review and monitor the ASC's future work programme and advise on priorities relating thereto', and to 'keep under review the status of the ASC's current projects'. The ASC work programme is referred to below.

Planning sub-committee
1.50 Functions include:

(a) Those referred to in the previous section;
(b) Advising on the need for research;
(c) Advising on the composition of working parties;
(d) Considering and reviewing documents and proposals before they are put to the ASC.

Research

1.51 Once a topic has been placed on the agenda, the progress of the project may start with the carrying out of a research study. The results of the study should help clarify the issues and provide a useful basis for future decisions.

Formation of a working party

1.52 Once the research study is available it will be considered by the ASC who will decide whether to go ahead. The first decision to make is whether the final pronouncement should be an accounting standard. The ASC should also decide what type of consultative document should be issued.

Consultative documents

1.53 The various types of consultative documents are considered in turn:

(a) *Discussion papers*. Unlike exposure drafts which must always be issued prior to a standard, discussion papers are optional. Discussion papers are exploratory in nature and do not set out the text of a proposed standard.

The paper sets out a discussion of the issues involved, as a means of seeking public comment. A discussion paper would not be published on a topic where the ASC had already decided how it would move forward.

(b) *Statements of Intent (SOI)*. An SOI is a public statement issued by the ASC setting out a brief summary of how the ASC intends to deal with a particular matter. For example, SOIs have been issued on current cost accounting, deferred taxation, goodwill and acquisitions and mergers. An SOI is intended to be much less detailed than an exposure draft. It attempts to focus attention on the main issues relating to a particular topic and on the accounting policies which are proposed. An SOI could be used to prompt public comment on a proposed course of action more promptly than a full-length discussion paper.

As with a discussion paper, the publication of an SOI is optional.

(c) *Exposure drafts (EDs)*. The ASC considers the publication of an ED to be essential. In order to stimulate comment an ED often contains a preface to the main text which sets out the background to the subject and some of the arguments for and against the proposals in the text. The procedures are adopted before an ED is published. They are equally relevant to a discussion paper or an SOI.

Initial feedback to the ASC

1.54 At an early stage, the working party presents the ASC with:

(a) The planned technical content of the documents (in outline form); and
(b) Its consultation plan.

The consultation plan
1.55 The plan will:
(a) Identify which specific groups may be affected;
(b) Set out plans for the early and continuous involvement of the CCAB;
(c) Make provision for consultation with users of accounts;
(d) Make provision for a public hearing (if appropriate);
(e) Include a press plan, as good press coverage of the development of a pronouncement encourages debate;
(f) Set out a timetable covering all aspects of the work leading up to the final standard.

The purpose of the above is to explain to various groups the proposals on which the eventual standard will be based and to receive evidence and hear representations regarding its acceptability.

Technical drafting and consultation by the working party
1.56 Once it is established what type of document is to be developed, the content and the necessary consultation, the working party proceeds with detailed drafting and consultation.

Involvement of the CCAB
1.57 The six CCAB bodies approve and enforce standards. Therefore, each body must be kept aware of progress at each stage.

Consideration by ASC and publication of an exposure draft
1.58 When the detailed drafting and consultations are completed, the findings of the working party are presented to the ASC for consideration. Once the ASC is satisfied with the ED, it will approve it for publication.

Exposure period
1.59 This normally lasts for six months. During this period, many commentators formulate their comments and submit them in writing to the ASC. The working party will meet the technical committees of the CCAB bodies. Also, at the end of the exposure period, the ASC may decide to hold a public meeting.

Thus, comments are received from as many different directions as possible, particularly from those affected by the proposed standard.

Finalisation and issue of a standard
1.60 Once the redrafting and consultative work has been completed, a final draft is submitted to the ASC. Subject to any changes, this will usually be approved.

The draft must then be sent to the Councils of the six CCAB bodies for their approval, since it is they who approve it and not the ASC.

UNDERSTANDING ACCOUNTING STANDARDS

Guidance notes, appendices to standards and technical releases
1.61 Guidance notes and appendices do not form part of the standard. They provide non-mandatory guidance.
A technical release gives background information and is normally issued with a standard.

Review and revision of standards
1.62 From time to time, the ASC must decide whether or not a standard should be revised, possibly as a result of company law changes or because the standard has become out of date in some other respect. The way the standard is revised will depend on circumstances:
(a) A discussion paper may need to be issued in order to determine *whether* a standard should be revised;
(b) If a standard is to be revised, either an exposure draft or a statement of intent should precede the standard.

1.63 The flowchart given in Fig. 1.1 sets out the main stages in the standard setting process. For simplicity it excludes reference to the fact that at each stage (for example, once the results of a research study are available but before a working party is formed) the status and progress of a project are reviewed by the ASC or the planning sub-committee, and a decision is made on the next stage of the project. The flowchart makes the assumption that no discussion paper or statement of intent is published.

STATEMENTS OF RECOMMENDED PRACTICE (SORPs)

Need for and status of SORPs
1.64 (a) There are occasions when issues arise which are of sufficient importance to require an authoritative pronouncement but which do not meet the criteria for an accounting standard.
Statements of recommended practice (SORPs) have been developed to fill the gap. A SORP is a stand-alone document that will not relate to a standard.
(b) SORPs will *not* be mandatory. However, they will be of such a quality and status as to be widely respected and compliance will be *encouraged*.
(c) If a company does not follow a SORP, the company will not be required to disclose the fact or the effect of the departure.
(d) SORPs will always take full account of the principles laid down in accounting standards.
(e) (i) *SSAPs* will relate only to matters of major and fundamental importance affecting the generality of companies.

THE REGULATORY BASIS OF ACCOUNTING STANDARDS

	Flowchart
	Identification of a topic
	Research study commissioned and carried out
Planning sub-committee appoints members, gives them terms of reference and explains what consultative documents should be prepared.	Working party formed
Working party develops and presents to ASC for approval: (a) technical point outline; and (b) consultation plan.	Initial feedback to ASC
Working party carries out (a) detailed development of draft and (b) procedures set out in consultation plan, including involvement of the CCAB.	Technical drafting and consultation
ASC discusses the draft and may require amendments to be made before publication.	Consideration of draft by the ASC
	Publication of exposure draft
	The exposure period
Normally a six month period in which letters of comment are received by the ASC and further consultation takes place.	Summary of comments and decision on future progress
Working party summarises and discusses comments received; makes recommendation to ASC on how the project should proceed.	Redrafting and further consultative meetings by working party
	Consideration of draft standard by ASC
Working party presents its final draft to ASC. ASC discusses it and may require amendments to be made before approving it.	Sent to CCAB councils
ASC forwards its approved draft standard to the councils of the six CCAB bodies with the recommendation that they approve it for publication as an accounting standard.	Draft standard considered and approved by six councils
	Standard issued by six councils

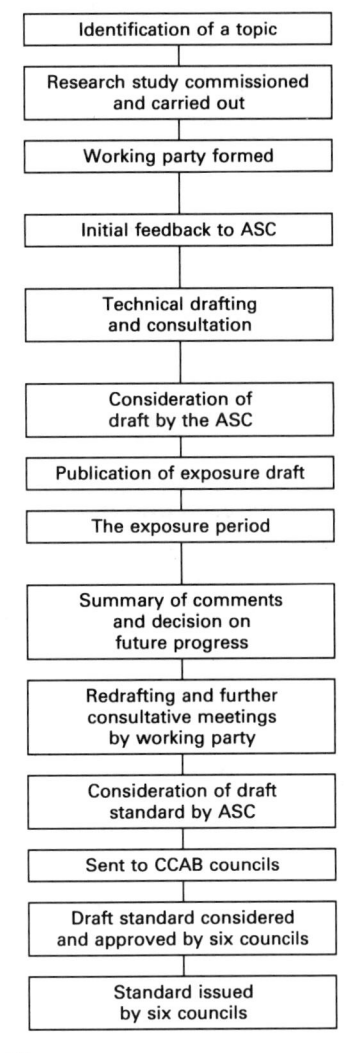

Figure 1.1 *The standard-setting process*

  (ii) *SORPs* will generally deal with either:

   (1) Matters of widespread application but not of fundamental importance; or
   (2) Matters which are of limited application (e.g. to a particular industry).
 (f) SORPs falling into category (e)(ii)(1) should be prepared by the ASC itself but those falling into category (e)(ii)(2) should be developed by

21

the industry concerned. The statement will then be reviewed by the ASC and then 'franked', i.e. approved as best practice.
SORPs referred to in (e)(ii)(2) above may be referred to as 'franked SORPs'.

Public sector
1.65 The ASC is currently identifying its role in the public sector, particularly for non-trading activities.
The ASC's role is one of encouraging and facilitating the setting of standards in the public sector, as well as assisting with the application of standards where they are relevant to public sector bodies.

Process
1.66 The process by which SSAPs and SORPs are prepared should be similar.

SORPs prepared by ASC
1.67 The process is similar to that set out above. However, it is *not* essential for the ASC to issue an exposure draft, but it must issue either an ED *or* a statement of intent.

Franked SORPs
1.68 (a) One of the major differences between the processes for the two types of SORPs lies in the identification of the topic.
For franked SORPs, the initiative for the development may come from either the industry concerned or the ASC.
The ASC will need to satisfy itself that all the following criteria are satisfied:
  (i) The proposal should be in respect of accounting in an industry of significant size;
  (ii) The industry on behalf of which the proposal is being made can be adequately defined;
  (iii) The proposal should be made by a group which is representative of large parts of the industry.

(b) The ASC will then issue the following guidelines:
  (i) Drafting of the statements should be by a working party which is representative of the industry, and which includes users of accounts;
  (ii) The preparation of the statement should involve wide consultation within the industry and publicly outside it;
  (iii) Before the final SORP is published, an exposure draft or a statement of intent should be published for comment;

THE REGULATORY BASIS OF ACCOUNTING STANDARDS

      (iv) The SORP should go some way to narrowing down the areas of differences in accounting within the industry in question;
      (v) The SORP must serve the public interest.
- (c) The working party will then proceed with its programme of initial research (where appropriate) and technical drafting and consultation.
- (d) Procedures carried out during and after the exposure period will be similar to those for EDs.
- (e) Once the working party has finalised its text, its draft statement will be submitted to the ASC. The ASC will set up a panel to review the draft. If the panel is satisfied, it will recommend the statement to the ASC.

If the ASC accepts the recommendation of the working party and if it believes that the SORP is in the public interest, then the SORP will include a report to the effect that:

      (i) The statement has been prepared by a group which is representative of the industry concerned; and
      (ii) The statement has been reviewed and franked as representing recommended practice for that industry.

The statement will be published by the industry concerned.
The above procedures may be varied at the discretion of the ASC.

CONCLUSIONS AND SUMMARY

1.69 The principal conclusions published in the report were as follows:

- (a) The standard-setting process was in need of review and was capable of improvement.
- (b) The essential characteristics of future accounting standards will be that:
    - (i) They are prepared by the ASC but issued and enforced by the six members of the Consultative Committee of Accountancy Bodies (CCAB);
    - (ii) They deal only with matters of major and fundamental importance affecting the generality of companies, and will therefore be few in number;
    - (iii) They are applicable to all accounts which are intended to give a true and fair view.
- (c) The revised standard-setting covers matters which relate both to the general work of the ASC and to the development of specific standards. Effective consultation and communication is seen as an essential element of both these aspects of the process.

(d) A new form of consultative document, to be called the Statement of Intent (SOI), is to be introduced; this will enable the ASC to indicate at an early stage how it proposes to deal with a particular accounting matter.
(e) The ASC has decided not to issue interpretations of accounting standards.
(f) A new category of final pronouncement, the Statement of Recommended Practice (SORP), is to be introduced. A SORP will be issued when a need is seen for a pronouncement on a specific topic, but when that topic does not meet all the criteria for an accounting standard. Although companies will be encouraged to comply with SORPs, compliance will, unlike standards, not be mandatory. Thus, there will in future be a hierarchy consisting of legal requirements for accounts, accounting standards and SORPs.
(g) A sub-category of SORPs is to be introduced called 'franked SORPs'. These will generally relate to topics of limited application, for example a specific industry. The work on franked SORPs will generally be undertaken by a working party drawn mainly from the industry concerned, but its work will be overseen and be subject to review by the ASC. The final approved document will be published by the industry concerned.

ASC WORK PROGRAMME

1.70 As was mentioned above, the ASC proposes from time to time (probably annually) to invite public comment on its work programme. The first occasion on which this took place was May 1984, Technical Release 549 stated:

'It should be borne in mind that the volume of work undertaken by the ASC is determined by the governing bodies through their decision on the ASC's budget and level of staffing. This invitation to comment is not concerned with the volume of work to be undertaken by the ASC but with the determination of priorities at a given level of activity'.

Arguments for and against the setting of mandatory accounting standards

1.71 The failure of SSAP 16 on Current Cost Accounting and a number of revisions of the Standard on deferred tax has led to discussion on whether standards should no longer be mandatory. Arguments for and against the setting of mandatory standards are listed below:

Arguments for the setting of mandatory accounting standards

(a) This would bring some statutorily imposed uniformity into financial accounting practice. The absence of such regulation would mean that, within the bounds of prescription under the Companies Act and any other relevant legislation, the amount and quality of information disclosed in financial statements, as well as the computation of monetary amounts included therein, would be left to the judgement of accountants, acting as advisers to the directors responsible for producing the statements, and checked only by the auditors, themselves similarly circumscribed.

(b) Regulation of the preparation and presentation of information in financial statements is a necessary pre-requisite of securing equitable treatment of investors and others external to the management of an enterprise. The accounts are the principal source of information about the enterprise's affairs, and without strong regulatory arrangements there would be little assurance that external interests are being fairly dealt with by the directors, the preparers of the statements. Legislation offers some safeguards, but Parliament cannot pronounce on matters of detailed accounting practice, nor can it keep abreast of current developments. A more flexible system is required, furnished by representatives of the accountancy profession, preferably with full statutory support, such as exists in Canada.

(c) The standard-setting process requires ongoing and systematic thought about the accounting process, its conceptual basis, its detailed applications, and the developing role of accounting in the economy and society at large. It is hard to see how this function could be performed efficiently other than within a professional context, thereby acquiring respect and compliance on the part of accountants. Parallel efforts by the academic community or any other agency external to the profession are unlikely to gain comparable support.

(d) Failure by the profession to regulate accounting practices would invite the intervention of government in the detailed regulatory process.

Arguments against the setting of mandatory accounting standards

(a) Regulation by a semi-official body is calculated to fetter the judgement of accountants in responding to the problems which arise daily. There is the danger that, as in the United States to an increasing extent, a 'recipe book' approach to accounting practice may become dominant. Solutions to specific problems are looked up in a book of rules, and applied mechanically without regard to the special circumstances of the case. Accountants should be well-qualified to resolve such issues by reference to their own training, expertise and grasp of accounting principles.

(b) Approval by the standard-setting body of one solution and rejection of another, which may be equally arguable, will discourage original thought and reduce accounting to a mechanical discipline.

(c) Too much reliance on regulation and too little on judgement will debase the quality of accounting practice, and will ultimately discourage persons of high intelligence from entering or remaining in the profession. In time this could lower the status of accountancy to that of mere bookkeeping and filling-in of forms, through excessive government prescription of accounting procedures.

(d) The determination of accounting standards demands powers and resources which a self-regulating profession simply does not possess. The sanction available to it in the event of non-observance of standards, i.e. qualification of audit reports, amounts to little more than a mild rebuke and holds no terror to a powerful Board, particularly if, based on legal advice if necessary, no Companies Act infringement occurs. If a standard is widely defied (as was the case with SSAP 11 and SSAP 16), the standard-setting body can do no more than conclude that it is inappropriate and unenforceable, and withdraw it.

Small companies and accounting standards

1.72 Views have been expressed that small companies should be exempted from the requirements of the accounting standards. Arguments for and against this view are set out below:

1 Arguments for the 'universal' application of accounting standards:

(a) All company accounts must carry an audit report which expresses an opinion on whether or not they show a true and fair view. If a certain standard is required to show a true and fair view for large companies, it must be needed equally to show a true and fair view for small companies.

(b) The application of accounting standards in relation to small or large companies help significantly:

   (i) to implement the requirements of the CA 1985;

(ii) to prescribe methods of sound accounting which go a long way towards narrowing the areas of difference and variety in the accounting treatment of the matters with which they deal and thus promote comparability; and
(iii) to prescribe suitable and adequate disclosure of items contained in financial statements in order to provide a reader with a true and fair view of the financial position and profit or loss for the period.
(c) A distinction between companies according to size is bound to involve an arbitrary cut-off point which would be hard to defend.
(d) The typical small company relies, to a large extent, on its auditors, acting as accountants, to prepare the financial statements. A second level of reporting requirements would have to be applied by the auditing firm which could lead to increased costs for the small company to bear.
(e) Although the CA 1985 gives small companies the right to file 'modified' accounts, containing much less information than full accounts, with the Registrar of Companies, this does not of itself reduce costs faced by such companies, because full accounts must still be prepared, audited and distributed to shareholders. The full accounts of these companies are also used outside the company – for example, by banks and the Inland Revenue. Therefore, for the benefit of all interested parties, small companies should comply with the accounting standards, at least until such time as the Government resolve the question of whether small companies should be relieved of the need to have their accounts audited.

2 Arguments against the 'universal' application of accounting standards:

(a) The concept of the true and fair view needs to be modified to a certain extent by cost–benefit considerations. The cost of preparing financial information is proportionately greater for smaller companies than for larger ones. The benefit for large companies is usually greater than for small companies as large companies have a large number and variety of users.
(b) The small companies find compliance with accounting standards burdensome. An example of this is SSAP 15 on accounting for deferred tax. Some small companies ignore standards which appear to be burdensome, thus bringing the standard setting process into disrepute. This can be avoided by giving appropriate exceptions.
(c) SSAP 10 on Statements of Source and Application of Funds applies only to companies with a turnover of £25,000 or more. SSAP 3 on earnings per share applies only to companies quoted on a recognised

UNDERSTANDING ACCOUNTING STANDARDS

stock exchange. There is thus no reason why small companies should not be exempted selectively from the requirements of particular accounting standards. The CA 1985 defines companies according to their size. The definition of small company contained in S.248 of the CA 1985 could be used to establish a cut-off point for this purpose.
(d) The main users of a small company tend to be its directors (who in many cases also are its owners) who have little awareness of the term 'Statements of Standard Accounting Practice'. They place little reliance on the accounts, and are primarily interested in reducing compliance costs.
(e) The argument that a two tier system of reporting requirements is likely to increase costs for small companies is hardly valid. It may do so initially but should lead to a reduction in costs in time as reporting becomes simpler.

Questions

1   Examine the concept of a 'true and fair' view in the context of financial reporting in the UK and briefly discuss its implications in relation to accounting standards.

2   (a) What are the objectives of the Accounting Standards Committee and to what extent do you consider they are being achieved?
    (b) What are 'Statements of Recommended Practice' (SORP) and how may they be expected to influence financial reporting?

3   The report 'Setting Accounting Standards' (Accounting Standards Committee 1981) affirmed that accounting standards are necessary and will continue to be necessary in order to complement the statutory regulations.
Required:
Do you agree with the statement? State your reasons.

4   Accounting standards can be categorised as follows:
Type 1: description of accounting practice;
Type 2: presentation;
Type 3: disclosure;
Type 4: valuation and profit measurement.
Required:
(a) Give one example of an SSAP that belongs to each category and briefly justify your categorisation of it.

THE REGULATORY BASIS OF ACCOUNTING STANDARDS

(b) What do you consider is the essential problem that each category seeks to overcome?

(c) How successful have each of these categories of standard been and why?

5   The setting of mandatory accounting standards by a semi-official body representative of the accountancy profession began in the United Kingdom and the Republic of Ireland in 1970. Doubts have recently been expressed about the practical workings of the standard-setting process, and about the usefulness of standard-setting in general.

Required:

(a) Set out arguments *both* FOR and AGAINST the setting of mandatory accounting standards by bodies representative of professional accountants; and

(b) appraise the 1983 proposals of the UK/Irish Accounting Standards Committee for the issuing of Statements of Intent (SOI) and Statements of Recommended Practice (SORP), in addition to the documents already issued by the ASC.

Chapter 2
Accounting principles

SSAP 2 – Disclosure of Accounting Policies

2.1 Although this was not the first Accounting Standard, it has always been regarded as the most fundamental. It explains some of the assumptions on which all other Standards rest, and its importance and widespread recognition and acceptance was duly acknowledged when the CA 1981, consolidated in the CA 1985, incorporated under 'Accounting Principles' the essential concepts first formulated in the UK in SSAP 2.

2.2 It can be said that SSAP 2 explains the very language of accounting, or that which must be taken for granted without question, as the foundation stone upon which all other arguments are staged.

2.3 It should not, however, be regarded as a substitute for a conceptual framework for accounting. Such a framework, slow in development and even slower in acceptance, requires recognition of accounting applications and the needs of respective user groups; whereas SSAP 2 provides no more than a description at the most basic level of the linguistic building bricks with which financial statements, as we have come to know and accept them for the general purposes of stewardship accounting, are constructed.

2.4 The Standard deals with three matters developmentally: *concepts*; *bases*; and *policies*.

2.5 The fundamental accounting concepts (referred to as 'accounting principles' in the CA 1985) are *going concern, prudence, consistency*, and *accruals* (sometimes known as the 'matching' concept). The CA adds a fifth: the amount of each individual asset or liability included in the aggregate amount of any item in the accounts is to be determined separately.

2.6 This means that compensatory inaccuracy as between items included in an omnibus total or sub-total is not permitted; nor is it permissible to set-off debits and credits, resulting in their mutual omission.

ACCOUNTING PRINCIPLES

2.7 Fundamental though these general principles are, the Act allows for departure in unspecified circumstances, but insists that there must be 'special reasons', and that the directors must disclose in the accounts (a) particulars of any such departure, (b) the reasons for it, and (c) its effect.

2.8 The fifth principle ('aggregation'), included in the Act but not part of SSAP 2, is further supported and amplified in para (5) of the Fourth Schedule to the Act, which stipulates that amounts representing assets or income may not be set off against amounts representing liabilities or expenditure (as the case may be), or vice versa.

2.9 It will be observed that the nature of the going concern concept is wholly different from that of the other concepts included in SSAP 2. The assumption that the company is a going concern has to be *justified* in order to satisfy compliance; whereas in all other cases it is a *departure that would have to be justified*.

2.10 This is not to say that a departure from the going concern assumption would require no justification; rather that such accounts (unless drawn up by a liquidator rather than by directors for publication) are unlikely to see the light of day as stewardship accounts giving a true and fair view. In this sense the going concern concept is the most fundamental of all.

2.11 There are no circumstances in which adherence to the requirement to match costs and benefits, to employ consistent treatment, or to exercise prudence, require any prior justification. But the moment that the company cannot justifiably be regarded as a going concern the entire accounting exercise dissolves in pointlessness – perhaps to be resurrected in accordance with a wholly different set of rules, for a select and limited readership, by a liquidator at a later point in time.

2.12 The accounting concepts, if correctly applied, clearly require no disclosure *per se*. After all, one can hardly imagine any alternative set of groundrules: for prudence, perhaps 'optimism'? For accruals, perhaps 'optional matching'; for consistency, obviously 'inconsistency'; and, finally, the 'gone' concern concept.

2.13 The Standard explains that the basic concepts are capable of practical implementation in a variety of ways, depending upon the nature of the transactions or balances in question, the nature of the business, and the particular circumstances prevailing. The methods by means of which the concepts may correctly be applied are referred to in SSAP 2 as 'accounting bases', and it is accepted that a range of such bases may exist.

UNDERSTANDING ACCOUNTING STANDARDS

2.14 The specific accounting bases selected by the directors as being most appropriate to the business and, of course, most likely to result in a true and fair view being given if used when preparing the company's financial statements, are known as the 'accounting policies'. It is these that both the Standard and the CA require to be disclosed. This is natural enough, given the range of permissible bases, and without explicit disclosure the accounts would lack inherent intelligibility and comparability in relation to other accounts, of other companies and of the same company in other financial periods.

2.15 The Standard recognises that while the accounting concepts are inter-related, it is possible that they could be in conflict. For example, it may be expected that a particular asset has an expected useful life, at a given usage level, of ten years if properly serviced and maintained. It may, however, be prudent to recognise, based on knowledge of the technology currently being developed, that obsolescence after five years is a strong possibility, especially if past experience supports such a view.

2.16 The normal application of the accruals concept would suggest that the cost of the asset should be charged over the ten successive accounting periods in which the benefits of its use are likely to be recorded. For reasons of prudence, however, the Standard requires that in this case a five-year period should be used, giving rise to higher depreciation charges throughout.

2.17 The accruals concept, taken on its own, assumes that the asset in question will be used in the business for the whole of its expected useful life, as estimated by the directors and, as we have seen, reduced to reflect obsolescence as a risk additional to straightforward wear and tear. The latter is intrinsic to the physical nature of all tangible assets, and is reflected in periodic depreciation charges calculated to allocate the cost (either historic or current, depending on the convention being used) of assets to the periods in which their use creates a benefit.

2.18 Obsolescence, by contrast, reduces the expected useful life of an asset for reasons wholly independent of the asset's use in the business, and is usually caused by external technological developments. Its practical impact is that the net relevant cash flows capable of being derived from the asset's use over its effective life (including any residual value at the end thereof) are less than its cost or written down book value, and the latter must be reduced accordingly.

2.19 We may refer to the present value of future net income flows as the asset's economic value. When its economic value, or the value of continuing to use it, is exceeded by its net realisable value, its disposal would normally be indicated.

2.20 The foregoing serves merely to illustrate the practical relationship between the twin concepts of accruals and prudence respectively. The other two require little further commentary. There are, of course, occasions when a departure from the consistency principles is not only justified but necessary; such as on the introduction of a new Accounting Standard requiring a change of policy.

2.21 In the USA the principle of 'preferability' is used, whereby changes of accounting policy are permitted only if (with the auditor's concurrence) the new policy is preferable to the existing one. The difficulty, of course, has always been to establish how preferability should be assessed, and from whose standpoint. Pending the widespread acceptance of a conceptual framework, no objective yardstick is available whereby such preferences may be judged.

2.22 The UK legal attitude has, both in statute and in common law, always been to impose the apparently *subjective* measure of the actions or expectations of 'the reasonable man' as the closest available measure of *objective* truth and fairness. While this is a convenient and practical device, and has served the coherent development of common law for several centuries, it suffers in our present context from one particular omission: we do not know whether 'the reasonable man' (an abstraction recognised by all minds despite none of us having ever met such a saintly figure!) is a shareholder, depositor, debenture holder, trade creditor, member of the management team, tax inspector, or other interested party.

2.23 In other words, while we have no multidimensional conceptual framework which both acknowledges and embraces the varying, and potentially conflicting, interests of respective users of financial statements, we are obliged to make do with a set of surrogate rules which, while fitting one particular set of circumstances, will require adaptation when these alter. So the rules proliferate, in a seemingly endless set of circumstantially generated permutations, each representing yet another variation on the same general theme of our basic accounting concepts.

2.24 Consistency must be understood to relate to the accounting policies themselves, rather than the details of their application. A reduction in the period over which the cost of an asset is written off does *not* represent a change of depreciation policy; nor does it represent a breach of the consistency principle. The policy of charging the cost against the revenues of respective accounting periods (by means of a specified method such as 'straight line', 'reducing balance', etc.) remains consistently in force despite the alteration in write-off period due to changed circumstances.

2.25 Extended reference has already been made to the going-concern concept. Its meaning and significance is well appreciated in practice, and auditors are familiar with the procedures whereby any apparent danger signals are evaluated by reference to post balance sheet events, directors' explanations, future production plans, cash flow and profit forecasts, and the trade outlook in general. The effect of the principle itself is that the accounts are drawn up on the assumption that the business will continue indefinitely or, stated more specifically, that all non-monetary balance sheet asset values will, in the due unfolding of time, yield benefits of similar amount or more, while all liabilities will continue to be met on their due dates.

2.26 Seen thus, a balance sheet, being a mixture of equity, monetary and non-monetary items, represents the *lowest* of economic value, cost and net realisable value of all non-monetary items, plus or minus the difference between monetary assets and liabilities.

2.27 The moment this perception of continuity is replaced by one of untimely cessation, all prior assumptions collapse and realisable values become operative. In practice this means that assets are realised piece-meal on a break-up basis by the liquidator (or receiver for debenture holders, if there is any possibility of saving the business in its drastically pruned form) for whatever proceeds can be obtained on a forced sale. The full meaning of the going concern concept can easily be grasped when contrasted with such dire circumstances.

Other accounting assumptions

The Business Entity
2.28 This assumption holds that each business is an accounting unit, separate and distinct from its owners and other businesses. The transactions of the business are to be reported, rather than the transactions of the business' owners. This assumption recognises the stewardship function, i.e. the fiduciary responsibility of management to shareholders.

The Unit-of-Measure
2.29 The accounting information is measured in terms of money. It is further assumed that the value of money remains stable.

ACCOUNTING PRINCIPLES

The accounting period

2.30 This assumption holds that financial reports depicting the changes in wealth of a business should be disclosed periodically. Most companies use an accounting period that corresponds to a calendar year of 12 months.

The concept of materiality in accounts

Introduction

2.31 The use of the word 'material' in relation to accounting matters is intended to give scope to a reasonably wide interpretation according to the variety of circumstances which can arise. It is not possible or desirable, therefore, to give a precise definition of such an expression. By literal definition the adjective 'material' can vary in meaning from 'significant' to 'essential'. In an accounting sense, however, a matter is material if its non-disclosure, mis-statement or omission would be likely to distort the view given by the accounts or other statement under consideration.

General accounting requirements

2.32 The principle of materiality is and has always been fundamental to the whole process of accountancy, and is not therefore confined to statutory requirements. The whole process of preparing accounts consists of the aggregation, classification and presentation of all the transactions in such a way as to give a true and fair view of the results for a period and of the position at a specified date. Each of these processes involves the application of the principle of materiality. Questions of materiality arise in simple receipts and payments accounts or detailed profit and loss accounts as they do in any other kind of accounts.

Interpretation

2.33 The interpretation of what is 'material' is a matter for the exercise of professional judgment based on experience and the requirement to give a true and fair view. Some general considerations are set out below, but their application will depend upon the context in which a matter falls to be judged.

Application

2.34 The question of materiality can arise in various circumstances, including whether or not:

(a) an item should be disclosed:
    (i) by description in an omnibus item;
    (ii) separately;

(iii) as an important reservation or a matter of deliberate emphasis in presentation (e.g. profit of the year before deducting special loss);
(b) an error or oversight needs correction;
(c) a method of computation, basis or formula properly allows for relevant factors.

The application of the term 'material' to any item will include consideration of:

(a) the amount itself, in relation to:
   (i) the overall view of the accounts;
   (ii) the total of which it forms or should form a part;
   (iii) associated items (whether in the profit and loss account or in the balance sheet);
   (iv) the corresponding amounts in previous years;
(b) the description, including questions of emphasis;
(c) the presentation and context;
(d) any statutory requirements for disclosure.

2.35 Materiality can be considered only in relative terms. In a small business £500 may be material, whereas £1 million may not be material in classifying the expenditure of a very large undertaking, especially as too much elaboration could obscure the true and fair view. Those responsible for preparing and auditing accounts have to decide which, out of the many facts available to them, are the ones that have a real bearing on the true and fair view which the accounts must give. In some circumstances, a difference of about 10% might be acceptable, but in other circumstances a difference as low as 3% might be too much. While percentage comparisons can, properly used, constitute useful broad guides, it must be kept in mind that they are no more than rough rules of thumb, and should not be applied indiscriminately without regard to particular circumstances.

Context – precision v latitude
2.36 An item may be material, in either a general or a particular context. The general context refers to the true and fair view given by the statement as a whole. The particular context relates to the total of which an item forms or should form part and any directly associated items. If an item is not material in the general context, the degree of latitude acceptable in the particular context may depend upon its nature. There is an important distinction between cases where the amount at issue is arrived at on the basis of assumption and exercise of judgment and those where it is capable of precise and objective determination.

2.37   On the one hand, there are items such as depreciation where some measure of arbitrary assessment can be inherent in determining the amount to be written off in any one year. A margin of error which is high in relation to the item itself might be acceptable, if it is acceptable when viewed in the context of the profit and of the associated balance sheet item. On the other hand, items such as directors' emoluments, audit fees and investment income may have a particular interest or importance to shareholders, so that an error which might be trivial in the general context, and indeed may not be large in relation to the item itself, might nevertheless be considered material. It is relevant to observe that these items are usually capable of precise measurement, so that any departure from the exact figure would call for some justification. Indeed, in the case of directors' emoluments, the directors' fiduciary relationship inhibits any latitude in this respect.

Miscellaneous factors

2.38   (a) *Degree of approximation*. The degree of estimation or approximation which is unavoidably inherent in arriving at the amount of any item may be a factor in deciding on materiality. Examples include contingency provisions, stock and work in progress, and taxation provisions.

(b) *Losses or low profits*. The use of the profit figure as a point of comparison tends to be vitiated when the profits are abnormally low or where there is a loss; when judging the materiality of individual items in the profit and loss account the more normal dimensions of the business have to be considered.

(c) *Relative materiality*. The view given by accounts may sometimes be affected by the trend of profit, or turnover, and of various expense items. An inaccuracy which might not otherwise be judged to be material could have the effect of reversing a trend, or turning a profit into a loss, or creating or eliminating the margin of solvency in a balance sheet. Where an item affects such a critical point in accounts, then its materiality has to be viewed in that narrower context.

Materiality is a relative factor and each case must be looked at on its individual merits. Percentage differences are often useful guides to materiality, and the figure most often given for the point at which a difference becomes material is 5 per cent . But if a difference of say 5 per cent is material to the item specifically being reviewed, this does not necessarily mean that it is material within the context of the accounts as a whole; equally, the converse may be true in that a change in the valuation of the stock, which is immaterial *per se*, may dramatically affect the profit. It is necessary to consider the effect that this difference would have on:

UNDERSTANDING ACCOUNTING STANDARDS

    (i) shareholders' funds;
    (ii) total assets;
    (iii) net profit; and
    (iv) turnover.

    If the item is not material in the general context, the degree of latitude acceptable in the particular context may depend upon its nature.

    It is usual to consider materiality in relation to the largest possible base, e.g. turnover or gross assets, for purposes of determining 'high value' items and sampling intervals in an auditing context.

(d) *Disproportionate significance.* An item of small amount may nevertheless be of material significance in the context of the company's particular circumstances, especially if the context would lead the reader to expect the item to be of substantial amount.

(e) *Offset and aggregation.* It frequently happens that two items, which might each be material taken separately, will be of opposite effect. Care should be taken before offsetting such items. For example, a profit arising as a result of a change in the basis of accounting should not be offset against a non-recurring loss. It may also be necessary, where there are a large number of small items, for them to be aggregated to ascertain if they are material in total. The principle of 'aggregation' now required under the CA 1985 precludes the setting-off of items, e.g. bank overdrafts and balances in hand.

5. Substance over form

2.39 This assumption requires that the transactions in accounts must be recorded in accordance with their economic substance rather than their legal form. There are a number of applications of this assumption and some of them are discussed below:

(a) Consolidated financial statements

2.40 The assumption here is that two or more legally separate entities are treated as one economic unit. In form they are distinct companies, but, in substance, they are viewed as one because of the control exercised by the parent company and other factors. The purpose of consolidated financial statements is to reflect transactions between the consolidated entity and outside parties, such as customers. Therefore, transactions among the related companies (inter company transactions) do not affect the financial statements. To issue consolidated financial statements, the parent company must control the subsidiary companies.

(b) The equity method of accounting for investments

2.41 This involves increasing or decreasing the investment account for the investor's share of the investee's reported earnings or losses and decreasing the investment account when the investor receives dividends from the investee. The investor's earnings, therefore, are increased by the investee's reported earnings for the period (substance), whether or not these earnings are actually distributed by the investee (form). In other words, substance is recognised over form for reporting an investor's share of an investee's earnings.

2.42 The equity method is assumed to be appropriate if an investor can influence the operating or financial decisions of the investee. In form, such influence implies ownership of more than 50 per cent of the voting shares of the investee. In substance, though, such influence can be present even if the share ownership in the investee is less than 50 per cent. Again, substance prevails over form because the equity method of accounting for investment is required when an investor is in a position to exercise significant influence over the investee.

(c) Financial lease in the books of lessee
2.43 This must be recorded in the books of lessee as if he is acquiring the asset.

2.44 The asset and related obligation (liability) initially must be included in the lessee's accounts at a fair value or the present value of future rents and other payments. The lessee would then charge interest and depreciation (instead of rent) to profit and loss account each year. In form, this is a lease or rental agreement; in substance, it is equivalent to a purchase because certain criteria are met. In the absence of these established criteria, the lease is treated as an operating lease with no capitalisation required and rent charged to the profit and loss account annually.

2.45 This decision on whether or not to record the acquisition of an asset and incurrence of a liability is based on the substance of what the lessee is assumed to be acquiring. If the lessee is assumed to be acquiring equity in the asset, the lease should be considered a purchase. If the lessee is assumed to be acquiring current service value of the asset, the lease should not be considered a purchase.

SSAP 17 – Post balance sheet events

2.46 The purpose of this Standard is to prescribe a uniform accounting treatment of events which, although occurring after the balance sheet date, have an effect on the financial statements in question. Without such standardised treatment directors of companies would be subject to the understandable temptation to adjust the accounts to reflect only those subsequent events which have a favourable effect.

2.47 The Standard's recognition of 'adjusting' and 'non-adjusting' events is reflected in the CA 1985, in which 'Accounting Principles' to be used in preparing accounts are described and these include the following in the paragraph on Prudence: '... *provision is to be made for all liabilities and losses which have arisen or are likely to arise in respect of the financial year, including those which become apparent only after the balance sheet date and before it is signed'*.

2.48 Although the Act makes no reference to assets or gains which become apparent after the balance sheet date, it does not specifically prohibit their accrual; while SSAP 17 applies to both *'favourable and unfavourable'* events alike – insisting, of course, that prudence is exercised in all situations requiring the exercise of judgment.

2.49 It should also be noted that the Act's reference to post balance sheet events includes a time-frame which coincides precisely with that defined in SSAP 17: these are events which occur between the date of the balance sheet and the date on which the accounts are approved (signed) by the directors.

2.50 This requirement may, however, present problems for the auditors, who should sign the audit report after the directors have approved the accounts. The directors may choose to ignore events which occur subsequent to signing, even if those events would have been relevant to the accounts had the latter still been unsigned. Presumably, however, the 'true and fair' override requirement would prevail in the case of any material event. This is obviously an area in which the auditor's own independent judgment is essential.

2.51 Even if the accounts and audit report have been signed, it may be necessary to amend them and re-approve them if a material subsequent event occurs which impinges on the truth and fairness of the view presented by the accounts. An Auditing Guideline on this subject has been published, *Guideline 402: Events after the Balance Sheet Date*, to which reference should be made if required.

2.52 The Standard on Post Balance Sheet Events defines adjusting events as those *'which provide additional evidence of conditions existing at the balance sheet date'*. Adjusting events, by definition, require changes in amounts to be included in the financial statements. The appendix to the Standard provides a list of examples.

2.53 Non-adjusting events are defined inversely as *'post balance sheet events which concern conditions which did not exist at the balance sheet date'*. Again, examples are given in the Appendix. Non-adjusting events, if material, require disclosure in the notes to the accounts but, again by definition, do not warrant any changes to be made to the accounts themselves.

2.54 The Standard makes it clear that an event which would ordinarily be classified as non-adjusting will justify treatment as adjusting only if its effect is to indicate that the application of the going concern assumption to the whole or material part of the business may no longer be appropriate.

2.55 The requirement to disclose material non-adjusting events by way of note is extended by the Standard to catch instances of 'window-dressing'. Disclosure is required of *'the reversal or maturity after the year end of a transaction entered into before the year end, the substance of which was primarily to alter the appearance of the company's balance sheet'*.

2.56 Although the definitions given in the Standard of adjusting and non-adjusting events are straightforward enough, arguments persist on their practical application, which can have a dramatic impact on the financial statements as presented and duly published.

2.57 The examples provided in the Appendix to the Standard, although not part of the Standard and included for guidance only, leave far too much room for interpretation. The examples of adjusting events include 'the receipt of proceeds of sales after the balance sheet date or other evidence concerning the net realisable value of stocks'. This example should, of course, have gone on to state that the net realisable value *at the year end* is in question, rather than subsequently. Post balance sheet sales at less than cost could be non-adjusting events if it is known that the fall in value of stocks is wholly attributable to circumstances which did not exist at the year end.

2.58 Similarly, the examples of non-adjusting events include *'closing a significant part of the trading activities if this was not anticipated at the year end'*. It would have been preferable if the example had referred to a closure which *could not reasonably* have been anticipated, since this endows the example with a measure of objective determination.

UNDERSTANDING ACCOUNTING STANDARDS

2.59 Company directors will often swear that they did not in fact anticipate an adverse eventuality which, at the balance sheet date, was patently unavoidable, and known to be so to all affected thereby. Yet their acknowledged blindness to it, on the face of it, entitles them to treat it as non-adjusting. This is another area in which auditors have a clear duty to determine whether the directors are merely seeking to avoid having to make unwelcome changes in the financial statements.

2.60 Other than in such marginal instances there should be little difficulty in applying the Standard's definitions. All insured losses caused by fire or flood after the year end are, of course, non-adjusting events and their consequences for the company should, if judged material, be disclosed by way of note. The cause of loss is the event itself, not the condition of underinsurance. If the loss had been fully insured, including consequential effects, the event would have had no effect on the accounts anyway.

2.61 Currency or commodity price hedging by means of future contracts may cause problems. The loss or gain may crystallise after the year end, but it is often very difficult to establish whether the 'condition' giving rise to the eventual result existed at the year end date. It can only be suggested that, in the case of material losses, the prudent course is to make full provision, irrespective of the fact that the company's open position at close of business at its year end showed a favourable margin.

2.62 Another area of difficulty concerns management decisions before the year end, but implemented after date. What is the 'condition' at the year end? The Standard fails to answer this, but merely notes that the preliminary consideration of a matter which may lead to a future board decision is not within the scope of the Standard. It is, however, doubtful whether a board decision on its own to, say, sell an investment in a subsidiary, or to issue new shares, is sufficient to justify treatment as an adjusting event. A legal or otherwise binding commitment to complete the transaction in question should, at very least, be in force before the year end.

SSAP 18 – Accounting for contingencies

2.63 Both in law and according to this Standard the nature of any material contingent liability which exists at the balance sheet date must be disclosed, together with an estimate of its amount. The Standard, however, extends its provisions to cover contingent assets and gains also,

ACCOUNTING PRINCIPLES

and requires the uncertainties affecting the ultimate outcome to be disclosed. Since the determination of the outcome of any year-end contingency necessarily occurs at a later date, SSAP 18's provisions are inseparable from those of SSAP 17, which we have already considered. These two Standards should therefore be regarded together.

2.64 Examples of contingent liabilities are (a) bills of exchange receivable which have been discounted with recourse; (b) pending litigation; (c) financial guarantees on behalf of other parties; and (d) product warranties issued to customers, and still unexpired.

2.65 Examples of favourable contingencies are (a) insurance claims in respect of losses already incurred; (b) litigation likely to benefit the company, acting as plaintiff; (c) the alteration of contract terms in the company's favour; (d) compensation in respect of foreign assets previously nationalised or sequestrated.

2.66 The Standard, wisely, avoids any attempt to determine categorically when the outcome of a contingency is sufficiently clear to warrant adjustment to the accounts. The Auditing Practices Committee of the CCAB, in its publication *True & Fair*, did, however, offer the following guidance on a 'rule of thumb' basis, which should be regarded as no more than a helpful starting point for evaluating particular situations.

Likelihood of crystallisation	Contingent Assets	Contingent Liabilities
1. Remote	Do not disclose	Do not disclose
2. Possible – Probable	Do not disclose	Disclose by way of note (CA 1985)
3. Highly probable	Disclose by way of note	Make specific provision
4. Virtually certain	Accrue	Make specific provision

2.67 The above guide serves to indicate when it is permissable to recognise gains, either by note or by accrual in the accounts, and when it is permissable to allow losses or liabilities merely to be noted, as opposed to being provided for in the accounts. In other words, it is necessary always to give careful consideration to the question of whether a potential gain or loss is genuinely a contingency at all.

2.68 If a post balance sheet event, for example the meeting of a bill receivable discounted before the year end, demonstrates that no liability to the bank can arise, there is no purpose served in including the bill in any contingency note. Even though the favourable outcome was not *known* at the balance sheet date, the actual condition at that date was without risk, as proved by the subsequent event. The contingency of dishonour was therefore more apparent than real, and any note of it would serve no purpose – except perhaps to indicate to readers the normal *level* of contingency that operates during the year, if such is indeed the case. Even then, the note should state that the bills in question have in fact been met by their acceptors in full, after the year end.

2.69 Similarly, any contingent liability which is, by its very nature, matched upon crystallisation by an equivalent gain or asset, should not be noted. Unawarded contracts for which tenders have been submitted prior to the year end will, if won, result in both extensive costs and, presumably, commensurate profits. There is therefore no point whatever in noting the costs contingent upon the award being granted – unless it is known that the income will be insufficient to meet the probable costs; in which event one can but wonder why the tender has not been withdrawn!

2.70 (The true financial outlook may, of course, have been revealed only after the award of the contract has been made: in such a case, however, it is probable that full provision in the accounts is required. A contingency note would not be adequate, since the post balance sheet award represents the crystallisation of all that was contingent when the accounts were first drafted.)

Off-balance sheet finance

2.71 This chapter on accounting standards and the law would be incomplete without reference to the particularly critical issue of material assets and liabilities being disclosed by way of notes to accounts rather than being reflected in the accounts themselves – a syndrome which has become popularly known as 'off balance sheet finance'.

2.72 It was in the 1978 Department of Trade Inspectors' Report on *Court Line*, the failed travel group, that attention was first drawn to the use of notes in financial reports as a means of redressing deficiencies in the accounts themselves. The Inspectors were appointed under the CA after the group collapsed with a massive deficiency despite its most recent accounts, published only a few months earlier, having declared a pre-tax profit of £4.7 million.

2.73 This 'accounting profit' was largely a result of the company's accounting policies (rather than its trading!) yet they were by no means hidden from view. The following was published openly under its accounting policies and illustrates a determination to boost profits, come what may: *'(Group) profit before taxation includes the profit arising on work carried out by one group company on improvements to the ships of another in whose accounts the work done has been capitalised at £609,000'.*

2.74 Instead of eliminating from group results all profits attributable to inter-company trading, the policy blatantly declared their inclusion. The company's 'more credits than debits' philosophy is, of course, enforced by telling us that the company receiving the service had capitalised its cost rather than writing it off. Nor do we know the size of the profit element in the £609,000. With policies like these, one might cynically ask, does one actually need to trade?

2.75 In response to this situation the Inspectors commented: *'It does not seem to us therefore sufficient to adopt an accounting treatment in arriving at the figure of profit and rely on disclosure of that treatment in the notes for the truth and fairness of the profit. The average reader of the accounts looks to the stated profit figure and places less reliance on the accompanying notes'.*

2.76 It is a comment on our notions of progress that ten years after those words were published, the ACS has published an exposure draft (ED42: Special purpose transactions) on the 'off-balance sheet finance' theme, whose central debate is remarkably similar to that posed above: the validity of notes as an antidote to otherwise deficient report. The current Chairman of ASC has declared: *'You can't cure a defective balance sheet with yards and yards of footnotes'*, which is a more forthright way of making the identical point to that highlighted by the *Court Line* Inspectors.

2.77 The context, to be fair, is different. But it nevertheless demonstrates an anomaly in financial reporting that has fully emerged as a public issue only very recently. While the all embracing 'true and fair' criterion has been a legal requirement since the CA 1948 (which preferred this phrase to the unattainably precise 'true and correct' formula which preceded it) its interpretation has not apparently extended to a requirement that the commercial or economic substance of transactions take precedence over their legal form.

2.78 While the CA 1985 declares 'going concern', 'consistency', 'prudence' and 'accruals' to be fundamental accounting principles, it fails to add a requirement that the commercial substance of a transaction or arrangement shall take priority over its legal form. Such advantage has been taken of this omission that the Institute published a Technical Release (TR 603) identifying three commonly found situations in which accounting treatment is determined by reference to legal form rather than commercial substance:

(i) *Non-subsidiary 'dependent' companies*
A separate entity is set up in a way that, although it is under the control of the 'parent', it is not legally a subsidiary. Assets and liabilities are then transferred from the parent to the dependent company with the clear intention that they be excluded from the consolidated accounts. The effect may be that gearing (and hence the apparent return on capital) of the group is improved.

(ii) *Sale and repurchase*
Trading stock is sold to a friendly entity with an option to buy back, the deal constructed so that the option is virtually certain to be exercised. Both the stock and the related repurchase obligation (in effect the 'finance' provided by the temporary holder of the stock) are excluded from the balance sheet of the seller, and the difference between the original sale price and buy-back price (effectively the finance charge) is charged as part of the cost of sales as and when the item is finally sold to an independent third party. Any 'profit' on the original transfer is treated as realised immediately, while no financing costs or obligations appear at any time.

(iii) *Consignment stocks*
Manufacturers consign stocks to dealers under a variety of schemes. The purchase price is payable only on sale to a third party, and is carefully calculated to reflect the period of stock holding. The manufacturer is effectively financing the trading stock of the dealership, yet neither the stock nor the loan is reflected in the dealer's balance sheet, and the trading results reveal no financing cost.

2.79 The ASC realises that the current off-balance sheet finance issue is possibly the most serious it has faced, and an unsuccessful outcome could present a crisis of credibility which our regime of self-regulation could not survive.

2.80 The real problem is that this type of creative accounting is self-perpetuating: companies which secure improved gearing and return on assets employed also cause a change in market expectations of what these hallmark ratios should be. By the same token those who fail to achieve

ACCOUNTING PRINCIPLES

them are marked down, but will soon jump on the accounting policy merry-go-round – thereby obliging those already on it to go for still more inventive schemes, just to stay ahead.

2.81 The ASC has disclosed in its exposure draft (ED42) an outline of the type of solution it will propose. Quite correctly, it has overridden all interpretive subtleties and come out firmly for substance over form as an essential ingredient of a true and fair view. And no compromises!

2.82 So fundamental are the issues involved that the draft even provides new definitions of assets and liabilities. All familiar connotations of legal ownership and control are side-stepped on the basis that they have shown themselves to be a fertile breeding ground for ill-disguised invention and contrivance.

2.83 Instead we shall probably be required to consider assets in terms of 'probable future economic benefits'; and liabilities as 'probable future sacrifices'. For example, in considering transactions affecting assets already on the balance sheet, the main issue will be whether, as a consequence of those transactions, the assets have been disposed of or merely refinanced. Debt factoring is a classic illustration of the former since no future benefit remains after the proceeds of the sale of debts have been received – although there may be a disclosable contingent liability, depending on any recourse terms in respect of debts which may prove worthless. The difference between proceeds and face value will, of course, be written off as a finance charge.

2.84 By contrast, any arrangement whereby stock is transferred to a third party on terms which ensure that the transferor company continues to receive the benefits arising from it, indicates that the asset had simply been refinanced. It should therefore remain on the balance sheet irrespective of the legal ramifications which underpin the arrangement itself.

2.85 The ASC's approach to disentangling complex arrangements is similar to that used by the Inland Revenue in determining whether the intermediate steps or transactions in a series have any independent commercial justification. If they do not, they are set aside as having no purpose other than tax avoidance or mitigation. By reference to a 'reasonable accounting analogy' a complex transaction can be compared with a simple equivalent whose effect, although more directly achieved, is otherwise indistinguishable.

2.86 A sale and repurchase arrangement may, for example, have the same commercial effect as a secured loan. The principle of using a

47

reasonable accounting analogy would therefore dictate that the arrangement be accounted for in the same way as a secured loan. The supporting disclosure of relevant details would be given in notes which, in this context, are providing supporting rather than primary information.

2.87 Quoting once again the words of the ASC Chairman, these proposals *'represent the foundations of a standard that will ensure that financial statements continue to give a fair presentation of the risks and rewards underlying a company's financial position'*.

2.88 The establishment of these accounting criteria, which effectively re-evaluate the conceptual basis on which financial reporting is structured, will produce predictably vehement opposition – not least from those companies who have most to lose from the abandonment of creative schemes already in full swing. If the ASC's proposals proceed to full implementation these companies will be required to tell the world about the substance of transactions and superstructures which have previously been revealed only in terms of their outline form.

2.89 They will also be obliged to publish full reconciliations between the two positions at the implementation date, possibly involving prior-year adjustments and restated comparative amounts. It thus promises to be an interesting development for all concerned!

Conceptual framework of accounting

2.90 As stated earlier, SSAP 2 should not be regarded as a substitute for a conceptual framework of accounting. Arguments for and against establishing a conceptual framework of accounting *before* proceeding to the standards are set out below:

Arguments for establishing a logical and coherent framework of accounting before proceeding to accounting standards:

(i) There is a close relationship between theory and practice. If theory is without potential relevance to practice, it cannot be sound theory. Those who decry theory in general as having no practical relevance either do not understand theory, or they rely on unsupported argumentation presented in the guise of theory.

(ii) A conceptual framework would advance the expression of generally accepted accounting principles. To formulate standards on specific issues without first constructing, by induction from practice, a set of basic postulates or axioms (such as entity and money measurement), and deriving from them a hierarchy of principles (such as assumptions, working rules, conventions, etc.) would leave accounting without the foundation of rational principles.
(iii) Such a framework would help to narrow the areas of difference in appropriate practice and achieve comparability between financial statements of different companies, or even of the same company, in different periods.
(iv) A framework would provide a reference point when facing unsettled and controversial issues, and would provide a basis for understanding the broad fundamentals of accounting and for its future development.

Arguments against a logical and coherent framework of accounting before proceeding to accounting standards

(i) There is little evidence that a framework would necessarily lead to the expression of generally accepted accounting principles, or narrow the areas of difference in practice. Some Standards based on 'theory' have been abandoned (SSAP 7 and SSAP 16).
(ii) It tends to create a rigid framework of rules which may not be appropriate in all the circumstances.
(iii) Financial statements are needed by a variety of users, and it is never certain that a single conceptual framework can be devised to suit all users – whose interests may well be in conflict.
(iv) Given this diversity of user requirements, there may well be a variety of SSAPs, each produced for a different purpose (and with different concepts as a base).
(v) It is not clear that a conceptual framework will render the task of devising and implementing standards any easier than it is now.

Profits available for distribution

2.91 The introduction of prescriptive accounting in the CA 1981 (the UK implementation of the EC Fourth Directive) caused particular difficulty in the area of profit determination by stipulating that only 'realised' profits may be included in the profit and loss account, and providing a circuitous definition raised more questions than it answered.

UNDERSTANDING ACCOUNTING STANDARDS

2.92 The concept of realised profits is not new, of course. It was, for example, declared in *Foster v New Trinidad Lake Asphalte Co. Ltd.* [1901] 1 Ch 208 and even earlier cases that capital profits may be distributed provided that (i) the company's articles permit this; (ii) the surplus remains after all the other assets are fairly revalued; and (iii) the surplus is *realised*.

2.93 In the case of *Dimbula Valley (Ceylon) Tea Co. Ltd v Laurie* [1961] Ch 353, (1961) 1 A11ER 769, it was held that an *unrealised* revaluation surplus could, with certain safeguards (such as a professional revaluation of all assets), be used to pay a cash dividend on the 'grounds' that *if any reserve arising from a revaluation could not be distributed, it likewise could not be capitalised; only that which could be distributed in dividends can be capitalised.*

2.94 The *Dimbula* case was decided just in time for Lord Jenkins and his company law reform committee to condemn roundly its notion of basing cash distributions on a valuation, however well it is apparently supported. The *Dimbula* judgement was also notable in flying in the face of the sound Scottish decision in *Westburn Sugar Refineries Ltd v IRC* (1960) 39 PC 45, (1960) TR 105 only months earlier, in which Lord Sorn soberly and simply observed: 'In my view, capital profits are not distributable until they are realised'.

2.95 While the debate on distributable profits continued in the realm of case law, it was notably absent from the statutes – apart from the question-begging clause in Table A (CA 1948) stating that *'dividends shall not be paid otherwise than out of profits'*. The UK implementation of the EC Second Directive demanded, however, that the requirements designed to protect companies' capital should incorporate specific rules on profits available for distribution. These were embodied in the CA 1980.

2.96 These rules are now included in the 1985 consolidating Act, and effectively overrule the *Dimbula* case referred to above. Section 263, which applies to all companies, states that distributions may be made only from profits available for the purpose. These are, in effect, the company's accumulated, realised profits (not otherwise utilised by distribution or capitalisation); *less* its accumulated, realised losses (so far as not previously written off).

2.97 The Act makes it clear that
(i) a provision shall be treated as a realised loss;
(ii) capitalised development expenditure shall be treated as a realised loss unless the directors have justifiable special reasons (to be disclosed) why it should not be so treated;

ACCOUNTING PRINCIPLES

(iii) any unrealised profit included in the amount of previously revalued fixed assets shall be deemed to be realised on a piecemeal distribution *in specie* of those assets;
(iv) depreciation attributable to the uplift on revaluation shall be deemed to be realised profits.

2.98 The logic of the latter provision is that part of the unrealised revaluation reserve created by the revaluation has become realised by consumption, the asset in question having been used throughout the accounting period and having therefore been subject to normal wear and tear. For this reason a sum equivalent to the depreciation on the uplift should be transferred from unrealised to realised revaluation reserves in the balance sheet, and disclosure thereof made in the 'movement on reserves' note.

2.99 We see from this that this branch of legislation has created a clear distinction (which did not exist in statute law prior to the 1980 Act) between accounting profit (or 'true and fair' profit) and distributable profit, each arising from its own framework of rules – the former based largely on SSAPs, the latter on the statutory rules outlined above. They are from time to time in conflict; for example, SSAP 20 requires that long-term foreign exchange gains and losses should *both* feature in the profit and loss account, irrespective of whether realised. The Act, of course, prohibits the inclusion of unrealised profits in the profit and loss account.

2.100 Conflicts of this type render it necessary to invoke the Act's 'true and fair' override, an option resented by the Department of Trade and Industry (DTI) if used, as they put it, as a recourse of first, rather than last, resort. They are particularly concerned about its use in the context of long-term contracts in progress, the valuation of which must, according to SSAP 9, include profit attributable to the proportion of contract work completed to date. This results in unrealised profit (a) being included in the profit and loss account; and (b) inflating the current asset amount of work in progress in the balance sheet above 'purchase price or production cost'.

2.101 As the chapter on this standard explains, the ED 40 solution to this legal problem may cause unrealised profit to be included in debtors rather than in work in progress, and this therefore becomes questionable on other grounds, such as the effect on accounts interpretation from the standpoint of banks and investment analysts.

2.102 Section 270 of the Act provides that the right of a company to make a distribution, and the amount of any distribution, is to be determined by reference to accounts complying with specific requirements. The accounts are *the most recent audited accounts*, made up as at the company's accounting reference date, or, if the distribution would not be permitted by reference to these accounts, more recent interim accounts. The accounts must carry an *unqualified audit report* or *a statement in writing*.

2.103 This means broadly that either a 'clean' opinion is given for the balance sheet being audited or, in the case of a qualified report, *a written statement* (laid before the members in general meeting) that the qualification is not material in determining the propriety of the company's proposed distribution.

2.104 This 'balance sheet approach' to determining distributable profits of public companies provides a curious contrast with the 'profit and loss account approach' already explained as applicable to *all* companies. Is there really any difference? The public company criterion seems to be, in essence, that any distributions may be made from a company's realised reserves only – which is exactly what the general requirement is saying.

2.105 What of revaluation deficits? By their nature they are unrealised losses and surely, therefore, this constitutes the difference between the general and the plc rules respectively? The former make no allowance for unrealised losses, whereas a plc would have to take them into account.

2.106 This answers the problem on the face of it, but let us briefly consider its practical application. A revaluation deficit simply represents the measure of past underdepreciation, for which the obvious and necessary remedy is to increase the depreciation provision accordingly. By definition, however, as already explained, a provision must be regarded as a *realised* loss, and this therefore places both private and public companies on the same footing in this regard.

2.107 The real answer seems to be that if the revaluation deficit relates to a *non-depreciable* asset (such as freehold land or a portfolio of investments), and is incorporated in the accounts, a private company would be at liberty to *add back* to its accumulated realised profits any amount previously written off as a consequence of that revaluation in arriving at its distributable profit (but obviously not altering its accounting profit). A plc is not, of course, legally able to make such an adjustment.

2.108 The foregoing will serve to illustrate why it was felt important to provide a statutory definition of 'realised profits', and this was included

ACCOUNTING PRINCIPLES

in the 1981 Act. The Act's description of the 'prudence' principle, which is the passage that precludes the inclusion of unrealised profits in the profit and loss account, is followed by the tortuously worded, barely intelligible and conceptually unsound 'definition' which follows:

'It is hereby declared for the avoidance of doubt that in relation to a company's accounts realised profits are references to such profits of the company as fall to be treated as realised profits, for the purposes of those accounts, in accordance with principles generally accepted with respect to the determination for accounting purposes of realised profits at the time when these accounts are prepared'.

2.109   One can but speculate on how that definition might have read if it had been for the *creation* rather than *avoidance* of doubt! Perhaps its worst failing is its implicit assumption of the existence of generally accepted accounting principles for determining realised profits.

2.110   We have seen that there is a substantial body of judicial case law in this area, but certainly no set of accounting rules on the subject. Accounting standards are designed with a true and fair view in mind, but this is by no means the same as the determination of realised profits, which is, after all, a *particular* accounting application and is notoriously elusive of resolution as we have seen. Indeed, we have also noted that distinct differences between the two frameworks may arise all too easily.

Questions

1. (a) What do you understand by the terms accounting concepts, accounting bases and accounting policies? Explain the relationships between them.
   (b) Why is the disclosure of accounting policies by companies considered to be desirable?

2. The word 'materiality' is used frequently in company law and in Statements of Standard Accounting Practice.
Required:
Briefly explain the concept of materiality, and state what criteria may be used to assess whether an item is material.

3. Accounting standards appear to be based on generally accepted accounting principles arrived at by consensus.

Required:
(a) Analyse and compare the said principles, insofar as they apply in the UK.
(b) Argue the cases for and against the assertion that, before proceeding to specific standards, the Accounting Standards Committee should have worked out a logical and coherent framework of accounting, from which individual standards can be derived.

4. 'Financial statements should be prepared on the basis of conditions existing at the balance sheet date'. (SSAP 17 *'Accounting for Post Balance Sheet Events'*.)
(a) Recognising the possibility of time lags in establishing what conditions actually exist at the balance sheet date, how does SSAP 17 seek to ensure that financial accounts are prepared in accordance with this rule?
(b) How does SSAP 17 seek to ensure that financial accounts prepared in accordance with this rule are not misleading?

Your answer should include THREE examples relating to (a), and a further THREE examples relating to (b).

Chapter 3
Extraordinary Items and Prior Year Adjustments

Concept of profit

3.1 There are two concepts of profit for a particular period. The treatment of extraordinary and prior period items depends on the concept adopted.

3.2 Under the 'Current Operating Performance' concept, the profit and loss account for the year will include only the normal recurring activities of the company. The extraordinary and prior year items will be excluded from the profit and loss account for the year and will be recorded as part of movement on reserves. Proponents of this concept argue that since the current operating performance profits forms the basis for calculating earnings per share, which is a component of the price–earnings ratio, such a profit figure will be most useful to shareholders and others for comparing the effectiveness of management, both over time and between companies, and for predicting the company's future earning power. It should, however, be remembered that normally only listed companies, a very small proportion of the total, will produce earnings per share information.

3.3 The alternative view, the 'All-Inclusive' concept, advocates that all movements between opening and closing revenue reserves should be reflected in the profit and loss account. The profit and loss account for the year will include and show separately all extraordinary items which are recognised in that year and all prior year items.

3.4 The original and revised versions of SSAP 6 have both adopted the 'All-Inclusive' concept and put forward the following reasons for adopting this concept:
1. by segregating extraordinary items for separate disclosure, the current operating profit (profit on ordinary activities) can be shown as an element of the all-inclusive profit (profit for the financial year);
2. inclusion and separate disclosure of extraordinary and prior year items will enable the profit and loss account for the year to give a better view of a company's profitability and progress;

3. exclusion, being a matter of subjective judgement, could lead to variations and to a loss of comparability between the reported results of companies; and
4. exclusion could result in extraordinary and prior year items being overlooked in any consideration of results over a series of years.

3.5 One of the objectives of the original SSAP 6 was that of full disclosure, i.e. all profits and losses recognised in the year should be accounted through the profit and loss account for the year and not through reserves (except unrealised surpluses on revaluation of fixed assets). In this respect the original standard has been successful. The adoption of the 'All-Inclusive' concept meant that a profit and loss account based on this concept was more objective since there is no subjective decision involved in what should and should not be excluded from the statement, although subjectivity still applies to the classification of items within the profit and loss account.

3.6 The revised standard requires that 'all profits and losses recognised in the financial statements should be included in the profit and loss account, except for those items which are specifically permitted or required by this or other accounting standards to be taken directly to reserves or, in the absence of relevant accounting standard, specifically permitted or required by law to be taken directly to reserves.

3.7 The profit and loss account should show separately in order:
(a) profit or loss on ordinary activities;
(b) the extraordinary profits or loss recognised in the financial statements for the year; and
(c) the profit or loss for the financial year.

Dividends and other appropriations should be shown after and deducted from the profit or loss for the financial year'.

Extraordinary items

3.8 The original SSAP 6 defined extraordinary items as those which derive from events or transactions outside the ordinary activities of the business and which are both material and expected not to recur frequently or regularly.

3.9 SSAP 6 in its explanatory note states that extraordinary items derive from events outside the ordinary activities of the business; they do not include items of abnormal size and incidence which derive from the

EXTRAORDINARY ITEMS AND PRIOR YEAR ADJUSTMENTS

ordinary activities of the business. Neither do they include prior year items merely because they relate to a prior year. The classification of items as extraordinary will depend on the particular circumstances – what is extraordinary in one business, or in one period, will not necessarily be extraordinary in another.

3.10 The Revised SSAP 6 (1986) provides for more restrictive criteria than the original SSAP 6 for determining whether an item may be classified as extraordinary. It does this in three ways:

1. The definition in the original SSAP 6 is not changed significantly, but a definition of 'ordinary activities' is introduced. The Revised SSAP 6 defines extraordinary items as being material items which derive from events or transactions that fall outside the ordinary activities of the company and which are therefore not expected to recur frequently or regularly. They do not include exceptional items nor do they include prior year items merely because they relate to a prior year.

    Ordinary activities are any activities which are usually, frequently or regularly undertaken by the company and any related activities in which the company engages in furtherance of, incidental to, or arising from those activities. They include, but are not confined to, the trading activities of the company.

    The revised standard does not clearly define an extraordinary event only defining it as an event giving rise to an extraordinary item. Critics will say it is evading the fundamental problem of defining the event by reference to its result. The definition of ordinary activities means that anything that is not extraordinary is ordinary. Profit on sale of fixed assets will be part of ordinary activities unless it arises because of an event which gives rise to an extraordinary item.

2. It gives a list of examples of extraordinary and exceptional items. Extraordinary items could be material profits or losses arising from the following:

    (a) the discontinuance of the business segment, either through termination or disposal;
    (b) the sale of an investment not acquired with the intention of resale, such as investments in subsidiary and associated companies;
    (c) profits or losses on the disposal of fixed assets if the event which gave rise to the disposal is an extraordinary event;
    (d) provision made for the permanent diminution in value of a fixed asset because of extraordinary events during the period;
    (e) the expropriation of assets; and
    (f) a change in the basis of taxation, or a significant change in Government fiscal policy.

57

UNDERSTANDING ACCOUNTING STANDARDS

The list of examples is not intended to be exhaustive. The list of extraordinary and exceptional items will reduce the inconsistencies in their treatment.
3. The revised standard gives guidance on terminated activities, distinguishing between 'the discontinuance of a significant business segment' which is extraordinary and other reorganisations, which are not. Illogically, perhaps, counterpart costs relating to the *commencement* of a new business segment or activity are not mentioned in the revised Standard.

Presentation

3.11 The revised SSAP 6 also tightens disclosure requirements by comparison with the original version. This is achieved as follows:

1. The presentation of extraordinary items in the profit and loss account is standardised. In the original SSAP 6, there was guidance in the Appendix only. The Revised SSAP 6 requires the extraordinary items to be shown in the profit and loss account following the ordinary results but before deducting any appropriations such as dividends paid or proposed.
2. It gives guidance on the treatment of individual elements of income and expenditure which derive from a single extraordinary item and when there are a number of extraordinary items in a single year. Revised SSAP 6 requires individual elements of income and expenditure which derive from a single extraordinary event to be aggregated and disclosed as one extraordinary item. When there is more than one extraordinary item, each must be disclosed separately.
3. The Revised SSAP 6 incorporates the legal requirement to disclose the tax on extraordinary profit or loss separately. It also requires the minority share of extraordinary profit or loss to be disclosed separately.

3.12 The revised standard prescribes a method for calculating tax on extraordinary profit or loss known as the 'with and without' treatment. This involves computing tax charges with and without extraordinary profit or loss and attributing the difference to the extraordinary items. This method ensures that the earnings per share will be the same whether or not there were any extraordinary items.
A simple illustration on this is as follows:

Profit on ordinary activities before taxation	£550,000
There is no franked investment income.	
Extraordinary Loss (relates to income)	£100,000
Rate of corporation tax = 35% on profits over £500,000	

EXTRAORDINARY ITEMS AND PRIOR YEAR ADJUSTMENTS

1. Tax computation with extraordinary items (ACTUAL):
   Taxable profits = £450,000
   Profits are less than £500,000 therefore marginal relief will apply.
   The Corporation Tax payable on the above profits = £156,750
2. Tax computation with extraordinary items (NOTIONAL)
   Taxable profits = £550,000
   The Corporation Tax payable @ 35% = £192,500

The difference between 1 and 2 = £35,750 which is tax on extraordinary items.

Tax on profit on ordinary activities =	£192,500
Tax on profits, including extraordinary items =	£156,750
Tax relief on extraordinary items =	£35,750

The tax effects of an extraordinary item should be treated as extraordinary even though an extraordinary item and its tax effects are recognised in different periods.

3.13 Major tax changes were introduced in the FA 1984. Prior to the FA 1984, first year allowances on most types of capital expenditure stood at 100%. These rules were changed in FA 1984, and are as follows:

Year ended	Rate of Corporation Tax	FYAs	WDA
31/3/1984	50%	100%	–
31/3/1985	45%	75%	25% pa
31/3/1986	40%	50%	25% pa
31/3/1987	35%	–	25% pa

This gradual phasing out of first year allowances has eroded the hard core of timing differences retained by many companies as the assets depreciate and timing differences reverse. After 1/4/1986 first year allowances ceased and writing down allowances of 25 per cent (reducing balance) are available. Thus after 1986, originating timing differences will be much lower in amount and in anticipation of this there is likely to be an increase in the amount of deferred tax provided. Many companies did not provide deferred tax prior to FA 1984 because the projection forecasts were prepared on the assumption that the first year allowances would continue at 100%. With the changes in FA 1984, a number of companies would have had to provide deferred tax in 1984 on timing differences which arose in prior periods. This provision for deferred tax arises because of a fundamental change in fiscal policy and should be treated as an extraordinary item.

3.14 ED 36 proposed that the earnings per share (EPS) figure should be stated both before and after extraordinary items. This would have

UNDERSTANDING ACCOUNTING STANDARDS

meant a disclosure in some cases of up to 16 different EPS in one set of accounts. This requirement was dropped by the revised standard as it was argued that the reasoning behind the separation of extraordinary items from profit on ordinary activities was to eliminate 'distortions'.

Illustration on Presentation

3.15 The Appendix to Revised SSAP 6 gives the following illustration on presentation:

Appendix

This appendix is illustrative only and does not form part of the statement of standard accounting practice.
Example of a consolidated profit and loss account and certain related notes to the accounts
Profit and loss account

	Note	1986 £000	1985 £000
Turnover	2	183,000	158,000
Cost of sales		106,140	86,900
Gross profit		76,860	71,100
Distribution costs and administrative expenses	3	57,160	52,500
Profit before exceptional item		19,700	18,600
Exceptional item – loss on major contract	4	8,600	–
Profit on ordinary activities before taxation	5	11,100	18,600
Tax on profit on ordinary activities	6	4,500	7,400
Profit on ordinary activities after taxation		6,600	11,200
Minority interests	7	400	370
Profit attributable to members of the holding company		6,200	10,830
Extraordinary loss after taxation	8	595	1,020
Profit for the financial year		5,605	9,810
Dividends	9	4,410	4,200
Retained profit for the year	10	1,195	5,610

Movements on reserves are set out in Note 10

60

EXTRAORDINARY ITEMS AND PRIOR YEAR ADJUSTMENTS

	1986 £000	1985 £000
Extracts from notes		
4. Exceptional item		
Exceptional loss on major contract in Middle East	8,600	–
8. Extraordinary loss after taxation		
Extraordinary income		
Profit on sale of head ofice	1,030	–
Extraordinary charges		
Provision for costs of closure of x division	–	1,700
Provision for costs of closure of y division	2,700	–
	2,700	1,700
Extraordinary loss	1,670	1,700
Tax relief on extraordinary loss	670	680
	1,000	1,020
Less minority share of provision for closure costs	405	–
Extraordinary loss after tax	595	1,020
10. Movements on reserves	*Profit and loss account* £000	*Revaluation reserve* £000
(a) Consolidated		
At 1 January – as previously reported –	48,890	23,400
prior year adjustment (see below)	450	–
– as restated	48,440	23,400
Retained profit for the year	1,195	–
	£49,635	23,400

The prior year adjustment represents the effect of a change in the accounting policy for goodwill. Goodwill, which was previously carried in the balance sheet as a permanent item, is now as a result of the introduction of SSAP 22 'Accounting for goodwill' written off against reserves immediately on acquisition, this being the preferred treatment under that standard. This adjustment has no effect on the reported profit of either of the years under review. Goodwill of £450,000 previously carried in the balance sheet has therefore been written off against retained profits at the beginning of 1985.

Alternative treatments

3.16 Some companies have adopted one of the following alternative treatments:
(a) They have shown extraordinary items as part of the profit or loss for the year, but after dividends. This treatment is based on the argument that extraordinary items do not affect a company's dividend policy since this is dependent on the trend of results from ordinary activities, the directors' view of current trading and prospects and the cash resources and underlying stability of the business.
(b) They have completely excluded extraordinary items for the profit or loss for the year and have shown them as reserve movements immediately below the profit and loss account. This treatment is based on the view that profit or loss after extraordinary items is a meaningless figure which combines two radically different elements, the results of ordinary activities and those of extraordinary activities.

ASC opinion

3.17 The ASC obtained legal advice on the various presentations used by companies and the opinion was:
(a) the inclusion of retained profits in the profit and loss account to offset extraordinary items was inconsistent with company law;
(b) as extraordinary items are covered by the formats prescribed by company law, they cannot be accounted for as a reserve movement.

Exceptional items

3.18 The original SSAP 6 did not define exceptional items. The revised SSAP 6 defines them as 'material items which derive from events or transactions that fall within the ordinary activities of the company and which need to be disclosed separately by virtue of their size or incidence if the financial statements are to give a true and fair view'. The revised standard gives examples of items which may be exceptional if they are material:
(a) redundancy costs relating to a continuing business segment;
(b) reorganisation costs unrelated to the discontinuance of a business segment.
The revised standard in its explanatory note states that 'programmes of reorganisation which, although involving redundancies and a reduction in the level of activities, do not amount to the discontinuance of a business segment are not extraordinary. Such reorganisations are a normal business process and therefore form part of the ordinary activities of a company. Their costs are charged in arriving at profit or loss on ordinary activities, and shown as exceptional item if material';

(c) previously capitalised expenditure on intangible fixed assets written off other than as part of a process of amortisation.
One example of this would be development expenditure which was capitalised when the conditions under SSAP 13 were satisfied. If, in future, these conditions are no longer valid, the amount of development expenditure capitalised should be written off to the profit and loss account and disclosed as an exceptional item if material;
(d) amounts transferred to employee share scheme. These amounts would be in respect of employees giving up pay increases or bonuses and therefore, should be treated as exceptional items, if material;
(e) profit or losses on the disposal of fixed assets. The revised SSAP 6, in its explanatory note, states 'A material surplus or deficit on disposal of a fixed asset, including property, will be disclosed as either exceptional or extraordinary, classified according to the nature of the event which gave rise to the disposal';
(f) abnormal charges for bad debts and write-offs of stock and work in progress;
(g) abnormal provisions for losses on long term contracts;
(h) surpluses arising on the settlement of insurance claims;
(i) amounts received in settlement of insurance claims for consequential loss of profits.

3.19 The original standard had no specific requirements regarding the disclosure of exceptional items. The revised standard requires exceptional items to be reflected in the ascertainment of profit or loss on ordinary activities and to be disclosed separately in the financial statements to give a true and fair view.

Prior year adjustments

3.20 The original standard defined prior year adjustments as being those material adjustments applicable to prior years arising from changes in accounting policies and from correction of fundamental errors. They do not include the normal recurring corrections and adjustments of accounting estimates made in prior years.

3.21 The definition is fairly precise. A change in accounting policy can only be justified on the ground that the new policy is preferable to the one it replaces because it will give a fairer presentation of the results and of the financial position of the business. Corrections of fundamental errors arise when in exceptional circumstances accounts may have been issued containing errors which are of such significance as to destroy the true and fair view and hence the validity of those accounts and which would have led to their withdrawal had the errors been recognised at the time.

3.22 The definition of fundamental errors in the original standard did not cover those items which, whilst relating to past periods, would materially distort the financial statements of both present and future periods, if they are not accounted for as prior year adjustments. The working party reviewing SSAP 6 recommended that the definition of fundamental error should be extended to cover the effect on the financial statements both present and future. An example of an item relating to past periods but which materially distorts the financial statements of both present and future periods would be fully depreciated assets which are still in use. The working party reviewing SSAP 12 recommended that these assets should be reinstated through a prior year adjustment.

3.23 The proposals of the working party have not been incorporated in the revised standard, which retains the definition given in the original standard.

3.24 The original standard referred to the need to set out a statement of retained profits showing any prior-year adjustments immediately following the profit and loss account for the year, but it was unclear whether this requirement applied in all cases or only when there was a prior-year adjustment. The revised standard requires prior year items to be adjusted against the opening balance of retained profits or reserves. A statement of movement on reserves (including the movement on retained profit and loss account) should be disclosed. If this statement does not immediately follow the profit and loss account, reference should be made on the face of the profit and loss account as to its location in the notes.

Terminated activities

3.25 It is common practice for companies to treat costs associated with termination as extraordinary. The revised standard clarifies this further. It makes a distinction between the reorganisation of activities, which may involve a reduction in the scale of activities and the termination of activities. The revised standard states 'Programmes of reorganisation which, although involving redundancies and a reduction in the level of activities, do not amount to the discontinuance of a business segment are not extraordinary. Such reorganisations are a normal business process and therefore form part of the ordinary activities of a company. Their costs are charged in arriving at profit or loss on ordinary activities, and shown as exceptional items if material'.

3.26 A provision will be required for the consequences of all decisions taken up to the balance sheet date. This will be the net sum of all debits and credits from some or all of the following items:

(a) redundancy costs (net of government contributions);
(b) cost of retaining key personnel during the run-down period;
(c) profit or losses arising from the disposal of assets, including anticipated ongoing costs such as rent, rates and security;
(d) pension costs;
(e) bad and doubtful debts arising from the decision to close;
(f) all debits and credits arising from trading after the commencement of implementation; and
(g) any losses due to penalty clauses in contracts.

'These provisions are not being prevented from being treated as extraordinary items merely because they occur and are recognised over a number of accounting periods where this is either the ongoing result of a single decision or because of a number of separate decisions'. The revised standard requires the disclosure of the normal results of discontinued operations prior to the termination which were included in profit on ordinary activities.

Revaluation and realisation of fixed assets

3.27 ED 16 (Supplement to 'Extraordinary items and prior year adjustments') required unrealised surpluses on revaluations of fixed assets to be credited directly to reserves. It also required any unrealised deficits on revaluations of fixed assets to be debited to the profit and loss account of the year to the extent that they exceed any surplus held in the reserves and identified as relating to previous revaluations of the same assets. ED 16 stated that when fixed assets are realised, the surpluses or deficits compared with the book value should be recognised in the profit and loss account for the year. Any reserve identified as being in respect of previously unrealised surpluses on the revaluation of those assets thereby becomes a realised surplus but should not be reported as part of the profit for the year.

3.28 The working party on the review of SSAP 6 recommended the same treatment as proposed in ED 16. However, it pointed out two problems associated with the recommended treatment:

(1) a company's results may be materially affected by the fact that it has previously revalued a property which it has now disposed of or by the timing of any such revaluation. This will lead to lack of comparability between companies and the results of earlier years.

UNDERSTANDING ACCOUNTING STANDARDS

(2) it is not consistent with the 'All-Inclusive concept' as an element of profit which has now become realised but will never be recognised in the profit and loss account.

3.29 ED 36 took exactly the same view as the Review and ED 16 on revaluations, but proposed a different treatment on realisation of fixed assets. It stated 'when fixed assets are disposed of, the surpluses on deficits in the profit and loss account should be based on the difference between sale proceeds and depreciated original cost. Any reserve identified as being in respect of previously unrealised surpluses on the revaluation of those assets thereby becomes a realised surplus and will be included as part of the profit on disposal included in the profit for the year, but should be disclosed separately where material'.

3.30 ED 36 preferred this treatment because it ensures that the whole of the difference between sale proceeds and original cost will pass through the profit and loss account over the lifetime of the asset, rather than part of this difference being taken directly to reserves when the asset was revalued.

Example

Year end 31/12 Fixed Asset: Cost £100,000
Life 10 years

Year end 2   Cost £100,000
    Accumulated
      depreciation   £20,000
    Net book value   £80,000

1 January Yr 3   Asset is revalued to £120,000. This will give an unrealised revaluation surplus of £40,000.

Year 3   P & L A/c   £120,000 ÷ 8 years =   £15,000
                                        Revaluation reserve   £40,000

Year end 3 Net book value = £105,000 Realised through
                                       consumption (1/8)   £5,000
                                       Unrealised (will   £35,000
                                       become realised
                                       either through use
                                       or sale)

The asset is sold for £110,000 on the 1st day of Year 4.
Yr 4
P & L A/c: There will be a profit on sale of fixed assets.

ED 16/SSAP 6 (Review) Approach

3.31   Profit on sale = Selling price less Net book value at point of sale
                        = 110,000 − 105,000
                        = £5,000

£5,000 will go through P & L A/c for Year 4
£35,000 which was previously unrealised now becomes realised through a sale. It will remain on the balance sheet as part of realised reserves.

This treatment will cause the following two problems:
 (i) a company's results may be materially affected by the fact that it has previously revalued an asset which it has now disposed of, or by the timing of any such valuation – there will be a loss of comparability between a company which revalues its assets and one which does not.
 (ii) the proposed treatment will result in an element of profit becoming realised but never being recognised in the P & L A/c, i.e. contrary to the All-Inclusive concept.

ED 36 Approach

Profit on sale = selling price less depreciated original cost.
              = 110,000 − (100,000 − 30,000)
              = £40,000

OR: Same as ED 16 Approach + Release £35,000 to P & L A/c from reserves
              = £5,000 + £35,000 = £40,000.

Disclose (if material) as having been included in unrealized reserves in earlier years.

This approach is consistent with the All-Inclusive Concept and will afford better comparisons.

3.32 The revised standard has, however, deferred the entire issue of revaluation and realisation of fixed assets for the following reasons:

1. Opinion is divided among commentators as to which of the methods described above constitutes best practice.
2. There is no clear solution to the issues involved.
3. The subject of revaluations and the sale of revalued assets is not central to SSAP 6.
4. The ASC's work programme covers the topic of fixed assets and revaluations which would inevitably cover these points and it is believed that this would be a better medium by which to resolve this conceptually difficult question. The ASC recently brought forward the priority of the fixed assets and revaluations project and work has now begun.

Reserve movements

3.33 The original standard restricted reserve movements to unrealised surpluses on revaluation of fixed assets and prior year adjustments. A number of subsequent standards have varied this rule (e.g. SSAPs 19, 20 and 22). In each case reference should be made to the chapter which deals with the SSAP in question for information on treatment of reserve movements.

3.34 Company Law also allows reserve movements in certain instances (e.g. S130 CA 1985 – use of share premium account; S160–162 CA 1985 transfer to capital redemption reserve when own shares are purchased on redeemed out of distributable profits). The revised SSAP 6 requires that all profits and losses are to be accounted for in the profit and loss account unless this conflicts with legislation or another SSAP.

3.35 The revised standard requires all reserve movements, including the movement on retained profits to be disclosed in a single statement of movement on reserves. The standard requires that reference should be made on the face of the profit and loss account for the year to where the statements can be found if it does not immediately follow the profit and loss account.

Questions

1. SSAP 6: Extraordinary items and prior year adjustments has regulated the matters mentioned in the title since 1974. It was recently revised by the Accounting Standards Committee.
Required:
(a) State how far the revised SSAP 6 upholds the principles of the original SSAP 6, and how far it modifies or adds to them.
(b) ED 36 recommended the treatment of profits and losses on disposal of revalued assets. Discuss the treatment proposed by ED 36 and give reasons why it was not incorporated in the revised SSAP 6.

2. The main objective of SSAP 6 Extraordinary Items and Prior Year Adjustments is to prevent reserve accounting and yet both SSAP 20 on Foreign Currency Translation and SSAP 22 on Accounting for Goodwill allow a form of reserve accounting.
Required:
(a) State why the Accounting Standards Committee allows direct transfers to reserves in SSAPs 20 and 22.
(b) Discuss the assertion that such departures are evidence of an inconsistency between SSAPs.

Chapter Four
Accounting for Depreciation

Conceptual background

4.1 SSAP 12: Accounting for depreciation, issued in 1977, codified and tightened best accounting practice as it existed then. It required that provision for depreciation of fixed assets having a finite useful life should be made by allocating the cost (or revalued amount) less estimated residual values of the assets as fairly as possible to the periods expected to benefit from their use. The omission of depreciation charge on the grounds that the market value was greater than the net book value was no longer acceptable. The above requirement of SSAP 12 meant that the buildings which have a limited useful life also had to be depreciated.

4.2 The disclosure requirements of the CAs 1948 to 1967 on depreciation did not go far enough to helping users make decisions. These Acts required the companies in their published accounts to make the following disclosures regarding depreciation:
(1) Charge for the year
(2) Accumulated depreciation carried forward at the end of the year.

This was to some extent corrected in SSAP 12 which, in addition to the CA, required companies to disclose the method and rate (or estimated useful life) of depreciation.

4.3 SSAP 12 also gave guidance on the following accounting problems:
 (i) changes in the method of depreciation;
 (ii) revisions of estimated useful life;
 (iii) revaluations of fixed assets; and
 (iv) irrecoverable amounts.

4.4 SSAP 12 defined depreciation as being the measure of the wearing out, consumption or other loss of value of a fixed asset whether arising from use, effluxion of time or obsolescence through technology and market changes.

4.5 The approach adopted by the original SSAP 12 was that of the matching or accruals principle, whereby fixed assets are viewed as deferred costs which will earn revenue over a number of periods, and the depreciation charge is the cost consumed in a particular period to earn revenue in that period. SSAP 12 states 'Depreciation should be allocated to accounting periods so as to charge a fair proportion to each accounting period during the expected useful life of the asset'.

4.6 In theory there are at least three other possible reasons for the provision of depreciation but SSAP 12 did not deal with or consider them:
(1) reflecting in accounts a loss in the value of fixed assets;
(2) provision for the future replacement of fixed assets which are in use; and
(3) allocation of the cost of fixed assets between accounting periods.

4.7 The assessment of depreciation, and its allocation to accounting periods, involves the consideration of the following factors:
(a) the cost or revaluation of the asset;
(b) the residual value;
(c) the useful life; and
(d) the depreciation method.

The cost or revaluation of the asset

4.8 SSAP 12 made no attempt to define the cost of the fixed asset. This question was first dealt with in the CA 1981 (now consolidated in the CA 1985) which states that the cost of an asset carried at historical cost would comprise purchase price or production cost. Purchase price is the actual price paid plus any expenses incidental to the acquisition and includes any consideration (whether cash or otherwise) given in respect of an asset. Production cost includes raw materials, consumables and direct production costs. A reasonable proportion of indirect production costs and interest on capital borrowed to finance production of the asset may also be included. Where there is no record of the purchase price or production cost of an asset or this information cannot be obtained without unreasonable expense or delay, the value shown in the earliest available record after the acquisition of the asset may be regarded as cost.

4.9 This definition of the cost in the CA causes certain difficulties in the case of self-constructed fixed assets as a basis of allocation of overheads will have to be determined and this may lead to subjectivity in identification of this cost.

The residual value

4.10 This is the amount which the enterprise could expect to recover at the end of the asset's useful life irrespective of its condition. Residual value can only be estimated and is highly subjective. In practice, if there is no reason to believe that it will be material, it should be treated as nil.

The useful life

4.11 An asset's life may be:
(a) pre-determined, as in leaseholds;
(b) directly governed by extraction or consumption;
(c) dependent on the extent of use; or
(d) reduced by obsolescence or physical deterioration.

Since the purpose of depreciation under SSAP 12 is to allocate the cost of an asset over its useful life, it is important that the life should be assessed as accurately as possible. The assessment of the useful life of assets poses the greatest problem, since this assessment depends upon an estimate of the extent and pattern of future use. One possible approach in identifying the useful life is to take account of the net relevant cash flow. The net relevant cash flow will be affected by the age and usage of the asset, and so management will need to consider the optimum usage. Once the management has indicated likely usage, the accounting treatment can be determined. The term net relevant cash flow pattern may take account of the following receipts and payments:

(i) initial capital outlay;
(ii) repairs and maintenance payments (as affected by age and use);
(iii) cash receipts and benefits (as affected by above (i));
(iv) residual value (as affected by above (i)–(iii)).

The depreciation method

4.12 SSAP 12 did not specify the method of allocation which should be used, leaving this decision to the discretion of management. 'Management has a duty to allocate depreciation as fairly as possible to the periods expected to benefit from the use of the asset and should select the method regarded as most appropriate to the type of asset and its use in the business'.

The two most commonly employed methods are the straight-line method and the reducing balance method.

4.13 Since SSAP 12 did not specify the method of allocation which should be used, it raised a question as to whether methods of depreciation for tangible fixed assets in particular industries should be standardized. It will be difficult for any accounting standard to lay down formulae on rates of depreciation for particular assets or industries. However, greater guidance could be given, industry by industry, either in the Appendix to the Accounting Standard or in Statements of Recommended Practice (SORPs) and this will allow the depreciation methods to be used within an industry to become more uniform, and render the accounts of different companies within the industry more comparable.

SSAP 12 (as Revised in 1987)

4.14 The original standard issued in 1977 was revised in 1987. ED 37, issued in 1985, gave the following reasons for the revision:

1. Experience in the years since the issue of SSAP 12 has highlighted certain practical problems which were not specifically addressed in the original standard. Some of the practical problems highlighted included those of useful life, supplementary depreciation, split depreciation, etc.
2. The CA 1981 inserted into the CA 1948 a requirement that companies should depreciate any fixed assets with a limited useful economic life. Consequently, the failure by companies to provide depreciation in such cases is, in material cases, in breach of the law. It could be argued that because of this company law requirement the need for SSAP 12 has now disappeared. The ASC believes, however, that the company law provisions, which set out the legal framework, are complemented by those of SSAP 12, which deal with the practicalities of accounting for depreciation.
3. As part of its programme of reviewing existing standards the ASC set up a working party to review SSAP 12.
4. The original SSAP 12 was primarily concerned with the provision of depreciation in historical cost accounts. The revised standard also applies to any accounting for price level changes.
5. Although, as already stated, there were some theoretical objections to including assets at revalued amounts in historical cost accounts, the ASC encourages this practice. Factors in favour of this approach include the fact that the inclusion of assets at revalued amounts is a means of compensating for one of the limitations of historical cost accounts and can provide useful and more relevant information for users of accounts.

The ASC does not anticipate that the revision of SSAP 12 will result

ACCOUNTING FOR DEPRECIATION

in any significant changes in the way in which most enterprises account for depreciation. The revision is intended to clarify the provisions of the existing standard and to codify best practice. The underlying principle of the revised standard remains the same as that in the original standard.

Standard accounting practice

1. Scope

4.15 The revised standard applies to all fixed assets other than investment properties, goodwill, development costs and investments.

2. Definitions

4.16 The revised standard defines 'depreciation as being the measure of the wearing out, consumption or other reduction in the useful economic life whether arising from use, effluxion of time or obsolesence through technological or market changes'.

4.17 There is a change in the definition of depreciation from the one which was stated in the original standard. The term 'loss in value of fixed asset' in the original definition quite often caused confusion as to the real meaning of depreciation. It gave the impression that providing depreciation was a means of valuing the fixed assets. The new definition is much more in line with the application of the accruals concept. The emphasis is now on allocating 'cost' (whether historic or current) rather than measuring a loss of value.

4.18 The useful economic life of an asset is defined as the period over which the present owner will derive economic benefit from its use.

4.19 Residual value is the realisable value of the asset at the end of its useful life in its present ownership, based on prices prevailing at the date of acquisition or revaluation, where this has taken place. Realisation costs should be deducted in arriving at the residual value.

3. Provision for depreciation

4.20 'Provision for depreciation of fixed assets having a finite useful economic life should be made by allocating the cost (or revalued amount) less estimated residual value of the assets as fairly as possible to the periods expected to benefit from their use. The depreciation methods used should be the ones which are the most appropriate having regard to the types of asset and their use in the business.

4.21 'The accounting treatment in the profit and loss account should be consistent with that used in the balance sheet. Hence, the depreciation charge in the profit and loss account for the period should be based on the carrying amount of the asset in the balance sheet, whether historical cost or revalued amount. The whole of the depreciation charge should be reflected in the profit and loss account. No part of the depreciation charge should be set directly against reserves. Supplementary depreciation, namely that in excess of depreciation based on the carrying amount of the assets, should not be charged in the profit and loss account. This does not, however, preclude the appropriation of retained profits to, for example, a reserve specially designated for replacement of fixed assets.'

4.22 The revised standard does not specify the method of allocation which should be used, leaving this decision to the discretion of management. However, the explanatory notes to the standard points out that there is a range of acceptable depreciation methods.

4. Supplementary depreciation

4.23 As mentioned in 4.21 above, to compensate for the effect of price changes, a practice has developed in certain cases of making a supplementary depreciation charge without a corresponding revaluation of assets concerned.

EXAMPLE

Fixed Asset cost £100,000 Residual Value = 0
Useful Life 10 years Straight Line method.
Year end 2:
Accumulated
Depreciation: £20,000

The company decides to provide supplementary depreciation as from year 3. Replacement cost of this asset at the start of year 3 =£120,000
Accounts for year 3:
P & L A/c– normal charge = £100,000/10 =   £ 10,000
    – supplementary depreciation* =   £ 5,000
        Total charge   £ 15,000

* Difference between depreciation charge based on replacement cost (£120,000/8 = £15,000) and historic cost depreciation (£10,000) is £5,000.

4.24 However, this asset will not be stated at its replacement cost on the balance sheet.

Balance sheet year end 3	£
Fixed Asset at cost	100,000
Less Accumulated depreciation	35,000
Net book value	£ 65,000

This treatment
  (i) does not charge depreciation fairly to the periods which benefit from the use of the assets,
  (ii) has the effect of distorting ratios like earnings per share and return on capital employed, and
  (iii) will lead to the existence in many companies' books of significant amounts of fully depreciated assets which are still in use.

4.25 The revised standard requires the whole of the depreciation charge to be reflected in the profit and loss account. This rules against the practice which charges supplementary depreciation on fixed assets to take account of the impact of inflation. This may be done only if the assets are revalued in the balance sheet. However, where assets are not revalued supplementary depreciation must be shown as an appropriation of profit to reserves and not as a cost in the year.

5. Revaluations in historical cost accounts

4.26 As discussed earlier, SSAP 12 requires the revalued amount to be written off over the remainder of useful life. SSAP 12 does not deal with the merits of or objections to revaluations on a partial basis in the historical cost accounts. In recent years the practice of revaluing fixed assets to bring the book figures more into line with current values has been increasingly adopted and has been particularly evident in the case of property assets. This practice of revaluations on a partial basis creates a 'hybrid' of historical cost accounting and current value accounting and there have been objections to this practice.

4.27 At one point an argument was presented that the practice of including revaluations in historic cost accounts should be prohibited on the grounds that current cost accounts had removed the need to reflect price changes in any form in the historical cost accounts. This argument, however, did not prevail.

6. 'Split' depreciation

4.28 The practice of 'split' depreciation has grown in recent years. At present the CA 1985, in the opinion of some legal experts, permits companies to 'split' depreciation and there is nothing in the original SSAP 12 to prohibit it. It works as follows:

Depreciation is calculated on the amounts shown in the balance sheet whether this is historic cost or a revalued amount. Where assets have been revalued, the depreciation charge is split into two parts. The depreciation which relates to historic cost is charged in the profit and loss account. That part of depreciation which relates to the revaluation is taken directly to reserves and offset against the revaluation surplus which was created when the asset was revalued.

EXAMPLE

Fixed Asset Cost =		£100,000
Life		10 years
Residual Value =		0
Straight Line Method		

Year end 2: Cost		£100,000
Accumulated depreciation		20,000
Net book value		£ 80,000

4.29 On 1st day of Year 3, the fixed asset is revalued to £120,000: Therefore Revaluation Surplus = £40,000; Depreciation for Year 3 = £120,000/8 years = £15,000 of which £10,000 will be charged in P & L A/c of Year 3 and £5,000 will be written off against revaluation reserve.

4.30 The ASC in the revised SSAP 12 has ruled against the practice of 'split' depreciation, even though it is permitted by the CA 1985 – although the Department of Trade and Industry has indicated in a Consultative Note (1986) that this was never the intention in the EEC Fourth Directive, and that the CA 1985 provisions will be altered to support the SSAP 12 revisions.

7. Asset lives

4.31 'It is essential that asset lives are estimated on a realistic basis. Identical asset lives should be used for the calculation of depreciation both on a historical cost basis and on any bases that reflect the effects of changing prices. The useful economic lives of assets should be reviewed regularly and, where necessary, revised. The allocation of depreciation to accounting periods involves the exercise of judgement by management in the light of technical, commercial and accounting considerations and, accordingly, requires regular review. When, as a result of experience or of changed circumstances, it is considered that the original estimate of the useful economic life of an asset requires revision, the effect of the change in estimate on the results and financial position needs to be considered. Usually, when asset lives are reviewed regularly, there will be no material distortion of future results or financial position if the net book amount is written off over the revised remaining useful economic life. Where, however, future results would be materially distorted, the adjustment to accumulated depreciation should be recognised in the accounts in accordance with SSAP 6: extraordinary items and prior year adjustments. This means that such an adjustment will usually be dealt with in arriving at the profit on ordinary activities. It will only be treated as an extraordinary item if it is derived from an extraordinary event such as the discontinuance of a business segment. The nature and amount of adjustment should be disclosed.' (Para. 18, SSAP 12 revised.)

4.32 The explanatory notes to the standard state that the review of asset lives would normally be undertaken at least every five years, and more frequently where circumstances warrant it. There would be few fully depreciated assets still in economic use if the lives are realistically estimated and reviewed regularly.

4.33 ED 37 retained the original SSAP 12 requirement that where asset lives are revised the undepreciated cost should be charged over the remaining revised life. The requirement in the revised standard is rather vague. If asset lives are estimated realistically and reviewed regularly any adjustment required on revision of asset lives should usually be so immaterial as not to distort future financial results if recognised over the remaining useful life. Since these amounts would be immaterial, no question arises as to whether they should be treated as extraordinary items or prior year adjustments, i.e. they would be included as part of profit on ordinary activities before tax. The treatment proposed for an adjustment which is likely to distort future results materially is unclear. The revised standard merely states that the adjustment to accumulated depreciation should be recognised in the accounts in accordance with SSAP 6. This raises the question of whether companies will be allowed to recompute depreciation on the basis of the revised useful life and write off to or credit the accounts with the difference between the book value arrived on the basis of the original estimate and the revised estimate. What is quite clear is that whatever adjustment is made, it will usually be dealt with in arriving at the profit on ordinary activities. It should not be treated as a prior year adjustment and it can be treated as an extraordinary item only if it is derived from an extraordinary event. No doubt the forthcoming standard on revaluation accounting will resolve these residual doubts. On the face of it, it would appear that at the end of the originally estimated useful life of an asset a revision to that life may be made, with the result that past depreciation could be re-credited in the profit and loss account. This is, of course, contrary to the spirit of the prohibition in the revised standard against writing back past depreciation following a revaluation. The loophole is created by revising the asset's useful life rather than its value.

4.34 The specific requirements in ED 37 to reinstate fully depreciated assets still in use has been abandoned by the revised standard. ED 37 required that where omission of depreciation on fully depreciated assets still in use resulted in a failure to give a true and fair view, these assets had to be reinstated. The amount reinstated had to be credited directly to reserves.

4.35 These fully depreciated assets still in use may be reinstated in the accounts in a slightly different manner under the provisions of the revised standard. This may be illustrated by an example:

Fixed Asset – Cost £100,000
– Estimated residual value 0
– Original estimate of useful life 5 years.

Year end 5	Cost	£100,000
	Accumulated depreciation	£100,000
	Net book value	—

4.36 The asset is fully depreciated at the end of year five. The company notes that this asset is still in use in year six and has an estimated further useful life of five years. Assuming that the amounts involved are material, the company is entitled to recompute the net book value at the end of year five on the basis of the revised estimated useful life and the difference between the revised net book value and the original book value would be credited to the profit and loss account and dealt with in arriving at the profit on ordinary activities.

At start of Year 6	£
Net book value on the basis of revised useful life	50,000
Net book value on the basis of original useful life	—
DIFFERENCE – to be credited to the profit and loss A/c	50,000

The entry will be:	£	£
DR Accumulated depreciation	50,000	
CR Profit and loss A/c		50,000

Under ED 37, the credit to the profit and loss account would have been recorded as part of reserve movements.

8. Commentary – Economic lives of assets

4.37 We have seen that the revised Standard requires the economic lives of assets to be reviewed regularly and, if necessary, revised. The effect of this policy would be to avoid the situation found to exist at British Leyland (as it then was) and described in the Ryder Report in 1975 prior to the government takeover. Almost half of all depreciable plant still in use had already been fully written off, resulting in a zero depreciation charge. How a normal charge for the use of those assets would have inflated the company's reported losses of £107 million was never calculated!

4.38 Were the assets in question prematurely depreciated in the books? Or was it just a case of the company continuing to use worn out assets because it could not afford to replace them?

4.39 It may seem academic now, but it appears that Leyland have never really escaped this particular syndrome. A note in their 1985 accounts, for example, reads:

'No depreciation and amortisation has been charged in arriving at results for the year in respect of certain tangible assets which originally cost £452 million and are still in service but fully depreciated. If depreciation and amortisation had been charged during the year on the cost of these assets at normal rates it would have amounted to approximately £80 million'.

4.40 The new Standard tells us that if asset lives are reviewed regularly there should be no material distortion of future results if the existing book amount is written off over the revised remaining useful economic life. If, however, the revision does create a material distortion of future results, an adjustment to accumulated (past) depreciation should be reflected in the profit and loss account. This opens a significant loophole, as already explained in our earlier illustration, and no doubt some companies will be quick to exploit it.

Permanent diminution in value of an asset

4.41 The asset should be written down immediately to its estimated recoverable amount, which should be written off over the remaining useful economic life of the asset. The 'recoverable amount' is the greater of net realisable value of an asset and, where appropriate, the amount recoverable from its further use. If at any time the reasons for making such a provision cease to apply, the provision should be written back to the extent it is no longer necessary. The standard is silent on provisions in respect of previously revalued assets, and presumably it is permissible to charge deficits against any previous revaluation surplus. SSAP 6 requires that if this write off arises from an extraordinary event and the amount is material, it should be shown as an extraordinary item. Otherwise it will be included as part of profit on ordinary activities.

Change in method

4.42 The revised standard states that such a change does not constitute a change of accounting policy. The rules to be adopted are the same as in the original standard. The change is allowed only on the grounds that the new method will give a fairer presentation of the results and of the financial position. The unamortised cost should be written off over the remaining useful life on the new basis commencing with the period in which the change is made.

Revaluations and past depreciation

4.43 The revalued amount should be written off over the remaining useful economic life. There is no change from the original standard. However, there is one further requirement in the revised standard: 'Depreciation charged prior to the revaluation should not be written back to the profit and loss account, except to the extent that it relates to a provision for permanent diminution in value which is subsequently found to be unnecessary'.

EXAMPLE
Fixed Asset: Cost £100,000   Residual Value = 0
Useful Life   10 years   Straight line method

Year end 2:	Cost	£100,000
	Accumulated depreciation	£ 20,000
	Net Book value	£ 80,000

The asset is revalued to £120,000 on the first day of Year 3.

4.44 The revised SSAP 12 does not permit the write back of £20,000 or part of it to the profit and loss account at the point of revaluation,

ACCOUNTING FOR DEPRECIATION

although it is permissible to transfer it to *realized* reserves in the balance sheet. The alternative treatments are as follows:

Unrealised revaluation surplus on the first day of Year 3 – taken to reserves – £40,000.

This surplus will become realised through consumption over the next eight years or through sale, if it takes place earlier. The annual depreciation charge for the next eight years (if asset is not sold) = £120,000 ÷ 8 years = £15,000.

The practice which some companies followed in the past was as follows: (now not permitted by the revised standard):

In Year 3 – Credit Profit and Loss account with £20,000 (depreciation which was provided up to the point of revaluation).

– recognise an unrealised revaluation reserve of £20,000 (which would then become realised over the next eight years, or through sale, if earlier).

Annual Profit and Loss account charge = £120,000 ÷ 8 = £15,000. The profit and loss account for Year 3 in this case can be manipulated by the timing of the revalution.

4.45 The practice of taking £20,000 of revaluation surplus to the profit and loss account is specifically prohibited by SSAP 12. However, some companies continue legitimately to treat this £20,000 as being realised through two years' consumption (and therefore, distributable) and record it as a movement between unrealised and realised reserves.

4.46 ED 37 required the difference between the net book amount prior to the revaluation and the revalued amount to be transferred to the revaluation reserve. There is no specific requirement for this in the revised standard. The reason the ASC has given for leaving this out of the revised standard is that there is an intention to have a separate standard on the revaluation and realisation of fixed assets.

4.47 The revised standard does not prescribe how frequently assets should be revalued but states that where a policy of revaluing assets is adopted the valuations should be kept up to date, and should take place at least every five years.

Commentary on revaluation problems

4.48 The ASC, as we have seen, found itself unable to prescribe a uniform accounting treatment for revaluations in its revision of SSAP 12. This is particularly disappointing since it was one of the principal reasons for the Standard's recent revision. Consequently several accounting options remain available until such time that a further set of prescriptions are produced following the recommendations of yet another working party. In the interim companies whose revaluations reveal a surplus over existing book values may account for it as they please, subject only to the CA 1985 prohibition against including unrealised gains in the profit and loss account. The surpluses should be taken directly to revaluation reserves.

4.49 There is, however, no standard definition of a surplus. Is it the difference between the revalued amount and (i) original cost, or (ii) written down value at the revaluation date? Both views are permissible, giving rise to widely differing transfers to revaluation reserve. If option (i) is exercised SSAP 12 does not permit the depreciation previously charged to be written back to profit and loss account. There is, however, no reason in law or in Standards to prevent its direct transfer to the company's realised reserves in the balance sheet – despite having arisen from nothing more reliable than a revaluation.

4.50 The Standard is adamant that once an asset is revalued the annual depreciation charge must be based on the new value rather than historic cost. In other words, profit and loss account charges must be based on balance sheet carrying amounts. This rule was introduced to counter the 'split depreciation' method, explained above, once adopted by Woolworths and Davy Corporation. In their 1984 accounts Woolworth Holdings noted the following change of policy:

'The charge for depreciation is now split, with that part based on the revaluation excess being charged directly to the revaluation reserve. This change in policy has had the effect of increasing profit on ordinary activities before taxation by £1.8 million.'

4.51 No reason was given for the change (apart from the obvious boost to profits) and it was heavily criticised by both the ASC and the DTI, who questioned its legality under the CA. It enjoyed the support of its auditors who, in turn, had previously sought counsel's advice. Whether or not the DTI intended it, paragraph 32, Schedule 4 to the Act states quite clearly that companies may limit the depreciation charge in the profit and loss account to that based on historic cost, provided they disclose the effect.

4.52 To quote: *'... the amount of any depreciation in respect of that asset included in any item shown in the profit and loss account ... may be the historical cost amount instead of the adjusted amount, provided that the amount of any difference between the two is shown separately in the profit or loss account or in a note to the accounts.'*

4.53 Woolworth selected the latter option, and disclosed the treatment with commendable clarity. This novel method, legitimate as we see, enables a company to reflect the good news in the balance sheet by incorporating assets at their uplifted revaluations, without the usual corresponding bad news in the profit and loss account in the form of a higher depreciation charge – a clear instance of having your cake and eating it. No longer, however, if the revised SSAP 12 is followed.

Disposals of revalued assets

4.54 The Standard remains ambivalent on the treatment of gains or losses on the disposal of previously revalued assets. Normally a reader of accounts would expect the gain or loss to represent the surplus of disposal proceeds over the asset's written down value at the date of sale. But the Standard explicitly encourages (until the issue of a separate Standard on revaluations) the gain or loss to be calculated by comparing the proceeds of sale with the 'depreciated original cost', i.e. what the written down value *would* have been but for the revaluation, enabling a far higher amount to be included in profits for the period in which the disposal occurs. Selectively timed disposals can therefore have a dramatic effect on reported results, and some companies have been quick to spot the opportunity.

4.55 In its accounts for the year to 31 January 1987 *Sears Holdings* reported substantially increased pre-tax earnings but part of the improvement arose from changes in depreciation methods. The change in the method of calculating disposal profits just described accounted for £4.1 million (including £1.6 million allocated to the previous period's comparative figures), and a further £5 million was produced by scrapping the usual depreciation charge on freeholds and long-leaseholds on the basis that estimated realisable values far exceed book values, giving rise to a zero depreciation charge. The latter was achieved without any change of policy, for reasons explained earlier.

Freehold land and buildings

4.56 'Freehold land does not normally require a provision for depreciation, unless it is subject to depletion by, for example, the extraction of minerals. However, the value of freehold land may be adversely affected by considerations such as changes in the desirability of its location and in these circumstances it should be written down.

4.57 Buildings are no different from other fixed assets in that they have a limited useful economic life, albeit usually significantly longer than that of other types of assets. They should, therefore, be depreciated having regard to the same criteria.'

4.58 This is likely to be one of the most controversial points in the new standard. As the market value of land and buildings continues to rise in a time of inflation, many companies have been reluctant to depreciate buildings. For many business people it is often difficult to see why they should reduce the amount attributed to land and buildings in the accounts when in fact the market price is increasing. The old SSAP 12 has this requirement in the explanatory note and not as part of the Standard Accounting Practice. Many companies interpreted this to be an encouragement to depreciate buildings rather than as a requirement to do so. In the revised standard, this requirement appears as part of the Standard Accounting Practice and it appears that the ASC is attempting to take a harder line on the subject.

4.59 This line in the revised standard is at variance with the approach taken in ED 37 where it appeared that the requirement to depreciate buildings was being relaxed when buildings were maintained to such a standard that:
(a) their estimated residual value was equal to or greater than their net book amount; or
(b) their estimated useful economic life was either infinite or such that any depreciation change would be insignificant.

4.60 The relaxation in ED 37 would have accommodated the breweries and hotel companies but the ASC has dropped this provision as it believes that any relaxation of the requirement to depreciate buildings would have been open to abuse. The only ground left to companies to exempt themselves from depreciating buildings is that of materiality.

Property assets – Commentary on Revised SSAP 12
4.61 When SSAP 12 was first introduced, directors complained that depreciation charges on property assets were totally unrealistic since general pressure to acquire good sites ensured that their values increased progressively. The ASC countered by pointing out that these increases were attributable to the sites rather than the buildings, which depreciate like every structure in the physical world. The spurious argument put forward by companies could, if logically extended, be used to justify a failure to provide for depreciation on, say, plant on the basis that the site on which it stood had risen in value.

4.62 Quite simply, the ASC would not countenance any exemption from the requirement to make a depreciation charge by virtue of an

ACCOUNTING FOR DEPRECIATION

incidental and wholly unconnected rise in a company's land values. But what if it could be shown that the buildings had indeed risen in value independently of the site? This, the ASC argued, would necessitate an increased depreciation charge rather than no charge at all, since the value ultimately to be replaced was that much greater. Thus the battle raged, and many company directors did their own thing with self-righteous impunity, blazoning their qualified audit reports as a mark of distinction: evidence of independence of mind and a refusal to succumb to the cerebral utterings of out-of-touch committees.

4.63 Some compromise was reached in 1981, but only in respect of investment properties. A new Standard, SSAP 19, was written in which these assets were excluded from the ambit of SSAP 12 provided that they are included in the balance sheet at their open market value, and that any revaluation deficit not covered by a previous surplus must be charged in the profit and loss account.

4.64 Ironically, the issue of SSAP 19 coincided with the CA 1981 which, in implementing the EC Fourth Directive, prescribed a mandatory depreciation charge for *all* tangible assets, with the sole exception of freehold land. To this day, therefore, companies with investment properties, despite complying with the Standard, are obliged to disclose a departure from statutory requirements, invoking the now infamous S228 'override' clause: that the departure is necessary in order to give a true and fair view. Although this requires the departure's effect to be quantified if practicable, few companies provide this information. Here, for example, is the relevant extract from the accounting policy on depreciation in the 1987 report and accounts of MEPC plc:

'No depreciation is charged on freehold or long leasehold properties in accordance with SSAP 19. The directors consider this accounting policy is necessary for the financial statements to show a true and fair view. It is not practicable to quantify the depreciation which might otherwise have been charged.'

Change of definition
4.65 In its most recent revision of SSAP 12 the ASC has, as we have seen, sensibly side-stepped further confrontation by introducing a subtle change in the Standard's definition of depreciation. It drops the phrase 'measure of ... loss of value', which lay behind the earlier arguments. Indeed, it avoids references to value altogether. The revised definition states instead that depreciation is the measure of any reduction in the useful economic life of a fixed asset, however caused. The effect of this change is that the cost of depreciable fixed assets (less estimated residual

UNDERSTANDING ACCOUNTING STANDARDS

values) must simply be allocated to the accounting periods which benefit from their use. The argument about any compensatory rise in value does not arise.

4.66 The principal advantage of the new definition is its comprehensive validity in all situations. Indeed, if it had been used in the original version of the Standard, SSAP 19 would hardly have been necessary. It applies to assets recorded in the balance sheet at historic cost, current cost or revalued amounts; it also applies to assets maintained to a high standard, such as property assets.

4.67 Essentially, it works like this:

	£
Balance sheet amount of asset	X (1)
less: Estimated residual value	X (2)
Depreciable amount	X (3)

The latter, (3), represents the amount to be charged against the profits of the accounting periods which benefit from the asset's use. There is no need to create exceptions for, say, hotel properties or licensed estate (tied public houses) which are maintained to such a high standard that, in the directors' opinion, their estimated residual value (2) will never fall below the amount at which they are included in the balance sheet (1). In such cases (3) will simply be zero or an immaterial sum, and hence there is no depreciation to allocate.

4.68 The Standard does stress, however, that present estimation of future residual values (2) should not anticipate future inflation: current values must be used. Further, such estimates should relate to residual values at the time the asset is disposed of by its present owners, rather than when the asset itself is eventually scrapped.

4.69 A hotel or property group may therefore present an asset profile like this:

ACCOUNTING FOR DEPRECIATION

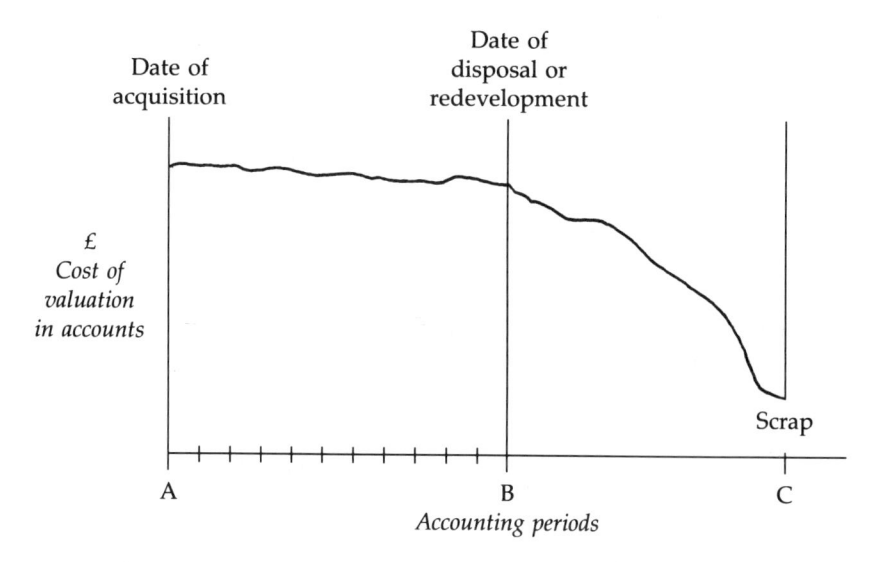

```
                  Date of
   Date of        disposal or
   acquisition    redevelopment

£
Cost of
valuation
in accounts
                                              Scrap
         +++++++++++
         A              B                       C
                 Accounting periods
```

The horizon of present ownership, i.e. the asset's useful economic life, lasts from A to B. The directors simply adopt and adhere to a policy of redeveloping or disposing of any property asset when the annual maintenance and repair costs (all of which are charged against profits as they are incurred) needed to preserve its present book value become uneconomic in relation to the revenues it can sustain. In the diagram this occurs at point B when, assuming the estimates have been accurate, no loss will occur on disposal or redevelopment. In the case of redevelopment the full costs (including demolition of existing structures) will be capitalised to establish a new point A, and the pattern recommences. The phase from B to C will occur only in the event of a disposal, but under different ownership and is therefore not our concern.

4.70 This philosophy has been variously translated into corporate accounting policies, of which the following extracts are typical:

Trusthouse Forte plc:

'It is the Group's practice to maintain the hotels in a continual state of sound repair and to extend and improve selected hotels from time to time and accordingly the directors consider that the lives of hotel buildings are so long and residual values so high that their depreciation is insignificant.'

Burton Group plc:

'It is the Group's policy to maintain its properties in a continual state of sound repair. In the case of freehold and long leasehold properties the directors consider that the lives of these properties and their residual values are such that their depreciation is not significant.'

Under the revised definition it will in future be unnecessary to formulate separate policies for property assets.

Disclosure
4.71
1. The following should be disclosed in the financial statements for each major class of depreciable asset:
   (a) the depreciation methods used;
   (b) the useful economic lives or the depreciation rates used;
   (c) total depreciation charged for the period;
   (d) the gross amount of depreciable assets and the related accumulated depreciation.
2. Where there has been a change in the depreciation method used the effect, if material, should be disclosed in the year of change. The reason for the change should also be disclosed.
3. Where assets have been revalued the effect of the revaluation on the depreciation charge should, if material, be disclosed in the year of revaluation.

SSAP 19: Accounting for investment properties

4.72   SSAP 19 defines an investment property as an interest in land and/or buildings:
(a) in respect of which construction work and development have been completed; and
(b) which is held for its investment potential, and rental income being negotiated at arm's length.

The following are not investment properties:
(a) A property which is owned and occupied by a company for its own purposes;
(b) A property let to and occupied by another group company.

4.73   SSAP 19 in its explanatory note states:
'A different treatment is, however, required where a significant proportion of the fixed assets of an enterprise is held not for consumption in the business operations but as investments, the disposal of which would not materially affect any manufacturing or trading operations of the enterprise. In such a case the current value of these investments, and changes in that current value, are of prime importance rather than calculation of systematic annual depreciation. Consequently, for the proper

ACCOUNTING FOR DEPRECIATION

appreciation of the financial position, a different accounting treatment is considered appropriate for fixed assets held as investments (called in this standard "investment properties")'.

4.74 SSAP 19 requires investment properties to be included in balance sheets at their open market value and exempts them (except for leased property having an unexpired term of 20 years or less) from the SSAP 12 requirement that depreciation should be provided.

4.75 The value of investment properties should be reassessed annually and SSAP 19 does not require the valuer to be professionally qualified or independent. Where investment properties represent a substantial proportion of the total assets of a major enterprise, their valuation should normally be performed by a professionally qualified person and should be confirmed by an external valuer at least every five years.

4.76 Changes in the revalued amounts of investment properties should be treated as movements in an Investment Property Revaluation Reserve unless the reserve is insufficient to cover a deficit, in which case the deficit should be charged to the profit and loss account.

Question

SSAP 12: Accounting for depreciation (revised 1987) makes a number of changes to SSAP 12 issued in 1977.
Required:
(a) Summarise the principal changes that the revised SSAP 12 has made to SSAP 12 issued in 1977.
(b) Give your views on the necessity of a revision of the original SSAP 12.

Chapter Five

SSAP 9 and ED 40: Stocks, work in progress and long-term contracts

Principles

5.1 Both SSAP 9 and ED 40, in their explanatory notes, state: 'The determination of profit for an accounting year requires the matching of costs with related revenues. The cost of unsold or unconsumed stocks will have been incurred in the expectation of future revenue, and when this will not arise until a later year it is appropriate to carry forward this cost to be matched with the revenue when it arises; the applicable concept is the matching of cost and revenue in the year in which the revenue arises rather than in the year in which the cost is incurred.'

5.2 The application of the matching principle requires an amount for closing stocks and work in progress to be carried forward at the end of each year, and the application of different methods to determine this amount can produce a wide range of results. SSAP 9 and ED 40 therefore seek to define practices for the valuation of stocks, to narrow the differences and variation in those practices, and to ensure adequate disclosure in the published accounts.

5.3 SSAP 9 and ED 40 require stocks to be stated at cost or, if lower, at net realisable value. Stocks comprise:

(a) goods or other assets purchased for resale;
(b) consumable stores;
(c) raw materials and components purchased for incorporation in products for sale;
(d) products and services in intermediate stages of completion other than long term contract balances;
(e) finished goods.

All the definitions of terms relating to stocks are exactly the same in both SSAP 9 and ED 40.

5.4 **Cost** is defined as being that expenditure which has been incurred in the normal course of business in bringing the product or service to its

SSAP 9 AND ED 40: STOCKS, WORK IN PROGRESS AND LONG-TERM CONTRACTS

present location and condition. This expenditure should include, in addition to cost of purchase, such costs of conversion as are appropriate to that location and condition.

5.5 **Cost of purchase** comprises purchase price including import duties, transport and handling costs and any other directly attributable costs, less trade discounts, rebates and subsidies.

5.6 **Cost of conversion** comprises:

(a) costs which are specifically attributable to units of production, i.e. direct labour, direct expenses and subcontracted work;
(b) production overheads;
(c) other overheads, if any, attributable in the particular circumstances of the business to bringing the product or service to its present location and condition.

5.7 **Production overheads**: These are overheads incurred in respect of materials, labour or services for production, based on the normal level of activity, taking one year with another. For this purpose each overhead should be classified according to function (e.g. production, selling or administration) so as to ensure the inclusion, in cost of conversion, of those overheads (including depreciation) which relate to production, notwithstanding that these may accrue wholly or partly on a time basis.

5.8 Direct material, labour and expenses are usually easy to recognise. Other overheads related to production are less obvious and both the Appendix to SSAP 9 and ED 40 give further guidance on this. The allocation of overheads will usually involve the exercise of personal judgement. Only production overheads (factory rent, rates, insurance) should be apportioned to units of production. These production overheads will include expenses which accrue on a time basis. Selling, distribution, finance, administration, general management costs which are period costs should not be allocated to units of production but should be written off to the profit and loss account. The Appendix to SSAP 9 states that the allocation of overheads included in the valuation of stocks needs to be based on the company's normal level of activity, taking one year with another. The governing factor is that the costs of unused capacity should be written off in the current year. In determining what constitutes 'normal' the following factors need to be considered:

(a) the volume of production which the production facilities are intended by their designers and by management to produce under the working conditions (e.g. single or double shift) prevailing during the year;

UNDERSTANDING ACCOUNTING STANDARDS

(b) the budgeted level of activity for the year under review and for the ensuing year;
(c) the level of activity achieved both in the year under review and in previous years.

5.9 This definition of the cost and what is to be included in the cost causes a number of problems in relation to production overheads:

(a) Both SSAP 9 and ED 40 require the allocation of fixed overheads like factory rent and rates (which accrue on a time basis) to the cost of stocks carried forward on the grounds that there is a direct future benefit associated with these costs (i.e. accruals concept).
Costs like rent and rates are period costs (i.e. they will be incurred regardless of whether goods are produced or not) and therefore, on the grounds of prudence, should be written off to the profit and loss account for the year in respect of which they are incurred. There is therefore a potential conflict with SSAP 2 which requires the prudence concept to prevail when there is a conflict with the accruals concept.
(b) The allocation of overheads included in the valuation of stocks will depend on the costing system which the company uses, and this may lack consistency with allocations made under other systems, and may require adjustment for variances.
(c) The allocation of overheads in the valuation of stocks needs to be based on the company's 'normal level of activity' – which is a very subjective term and different companies will interpret it in varying ways.

The differences and variations in practices for the valuation of stocks therefore still remain.

Methods of determining costs

Unit Cost

5.10 This is the cost of purchasing or manufacturing identifiable units of stocks. This is the purest form of identifying the cost but is impracticable where the volume of stocks or turnover in stocks is large and purchases are made in bulk at irregular intervals.

Average cost

5.11 Average cost = units of stock on hand × average price
Average price = $\dfrac{\text{Total cost of units}}{\text{Total number of units}}$

The average price may be arrived at by means of a continuous calculation, a period calculation or moving periodic calculation. This method may be appropriate where the volume of stocks is large.

First in, first out (FIFO)

5.12 The calculation of the cost of stocks and work in progress is on the assumption that the earliest purchases are taken to production or sold first and the stock in hand represents the latest purchases or production.

The advantages of this method are:

(a) The amount stated for the stock on the balance sheet is at its most recent purchase price.
(b) It is easy to value stock on this basis as the valuation procedure follows the physical movement of the stock.

The disadvantage of this method is that the current revenue may be matched with an out of date cost resulting in a profit figure which includes realised price level changes (i.e. realised holding gains). If these price level changes are spent, there will be a depletion in the physical capital of the business in real terms.

Last in, first out

5.13 The calculation of the cost of stocks and work in progress is on the assumption that the most recent purchases are taken to production or sold first and the stock in hand represents the earliest purchases or production.

5.14 The advantage of this method is that the current revenue is matched with the most recent cost of purchase resulting in a realistic profit as holding gains on price level changes are excluded from it. If in a particular period the number of units sold equals the number of units purchased, the cost of sales arrived at will equal the current cost of items sold.

5.15 There are two main disadvantages of this method:

(i) The value recorded on the balance sheet may be out of date and unrealistic.
(ii) There may be practical difficulties as a check will have to be kept on the physical stock level movements at each price level at which stocks have been purchased.

Base stock

5.16 The calculation of the cost of stocks and work in progress is on the basis that a predetermined quantity of stock is ascribed a fixed unit value (e.g. original cost) and any excess over this number is valued on the basis of some other method. If the number of units in stock is less than the predetermined minimum, the fixed unit value is applied to the number in stock.

5.17 Tate & Lyle use this method for valuing stock of raw sugar. A predetermined amount is valued at the original cost and the remainder on the FIFO basis. Their argument for valuing on this basis is that there is always a certain amount of sugar in the pipeline and this should therefore be considered as part of the fixed assets. In historic cost accounts, fixed assets are always recorded at their original cost, and therefore the amount of sugar in the pipeline should also be recorded at the original cost. The disadvantage of this method is that part of the stock on the balance sheet will be recorded at an out of date cost, although Tate & Lyle overcome this by revaluing the base stock at current prices prevailing at the balance sheet date, at the same time creating (or adjusting) revaluation reserve.

Replacement cost

5.18 The cost at which an identical asset could be purchased or manufactured. If the stocks and work in progress are carried forward at replacement cost and the replacement cost is greater than the historic cost, unrealised gains will be included in the resulting profit. However, the balance sheet will reflect a most up to date value. If the stocks and work in progress are valued at replacement cost and the replacement cost is less than the net realisable value which in turn is less than the cost, a loss greater than the one likely to be incurred will be included in the results.

5.19 In some instance, replacement cost may be the best measure of net realisable value, e.g. in respect of commodity sales.

Standard cost

5.20 The calculation of the cost of stocks and work in progress is on the basis of periodically predetermined costs calculated from management's estimates of expected levels of costs and of operations and operational efficiency and the related expenditure.

Adjusted selling price

5.21 Stock is valued at current selling prices less the normal gross profit margins. This method is commonly used by supermarkets and other retail businesses.

Compliance Summary

Method of cost determination	SSAP 9	Companies Act 1985
FIFO	Acceptable	Acceptable
Average cost	Acceptable	Acceptable
Unit cost	Acceptable	Acceptable
Adjusted selling price	Acceptable provided it gives reasonable approximation of actual cost	Acceptable
Replacement cost	Not acceptable under historical cost convention except in cases where it provides the best measure of net realisable value and net realisable value is less than cost	Acceptable under alternative accounting rules
Standard cost	Acceptable provided it is reviewed regularly and it gives reasonable approximation of actual cost	Acceptable
LIFO	Not acceptable as it does not usually bear a relationship to actual costs incurred	Acceptable
Base stock	Same as LIFO	Acceptable

Net realisable value

5.22 This is defined as the actual or estimated selling price (net of percentage of trade but before settlement discounts) less:

UNDERSTANDING ACCOUNTING STANDARDS

(a) all further costs to completion; and
(b) all costs to be incurred in marketing, selling and distributing.

5.23 Alternatively it may be thought of as the amount at which it is expected that stocks can be disposed of without creating a profit or a loss at the time of sale.

5.24 SSAP 9 and ED 40 require stocks and work in progress to be stated at net realisable value if it is less than the cost. The comparison of cost and net realisable value should be made in respect of each item of stock separately. Where this is impracticable, groups or categories of stock items which are similar will need to be taken together.

EXAMPLE

Category	Cost	Net realisable value	Stock at lower of cost and net realisable value
	£	£	£
A	100,000	80,000	80,000
B	150,000	180,000	150,000
C	200,000	230,000	200,000
	450,000	490,000	430,000

5.25 The net realisable value may be less than the cost for the following reasons:

(a) an increase in costs;
(b) a fall in selling price;
(c) obsolescence of products;
(d) a decision as part of a company's marketing strategy to manufacture and sell products at a loss – 'loss leader'; or
(e) error in production or purchasing.

5.26 The following should be taken into account when determining net realisable value:

(a) the age of stocks;
(b) movements during the past;
(c) expected future movements; and
(d) estimated scrap values of the stock.

5.27 Events between the balance sheet date and the date of completion of accounts also need to be considered in arriving at the net realisable value at the balance sheet date (e.g. a subsequent reduction in selling price).

SSAP 9 AND ED 40: STOCKS, WORK IN PROGRESS AND LONG-TERM CONTRACTS

Disclosures

5.28 The accounting policies which have been used in calculating cost and net realisable value should be stated.

5.29 Stocks and work in progress should be sub-classified in balance sheet or in notes to the financial statements in a manner which is appropriate to the business and so as to indicate the amounts held in each of the main categories.

Long-term contracts

5.30 IAS 11: Accounting for construction contracts states that there are two methods of accounting for contracts:
(a) *the percentage completion method*: under this method revenue is recognised as the contract activity progresses. The costs incurred in reaching the stage of completion are matched with this revenue, resulting in the reporting of results which can be attributed to the proportion of work completed. Provision is made for losses to the stage of completion reached, and also for losses on the remainder of the contract, in accordance with prudence principle. The amount of revenue recognised is determined by reference to the stage of completion of the contract activity at the end of each accounting period. The stage of completion can be measured by calculating either:
  (i) the proportion that costs incurred to date bear to the estimated total costs of the contract; or
  (ii) the proportion that value of work certified bears to the contract price.
In short:

Revenue recognised = % of completion × total estimated revenue

$$\% \text{ of completion} = \frac{\text{costs incurred to date}}{\text{total estimated costs}}$$

OR

$$\frac{\text{value of work certified}}{\text{contract price}}$$

Total estimated revenue = contract price − total estimated costs.
The advantages of this method are:
  (i) it complies with the accruals concept;
  (ii) it reflects revenue in the accounting period during which activity was undertaken to earn such revenue, thus giving a better view

97

of profitability and progress of the company. The earnings figure reported in the profit and loss account can be used for predictive purposes.

The disadvantages of this method are:

(i) it is contrary to the prudence concept, as it recognises revenue before the work is completed;
(ii) it is subject to a risk of error in making estimates, such as the determination of stage of completion, total estimated costs and total estimated revenue;
(iii) the recognition of revenue prior to work being completed may cause cash flow problems for the company, as tax and dividends may have to be paid out of this revenue without knowing whether the company will ultimately make a profit or loss on this contract in the future.

(b) *the completed contract method*: under this method, revenue is recognised only when the contract is completed or substantially completed. Provision is made for any losses to date and those which are foreseeable.

The advantages of this method are:

(i) it complies with the prudence concept;
(ii) no estimates are required in the estimation of revenue earned on contracts incomplete at the balance sheet date.

The disadvantages of this method are:

(i) it may be excessively prudent;
(ii) it is contrary to the accruals concept;
(iii) the profit and loss account does not reflect the revenue earned in the period in which activity was undertaken to earn such revenue;
(iv) the results do not give an accurate picture of the progress of the company during the period.

The SSAP 9 approach

5.31 SSAP 9 defines a long-term contract as being one which has been entered into for the manufacturing or building of a single substantial entity or the provision of a service where the time taken to manufacture, build or provide is such that a substantial proportion of all such contract work will extend for a period exceeding one year. SSAP 9 requires that the amount at which long-term contract work in progress is stated in financial statements should be:

SSAP 9 AND ED 40: STOCKS, WORK IN PROGRESS AND LONG-TERM CONTRACTS

	£
cost	X
plus: any attributable profit	X
	X
less: any foreseeable losses	(X)
	X
less: progress payments received and receivable	(X)
BALANCE SHEET VALUE	X

5.32 If anticipated losses on individual contracts exceed costs to date less progress payments received and receivable, such excesses should be shown separately as provisions. SSAP 9 defines foreseeable losses as being those which are currently estimated to arise over the duration of the contract (after allowing for estimated remedial and maintenance costs, and increases in costs as far as not recoverable under the terms of the contract). This estimate is required irrespective of:

(a) whether work has yet commenced on such contracts;
(b) the proportion of work carried out at the accounting date; and
(c) the amount of profits expected to arise on other contracts.

The definition of cost is the same as for stocks (see the discussion on stocks above).

5.33 As can be seen, SSAP 9 has adopted the percentage of completion method. SSAP 9 attempts to reflect the four fundamental concepts stated in SSAP 2:

(i) *accruals concept* – contract activity may extend over several years. It is therefore argued that in order to give a true and fair view of the results of the year over which the activity takes place, profit should be allocated over these years. A misleading view could be given if contract profits were not recognised until completion of the contract. Some years might then show substantial profits, others substantial losses and incorrect interpretations might be placed on the company's progress;

(ii) *prudence concept* – it may not be possible to predict accurately the outcome of a contract until the contract is well advanced. The prudence concept requires a company to determine the earliest point at which contract profits may be brought into the profit and loss account. Uncertainties include those relating to costs and the date when the contract will be completed. As time passes, the picture gradually unfolds and the uncertainties diminish. If, however, it is expected that there will be a loss on a contract as a whole, provision should be made for the whole of loss as soon as it is recognised;

(iii) *going concern* – a company should ensure that it has adequate resources (particularly finance) to complete the contract work;
(iv) *consistency* – similar contracts should be treated in a consistent manner, both within a particular year and between successive years.

Calculating attributable profit

5.34 The stages referred to in SSAP 9, Appendix 1, may be summarised as follows:

(a) *Calculate total costs to date* (A)
   (i) Costs relating directly to a specific contract
   - site labour costs, including supervision
   - materials used for project construction
   - depreciation of plant and equipment used on a contract
   - costs of moving plant and equipment to and from a site.
   (ii) Costs relating to general contract activity, but which can be allocated to specific contracts
   - insurance
   - design and technical assistance
   - construction overhead.

   General administration and selling costs and research and development costs should not be included. Nor should depreciation of idle plant and equipment.

   Interest payable on borrowed money should not normally be included. However, where sums borrowed can be identified as financing specific long-term contracts, related interest costs may be included. The fact and the amount of the interest should be disclosed.
(b) *Calculate estimated further costs to complete* (B)
   Estimated further costs should take into account expected future increases in wages, materials, and overhead costs except where these are recoverable from the customer under the terms of the contract.
(c) *Calculate estimated future costs of rectification and guarantee work and any other future work to be carried out under the terms of the contract* (C)
(d) Therefore estimated total costs to completion are (A + B + C).
(e) *Calculate estimated total profit* (D)
   This is the excess of the sales value of contract over estimated total cost (A + B + C).
(f) *Should any profit be recognised?*
   Can the outcome of the contract be predicted with reasonable certainty? If the answer is yes, go on to calculate attributable profit.

SSAP 9 AND ED 40: STOCKS, WORK IN PROGRESS AND LONG-TERM CONTRACTS

(g) *Attributable profit* (E)

Attributable profit is effectively the cumulative profit earned to date. It is the proportion of estimated total profit (D) which prudently reflects the amount of work performed to date. To calculate (E) it is necessary to arrive at an indicator of progress, i.e. an assessment of the degree of completion of the contract.

(h) *Indicator of progress*

There are several possibilities:

(i) $\dfrac{\text{cost to date}}{\text{estimated total cost to complete}}$

(ii) $\dfrac{\text{work certified to date}}{\text{estimated contract price}}$

(iii) $\dfrac{\text{labour hours to date}}{\text{estimated total labour hours}}$

(iv) surveys which measure the physical work done.

Possibility (ii) may be suspect if architects' valuations are used – they do not necessarily reflect the value of work done. It is not uncommon in the construction industry deliberately to overvalue contracts in their early stages. This practice, known as front-end loading, is of course known to the customer! The problem from the accountant's viewpoint is that it can distort profit measurement.

Say approach (i) is used:

Cost to date	F
Estimated total cost	G

Therefore attributable profit (E) is calculated as:

$$\frac{F}{G} \times D$$

(i) *How much profit should be credited to this year's profit and loss account?*

Effect on this year's P/L account is:

Attributable profit	E
less profits recorded in P/L accounts of previous years, say,	H
Therefore this year's P/L account	I

SSAP 9 makes the important point that where a contract extends over several years, the estimated outcome will nearly always vary as a result of changed circumstances. As a result, the profit (or loss) recorded this year (I) will not necessarily represent the proportion of total profit appropriate to the work carried out this year. It may also reflect changed circumstances during the year which have affected the estimated total profit.

UNDERSTANDING ACCOUNTING STANDARDS

EXAMPLE

Harry Ltd. is carrying out a fixed price construction contract for a customer, William. Work started in 19X0 and is expected to be completed towards the end of 19X3. The information below relates to the first three years of the contract. The contract price is £960,000.

Year	Costs Incurred to date	Estimated further costs	Estimated total costs	Value of work certified	Progress payments received	Progress payments outstanding at year end
	£'000	£'000	£'000	£'000	£'000	£'000
19X0	100	650	750	130	100	45
19X1	350	420	770	470	260	50
19X2	605	205	810	768	260	70

Calculations of attributable profit

	Estimated total profit	Cost to date / total Cost	Value of work certified / sales price	Attributable profit 'cost' approach	Attributable profit 'value' approach
	£			£	£
19X0	210,000	No profit taken (contract outcome cannot be reasonably foreseen)			
19X1	190,000	$\frac{350}{770}$	$\frac{470}{960}$	86,364	93,021
19X2	150,000	$\frac{605}{810}$	$\frac{768}{960}$	112,037	120,000

Balance sheet extracts ('cost' approach figures)

	As at 31 December		
	19X0	19X1	19X2
	£	£	£
Cost	100,000	350,000	605,000
Attributable profit	–	86,364	112,037
	100,000	436,364	717,037
Progress payments received and receivable	145,000	410,000	690,000
Work in progress	(45,000)	26,364	27,037

SSAP 9 AND ED 40: STOCKS, WORK IN PROGRESS AND LONG-TERM CONTRACTS

Profit and loss account (one of the presentations used – SSAP 9 gives no specific guidance on this)

	Year ended 31 December			
	19X0	19X1	19X2	Total
	£	£	£	£
Turnover	100,000	336,364	280,673	717,037
Cost of sales	100,000	250,000	255,000	605,000
Operating profit	–	86,364	25,673	112,037

Notes
(1) Turnover is based on cost plus attributable profit. Assuming the contract is completed during 19X3, the turnover of the four years will add to £960,000 (the fixed contract price). The above approach must be adopted in any event as the Companies Act formats reconcile downwards arithmetically (turnover less cost of sales, etc.), and this is now required by ED 40.
(2) In the financial statements, amounts would be rounded to £'000 to avoid an impression of over-precision.
(3) It is assumed that the cost figures allow for anticipated contingencies and that the contract is sufficiently well advanced by the end of 19X1 to justify taking profits.
(4) Other approaches in assessing the degree of completion (e.g. the value certified/contract price approach) could be justified.

Other ways of calculating attributable profit

5.35 The approach outlined above is set out in Appendix 1 of SSAP 9. The appendix does not form part of the standard accounting practice and thus is not mandatory. Any approach can be justified provided that it 'fairly reflects the profit attributable to that part of the work performed at the accounting date'.

In the past, some companies have calculated the profit for a particular year as follows:

	£
Value of work to date	X
less cost of work to date	X
profit to date	X

This is then adjusted by arbitrary factors to reflect prudence, etc.

In examinations, unless indicated to the contrary, you are recommended to follow the approach in SSAP 9.

5.36 Other considerations

(a) *Approved variations.* These are equivalent to extras and will add on to the contract price. If the amount of this extra work has not been settled, a conservative estimate of the amount likely to be received, should be made. The cost of such work will already be reflected in the cost figure (A + B + C above) and the estimate should be added to the sales figure (contract price).
(b) *Penalties and claims against the contractor.* Provision should be made for penalties or claims arising out of delays in completion, etc.
(c) *Claims against the customer.* These could involve situations where the contractor has already incurred expenditure (reflected in costs, etc.) and is trying to get the customer to agree to an increase in the contract price. Such amounts should not be taken into account unless:
  (i) negotiations have reached an advanced stage;
  (ii) there is written evidence of the acceptability of the claim from the customer's viewpoint;
  (iii) there is an indication of the amount of money involved.
(d) *Contracts which can be divided into separate parts.* SSAP 9 points out that in some businesses, long-term contracts exist where the prices are determined and invoiced according to separate parts of the contract. SSAP 9 suggests that the most appropriate method of calculating profits is to treat each such part as a separate contract. IAS 11 makes a similar comment referring to a contract which may cover a number of individual projects, where costs and revenues can be separately identified.

5.37 Contracts which are expected to make losses

(a) *General principle.* As soon as it is expected that a particular contract will result in a loss, immediate provision should be made for the full amount of the anticipated loss (prudence concept). This effectively brings the value of the contract to net realisable value.
(b) *Loss-making contracts of a large magnitude.* In some cases, unprofitable contracts are of such a size that they are expected to absorb a considerable part of the company's capacity for a substantial period. The calculation of provisions for losses should take into account

related administration overheads likely to be incurred while the contracts are being completed.
(c) *Disclosure of provisions.* If anticipated losses on individual contracts exceed cost incurred to date less progress payments received and receivable, such excesses should be shown separately as provisions.

EXAMPLE

A contractor entered into a fixed price contract of £650,000. The contract is in a relatively early stage but it is already apparent that the contract will result in a loss. Costs incurred to date amount to £190,000 but estimated total costs amount to £830,000. Show how the contract would be disclosed in the balance sheet, assuming progress payments received amount to £75,000.

SOLUTION

	£	£
Anticipated losses on contract (830,000–650,000)		180,000
Costs incurred to date	190,000	
less progress payments invoiced	75,000	115,000
Excess to be shown as separate provision		65,000

5.38 Disclosure

(a) State the following amounts in the balance sheet:
 (i) cost plus attributable profit, less foreseeable losses
 (ii) cash received and receivable at the accounting date as progress payments on account of contracts in progress.
(b) If, on individual loss-making contracts, anticipated losses exceed cost incurred to date less progress payments received and receivable, the excess(es) should be shown separately as provisions.
(c) Accounting policies used in calculating attributable profits and foreseeable losses.

5.39 Problems with the SSAP 9 approach

(a) The recognition of revenue in SSAP 9 is based on the accruals concept, i.e. the revenue is recognised as the work progresses and not when it is completed. The prudence concept requires that revenue and profits are not anticipated, but are recognised by inclusion in the profit and loss account only when realised in the form either of cash or of other assets, the ultimate cash realisation of which can be assessed with reasonable certainty. There appears to be a conflict between the accruals concept and the prudence concept and in such instances SSAP 2 requires that the prudence concept must prevail.

(b) SSAP 9 defines attributable profit as being that part of the total profit currently estimated to rise over the duration of the contract (after allowing for likely increases in costs not recoverable under the terms of the contract) which fairly reflects the profit attributable to that part of the work performed at the accounting date. (There can be no attributable profit until the outcome of the contract can be assessed with reasonable certainty.) More simply, what SSAP 9 means is that the attributable profit will be based on the amount (or percentage) of work completed and there can be no attributable profit until the outcome of the contract can be assessed with reasonable certainty. SSAP 9 gives no guidance as to how this percentage of work completed may be computed and, as discussed earlier, there are several instances of this.

(c) There is a conflict with the CA 1985 in respect of the balance sheet presentation of long-term contracts. SSAP 9 requires long-term contract work in progress to be recorded in the balance sheet at 'cost plus any attributable profit, less any foreseeable losses and progress payments received and receivable'. Schedule 4 of the CA 1985 requires that 'the amount to be included in respect of any current asset shall be its purchase price or production cost (or its net realisable value if lower)'. Therefore, there is a conflict in relation to the profit element.

In practice, most companies affected by this conflict have invoked the true and fair override to justify the inclusion of the profit element. This causes two further problems. First, the true and fair override should not be used as a general solution, but only to meet the specific circumstances of a particular company. Second, if the true and fair view is invoked, disclosure of the departure with reasons, as well as the effect on financial statements, are required to be disclosed in the notes to the accounts.

There have been disagreements on how the effect of the departure should be disclosed. A typical example of this is the following note taken from the Trafalgar House accounts in 1985:

'The inclusion of attributable profit in work in progress is in accordance with SSAP 9. This constitutes a departure from the statutory valuation rules for current assets but is required by S 228(5) CA 1985 to enable the accounts to give a true and fair view. As progress payments cannot meaningfully be allocated between cost and profit, it is impracticable to determine the effect of the departure on the balance sheet carrying amount of contract work in progress'.

(d) SSAP 9 simply requires that attributable profit (if any) should be recognised in the profit and loss account and added to the cumulative cost of contract work in progress in the balance sheet. It ignores the question of how contract sales revenue and related costs should be recorded in the profit and loss account. In practice, a variety of methods has been used to determine the turnover disclosed in each accounting period. However, in many cases, this has not been derived from a formal integration of revenue, cost and balance sheet accounting.

(e) SSAP 9 requires that if anticipated losses on individual contracts exceed costs to date less progress payments received and receivable, such excess should be shown separately as provisions. The opinion amongst the preparers of the accounts is divided on whether this excess amount should be classified as provision or accrual.

The ED 40 approach

5.40 ED 40 defines a long-term contract as being one entered into for the manufacture or the building of a substantial entity or the provision of a service where the time taken to manufacture, build or provide is such that the contract activity falls into different accounting periods and normally is expected to extend for a period exceeding one year. However, the specific duration of performance may not be the sole distinguishing feature of such a contract and where the reporting entity is substantially engaged in contracts which extend for more than one year, it may not be appropriate to adopt a separate accounting policy for shorter-term contracts. This is a change in definition from SSAP 9, which rigidly defines long-term contracts as those in respect of which a substantial proportion of the work 'will extend for a period exceeding one year'. ED 40 states that the specific duration may not be its sole distinguishing feature.

ED 40 requirements

5.41 ED 40 requires that
(a) long-term contracts should be disclosed in the balance sheet as follows:
  (i) the amount of long-term contracts, at costs incurred, net of amounts transferred to cost of sales, after deducting foreseeable losses and applicable payments on account, should be classified

as 'long-term contract balances' and separately disclosed within stocks. The balance sheet note should disclose separately the balances of:
(1) net cost less foreseeable losses; and
(2) applicable payments on account;
  (ii) the balance of payments on account (in excess of amounts recorded as turnover and off-set against long-term contracts) should be classified as payments on account and separately disclosed within creditors;
  (iii) the amount by which recorded turnover is in excess of payments on account, should be classified as 'amounts recoverable on contracts' and separately disclosed within debtors;
  (iv) the amount by which the provision or accrual for foreseeable losses exceeds the costs incurred (after transfers to cost of sales) should be disclosed within either provisions for liabilities and charges or creditors as appropriate. The amount need not be separately disclosed unless material to the financial statements;
(b) consequent upon the implementation of this revised standard, the corresponding amounts in the financial statements will need to be re-stated on a comparable basis;
(c) the accounting policies which have been used in calculating turnover, cost, cost of sales, net realisable value, attributable profit and foreseeable losses (as appropriate) should be stated.

5.42 The definition of cost is the same as for stocks. The definitions of attributable profits and foreseeable losses also remain the same as for SSAP 9.

5.43 The effect of the above proposals is that the profit and loss account and balance sheet will be fully integrated. This is not the case with the existing SSAP 9. The existing practice under SSAP 9 is to 'build up debits' on each individual contract by reference to direct costs, allocated overheads and attributable profits, culminating in a 'carry-forward' to feature in the balance sheet (net of payments received). This 'carry-forward' relating to a particular contract is eliminated when the contract is determined to have been completed. SSAP 9 asserts the principle that attributable profit should be recognised by reference to the work done to date but does not detail any specific methods of achieving this requirement. The SSAP 9 approach of referring to principles rather than methods is perpetuated in ED 40. The ASC continues to believe that all suitable techniques which have been used under SSAP 9 to measure the value of work done and attributable profit should continue to be applied.

SSAP 9 AND ED 40: STOCKS, WORK IN PROGRESS AND LONG-TERM CONTRACTS

5.44 The ED 40 approach is similar to the IAS 11 approach. ED 40 requires revenues to be recognised as the contract activity progresses. The costs incurred in reaching the stage of completion are matched with this revenue, resulting in the reporting of results which can be attributed to the proportion of work completed. The balance sheet presentation is arrived at on a contract-by-contract basis as follows:

(a) Work in progress is stated in the balance sheet at total cost incurred, less the amount transferred to the profit and loss account in respect of work carried out to date (i.e. cost of sales). Amounts provided for anticipated losses are deducted from any remaining work in progress balances, with excesses shown separately as provisions or accruals as appropriate;

(b) Cumulative turnover (i.e. the total turnover recorded in respect of the contract in the profit and loss accounts of all accounting periods since inception of the contract) is compared with total payments on account. If turnover exceeds payments on account an 'amount recoverable on contract' is established and included in debtors. If payments on account are greater than turnover to date, the excess is classified as a deduction from work in progress with any residual balance in excess of this amount being classified with creditors.

5.45 The example opposite from the Appendix to ED 40 illustrates the financial statement presentation of long-term contracts following the principles set out in the exposure draft.

5.46 The proposed revision to SSAP 9 specifies a balance sheet presentation which takes account of amounts which have been transferred to the profit and loss account. There will be no effect on the profit and loss account because any attributable profit and foreseeable losses will be measured in the same way as under the existing standard. The ASC believes that the proposals in ED 40 will enable all companies which wish to present a 'true and fair view' by recognising attributable profits on long-term contracts to do so without fear of contravention of paragraph 22 of Schedule 4, CA 1985. The debtor balance termed 'amount recoverable on contracts' is believed to be a true debtor balance and is consistent with the existing practice of recognising turnover and profit on long-term contracts in the profit and loss account by reference to the value of work done. Also, legal opinion has confirmed that such a balance may appropriately be described as a debtor.

5.47 It is too early to say whether the ED 40 proposals will be accepted in full by companies, particularly those in the construction industry. Two potentially contentious points may arise:

(a) The lack of distinction in ED 40 between

UNDERSTANDING ACCOUNTING STANDARDS

	Contract Number					Balance Sheet Total	Profit & Loss Account
	1	2	3	4	5		
Recorded as turnover – being value of work done	145	520	380	200			1,245
Cumulative payments on account	(100)	(600)	(400)	(270)	(40)		
Classified as amount recoverable on contracts	45					45DR	
Balance (excess) of payments on account		(80)	(20)	(70)	(40)		
Applied as an offset against long-term contract balances – see below		60	20		20		
Residue classified as payments on account		(20)		(70)	(20)	(110)CR	
Total costs incurred	110	510	450	250	50		
Recorded as cost of sales	(110)	(450)	(350)	(250)			(1,160)
		60	100		50		
Provision/accrual for foreseeable losses				(40)	(30)		(70)
		60	100		20		
Classified as provision/ accrual for losses				(40)		(40)CR	
Balance (excess) of payments on account applied as offset against long-term contract balances		(60)	(20)		(20)		
Classified as long-term contract balances			80			80DR	
Gross profit or loss on long-term contracts	35	70	30	(90)	(30)		15

(i) progress payments in respect of completed work; and
(ii) advance payments by customers before work commences, as a form of contract funding to be settled at a later date.

SSAP 9 AND ED 40: STOCKS, WORK IN PROGRESS AND LONG-TERM CONTRACTS

This distinction is important in relation to government contracts, when tendering requires submission of accounts to facilitate the assessment of financial strength, based on defined balance sheet criteria;
(b) the relaxation of the 'long-term' definition. This may now affect comparability between the financial statements of different companies. Some may argue that *all* contracts based on customer specifications and which are incomplete at the balance sheet date should be accounted for in the manner specified in ED 40, thus abandoning the arbitrary time/length criterion.

Example of ED 40 approach

5.48 Builder Ltd commenced business on 1 June 1986 as building contractors. The following details relate to the three uncompleted contracts in the company's books on 31 May 1987.

CONTRACT NAME:	Apple £	Pear £	Plum £
cost of work to 31 May 1987	31,000	28,000	10,300
cost of work to 31 May 1987, as certified	30,470	27,280	9,640
value of work to 31 May 1987 as certified by contractees' architects	38,500	22,000	14,300
progress payments invoiced to 31 May 1987	33,000	17,600	11,000
progress payments received by 31 May 1987	27,500	17,600	11,000
Estimate of: final cost including future costs of rectification and guarantee work	33,000	38,500	66,000
Final contract price	41,800	30,800	88,000

Required:

(a) a statement showing calculations for each contract;
(b) to show, as an extract therefrom, the information which should appear in the profit and loss account for the year ended 31 May 1987 and the balance sheet as at 31 May 1987. The presentation should take into account the requirements of ED 40.

UNDERSTANDING ACCOUNTING STANDARDS

BUILDERS LTD. YEAR ENDED 31 MAY 1987

	CONTRACT			Balance Sheet	Profit & Loss a/c
	Apple £	Pear £	Plum £	£	£
Recorded as turnover – being value of work done	38,500	22,000	—		60,500
Cumulative payments due – progress payments invoiced	(33,000)	(17,600)	(11,000)		
Classified as amounts recoverable on contracts	5,500	4,400		9,900 DR	
Balance (excess) of payment on account			(11,000)		
Applied as an offset against long-term contract balances – see below			10,300		
Residue classified as payments on account	—	—	700	(700) CR	
Total costs incurred	31,000	28,000	10,300		
Recorded as cost of sales – cost of work certified	30,470	27,280	—		(57,750)
	530	720	10,300		
Provision/accrual for foreseeable losses	—	(2,420)	—		(2,420)
	530	(1,700)	10,300		
Classified as provision/ accrual for losses		1,700		(1,700)CR	
	530	—	10,300		
Balance (excess) of payment on account applied as offset against long-term contract balances			(10,300)		
Classified as long-term contract	530	—	—	530 DR	
Gross profit (or loss) on long-term contract	£ 8,030	£(7,700)	—		£330

Contract:

Apple: As this contract is almost complete and the outcome can be calculated with a reasonable degree of certainty, the profit can be recognised.

Pear: The loss to date of £5,280 is the net figure after deducting cost of sales of £27,280 from the turnover of £60,500. The total loss on this contract is likely to be £7,700 (£38,500 – £30,800). A further provision of £2,420 for foreseeable losses is required in the accounts.

Plum: As this contract is in its early stages, it is difficult to foresee whether an overall profit will ultimately accrue. For this reason, it may not be prudent to recognise any attributable profit.

BUILDERS LTD.
Profit and loss account for the year ended 31 May 1987

	£
Turnover	60,500
less cost of sales	(57,750)
Operating profit	2,750
less provision for foreseeable losses	(2,420)
	£330

Balance sheet (extract) as at 31 May 1987

CURRENT ASSETS	£	
STOCKS		
work in progress on long-term contracts	530	at lower of cost and NRV
DEBTORS		
Progress payments due	5,500*	
Amounts recoverable on contracts	9,900	

*This is progress payments invoiced of £33,000 for Apple less cash received of £27,500.

CREDITORS (amounts falling due within 1 year)

	£
Long-term contracts – payment on account	700
**Accrual for loss	1,700

**Alternatively this may be shown as a provision.

Question

SSAP 9 Stocks and Work in Progress is partly concerned with long-term contract work in progress.

Required:

(a) How does SSAP 9 justify the recognition of profits before completion of a long-term contract?

(b) How does SSAP 9 require the profits and losses on long-term contracts in progress to be calculated and disclosed in financial statements?
(c) Do you consider that the provisions in SSAP 9 concerning long-term contracts are consistent with the requirements of SSAP 2 'Disclosure of Accounting Policies' and the Accounting Principles stated in the Companies Act 1985?
(d) Discuss the proposals of ED 40: 'Stocks and Long Term Contracts'.

Chapter Six

SSAP 13 and ED 41: Accounting for research and development

SSAP 13: Accounting for Research and Development

6.1 SSAP 13 subdivides 'research and development' into three categories:
1. Pure Research;
2. Applied Research; and
3. Development.

The definitions of the above three categories have been based on those used by the Organisation for Economic Co-operation and Development and are as follows:

1. *Pure (or basic) research*: original investigation undertaken in order to gain new scientific or technical knowledge and understanding. Basic research is not primarily directed towards any specific practical aim or application.
2. *Applied research*: original investigation undertaken in order to gain new scientific or technical knowledge and directed towards a specific practical aim or objective.
3. *Development*: the use of scientific or technical knowledge in order to produce new or substantially improved materials, devices, products, processes, systems or services prior to the commencement of commercial production.

Accounting treatment

6.2 The accounting treatment will depend mainly on two fundamental accounting concepts:
(a) 'Accruals' concept – which requires that revenue and costs are accrued and are matched with one another to the extent that their relationship can be either established or justifiably presumed.
(b) 'Prudence' concept – which requires that revenue and profits are not anticipated until such time as they are realised either in the form of cash, or in the form of assets, where the ultimate cash realisation of those assets can be assessed with reasonable certainty.

Pure and applied research

6.3 SSAP 13 requires that expenditure on pure and applied research (other than the cost of fixed assets acquired or constructed in order to provide facilities for research and development) should be written off in the year of expenditure.

6.4 SSAP 13 treats these costs in much the same way as fixed overheads which would normally be written off to the profit and loss account on the grounds of prudence. SSAP 13 in its explanatory note states 'Expenditure incurred on pure and applied research can be regarded as part of a continuing operation required to maintain a company's business and its competitive position. In general, one particular period rather than another will not be expected to benefit and therefore it is appropriate that these costs should be written off as they are incurred'.

6.5 Pure research is not undertaken with any specific practical application in mind, although it may at a later stage result in practical benefits (such as new products, cost savings, and new techniques). Applied research is aimed at achieving a particular objective like say, the construction of a machine to perform a specific task, but at this stage the outcome of this research may not be ascertainable. Since no specific relationship can be identified between these costs and revenue (even though benefit exists), the cost should be written off in the year in which it is incurred.

Development expenditure

6.6 SSAP 13 does not specify the costs which should be included as part of development expenditure. As in the case of other fixed assets, it should include all the costs incurred to bring the item into its existing location and condition. This expenditure is generally undertaken where there is a reasonable expectation that specific commercial success and future benefits will result from the work.

6.7 SSAP 13 requires that, generally, development expenditure should be written off in the year of expenditure. However, SSAP 13 makes an exception to this requirement in stating that charging its cost *may* be deferred to future periods if the following conditions are satisfied:

(a) there is a clearly defined project; *and*
(b) the related expenditure is separately identifiable; and

SSAP 13 AND ED 41: ACCOUNTING FOR RESEARCH AND DEVELOPMENT

(c) the outcome of such a project has been assessed with reasonable certainty as to
   (i) its technical feasibility, and
   (ii) its ultimate commercial viability considered in the light of factors such as likely market conditions (including competing products), public opinion, consumer and environmental legislation; *and*
(d) if further development costs are to be incurred on the same project the aggregate of such costs together with related production, selling and administration costs are reasonably expected to be more than covered by related future revenues; *and*
(e) adequate resources exist, or are reasonably expected to be available, to enable the project to be completed and to provide any consequential increases in working capital.

6.8 The general rule is that the development expenditure should be written off in the year in which it is incurred. This is consistent with the prudence concept as there may be uncertainties regarding future benefits arising from the development expenditure incurred.

6.9 Some companies will make the writing off of this expenditure one of their accounting policies regardless of whether or not there is a future benefit. Other companies may, however, decide to capitalise the development expenditure and amortise it. SSAP 13 allows this expenditure to be deferred only if the conditions stated earlier are satisfied.

6.10 Conditions (a) and (b) require that a separate account is set up for each project and there is an analysis of all development expenditure between projects. Condition (c) (i) requires that the project must be technically feasible. This means that there can be no grounds for deferring expenditure on a project that is unlikely to be successful.

6.11 The assessment of the outcome of the project by an accountant is much more difficult as the accountant is ordinarily no judge of its technical feasibility and must accept the advice of engineers, chemists or other technologists.

6.12 Condition (c) (ii) requires that the project should be commercially viable. The question of 'ultimate commercial viability' is more within the sphere of the accountant. Before initiating the project, the directors will have studied the market for assessing the viability of the expected product (or the practical utility of the improved process), the probable profits (or cost savings), the factors (such as competing products or processes) likely to set limits to the profits or savings, and the possibilities of public or political objections to the project (e.g. the possible harmful side-effects of a new drug). The report and computations on all the above factors will need to be in considerable detail and available to the accountant, who must then make a judgement regarding the 'ultimate commercial viability' of the project. If he is convinced that the project will be commercially viable, he may wish to consider the matter further; otherwise the expenditure must be written off.

6.13 Condition (d) deals with the recoverability of the development expenditure on a long run. As in condition (c), the accountant will have to rely on the information provided by the directors to judge whether this expenditure will be recovered. Condition (e) requires that there must be adequate resources to carry the project to completion. This is largely a function of the overall viability of the company.

6.14 If the conditions stated in SSAP 13 are satisfied, then the development expenditure may be deferred to the extent that its recovery can reasonably be regarded as assured. The criteria for determining whether development expenditure may be deferred should be applied consistently from project to project and from year to year.

Deferred development expenditure

1. Amortisation
6.15 SSAP 13 requires that 'If development costs are deferred to future periods, their amortisation should commence with the commercial production of the product or process and should be allocated on a systematic basis to each accounting period, by reference either to the sale or use of the product or process or the period over which the product or process is expected to be sold or used'. The above requirement raises two questions:

(1) At what point should amortisation commence? and
(2) On what basis should the expenditure be amortised?

6.16 It is usually easy to decide on the year when the amortisation should begin but less easy to determine its time-pattern. Allocation on either sale/use basis or a time basis raises the question as to how long a time should be covered. The time-pattern could be determined on any one of the following basis:

(a) period over which the product/process is sold/used; or
(b) period over which the product/process is profitable; or
(c) period over which the product/process is dominant in the market or not superseded by technically superior alternatives.

SSAP 13 AND ED 41: ACCOUNTING FOR RESEARCH AND DEVELOPMENT

6.17 Most companies would fix a limit by reference to the criterion (b) or (c) in order to amortise over a reasonably short period of years. It is then necessary to choose between the following:

(a) Sales/use pattern (implying accelerated write off); or
(b) time pattern (straight-line method).

Sales/use pattern is more conservative, especially for products which make most money in the earlier years. The accountant must look at the circumstances of each case and apply judgement.

2. Annual Review

6.18 SSAP 13 requires that 'Deferred expenditure should be reviewed at the end of each accounting period and where the circumstances which have justified the deferral of the expenditure no longer apply, or considered to be doubtful, the expenditure, to the extent to which it is considered to be irrecoverable, should be written off immediately. Development expenditure once written off should not be reinstated even though the uncertainties which had led to its being written off no longer apply.'

6.19 The accountant's responsibilities do not end once it is decided to capitalise the development expenditure. As long as the project is going on, it must be reviewed at the end of each financial year.

6.20 An opinion must be formed as to whether the criteria stated in SSAP 13 regarding the capitalisation of development is found not to be technically feasible, it will be terminated and the expenditure to date must be written off to profit and loss account. If ultimate commercial viability is in question through the emergence of a successful competing product or through the passing of legislation banning or severely restricting the use of the product or process, the expenditure capitalised to date must be written off. Increased costs or cost overruns may also call into question the availability of adequate finance to carry through a project to completion. If there is any doubt on such matters, the expenditure must be written off at the year-end.

Fixed assets acquired to provide facilities for research and development

6.21 SSAP 13 requires that 'Fixed assets acquired or constructed in order to provide facilities for research and development over a number of accounting periods should be capitalised and written off over their useful life'.

6.22 The amounts written off should be included as part of research and development expenditure. It will be disclosed in the profit and loss account as part of the depreciation charge. Where the fixed asset is acquired for a specific project, it will be amortised over the term of the project.

Disclosures

6.23
(a) Movements on deferred development expenditure and the amount carried forward at the beginning and end of the period should be disclosed.
(b) Deferred development expenditure should be separately disclosed and should not be included in current assets.
(c) The accounting policy followed should be explained.

EXAMPLE

Three cases of Research and Development expenditure in the accounts of a pharmaceutical company:

Case 1

During the financial year, the company has spent £500,000 on a project to develop a drug to treat cancer. It is expected that it will take three years to establish whether or not the drug is likely to be effective, and if it is, it will take at least two years to produce a marketable product.

In this particular case there is a defined project and the costs are separately identifiable. But there is an uncertainty in relation to its technical feasibility and its commercial viability, i.e. it will take three years before it is known whether the drug will work and if it does, it will take at least another two years to develop a marketable product. Thus, the £500,000 spent in the current year should be written off to the profit and loss account.

Case 2

In previous years to date the company has spent a total of £2,000,000 on developing a new type of tranquilliser, and has carried this expenditure forward in the books. In the current year the project is completed at a cost of £400,000, and the drug is launched on the market, with sales of £1,500,000 in the second half of the year. It is expected that the new drug will lead the market for two years (from launching) before a successful competing product appears, with total sales in that time estimated at £10,000,000. The tranquilliser drug will remain marketable for another two years after that, with estimated further sales of £5,000,000 before it is withdrawn. The profits on the new drug are forecast at £8,000,000 in the first two years (£1,000,000 of this arising in the second half of the current

SSAP 13 AND ED 41: ACCOUNTING FOR RESEARCH AND DEVELOPMENT

year), and at £2,000,000 in the following two years – exclusive, in all cases, of development costs.

It appears that the conditions stated in SSAP 13 for capitalisation of development expenditure are satisfied in this particular instance. There is a clearly defined project – development of a new tranquilliser. The expenditure relating to the project can be separately identified and will amount to £2,400,000 by the end of the current year. The project has been successful and commercial production has been successful. The estimated profits of £8 million in two years, and £10 million in four years means that the project will be commercially viable and all development costs on the project will be recovered in the ordinary course of business. The project is now complete and no additional capital will therefore be needed for it. The capitalised development costs will be amortised from the second half of the year (when the drug is launched in the market) on any one of the following basis:

1. by reference to sales; or
2. the period over which the product is expected to be sold or used.

Amortisation on the basis of sales

6.24 The capitalised development expenditure of £2,400,000 may be written off on either of the following bases:

(a) on the basis of sales while the product is leading the market:

Sales in the second half of the year =	£1,500,000
Total estimated sales while the product is leading the market =	£10,000,000
Therefore amortisation in current year =	$\frac{£1,500,000}{£10,000,000} \times £2,400,000$
=	£360,000

(b) on the basis of sales while the product is on the market:

Total estimates sales while the product is on the market year =	£15,000,000
Therefore amortisation in current year =	$\frac{£1,500,000}{£15,000,000} \times £2,400,000$
=	£240,000

Amortisation on the basis of time

6.25 It may be written off either over two years (i.e. while the product is leading the market) or over four years (while the product is in the market).

Therefore over two years $-\dfrac{0.5}{2} \times £2,400,000 = £600,000$

or over four years $\quad -\dfrac{0.5}{4} \times £2,400,000 = £300,000$

The accountant will have to adopt a basis which is both appropriate and prudent.

Case 3
In previous years, the company has spent, and carried forward in its books, a total of £10,000,000 on developing a cure for influenza. During the current year it is decided to terminate this project, as test results in the current year have proved adverse.

The £10,000,000 previously capitalised in respect of the influenza case must now be written off as the project has not been successful. SSAP 6 (revised) specifically requires this expenditure to be included as part of profit on ordinary activities before taxation and disclosed as an exceptional item if material.

ED 41: Accounting for Research and Development

6.26 ED 41 in its preface states that 'The proposed revision does not make any changes to the rules regarding the treatment of research and development expenditure, that is, the circumstances in which the expenditure should be written off as incurred or may be deferred to future periods'. Therefore, the companies will continue to account for research and development as required by SSAP 13. The changes proposed are summarised as follows:

1. Companies are required to disclose the research and development costs charged to the profit and loss account in the current year, including the amount of any development costs amortised. The ASC believes that this will provide useful information to users of accounts.

2. The CA 1985 provides that development costs may be capitalised only in special circumstances. The Act does not define the special circumstances. The ASC sought the views of the Department of Trade and Industry (DTI) and the DTI have confirmed that the conditions set out in SSAP 13 (and now ED 41) satisfy the term 'special circumstances'.

3. SSAP 13 does not give any guidance on the type of activities that could be included in research and development. ED 41 gives examples of activities that could be included in research and development. These are:

SSAP 13 AND ED 41: ACCOUNTING FOR RESEARCH AND DEVELOPMENT

(a) experimental or theoretical work aimed at discovery of new knowledge;
(b) searching for applications of such work of other knowledge;
(c) formulation and design of possible applications of such work;
(d) testing in search for, or evaluation of, product or process alternatives;
(e) design, construction and testing of pre-production prototypes and models;
(f) design of product, processes, systems or services involving new technology or substantially improving those already produced or installed.

ED 41 specifically excludes the following from research and development:

(a) routine design, testing and analysis either of equipment or product for purposes of quality or quantity control;
(b) routine or periodic alterations to existing products or processes even though these may represent improvement;
(c) operational research;
(d) trouble-shooting in connection with break-downs during commercial production;
(e) legal and administrative work in connection with patent applications, records and litigation and the sale of licensing of patents;
(f) activity, including design and construction engineering, relating to the construction, relocation, rearrangement or start-up of facilities or equipment other than facilities or equipment whose sole use is for a particular research and development project.

4. The requirement in SSAP 13 to review annually the deferred development expenditure is retained in ED 41. In addition, ED 41 requires that this expenditure should be examined project by project.

5. The CA requirement to disclose capitalised deferred development expenditure as part of intangible fixed assets is incorporated in ED 41.

6.27   Comments

1. The exposure draft is silent on the CA provision that deferred development expenditure shall be treated as a realised loss for the purpose of determining profits available for distribution. The Act states that such treatment need *not* be followed if the directors can give special reasons to support their view. It is not known whether mere compliance with SSAP 13 (ED 41) is sufficient for this purpose and ED 41 offers no interpretation.

2. The proposed standard gives no guidance on the classification of the R & D charges in the profit and loss account within the CA 1985 formats. The most likely options are:
(a) Formats 1 and 3 – R & D as a separate item either with cost of sales, or below administration and distribution costs;
(b) Formats 2 and 4 – The R & D costs will be included within the relevant headings in the accounts and the total R & D cost disclosed in a note to the accounts.

The accounting policies must explain the treatment of R & D costs. ED 41 ensures compliance with the international standard IAS 9.

3. Any opposition to this change (i.e. disclosure of R & D costs) from companies heavily dependent on ongoing research (such as the major pharmaceutical companies) will be on the grounds that such disclosures could be harmful to the company's interests. This could arise in a number of ways, of which the following four are perhaps the most obvious:
(a) competitors of comparable size would be in a position to determine without great difficulty the size of the company's research budget, and even the proportion of total R & D costs regarded as abortive – particularly if research cost write offs are distinguished from annual amortisations of deferred development expenditure;
(b) financial analysts could make similar assessments of the company's performance in relation to its R & D commitment, and may draw unjustifiable and harmful conclusions concerning the future returns from current R & D outlays;
(c) political pressures could all too easily result from a comparison between a company's record of products which are either 'suspect' or known to have harmful side effects, and its R & D expenditure record;
(d) legal consequences of counsel for plaintiff in a 'harmful effects' case being able to cite with apparent authority a series of unfavourable comparisons with the R & D commitment of rival companies. This is particularly relevant following the Consumer Protection Act 1987 which has introduced product liability to the UK statute book, and provides only a 'state of the art' defence to charges of selling, manufacturing, supplying or importing products which prove ultimately to be defective or otherwise harmful.

In general terms, many will feel that this type of disclosure, if insisted upon, could easily prove to be the forerunner of further mandatory disclosures of a quasi-statutory nature which, either singly or collectively, could be severely detrimental to a company's *bona fide* interests. These, it will be held, should not be sacrificed or subjected to risk in order to provide readers of accounts with information of relatively little intrinsic worth.

SSAP 13 AND ED 41: ACCOUNTING FOR RESEARCH AND DEVELOPMENT

Question

(a) Discuss the criteria which SSAP 13 'Accounting for Research and Development' states should be used when considering whether research and development expenditure should be written off in an accounting period or carried forward.
(b) Discuss to what extent these criteria are consistent with fundamental concepts as defined in SSAP 2 'Disclosure of Accounting Policies'.
(c) Discuss the changes proposed in ED 41: Accounting for Research and Development.

Chapter Seven

SSAP 8: The Treatment of Taxation under the Imputation System in the accounts of companies

Corporation Tax

7.1   Corporation Tax is charged at a single rate on a company's income whether distributed or undistributed.

Corporation tax for the year = rate of corporation tax × taxable income. The entry for the corporation tax in the accounts will be:

DR Profit and Loss Account
CR Corporation Tax Account
with the amount of corporation tax payable.

There are specific dates on which this corporation tax will become payable. The due dates for corporation tax depend on the date on which the company was formed.

Companies formed prior to April 1965

7.2   Due date for corporation tax will be **1 January following April following the year end.**
EXAMPLE
A company formed prior to April 1965 has a year end 31 August.
For the year ended 31 August 1987:

Corporation tax on profits of the year ended 31 August 1987 will be payable on 1 January 1989.

The company will therefore have 16 months before having to pay its corporation tax on profits for year ended 31 August 1987. On the balance sheet this liability will be disclosed under the heading of Creditors (amounts falling due after more than one year).

The corporation tax on the profits for year ended 31 August 1986 will be due on 1 January 1988. Therefore, this liability will be still outstanding at 31 August 1987 and will be disclosed in the balance sheet under the heading of Creditors (amounts falling due within one year).

SSAP 8: THE TREATMENT OF TAXATION UNDER THE INPUTATION SYSTEM

Companies formed after April 1965

7.3 Due date for corporation tax will be **9 months from the balance sheet date.**

EXAMPLE

A company formed in 1976 has a year end 31 December.
For the year ended 31 December 1987:

Corporation tax on profits of the year ended 31 December 1987 will be payable on 1 October 1988. Since the company will always have less than 12 months from its balance sheet date to settle its corporation tax liability, it will be disclosed in the balance sheet under the heading of Creditors (amounts falling due within one year).

Dividends

7.4 SSAP 8 requires that dividends should be shown in the profit and loss account at the amount paid or payable to the shareholders and the related ACT (see below) should not be treated as part of the cost of the dividend.

Franked Investment Income

7.5 SSAP 8 requires that 'incoming dividends from United Kingdom resident companies should be included at the amount of cash received or receivable plus the tax credit.'

EXAMPLE

A Limited received a dividend of £7,500 from X plc (in respect of shares it holds in X plc) during the year ended 31 December 1987. Basic rate of income tax = 25%.

A Limited Books
Grossing up the dividend of £7,500 at rate of 25% = £7,500 $\times \frac{100}{75}$

$$= \underline{\underline{£10,000}}$$

Entry	£	£
DR Tax credit on franked investment income	2,500	
CR Dividend Income		2,500

A Limited's profit on ordinary activities before taxation will include dividend income of £10,000 and the tax credit of £2,500 will be written off to the profit and loss account as part of the tax charge.

UNDERSTANDING ACCOUNTING STANDARDS

Advance corporation tax (ACT)

7.6 When in an accounting period a company pays dividends to its shareholders, the company is required to make an advance payment of corporation tax (ACT). This ACT will normally be set off against the company's total liability for corporation tax on its income (but not on its chargeable gains) of the same accounting period.

EXAMPLE
A Limited
Year ended 31 December 1987.
Corporation tax on the profits for the year ended 31 December 1987 =
£100,000
Dividends paid in the year = £ 7,500
Basic rate of income tax = 25%
*Amount of ACT to be paid by the company = £7,500 × $\frac{25}{75}$ = £2,500

Total corporation tax liability	£100,000
To be paid in advance (ACT)	£2,500
To be paid on due date – mainstream corporation tax	£97,500
	£100,000

*The shareholder will be deemed to have suffered a tax $\frac{25}{75}$ on dividends at source.

Due dates for ACT payment

7.7 The return to be filed for ACT payments is called CT 61. A financial year is split up into four ACT quarters where the year end coincides with one of the quarter end dates. Any ACT payable on dividends paid within a particular quarter must be accounted for within 14 days from the quarter end date.

EXAMPLE
A Limited
Year end 31 December
There will be four ACT quarters as follows:

— 1 January to 31 March
— 1 April to 30 June
— 1 July to 30 September
— 1 October to 31 December

ACT on any dividends paid in say, the quarter ending 30 June will have to be paid by 14 July.

SSAP 8: THE TREATMENT OF TAXATION UNDER THE INPUTATION SYSTEM

Where the year end does not coincide with one of the quarter end dates, the year end date will become an additional date for a CT 61 return.

EXAMPLE
A Limited
Year end 31 August
Five periods for which the returns may be required.
— 1 January to 31 March
— 1 April to 30 June
— 1 July to 31 August   } the third quarter is split
— 1 September to 30 September } and the year end date becomes an additional date for a CT 61
— 1 October to 31 December

The CT61 return is required only for the periods in which dividends are paid.

Rules regarding ACT set off against corporation tax

Rule 1

7.8   Any ACT set off against a particular year's corporation tax must be ACT on dividends paid in that particular year.

EXAMPLE
A Limited was formed after April 1965.
For the year ended 31 December 1987:

Corporation Tax on 1987 profits   £100,000
Dividends: Interim paid on 30 June 1987 £3,750
Final proposed   £7,500

There were no dividends paid or proposed in 1986.
Basic rate of Income Tax = 25%.

1. Dividends paid and proposed
These will be shown in the profit and loss account at the amount paid or payable, i.e. £11,250.

2. Corporation Tax on 1987 profits

	£	£
DR Profit and Loss Account	100,000	
CR Corporation Tax Account		100,000

3. ACT on Interim Dividend paid
A Limited will have to pay ACT of £3,750 $\times \frac{25}{75}$ = £1,250 to the Inland

Revenue by 14 July 1987. This ACT will be treated as an advance against 1987 Corporation Tax as it is ACT on dividends paid in 1987.

	£	£
DR Corporation Tax	1,250	
CR Cash		1,250

ACT on 1987 Interim dividend to be treated as an advance against 1987 Corporation Tax.

4. 1987 Mainstream Corporation Tax

	£
Corporation Tax on 1987 profits	100,000
Less Advance Corporation Tax	(1,250)
1987 Mainstream Corporation Tax	£98,750

Since A Limited was formed after April 1965, 1987 Corporation Tax will be payable on 1 October 1988 and therefore will be separately disclosed in the balance sheet under the heading of Creditors (amounts falling due within one year).

5. Proposed Dividend on 31 December 1987

This dividend will most probably be paid sometime in 1988. ACT on this dividend of $\frac{25}{75} \times £7,500 = £2,500$ will have to be paid to the Inland Revenue within 14 days from the quarter end of the ACT quarter in 1988 in which the dividend is paid. This ACT needs to be provided as at 31 December 1987 as follows:

	£	£
DR ACT Recoverable	2,500	
CR ACT Payable		2,500

7.9   The recoverable amount can be set off against 1988 corporation tax only, as the dividends to which it relates will not be paid until 1988. At 31 December 1987, the ACT recoverable on proposed dividend will be shown as a deduction from the deferred tax balance (see Chapter 8). If there is no deferred tax balance, it will be separately disclosed in the balance sheet under the heading 'Current Assets – ACT recoverable after more than twelve months'. As stated earlier, this ACT recoverable can be set off only against 1988 corporation tax which will not be due until 1 October 1989 (i.e. 21 months from the Balance sheet date of 31 December 1987).

The payable amount will be due sometime in 1988 and therefore, will be disclosed in the Balance Sheet under the heading of 'Creditors (Amounts falling due within one year)'.

SSAP 8: THE TREATMENT OF TAXATION UNDER THE INPUTATION SYSTEM

Summary
A Limited
Profit and Loss Account for the year ended 31 December 1987

	£
Taxation	
UK Corporation Tax at %	100,000
Dividends: paid and proposed	10,250

Balance Sheet as at 31 December 1987

Creditors (Amounts falling due within one year):	
Proposed Dividends	7,500
ACT Payable	2,500
Mainstream Corporation Tax	98,750
Provision for Liabilities and Charges	
Deferred tax on timing differences	x
*Less ACT Recoverable on proposed dividend	(2,500)
	x

*If there is no deferred tax balance, it would be separately disclosed under the heading of Current Assets. There is a restriction on the amount of ACT which can be offset against deferred tax and this is discussed on the pages which follow.

Rule 2
7.10 There is a limit on the amount of ACT which can be set off against a particular year's Corporation Tax. The maximum amount of ACT which can be set off against a particular year's Corporation Tax is restricted to:

Basic rate of income tax × taxable income

EXAMPLE
A Limited
Year ended 31 December 1987

Taxable income	£ 500,000	
Dividends paid in the year	£ 450,000	
Rate of corporation tax	35%	
Basic rate of income tax	25%	
Dividends paid	£ 450,000	
Therefore ACT paid ($^{25}/_{75}$)	£ 150,000	
Corporation tax on 1987 profits		£ 175,000
ACT set off	£ 150,000	
Restricted to 25% × £500,000	(125,000)	(125,000)
Mainstream corporation tax for 1987		£50,000
ACT unrelieved in 1987	£25,000	

UNDERSTANDING ACCOUNTING STANDARDS

Treatment of unrelieved ACT

7.11 The unrelieved ACT on dividends paid in 1987 can be relieved either against the Corporation Tax of earlier years (with the maximum set off being restricted to basic rate of tax × taxable income of each such year) or against future corporation tax with no time limit. If the relief can be claimed against the previous year's corporation tax, ACT recoverable of £25,000 (which was unrelieved against 1987 corporation tax) will be carried forward as a debtor and separately disclosed under the heading of current assets. If the taxable income of the preceding year or years is insufficient to cover £25,000 (because of restriction on set off), then ACT of £25,000 should be carried forward *provided* enough income will be earned in the foreseeable future on which there will be corporation tax payable to cover this £25,000 and any ACT on dividends which may be paid in future. SSAP 8 does not specify the time period but states 'how long this future period should be will depend on the circumstances of each case, but it is suggested that where there is no deferred taxation account it should not extend beyond the next accounting period'.

7.12 Deferred tax is tax on timing differences (see Chapter 8). Corporation Tax on these timing differences will crystallise when the timing differences reverse in the future and an amount equal to the Corporation Tax payable on these timing differences will be released from deferred tax account to the profit and loss account. Since the existence of deferred tax means that Corporation Tax will be payable in the future, some or the whole of unrelieved ACT of £25,000 may be carried forward and shown as a deduction from the deferred tax balance. There is a restriction on the amount which may be shown as a deduction from deferred tax balance – the maximum amount which can be shown as a deduction from deferred taxation balance (excluding any deferred tax on chargeable gains) is restricted to the basic rate of tax × timing differences (excluding any capital gains) on which deferred tax has been provided. The unrelieved ACT in 1987 was £25,000. Grossing up this amount at the basic rate of income tax of 25% equals £100,000. Therefore, if deferred tax has been provided on a timing difference of more than £100,000 then the whole of unrelieved ACT of £25,000 can be carried forward and shown as a deduction from deferred tax balance. If, however, deferred tax has been provided on a timing difference of less than £100,000, say £80,000, then the amount of unrelieved ACT which may be carried forward and shown as a deduction from deferred tax balance is restricted to 25% × £80,000 = £20,000. Whether the balance of £5,000 can be carried forward as a current asset will depend on the company making sufficient profits and paying Corporation Tax on it in the next period to cover it with ACT on any other dividends in that period.

SSAP 8: THE TREATMENT OF TAXATION UNDER THE INPUTATION SYSTEM

7.13 This restriction on ACT set off against deferred tax also applies to ACT Recoverable on proposed dividends. The treatment of ACT on proposed dividend has been discussed earlier.

Irrecoverable ACT

7.14 Any irrecoverable ACT (i.e. ACT the recoverability of which is not reasonably certain and foreseeable) should be written off in the profit and loss account in which the related dividend is shown. In the above example, £25,000 will be written off to the profit and loss account if the company's budgets do not show sufficient profits and corporation tax in the future to cover it. SSAP 8 requires that amounts written off should be included as part of taxation on profits on ordinary activities and separately disclosed if material.

Rule 3

ACT on dividends and tax credit on franked investment income

7.15 A company which has received franked investment income (dividends) from a UK resident company can reduce the amount of ACT it has to pay on the dividends by the amount of tax credit on the franked investment income received. This is best illustrated by an example:

EXAMPLE
A Limited
Year end 31 December 1987
A Limited paid an interim dividend of £7,500 on 30 June 1987 and is proposing a final dividend of £30,000.
A Limited also received a dividend of £11,250 30 June 1987 from X plc, a UK company. There were no dividends paid or proposed in 1986.
Basic rate of income tax 25%
ACT Quarter Ending 30 June 1987
Dividend paid on 30 June 1987 £7,500
ACT on dividend of £7,500 = £7,500 × $\frac{25}{75}$ = £2,500

A Limited has also received a dividend of £11,250 on 30 June 1987 from a UK company and on which there is a tax credit of £3,750. Since this tax credit of £3,750 exceeds ACT payable of £2,500, no ACT will be paid in the quarter ending 30 June 1987. At 30 June 1987, there is a surplus tax credit of £3,750 − £2,500 = £1,250. There are two possibilities:

1. A Limited can ask for a refund but the refund is restricted to lower of:
(a) surplus tax credit = £1,250; and
(b) ACT paid in previous quarters within the same financial year
— which in this case is zero.

UNDERSTANDING ACCOUNTING STANDARDS

Therefore, no refund is due in this case. However, if there was a refund due and A Limited asked for it, the entry in A Limited's books would be:

DR ACT Recoverable
CR ACT Paid (or Corporation Tax)

i.e. the ACT already paid would be reduced by the recoverable amount. When the cash is received:

DR Cash
CR ACT Recoverable

Note: The above makes no difference to the way in which franked investment income is treated in the accounts.

Dividends received = £11,250

Grossing up at 25% = £11,250 $\times \frac{100}{75}$ = £15,000

Entries

		£	£
1.	DR Cash	11,250	
	CR Dividends Received		11,250
	Dividends received from X plc		
2.	DR Tax Credit on franked investment income	3,750	
	CR Dividends received		3,750
	Tax Credit on franked investment income		

Profit on ordinary activities before taxation will include dividends received of £15,000 and tax credit of £3,750 will be included as part of the tax charge.

2. Carry forward surplus tax credit and reduce any future ACT payable. The surplus tax credit at 30 June 1987 will reduce any future ACT payable.

At 31 December 1987, there is a proposed dividend of £30,000.

ACT on proposed dividend = £30,000 $\times \frac{25}{75}$ = £10,000

There is no need to provide this full amount of £10,000 as there is a surplus tax credit brought forward of £1,250.

Therefore, the amount of ACT which needs to be provided at 31 December 1987 = £10,000 − £1,250 = £8,750. The entry will be:

	£	£
DR ACT Recoverable	8,750	
CR ACT Payable		8,750
ACT on proposed dividend.		

SSAP 8 – Standard accounting practice

Profit and loss account

7.16 The following items should be included in the taxation charge in the profit and loss account and, where material, separately disclosed:

(a) the amount of the United Kingdom corporation tax specifying:
  (i) the charge for corporation tax on the income of the year (where such corporation tax includes transfers between the deferred taxation account and the profit and loss account these also should be separately disclosed where material);
  (ii) tax attributable to franked investment income;
  (iii) irrecoverable ACT;
  (iv) the relief for overseas taxation;
(b) the total overseas taxation, relieved and unrelieved, specifying that part of the unrelieved overseas taxation which arises from the payment or proposed payment of dividends.

If the rate of corporation tax is not known for the whole or part of the period covered by the accounts, the latest known rate should be used and disclosed.

Outgoing dividends should not include either the related ACT or the attributable tax credit.

Incoming dividends from United Kingdom resident companies should be included at the amount of cash received or receivable plus the tax credit.

Balance sheet

7.17 Dividends proposed (or declared and not yet payable) should be included in current liabilities, without the addition of the related ACT. The ACT on proposed dividends (whether recoverable or irrecoverable) should be included as a current tax liability.

If the ACT on proposed dividends is regarded as recoverable, it should be deducted from the deferred tax account if such an account is available for this purpose. In the absence of a deferred taxation account ACT recoverable should be shown as a current asset.

Unfranked income and payments

7.18 Dividends received by a company from a UK resident company are franked investment income. Similarly, dividends paid by a UK resident company are franked payments. These dividends are out of the

UNDERSTANDING ACCOUNTING STANDARDS

taxed income of the company. The company receiving them does not have to include them as part of taxable income and pay Corporation Tax on them. The company paying the dividends is not entitled to tax relief on them. There are certain types of income which a company may receive where income tax at basic rate has been deducted at source. The company is entitled to reclaim the income tax from the Inland Revenue and will pay Corporation Tax on the amount of income received and the related income tax which was deducted at source. This type of income which is received under deduction of income tax is called unfranked income. The company which pays this amount under deduction of income tax will have to pay over the income tax deducted to the Inland Revenue and it will be entitled to a Corporation Tax relief on the amount paid and related income tax deducted. These payments are called unfranked payments.

7.19   Examples of unfranked income are interest or royalties which are received after deduction of income tax at basic rate of tax. Similarly, unfranked payments are interest or royalties which are paid after deduction of income tax at basic rate of tax. Where a company has received income after deduction of income tax at basic rate, it will be able to reclaim this income tax from the Inland Revenue. The Corporation Tax will be payable on the gross amount (i.e. cash received and income tax). Similarly, where a company pays items like interest and royalties after deducting income tax, it will have to pay over the income tax deducted to the Inland Revenue and the company will be entitled to corporation tax relief on the gross amount. The due dates for payment of or reclaiming income tax are exactly the same as the due dates for ACT.

EXAMPLE
A Limited
Year End 31 December 1987

A Limited has in issue 10% Debentures £100,000 and the interest is paid on 31/3 and 30/9. The interest paid is under deduction of income tax. A Limited also received royalties (net of income tax) of £2025 on 31/3 and 30/9.
Basic rate of income tax 25%.

Quarter ending 31/3/87
Interest for the period 1/10/86 to 31/3/87 = 10% × £100,000 × $\frac{6}{12}$ = £5000.

Income Tax to be deducted at source = 25% × £5000 = £1250
Due to the Debenture holder = £3750
Royalties received on 31/3/87 = £2025
Income Tax deducted at source = $\frac{25}{75}$ × £2025 = £675

SSAP 8: THE TREATMENT OF TAXATION UNDER THE INPUTATION SYSTEM

Therefore Income Tax payable to Inland Revenue by 14 April 1987 = Income Tax deducted at source on interest paid less Income Tax suffered at source on royalties received = £1250 − £675 = £575.

Quarter ending 30/9/97
Similarly, £575 will be payable to the Inland Revenue by 14/10/87.

Ledger Accounts in the books of A Limited

Debenture Interest Account

	£		£
		1/1/1987 Balance B/Fwd	2,500
31/3/1987 Cash	3,750		
31/3/1987 Income Tax	1,250	31/12/1987 P & L A/C (10%	10,000
30/9/1987 Cash	3,750	× £100,000)	
30/9/1987 Income Tax	1,250		
31/12/1987 Balance C/F	2,500		
	12,500		12,500

Royalties receivable

	£		£
		31/3/1987 Cash	2,025
		31/3/1987 Income Tax	675
		30/9/1987 Cash	2,025
31/12/1987 P & L A/C	5,400	30/9/1987 Income Tax	675
	5,400		5,400

Income Tax Account (Inland Revenue)

	£		£
31/3/1987 Royalties	675	31/3/1987 Interest	1,250
14/4/1987 Cash	575		
30/9/1987 Royalties	675	30/9/1987 Interest	1,250
14/10/1987 Cash	575		
	2,500		2,500

Taxation in Accounts: A Detailed Example

7.20   As the accountant of FACT plc, you are responsible for the preparation of its accounts for publication. You have been presented with

UNDERSTANDING ACCOUNTING STANDARDS

an agreed trial balance at the year ended 30 September 19X6 including the following accounts which, whilst balanced, are incomplete due to the omission of the entries reflecting taxation.

Dividends Received

	£		£
19X6 30 Sept Balance C/Fwd	375	19X6 4 March Bank	375
		19X6 30 Sept B/Fwd	375

Royalties Receivable

	£		£
19X6 30 Sept Balance C/FWD	975	19X6 31 March Bank	450
		19X6 31 August Bank	525
	975		975
		19X6 30 Sept Balance B/Fwd	975

Taxation Account

		£			£
19X5	1 Oct Balance B/Fwd	3058	19X5	1 Oct Balance B/Fwd	35547
19X5	31 Dec Bank	3058			
19X6	1 Jan Bank	15489			
19X6	31 March Bank	600			
19X6	30 Sept Bank	575			
19X6	30 Sept Balance C/Fwd	12767			
		35547			35547
			19X6	30 Sept Balance B/Fwd	12767

Debenture Interest Payable

		£			£
19X6	31 Jan Bank	2250	19X5	1 Oct Balance B/Fwd	1000
19X6	31 July Bank	2250	19X6	30 Sept Balance C/Fwd	3500
		4500			4500
19X6	30 Sept Balance B/Fwd	3500			

SSAP 8: THE TREATMENT OF TAXATION UNDER THE INPUTATION SYSTEM

The following information is relevant

1. <u>Dividends received</u>. These arise from a 5% equity shareholding in a UK registered company quoted on the London Stock Exchange. The associated tax credit amounts to £125.
2. <u>Royalties receivable</u>. These were received under deduction of tax.
3. <u>Debenture interest payable</u>. The payments made are the half yearly instalments in respect of £80,000 7½% Mortgage Debentures, made on the due dates under deduction of income tax.
4. <u>Taxation Account</u>. Only payments to the Inland Revenue have been dealt with. The opening debit balance represents Advance Corporation Tax recoverable. The opening credit balance comprises the agreed Corporation Tax liability of £15,489, based on the accounting year ended 30 September 19X4; £17,000 the estimated liability for Corporation Tax based on the accounting year ended 30 September 19X5, and Advance Corporation Tax liability of £3,058.
5. The basic rate of Income Tax is to be taken as 25 per cent.
6. You need to deal with a proposal to provide for a dividend of £7,500 for 19X6. The 19X5 dividend was paid on 20 December 19X5, and associated ACT of £3,058 on 31 December 19X5.
7. The Corporation Tax liability based on the accounting year ended 30 September 19X6 is estimated to be £18,000, while the Corporation Tax liability for 30 September 19X5 had been agreed at £15,844.

You are required, using the information available:
(a) to continue and to complete the accounts by making the necessary entries; and
(b) to show by way of extracts therefrom how the resultant figures would be revealed in the published profit and loss account and balance sheet.

A detailed example: Solution

(a) *Completed accounts*

Dividends received

	£		£
		30/9/X6 Balance B/Fwd	375
30/9/X6 P & L A/C Dividends Received	500	30/9/X6 P & L A/C Tax Credit	125
	500		500

Dividend received of £375 is grossed up by the tax credit of £125. Gross dividend of £500 will be included in the profit on ordinary activities before

139

UNDERSTANDING ACCOUNTING STANDARDS

taxation. Tax credit of £125 will be written off as part of tax on profits on ordinary activities.

Royalties receivable

	£		£
		30/9/X6 Balance B/Fwd	975
		30/9/X6 Income Tax A/C	150
30/9/X6 P & L A/C	1300	30/9/X6 Income Tax A/C	175
	1300		1300

£450 of royalties received on 31/3/X6 is net of Income Tax deducted at source of $\frac{25}{75} \times £450 = £150$. The entry for the Income Tax is

	£	£
DR Income Tax Account	150	
CR Royalties Account		150

Inland Revenue becomes a debtor of £150.

Similarly, Income Tax deducted at source on royalties received on 31/8/X6 is $\frac{25}{75} \times £525 = £175$. This amount will be debited to the Income Tax Account and credited to the Royalties Account. The total amount of royalties which will be credited to the Profit and Loss Account equals £1300 and this amount will be included as part of the profit on ordinary activities before taxation.

Debenture Interest Payable

	£		£
30/9/X6 Balance B/Fwd	3500		
30/9/X6 Income Tax A/C	750		
30/9/X6 Income Tax A/C	750	30/9/X6 P & L A/C	6000
30/9/X6 Accrual C/Fwd	1000		
	6000		6000

The balance brought forward on 1/10/X5 is an accrual for two months ending 30/9/X5 ($\frac{2}{12} \times £6000 = £1000$). There are two interest payments under deduction of Income Tax during the year. The Income Tax deducted on each payment is $\frac{25}{75} \times £2250 = £750$. These amounts are owed to the Inland

SSAP 8: THE TREATMENT OF TAXATION UNDER THE INPUTATION SYSTEM

Revenue and the entry for each deduction of tax will be:

	£	£
DR Debenture Interest Account	750	
CR Income Tax Account (Inland Revenue)		750

The interest to be charged in the Profit and Loss Account equals 7½% × £80,000 = £6,000. The balance carried forward of £1000 at 30/9/X6 represents an accrual for the months of August and September 19X6.

Income Tax Account

	£		£
30/9/X6 Royalties	150	30/9/X6 Debenture Interest	750
30/9/X6 Taxation A/C	600		
30/9/X6 Royalties	175	30/9/X6 Debenture Interest	750
30/9/X6 Taxation A/C	575		
	1500		1500

In the quarter ending 31/3/X6, Income Tax deducted on interest paid was £750 and Income Tax deducted on royalties received was £150. The amount due to the Inland Revenue by 31/3/X6 was £750 − £150 = £600. This was paid on 31/3/X6 and debited to the Taxation Account. It is now transferred out of Taxation Account into Income Tax Account. Similarly, Income Tax paid of £575 (£750 − £175) on 30/9/X6 is transferred out of Taxation Account.

Taxation Account

	£		£
		30/9/X6 Balance B/F	12767
		30/9/X6 Income Tax A/C	600
		30/9/X6 Income Tax A/C	575
30/9/X6 P & L A/C − overprovision in 19X5	1156	30/9/X6 P & L A/C − Corporation Tax for the year ended 30/9/X6	18000
30/9/X6 ACT Recoverable on proposed dividend	2375	30/9/X6 ACT Payable on proposed dividend	2375
30/9/X6 *BALANCES C/FWD* Corporation Tax −		30/9/X6 *BALANCES C/FWD*	
year ended 30/9/X5	15844		
year ended 30/9/X6	18000	ACT Recoverable against	
ACT Payable on proposed dividend	2375	19X6 Corporation Tax	3058
		ACT Recoverable on proposed dividend to be offset against 19X7 Corporation Tax	2375
	39750		39750

141

UNDERSTANDING ACCOUNTING STANDARDS

The credit balance of £35,547 brought forward on 1/10/X5 is made up of the following:

	£
Corporation Tax year ended 30/9/X4	15,489
Corporation Tax year ended 30/9/X5	17,000
ACT payable on 19X5 proposed dividend	3,058
	35,547

7.21 FACT plc is evidently a pre-April 1965 company because at 1/10/X5 there are two years' Corporation Tax outstanding. The Corporation Tax of £15,489 on the profits of year ended 30/9/X4 is due on 1/1/X6 and the payment is reflected in the Taxation Account. The Corporation Tax on the profits of year ended is not due until 1/1/X7 and therefore, it will still be outstanding at 30/9/X6. £17,000 provided in 19X5 accounts was an estimate and the agreed figure with the Inland Revenue is now £15,844. The overprovision of £1,156 will now be written back to the Profit and Loss Account and included as part of tax on profit on ordinary activities. The 19X5 proposed dividend was paid on 20 December 19X5. The ACT on this was paid over on 31 December 19X5 and is already recorded in the Taxation Account.

7.22 The debit balance of £3058 brought forward on 1/10/X5 is ACT Recoverable on proposed dividend for the year ended 30/9/X5. Since this proposed dividend is paid in the year ended 30/9/X6, this ACT Recoverable can only be offset against Corporation Tax on profits of the year ended 30/9/X6. The Corporation Tax on profits of year ended 30/9/X6 is not due until 1/1/X8. Therefore, ACT Recoverable of £3058 will still be outstanding at 30/9/X6.

The Corporation Tax on profits for the year ended 30/9/X6 is £18,000. This provided in the accounts by making the following entry:

	£	£
DR Profit and Loss Account	18,000	
CR Corporation Tax Account		18,000

Since this Corporation Tax is not payable until 1/1/X8, it will be carried forward at 30/9/X6.

7.23 A dividend of £7500 is proposed at 30/9/X6. ACT will need to be provided on this proposed dividend. If no dividends had been received during the year, the amount of ACT would have been $\frac{25}{75} \times £7500 = £2500$. Since a dividend was received the tax credit of £125 available will reduce the amount of ACT Payable to £2375 (= £2500 − £125). The entry for ACT on proposed dividends is:

SSAP 8: THE TREATMENT OF TAXATION UNDER THE INPUTATION SYSTEM

	£	£
DR ACT Recoverable	2375	
CR ACT Payable		2375

7.24 The recoverable amount can only be offset against Corporation Tax on profits of year ended 30/9/X7 (which will not be due until 1/1/X9) or beyond and the payable amount will be settled in the year ended 30/9/X7.

(b) Extracts from the published accounts

Fact PLC
Profit and Loss Account for the year ended 30 September 19X6

	£	£
Turnover		x
Income from quoted investments		500
*Royalties received		1,300
Profit on ordinary activities before taxation		x
Taxation		
UK Corporation Tax @ %	18000	
Overprovision in 19X5	(1156)	
Tax credit on franked investment income	125	
Other taxes charged in the P & L A/C	x	
		(x)
Profit on ordinary activities after taxation		x
Dividends – proposed		(7500)
Retained profit for the year		x

*Disclose if material

Balance Sheet as at 30 September 19X6

	£
Creditors (Amounts falling due within one year)	
Proposed Dividend	7500
ACT Payable	2375
Mainstream Corporation Tax for year ended 30/9/X5	15844
	x

	£
Creditors (Amounts falling due after more than one year)	
Mainstream Corporation Tax for year ended 30/9/X6	14942
Provision for liabilities and charges	
Deferred tax on timing differences	x
Less ACT Recoverable on proposed dividend	(2375)
	x

Chapter Eight
SSAP 15: Accounting for deferred taxation

8.1 In any accounting period, profits stated in accounts may not necessarily equal the profits used for computing the liability to tax. There are two main reasons for the difference between accounting profits and taxable income:

1. Items which cause a 'permanent difference' between the two profits. An example of an item causing a permanent difference is disallowable expenditure for tax purposes like entertaining, which would be written off as an expense in the accounts.
2. Items which cause a timing difference between the two profits. Timing differences arise because certain items which are included in the financial statements for a period may be dealt with for tax purposes in a different period. Timing differences originate in one period and are capable of a reversal in one or more subsequent periods. Examples of items which cause timing differences are:
   (a) Short-term timing differences: These may arise from the use of the receipts and payments for tax purposes and the accruals basis in financial statements. Examples of short-term timing differences:
      (i) Interest – in the accounts, interest would be recognised on an accruals basis but in tax computation, it would be recognised on an actual basis.
      (ii) Provision for general bad debts provided in the accounts would not be allowable for tax purposes until it becomes 'specific'.
      (iii) Any provision for pension costs in accounts would not be allowable for tax purposes until paid.
   (b) Accelerated or deferred capital allowances. These timing differences arise when the capital allowances claimed in tax computations either exceed or are less than the related depreciation charged in the accounts for a particular period.
   (c) Revaluation surpluses on fixed assets, when they are incorporated in the balance sheet. The surpluses are recognised in the accounts but will be included in the tax computation only when the asset is realised and no rollover relief is claimed.
   (d) Profit on disposal of fixed assets which are subject to rollover relief. Profit will be recognised in the accounts at the point of disposal but

will be included in the tax computation only when no further rollover relief is available.
(e) Losses available for offset against future profits.

8.2 Timing differences originate in one period and are capable of reversal in one or more subsequent periods.

EXAMPLE 1:

A PLC acquires a fixed asset at cost of £500. The estimated useful life is 5 years. Depreciation is charged on a straight line basis and the asset has no residual value.

The asset attracts capital allowances (CAs) at a rate of 25% per annum on reducing balance.

	Accounts £	Tax £	Difference £	
Year 1 : Cost	500	500	—	
P & L A/c CAs	(100)	(125)	25	originating
Year end 1 : *NBV/WDV	400	375	25	
Year 2 : P & L A/c/CAs	(100)	(94)	(6)	Reversing
Year end 2 : *NBV/WDV	300	281	19	

*NBV = Net book value
WDV = Written down tax value.

If this fixed asset is the only item causing the timing difference there will be an originating timing difference of £25 in Year 1, i.e., the accounts profit will be £25 higher than the tax profit. In Year 2, the depreciation charge in the acounts will exceed the capital allowances in the tax computation by £6, giving a reversing timing difference, i.e. the tax profit will be £6 higher than the accounts profits. Eventually the asset will be written off both in the accounts and tax computation. The time taken to write the asset off in the accounts will be shorter than that taken in the tax computation. Once the asset has been completely written off both in the accounts and the tax computation, the total accounting profit will equal the tax profits (provided there are no other items causing the difference between the two profits).

SSAP 15: ACCOUNTING FOR DEFERRED TAXATION

EXAMPLE 2

A PLC acquires fixed assets at cost of £500 in Year 1 and £1,000 in Year 2. Other details are as in example 1.

	Accounts £	Tax £	Difference £	
Year 1: Cost	500	500	—	
P & L A/c/CAs	(100)	(125)	(25)	originating
Y/e NBV/WDV	400	375	25	
Year 2 Addition	1000	1000	—	
	1400	1375	25	
P & L/CAs	(300)	(344)	44	Net originating
Y/e 2 NBV/WDV	1100	1031	69	
Year 3 Addition	—	—	—	
P&L A/c/CAs	(300)	(258)	(42)	Net reversing
Y/e 2 NBV/WDV	800	773	27	

The net originating timing difference in Year 2 can be explained as follows:

	Depreciation Charge £	CAs £	Originating /(Reversal) £
Asset acquired in Year 1	100	94	(6)
Asset acquired in Year 2	200	250	50
	300	344	44

Similarily the net reversing timing difference in Year 3 can be explained as follows:

	Depreciation Charge £	CAs £	Originating /(Reversal) £
Asset acquired in Year 1	100	70	(30)
Asset acquired in Year 2	200	188	(12)
	300	258	(42)

In the above example, the originating timing difference arising in a particular year will increase the difference between the accounting profit and tax profit and the net reversing timing difference will reduce the difference between the accounting profit and tax profit. If no new assets are acquired from Year 3 onwards, in future years there will be a reversal of the timing difference of £69 which has been built up at the end of year 2.

However, if new assets are acquired from Year 3 onwards, there may be net originating or reversing timing difference depending on the amount of depreciation charge in the profit and loss account and capital allowances entitlement in the tax computation.

SSAP 15 defines deferred tax as the tax attributable to timing differences.

The Principles

8.3   There are three alternative approaches:

1. Full Provision Basis

This is based on the principle that financial statements for a period should recognise the tax effects, whether current or deferred, of *all* transactions arising in that period, i.e. the charge for taxation in the profit and loss account for the year should be based on the reported profit. A full provision for tax should also be made on any revaluation surplus recognised on the balance sheet.

Profit and Loss Account tax charge

= rate of corporation tax × Accounting Profit (adjusted for items causing permanent difference)
= rate of corporation tax × Taxable income (= corporation tax payable on current year's income)
+ rate of corporation tax × Timing differences arising in the year (= Transfer to/from deferred tax account)

The advantage of this approach is that the tax effect of timing differences can be objectively determined as the exercise is an arithmetical one. The disadvantage is that it can be an unrealistically prudent approach. Where a company is a going concern, there will be a core of timing differences which may never reverse and if tax is provided on these timing differences, profits will be understated and liabilities overstated, thus distorting the return on capital employed and gearing ratios.

2. Flow through (or nil provision) basis:

This is based on the principle that financial statements of a period should recognise the corporation tax payable on the results of only that period. Profit and loss account tax charge = rate of corporation tax × taxable

SSAP 15: ACCOUNTING FOR DEFERRED TAXATION

income (= Corporation Tax). The advantage of this method is that the tax charge for the year can be objectively determined. However, this method is regarded as contrary to the prudence concept as contained in SSAP 2 which requires that provision should be made for all known liabilities whether the amount of these is certain or is the best estimate in the light of information available. It is also contrary to the application of the matching concept as applicable to taxation – no tax being provided on that part of accounting profit which is recognised in the financial statements for the current period but which will crystallise in later accounting periods. The matching concept requires that the tax consequences of a transaction should be matched with the transaction itself and dealt with in the same accounting period. As in the full provision method, the return on capital employed and gearing ratios will be affected by the absence of any provision for deferred tax.

3. Partial Provision Basis

This method recognises the amount that will actually become payable. If an enterprise is not expected to reduce the scale of its operations significantly, it will often have a 'core' of timing differences (i.e. there will *always* be a difference between its total accounting profit and total taxable income) so that the payment of some tax will be permanently deferred on part of the accounting profits.

This is best illustrated by a simple example:

A company plans to spend £100,000 every year on fixed assets which attract first year allowances of 100% (assuming this to be available under current legislation) and have a useful life of five years.

Year	1	2	3	4	5	6
P & L A/c – Depreciation charge	£20,000	£40,000	£60,000	£80,000	£100,000	£100,000
First Year allowances	£100,000	£100,000	£100,000	£100,000	£100,000	£100,000
Originating Timing Difference (Reversing)	£80,000	£60,000	£40,000	£20,000	–	–

By the end of year four, the total timing difference between the accounting profit and taxable income equals £200,000. If there is no net reversal of timing difference from year five onwards (i.e. the company continues to spend £100,000 per annum on fixed assets, £200,000 worth of accounting profit is sheltered from tax by fiscal incentives). The partial provision method recognises that no provision for tax should be made in the accounts on these hard core timing differences. A provision for deferred tax will be made in the accounts only where it is likely that tax will become payable in the future as a reversal of timing differences.

Profit and loss account charge =
rate of corporation tax × taxable income (= Corporation Tax)
+ rate of corporation tax × Timing differences   (= Deferred Tax)
  arising in the year
  which are likely to
  reverse in the future

As these timing differences reverse, there will be a transfer from deferred tax account to the tax charge for the year.

(*Note:* the full first year allowances are included for illustrative purposes only: it is the principle which matters. Illustrations based on current legislation appear later in the chapter.)

8.4 Up-to-date financial plans and/or projections covering a period of years will be required to enable an assessment to be made of the likely pattern of future reversal of timing differences which have arisen in the current period. A regular review and revision of financial plans and projections will be required to take account of changes in circumstances or the availability of new information relating to previously budgeted amounts. The deferred tax on timing differences will be maintained on the basis of the most up-to-date information, and adjustment to the deferred tax balance will be made if and when the circumstances change or new information is available.

The best way to deal with this is to first identify the timing differences at the end of the year; then prepare up-to-date financial plans and/or projections to identify any future reversal of these timing differences. The deferred tax balance which should be carried forward at the end of the year should equal the rate of Corporation Tax × future reversal of the timing differences identified at the end of the year. The difference between the deferred tax balance at the year end and the opening balance will equal the additional provision required or the write back of deferred tax.

Deferred tax balance at the year end (based on future reversal of timing differences determined at the year end)	x
Less: Deferred tax balance at the start (based on future reversal of timing differences determined at the end of last year)	(x)
Additional provision or write back of deferred tax	x

8.5 If there is any surplus, this is recognised on the balance sheet and the same criteria will apply, i.e. provide for deferred tax on the amount of surplus to the extent that the corporation tax will become payable in the future. No provision for deferred tax will be required if the liability is unlikely to crystallise.

The advantages of this method are:

SSAP 15: ACCOUNTING FOR DEFERRED TAXATION

(a) The earnings figure is arrived at on the basis of the provision for tax being made on current accounting profits to the extent that it is likely to crystallise now or in the future. Therefore, earnings per share is computed on a realistic basis giving a realistic ratio for return on capital employed.
(b) The provision for tax in the balance sheet is on the basis of what is likely to crystallise. This will not distort the relationship between the debt and equity (i.e. gearing ratio).

The main disadvantage of this method is that a fair amount of subjectivity will be required in deciding whether or not a provision is required. The timing differences arising in the current year but which are likely to reverse in the future will have to be identified and this will require long term forecasting.

EXAMPLE 1
1. A company plans to spend £100,000 on fixed assets in one year only. These fixed assets attract 100% first year allowances and have a useful life of five years. Rate of corporation tax = 35%

Year	1	2	3	4	5
Cost	£100,000	—	—	—	—
P & L A/c	20,000	20,000	20,000	20,000	20,000
First Year Allowance	100,000	—	—	—	—
Originating/(Reversing) Timing Difference	80,000	(20,000)	(20,000)	(20,000)	(20,000)

The difference between the accounting profit and the taxable income in the first year will equal £80,000; accounting profit being higher by that amount. There is no corporation tax payable in the first year on the difference of £80,000 arising in that year but the corporation tax will become payable on this amount over the next four years by 35% × £20,000 = £7,000 per year. Since an additional profit of £80,000 is recognised in the accounts in the first year and on which corporation tax will become payable in the four subsequent years, a provision for deferred tax of 35% × £80,000 is required in that year. This provision will be reduced by 35% × £20,000 = £7,000 per annum over the next four years as corporation tax on this amount becomes payable, i.e. there will be a transfer from deferred tax account to the tax charge of £7,000 per year, over the next four years.

EXAMPLE 2
The only timing difference which a company has is due to accelerated capital allowances. At the end of year one, it has fixed assets with net book value of £1,000,000 and tax written down value of £700,000. Therefore, the total timing difference at the end of year one = £300,000

(i.e. net book value − tax written down value). The budgets at the end of year one show that £100,000 of this timing difference is likely to reverse over next five years.

Therefore, the provision for deferred tax required at the end of year one will equal 35% × £100,000 = £35,000. (Assuming a Corporation Tax rate of 35%.)

At the end of year 2:

Net book value	= £1,500,000
Tax written down value	= £1,100,000
Therefore Total Timing Difference	£ 400,000

The budgets prepared at the end of year two show that due to the changed circumstances of the company, no part of this timing difference is likely to reverse in the foreseeable future. Therefore, no deferred tax provision will be required to be carried forward at the end of year two. The provision for deferred tax made at the end of year one can now be written back.

Methods of Computation

8.6   (a) Liability Method

The deferred tax balance is maintained at the rate of corporation tax applicable in the periods when timing differences are expected to reverse. This will usually be the current rate of tax, unless the rates applicable in periods in which the timing differences are expected to reverse are known. The deferred tax provision will be subject to future adjustment if the taxation rates change or new taxes are imposed. The provision for deferred tax under this method is regarded as liability for tax payable in the future or as an asset representing recoverable tax. An example of this method of computation is as follows:

A Ltd. purchases fixed assets in Year 1 of £500
and in Year 2 of £1,000.

These fixed assets attract (say) first year allowances (FYAs) of 100% and have a useful life of five years. There are no other timing differences.

Year	Rate of corporation tax
1	50%
2	60% (not known in Year 1)
3	55% (not known in Years 1 and 2)

SSAP 15: ACCOUNTING FOR DEFERRED TAXATION

Year	Accounts	Tax computation	Differences originating/ (reversing)	Rate	Transfer to/ (from) deferred tax account
	£	£	£	%	£
1 Cost	500	500	—		—
P & L A/c/ FYAs	(100)	(500)	400	50%	200
C/Fwd	400	—	400	50%	200
2 Adjustment for increase in rate of Tax = 10% × £400 (Therefore additional P & L A/c Charge)					40
	400	—	400	60%	240
Additions	1000	1000	—		—
	1400	1000	400		240
P & L A/c FYAs	(300)	(1000)	700	60%	420
C/Fwd	1100	—	1100	60%	660
3 Adjustment for decrease in rate of Tax = 5% × £1,100 = (Therefore £55 credit to P & L A/c)					(55)
	1100	—	1100	55%	605
P & L A/c/FYAs	(300)	—	(300)	55%	(165)
C/Fwd	800	—	800	55%	440

Summary

Year	P & L A/c charge/(credit)	Timing Difference @ year end	Rate of Tax	Provision C/Fwd
	£	£	%	£
1	200	400	50%	200
2	460	1,100	60%	660
3	(220)	800	55%	440

8.7 (b) Deferral Method

Deferred tax provision on timing differences arising in the period is made at the rate ruling in that period and no subsequent adjustments are made in future periods if the rates change. The reversals come out at the original rate. Taking the same example as in the liability method, the deferred tax account will be treated in the following way:

UNDERSTANDING ACCOUNTING STANDARDS

Year	Originating/(reversing) timing difference £	Rate %	P & L A/c charge/(credit) £	Provision c/fwd £
1	400	50%	200	200
2	(100)	50%	(50)	
	800	60%	480	630
3	(100)	50%	(50)	
	(200)	60%	(120)	460

SSAP 15 (Revised 1985) approach

8.8 The fundamental statement of principle in SSAP 15 is that *'tax deferred or accelerated by the effect of timing differences should be accounted for to the extent that it is probable that a liability or asset will crystallise and tax deferred or accelerated by the effect of timing differences should not be accounted for to the extent that it is probable that a liability or asset will not crystallise'*.

8.9 The revised standard requires that a provision for deferred tax should be made only to the extent that it is probable that it will crystallise, and *no* provision for deferred tax should be made to the extent that it is probable that it will not crystallise. The revised standard recognises that the result after tax is widely regarded as an important indicator of performance and this result will be distorted by accounting for deferred tax where it is probable that an asset or liability will not crystallise (e.g. the full provision basis) or by failing to account for deferred tax where it is probable that an asset or liability will crystallise (e.g. nil provision basis). Therefore the standard requires that deferred tax should be accounted for under the 'partial provision' basis in respect of the net amount by which it is probable that any payment of tax will be temporarily deferred or accelerated by the operation of timing differences which will reverse in the foreseeable future without being replaced. This 'partial provision' approach is based on an assessment of what will actually materialize. The adoption of this principle is consistent with:

(a) SSAP 18: Accounting for Contingencies – 'to provide for a material contingent loss or liability when it is probable that a future event will confirm the loss or liability which can be estimated with reasonable accuracy at the date on which the financial statements are approved by the board of directors'.

(b) Companies Act 1985 (Schedule 4, Para 89) to account for 'any amount retained as necessary for the purpose of providing for any liability or loss which is either likely to be incurred, or certain to be incurred but uncertain as to amount or as to date on which it will arise'.

SSAP 15: ACCOUNTING FOR DEFERRED TAXATION

Criteria for assessing whether deferred tax liabilities or assets will or will not crystallise

8.10 SSAP 15 states that the assessment of whether deferred tax liabilities or assets will or will not crystallise should be based on reasonable assumptions which take into account all relevant information available up to the date on which the financial statements are approved by the board of directors, and also the intentions of management.

8.11 It is possible to identify the following criteria upon which this assessment should be based, even though a considerable degree of judgement is required in making this assessment:

(a) Up-to-date financial plans and/or projections covering a period of years sufficient to enable an assesment to be made of the likely pattern of future tax liabilities. A regular review and revision of financial plans and projections by management will be necessary to take account of changes in circumstances or the availability of new information relating to previously budgeted amounts. The revised standard does not specify the period which financial plans and projections should cover. The appendix to the Standard gives some guidance on this. 'The combined effect of timing differences should be considered when attempting to assess whether a tax liability will crystallise, rather than looking at each timing difference separately.......... The period may be relatively short – say three to five years – where the pattern of timing differences is expected to be regular. However, it may need to be longer for an enterprise with an irregular pattern of timing differences.' If a company budgets for a fixed amount of capital expenditure, financial plans and projections covering 3 – 5 years will suffice. If the pattern of capital expenditure is likely to vary from year to year, a period longer than five years may have to be considered. An absence of fully developed plans would not, however, automatically justify a full provision.

(b) The Intentions of Management: Obviously these intentions would be reflected in financial plans or projections. However, it is also important to consider the circumstances affecting the company. A company may justify the absence of a deferred tax provision on the grounds that it intends spending certain amounts on capital expenditure every year which would give rise to a net originating timing difference each year. Before accepting this proposition, it is necessary to consider the ability of the company to implement the programme in terms of available financing, manpower and the technological skills which may be required, as well as the market situation governing the sale of its products.

(c) Pattern of future tax liabilities: These will depend on the rates of tax expected to be applicable in periods in which timing differences are likely to reverse. A company may at present be paying tax at small company rates but its plans and forecasts show that it will be taxed at large company rates in the future. In this case the deferred tax provision on timing differences arising now but likely to reverse in the future will be at large company rates.

It should similarly be noted that external fiscal policies can have a dramatic bearing on both the amount and incidence of deferred tax provisions. A policy of phasing out first year allowances while lowering tax rates is an example of this.

8.12 SSAP 15 requires that the provision for deferred tax liabilities should be reduced by any deferred tax debit balances arising from separate categories of timing differences and any advance corporation tax (ACT) available for offset against those liabilities. Care should be taken that offset of debit balances against credit balances on deferred tax be restricted to what is permitted by tax legislation. Since ACT recoverable is not allowed to be offset against a chargeable gain, ACT recoverable on a proposed dividend should not be offset against a deferred capital gains tax charge arising from a revaluation surplus.

Method of computation

8.13 As demonstrated earlier, there are two methods of computation for deferred tax. SSAP 15 rejects the deferral method as it is not consistent with the partial provision basis. It requires the liability method to be used as this attempts to quantify and recognise the actual amount which will crystallise in the future. The advantages of making this method mandatory are:
(a) it ensures comparability between companies; and
(b) it facilitates consistent classification of deferred tax in the balance sheets of companies.

Differences between the original SSAP 15 and revised SSAP 15

8.14 (1) There is a change in emphasis in the revised standard even though both are based on partial provision basis. The original SSAP 15 required that:
(a) Deferred tax should be accounted for in full on all short term timing differences.

SSAP 15: ACCOUNTING FOR DEFERRED TAXATION

(b) Deferred tax should be accounted for on the tax effects of all other originating timing differences of material amount, except for those that can be demonstrated with reasonable probability to continue in the future.

The criteria in the original standard introduced an unwanted bias into the standard. Many smaller companies who continued to provide deferred tax on the full provision basis (a requirement of the now withdrawn SSAP 11) did not have to justify it. It was accepted that this was done because the financial plans and forecasts were not available and therefore, on the grounds of prudence, a full provision was required, even though it was confirmed later that the provision was excessive. The companies that wished to leave some or all of the potential liability had to give justification for it. The revised Standard requires that the provision for deferred tax must be on the basis that it is probable that it will crystallise and no provision should be made to the extent that it is probable that it will not crystallise. Detailed financial plans and forecasts will be required for justifying the treatment adopted in the financial statements.

8.15 (2) As stated in (1) above, it was a requirement of the original Standard that deferred tax should be accounted for on all short-term timing differences. Experience has shown that the reversal of short-term timing differences does not automatically lead to crystallisation of tax liabilities. An accrual of interest receivable at the end of the year does not necessarily mean that the tax on this interest will be automatically payable next year when it is received. There may be trading losses available in the next period against which the interest may be offset; thus extinguishing the tax liability. The revised Standard requires all timing differences to be considered together when assessing whether a tax liability will crystallise. The revised Standard requires that where short-term timing differences are replaced by similar timing differences in the next accounting period, no provision should be made as such replacement postpones the crystallisation of the liability.

8.16 (3) The original Standard required companies to assess the likelihood of any liability crystallising by reference to a minimum period of three years. This, in practice, became a maximum period. The revised Standard requires this to be assessed by reference to their own particular circumstances.

8.17 (4) In the original Standard, the justification required for carrying forward a debit deferred tax balance on ACT was that there should be 'a reasonable certainty' of their recovery in future periods.

The requirement has been refined in the revised Standard:

Debit balances on deferred tax account due to trading losses and other timing differences should be carried forward only if they are 'expected to be recoverable without replacement equivalent debit balances'. As to ACT on dividends payable or proposed, the debit balance should be carried forward to the extent it is foreseen that sufficient corporation tax will be assessed on the profits or income of the succeeding accounting period, against which ACT is available for offset. The excess ACT debit balances on dividends paid should be written off unless their recovery is assured beyond reasonable doubt.

8.18 (5) The original Standard allowed both the liability method and deferral method of computation. The revised Standard rejects the deferral method as it is not consistent with the partial provision basis.

Accounting for deferred tax on timing differences

Short-term timing differences

8.19 The revised Standard requires the combined effect of timing differences to be considered when attempting to assess whether a tax liability will crystallise, rather than looking at each timing difference separately. The Appendix to the Standard gives a list of items which may cause short-term timing differences:

(a) interest receivable accrued in the accounting period, but taxed when received;
(b) dividends from foreign subsidiaries accrued in a period prior to that in which they arise for tax purposes;
(c) intra-group profits in stock deferred upon consolidation until realisation to third parties;
(d) interest or royalties payable accrued in the accounting period, but allowed when paid;
(e) pension costs accrued in the financial statements but allowed for tax purposes when paid or contributed at some later date;
(f) provisions for repairs and maintenance made in the financial statements but not allowed for tax purposes until the expenditure is incurred;
(g) general bad debt provisions not allowed for tax purposes unless and until they become 'specific';
(h) provisions for revenue losses on closing down plants or for costs of reorganisation upon which tax relief is not obtained until the costs or losses are incurred; and

SSAP 15: ACCOUNTING FOR DEFERRED TAXATION

(i) revenue expenditure deferred in the financial statements, such as development or advertising, if it is allowed for tax purposes as it is incurred.

8.20 The revised Standard also requires that where short-term timing differences are replaced by similar timing differences in the next accounting period, no provision should be made as such replacement postpones the crystallisation of the liability. An example of this would be where a company holds a debenture of £100,000 to be redeemed in Year 2000 and on which it earns interest at 10%. The company's year end is 31 December and it receives interest on 31 March and 30 September. At 31 December each year, the company will accrue interest receivable of £2,500. No deferred tax provision will be required on this timing difference of £2,500 as it will be replaced by an equivalent amount at the end of the following year.

Accelerated capital allowances

8.21 These timing differences arise from the availability of capital allowances in tax computations which are in excess of the related depreciation charges in financial statements. The reverse may also occur whereby the depreciation charge in financial statements exceeds the capital allowances available in tax computations. A number of different situations will have to be considered to see whether or not a tax liability will crystallise in the future:

(a) The Appendix to SSAP 15 states 'In many businesses, timing differences arising from accelerated capital allowances are of a recurring nature and reversing differences are themselves offset, wholly or partially, or are exceeded, by new originating differences, thereby giving rise to continuing tax reductions on the indefinite postponement of any liability attributable to the tax benefit received. Thus an enterprise having a relatively stable or growing investment in depreciable assets can take tax relief year by year on capital expenditure. This tax relief may equal or exceed the additional tax which would otherwise have been payable in consequence of the reversal of the originating timing differences through depreciation.'

No deferred tax provision is therefore required where the company's investment pattern is stable or expanding, giving rise to future tax relief on the expenditure (as it is made) which exceeds the additional tax payable on reversing timing differences. Also no deferred tax provision may be required where the rate of capital allowances exceeds the rate of depreciation on fixed assets. This is best illustrated as follows:

UNDERSTANDING ACCOUNTING STANDARDS

EXAMPLE

A PLC: Year end 31 December
Writing down allowance (per annum) 25% (reducing balance)
Straight line rate of depreciation (per annum) 10%
As at 31 March 1987, A PLC's capital expenditure projections show the following:

Year ended 31 March	£
1988	8,000
1989	11,000
1990	12,000
1991	15,000

WDV (for tax purposes) brought forward as at 1 April 1987 = £22,000
COST brought forward as at 1 April 1987 = £54,400
Accumulated depreciation brought forward as at 1 April 1987 = £12,760

There are no other timing differences.

Capital allowances

Year ended 31 March	1988 £	1989 £	1990 £	1991 £
WDV b/f	22,000	22,500	25,125	27,844
Additions	8,000	11,000	12,000	15,000
	30,000	33,500	37,125	42,844
WDA @ 25%	7,500	8,375	9,281	10,711
WDV c/f	22,500	25,125	27,844	32,133

Fixed assets and depreciation:

	1988	1989	1990	1991
Cost b/f	54,400	62,400	73,400	85,400
Additions	8,000	11,000	12,000	15,000
Cost c/f	62,400	73,400	85,400	100,400
Depreciation b/f	12,760	19,000	26,340	34,880
Charge @ 10% pa on straight line basis	6,240	7,340	8,540	10,040
Depreciation c/f	19,000	26,340	34,880	44,920
Net book value c/f	43,400	47,060	50,520	55,480

Comparing projected capital allowances and projected depreciation charges:

	Capital Allowances £	Depreciation charges £	Net originating timing differences £
1988	7,500	6,240	1,260
1989	8,375	7,340	1,035
1990	9,281	8,540	741
1991	10,711	10,040	671

As no net reversal of timing differences is anticipated prior to 1991 (a reasonable forward projection), no provision for deferred tax should

AUDITING

SSAP 1 - ACCOUNTING FOR ASSOCIATED COMPANIES *

SSAP 2 - DISCLOSURE OF ACCOUNTING PRINCIPLES

SSAP 3 - EARNINGS PER SHARE

SSAP 4 - ACCOUNTING FOR GOV'T GRANTS *

SSAP 5 - VALUE ADDED TAX

SSAP 6 - EXTRAORDINARY ITEMS + PRIOR YEAR ADJUSTMENTS

SSAP 8 - TREATMENT OF TAX UNDER THE IMPUTATION SYSTEM IN THE ACCOUNTS OF COMPANIES

SSAP 9 - STOCKS + LONG TERM CONTRACTS

SSAP 10 - STATEMENT OF SOURCE + APPLICATION OF FUNDS

SSAP 12 - DEPRECIATION

* SSAP 13 - RESEARCH + DEVELOPMENT
* SSAP 14 - GROUP ACCOUNTS
* SSAP 15 - DEFERRED TAX
  SSAP 17 + 18 - POST BALANCE SHEET EVENTS + CONTINGENCIES
* SSAP 19 - INVESTMENT PROPERTIES
* SSAP 20 - FOREIGN CURRENCY TRANSLATION
* SSAP 21 - LEASE + HP CONTRACTS
* SSAP 22 - GOODWILL
* SSAP 23 - ACQUISITIONS + MERGERS
* SSAP 24 - PENSION COSTS

* - NOT DETAILED - BREIF KNOWLEDGE

SSAP 15: ACCOUNTING FOR DEFERRED TAXATION

be made provided there is no known indication of projected reversals in 1992 or beyond.

(b) Appendix to SSAP 15: 'Where for economic or other reasons a spasmodic or highly irregular pattern of capital allowances is forecast, a substantial period of time will need to be considered in attempting to assess whether a tax liability will crystallise. Where there is a declining availability of capital allowances, any originating timing differences will usually reverse, and deferred tax should be provided unless it is probable for other reasons that no tax liability will crystallise'.

EXAMPLE

A PLC Year end 31 March.

As at 1/4/87 : Accounting Net book value b/fwd	£27,630
:Tax written down value b/fwd	£19,487

Corporation tax @ 35%
Writing down allowance @ 25%
Depreciation @ 40% per annum on reducing balance.
As at 31 March 1987, A PLC's capital expenditure projection show the following:

Year ended 31 March	£
1988	10,000
1989	16,000
1990	18,000
1991	25,000

There are no other timing differences.

Capital allowances computation:

Year ended 31/3	1988 £	1989 £	1990 £	1991 £
WDV b/fwd	19,487	22,115	28,586	36,940
Additions	10,000	16,000	18,000	25,000
	29,487	38,115	46,586	61,940
WDA at 25%	7,372	9,529	11,646	15,485
WDV c/fwd	22,115	28,586	36,940	46,455

Fixed assets and depreciation:

Year ended 31/3	1988 £	1989 £	1990 £	1991 £
NBV b/f	27,630	22,578	23,147	24,688
Additions	10,000	16,000	18,000	25,000
	37,630	38,578	41,147	49,688
Depreciation charge @ 40% pa on reducing balance	(15,052)	(15,431)	(16,459)	(19,875)
NBV c/f	22,578	23,147	24,688	29,813

161

Comparing projected capital allowances and projected depreciation charges:

	Capital allowances £	Depreciation charges £	Net reversing timing differences £	Cumulative reversing timing differences £
1988	7,372	15,052	7,680	7,680
1989	9,529	15,431	5,902	13,582
1990	11,646	16,459	4,813	18,395
1991	15,485	19,875	4,390	22,785

The comparison at 31 March 1987 of accounts net book value and tax written down value shows:

	£
Accounts net book value	27,630
Tax written down value	19,487
Total timing difference	8,143

Since the whole of this timing difference appears likely to reverse in the future, a deferred tax provision of 35% × £8,143 = £2,850 should be made at 31 March 1987.

Revaluation of assets

8.22 Appendix to SSAP 25: 'When a fixed asset is revalued above cost a timing difference potentially arises in that, in the absence of rollover relief, tax on a chargeable gain may be payable if and when the asset is disposed of at its revalued amount. Where it is probable that a liability will crystallise, provision for tax payable on disposal is required to be made out of the revaluation surplus, based on the value at which the fixed asset is carried in the balance sheet'.

Non-depreciable assets revalued upwards
(a) No deferred tax provision is required if there is no intention to discontinue or dispose of the assets on the business
(b) Provision for deferred tax should be made where a decision has been taken to dispose of the asset. The deferred tax should be provided out of the revaluation surplus.

Depreciable assets revalued upwards
Where a depreciable asset is revalued upwards, a timing difference will arise which will reverse either: if and when the asset is disposed of at its revalued amount provided no rollover relief is claimed or, if it is not disposed of, as it is subsequently depreciated (i.e. as it becomes realised).

SSAP 15: ACCOUNTING FOR DEFERRED TAXATION

Provision for deferred tax would be required, but will be released to the credit of the tax charge over the remaining life of the asset.

EXAMPLE

A PLC (year end 31 December) acquired an industrial building on 1 January 1985 for £100,000. A PLC depreciates its building over 50 years on a straight line basis and is entitled to industrial building allowance (IBA) at 4% pa on straight line basis. A PLC revalues this building at £125,000 on 1/1/1987. There are no other items which cause timing differences.

	Accounts £		Tax £
1/1/85 cost	100,000		100,000
1985 P & L A/c	2,000	IBA	4,000
1986 P & L A/c	2,000	IBA	4,000
31/12/86 NBV	96,000	WDV	92,000
1/1/87 Revalued to	125,000		
Revaluation surplus	29,000		

As at 1/1/1987:

	£
Book value	125,000
Less: Tax written down value	92,000
Total Timing Difference	33,000

	£
Therefore Potential amount of tax liability as at 1/1/1987:	
(i) Capital gains tax on £25,000 @ 30%	8,750
plus (ii) Tax on Timing Difference of £8000 @ 35%	2,800
	11,550

The above ignores indexation allowance. If the asset were sold on 1/1/1987 a capital gains tax of £8,750 on a profit of £25,000 @ 35% would crystallise and £8,000 claimed as industrial building allowances would become a balancing charge on which the Corporation Tax would become payable at 35%.

Accounts

			£
1/1/87	Revaluation Surplus		29,000
	Less transfer to deferred tax		7,500
	Deferred tax on capital gain		(8,750)
	Deferred tax on balancing charge		(1,400)
1/1/87	Net surplus		£18,850

The deferred tax on timing differences due to accelerated CAs of £4,000 @ 35% will have been provided in the first two years (assuming that they are likely to reverse in the future).

SSAP 12 requires the revalued amount to be written off over the remainder of useful life, i.e. 48 years in this case. If there is no intention to dispose of the asset, the deferred tax provision on revaluation reserve will be released to the credit of the tax charge in the profit and loss account over the period in which the asset is subsequently depreciated, i.e. 48 years. Therefore, the additional provision required on 1/1/87 = 11,550 − 1,400 = £10,150. The £10,150 is made up of capital gains tax of £8,750 and the balancing charge of £1,400.

P & L A/c

	Depreciation charge	Transfer from deferred tax on revaluation surplus
1987	1/48 × £125,000 = £2,604	1/48 × £8,750 = £182
1988	1/48 × £125,000 = £2,604	1/48 × £8,750 = £182

Therefore the net transfer in 1987 will be as follows: £

Deferred tax on accelerated capital allowances = 2000 @ 35%   700
less: transfer from deferred tax:
  on revaluation surplus   (182)
  on balancing charge = 1400 ÷ 23 years @ 35%   (21)
    497

Non-depreciable assets revalued downwards

A capital loss will arise for tax purposes if and when the asset is disposed of at its revalued amount. A capital loss can be utilised only if a chargeable gain arises on disposal of another asset during or after the accounting period in which the loss arises. An originating timing difference therefore arises if the revaluation deficit is recognised in the profit and loss account rather than by adjustment through reserves. A deferred tax asset should not normally be recognised in the interests of prudence. However, the tax effect of the downward revaluation may be recorded if:

(a) deferred tax has been provided on upward revaluations either in the same or past accounting periods; and
(b) it can be demonstrated that a chargeable gain will be available against which to utilise the loss.

Depreciable assets revalued downwards

The treatment will be similar to accelerated capital allowances (see p.159).

Revaluations not incorporated in the accounts

8.23 SSAP 15 requires that, where the value of an asset is not incorporated in the balance sheet but is given elsewhere such as in a note, the tax effects, if any, which would arise if the asset was realised at the noted value should also be shown. This also applies where the value is given in the directors' report instead of in the notes.

Deferred tax debit balances

8.24 SSAP 15: 'Deferred tax net debit balances should not be carried forward as assets except to the extent that they are expected to be recoverable without replacement by equivalent debit balances'. Deferred tax debit balances represent future tax benefits attributable to timing differences and may arise from:
(a) trading losses
(b) capital losses
(c) some of the items causing short term timing differences, i.e. accrued interest payable, general bad debt and stock provisions.

Trading losses

8.25 The Appendix to SSAP 15 states that the tax effect of a current trading loss should be treated as a recoverable asset only when:
(a) the loss results from an identifiable and non-recurring cause; and
(b) the enterprise has been consistently profitable with any past losses being more than offset by profits in subsequent periods; and
(c) it is assumed beyond reasonable doubt that future taxable profits will be sufficient to offset the current loss during the carry forward period prescribed by tax legislation.

EXAMPLE 1

Fred Ltd has no originating or reversing timing differences in 1986 or 1987, i.e. reported accounting profit also equals the profit on which tax is assessed. The balance on deferred tax account at 1/1/86 was £190,000. Trading losses in 1986 amounted to £160,000. In 1987, trading profits amounted to £190,000. The movement on deferred tax account over the two years would be as follows:

	£
Balance at 1/1/86	190,000
1986: Notional tax relief on loss (35% × 160,000)	56,000
Balance at 31/12/86	134,000
1987: Deferred tax reinstated (35% × 160,000)	56,000
Balance at 31/12/87	190,000

UNDERSTANDING ACCOUNTING STANDARDS

Profit and loss accounts	1986		1987	
	£	£	£	£
Profit (loss) on ordinary activities before tax		(160,000)		190,000
Taxation:				
Corporation tax	—		(10,500)	
Deferred tax	56,000	56,000	(56,000)	(66,500)
Profit (loss) on ordinary activities after tax		(104,000)		123,500

Calculation of corporation tax
(35% × (190,000 − 160,000)) = £10,500

EXAMPLE

Harold Ltd's reported and tax-adjusted results are as follows:

	1986	1987
	£	£
Accounting profit (loss)	(70,000)	160,000
Net originating timing differences due to accelerated capital allowances	(8,000)	(11,000)
Tax-adjusted profit (loss)	(78,000)	149,000

Balance on deferred tax account at 1/1/86 was £65,000. Show how the above information would be treated under SSAP 15 assuming that there are no other items which cause timing differences.

Deferred tax calculations

	£	£
Balance at 1/1/86		65,000
1986: *Tax value of timing difference		
35% × 8,000	2,800	
Future benefit of tax losses		
35% × (78,000)	(27,300)	(24,500)
Balance at 31/12/86		40,500
1987: *Tax value of timing difference		
35% × 11,000	3,850	
Tax value of tax loss relieved against current year profits	27,300	31,150
Balance at 31/12/87		71,650

SSAP 15: ACCOUNTING FOR DEFERRED TAXATION

Profit and loss accounts

	1986		1987	
	£	£	£	£
Profit(loss) on ordinary activities before taxation		(70,000)		160,000
Taxation:				
Corporation Tax	—		(24,850)	
Deferred Tax	24,500	24,500	(31,150)	(56,000)
Profit(loss) on ordinary activities after taxation		(45,500)		104,000

Calculation of corporation tax
35% × (149,000 − 78,000) = £24,850

*This calculation assumes that the timing differences arising due to the accelerated capital allowances will reverse in the future.

Capital losses

8.26 Appendix to SSAP 15:

'Deferred tax relating to capital losses may be treated as recoverable when:
(a) a potential chargeable gain not expected to be covered by rollover relief is present in assets which have not been revalued in the financial statements to reflect that gain and which are not essential to the future operations of the enterprise; and
(b) the enterprise has decided to dispose of these assets and thus realise the potential chargeable gain; and
(c) the unrealised chargeable gain (after allowing for any possible loss in value before disposal) is sufficient to offset the loss in question, such that it is assured beyond reasonable doubt that a tax liability on the relevant portion of the chargeable gain will not crystallise.'

Short-term timing differences

8.27 No deferred tax asset should be recognised when short term timing differences reverse but are replaced by equivalent amounts. The combined effect of all the timing differences should be considered when attempting to assess whether the deferred tax asset due to short-term timing differences will be realised.

UNDERSTANDING ACCOUNTING STANDARDS

Advance corporation tax (ACT)

8.28 ACT recoverable should be offset against deferred tax liabilities in so far as the ACT recoverable is available for offset against those liabilities. The amount of ACT recoverable which may be offset against deferred tax liability is restricted to basic rate of tax (currently 25%) on the amount of timing difference (excluding chargeable gains) on which the deferred tax balance is based.

EXAMPLE 1
No restriction of ACT set off.
On 31/12/87

	£		£
Timing difference on which deferred tax has been provided	400,000	@ Corporation Tax rate of 35%	140,000
Dividends	150,000	ACT Recoverable against future Corporation tax @ $25/75^{th}$	(50,000)
Therefore net deferred tax credit			90,000

The full amount of ACT recoverable can be set off against the deferred tax balance as this is less than the maximum set off which is restricted to 25% × £400,000 = £100,000.

EXAMPLE 2
Restriction of ACT set off – limit of 25% × timing difference on which deferred tax has been provided.
On 31/12/1987

	£		£
Timing difference on which deferred tax has been provided	150,000	@ Corporation Tax rate of 35%	52,500

SSAP 15: ACCOUNTING FOR DEFERRED TAXATION

Dividends	135,000	ACT Recoverable against future Corporation tax @ $25/75^{th}$	45,000
Maximum ACT set off is restricted to 25% × £150,000			37,500
Therefore net deferred tax credit balance equals (52,500−37,500)			15,000
Leaving ACT Recoverable (45,000−37,500)			7,500

This ACT recoverable of £7,500 may be shown as an asset subject to the following:

(a) If, as above, there is insufficient deferred tax to cover recoverable ACT, it may be carried forward as a debit balance provided it is foreseen that sufficient corporation tax will be assessed on the profits or income of the succeeding accounting period, against which the ACT is available for offset.

EXAMPLE
Restriction of ACT carry forward due to insufficient corporation tax in next accounting period:

*Unrelieved ACT in respect of dividends paid, payable or proposed in 1987	Dividends £36,000 @ $\frac{25}{75}$ ACT		£12,000
Estimated Profits in 1988	£32,000	Tax rate 35%	£11,200
Maximum ACT recoverable against 1988 Corporation tax 25% × £32,000 =			£8,000
Therefore ACT recoverable carried forward as an asset in 1987			£8,000
ACT written off to P & L A/c (12,000 − 8,000)			£4,000

*not otherwise offset against a deferred tax credit balance.

169

(b) *ACT brought forward from previously paid dividends:*
Net debit balances falling under this heading should be written off unless their recovery is assured beyond reasonable doubt. This recovery would have to be out of the corporation tax on profits or income of the next accounting period.

Disclosure of deferred tax in financial statements

8.29   Profit and loss account

1. Deferred tax relating to the ordinary activities of the enterprise should be shown separately as a part of the tax on profit or loss on ordinary activities, either on the face of the profit and loss account or in a note.
2. Deferred tax relating to any extraordinary items should be shown separately as part of the tax on extraordinary items, either on the face of the profit and loss account or in a note.
3. The amount of any unprovided deferred tax in respect of the period should be disclosed in a note, analysed into its major components.
4. Adjustments to deferred tax arising from changes in tax rates and tax allowances should normally be disclosed separately as part of the tax charge for the period. However, the effect of a change in the basis of taxation, or of a significant change in Government fiscal policy, should be treated as an extraordinary item where material (see Chapter 3 on SSAP 6).

8.30   Balance sheet

1. The deferred tax balance, and its major components, should be disclosed in the balance sheet or notes.
2. Transfers to and from deferred tax should be disclosed in a note.
3. Where amounts of deferred tax arise which relate to movements on reserves (e.g. resulting from the expected disposal of revalued assets) the amounts transferred to or from deferred tax should be shown separately as part of such movements.
4. The total amount of any unprovided deferred tax should be disclosed in a note, analysed into its major components.
5. Where the potential amount of deferred tax on a revalued asset is not shown because the revaluation does not constitute a timing difference, the fact that it does not constitute a timing difference and that tax has therefore not been quantified should be stated.

SSAP 15: ACCOUNTING FOR DEFERRED TAXATION

6. Where the value of an asset is shown in a note because it differs materially from its book amount, the note should also show the tax effects, if any, that would arise if the asset were realised at the balance sheet date at the noted value.

Groups

8.31 Where a company is a member of a group, it should, in accounting for deferred tax, take account of any group relief which, on reasonable evidence, is expected to be available and any charge which will be made for such relief. Assumptions made as to the availability of group relief and payment therefore should be stated. Deferred tax in respect of the remittance of overseas earnings should be accounted for in accordance with the provision of this statement. Where deferred tax is not provided on earnings retained overseas, this should be stated.

8.32 Illustration of presentation in accounts

Profit and loss account
for the year ended 31 December 1987

	Notes	1987 £'000	1986 £'000
Turnover		x	x
Profit on ordinary activities before taxation		x	x
Tax on profit on ordinary activities	1,2	(x)	(x)
Profit on ordinary activities after taxation		x	x
Dividend paid and proposed		(x)	(x)
Profit retained for the financial year		x	x
Statement of retained profits(to be included as part of reserve movements)			
Retained profits at 1 January 1987		x	x
Profit retained for the financial year		x	x
Retained profits at 31 December 1987		x	x

Balance sheet 31 December 1987

	Notes	1987 £'000 £'000	1986 £'000 £'000
Fixed assets			
Tangible assets		x	x
Current assets			
Stocks		x	x
Debtors		x	x
		x	x

UNDERSTANDING ACCOUNTING STANDARDS

	Notes	1987 £'000	1987 £'000	1986 £'000	1986 £'000
Creditors: amounts falling due within one year	3	(x)		(x)	
Net current assets			x		x
Total assets less current liabilities			x		x
Provisions for liabilities and charges	4		x		x
Capital and reserves					
Called up share capital		x		x	
Revaluation reserve		x		x	
Profit and loss account		x	x	x	x
			x		x

Relevant extracts from Notes to the Accounts

Accounting policy – deferred taxation

8.33   Tax deferred or accelerated is accounted for in respect of all material timing differences to the extent that it is probable that a liability or asset will crystallise. Timing differences arise from the inclusion of items of income and expenditure in tax computations in periods different from those in which they are included in the accounts. Provision is made at the rate which is expected to be applied when the liability or asset is expected to crystallise. Where this is not known the latest estimate of the long-term tax rate applicable has been adopted.

8.34   No provision is made for the taxation liability which might arise on the gain that would be realised if the revalued freehold buildings were disposed of at the amounts shown in the balance sheet. In view of the company's policy of expansion and continued ownership of its assets, it is not probable that a liability will arise in the foreseeable future.

8.35   The amount of unprovided deferred tax is disclosed in a note to the accounts, calculated at the best estimate of corporation tax rates in the longer term and analysed into its major components.

Tax on profit on ordinary activities

8.36   The tax charge is based on the profit on ordinary activities for the year and comprises:

	1987 £'000	1986 £'000
United Kingdom corporation tax at 35%	x	x
Deferred tax	x	x
	x	x

Creditors: amounts falling due within one year

	1987 £'000	1986 £'000
Trade creditors	x	x
Other creditors including taxation and social security (see (a) below)	x	x
Proposed dividend	x	x
	x	x

(a) 'Other creditors including taxation and social security' is made up as follows:

	£'000	£'000
United Kingdom corporation tax	x	x
Advance corporation tax on dividends	x	x
	x	x
Social security	x	x
	x	x

Provisions for liabilities and charges

Deferred taxation

	1987 Provision made £'000	1987 Full potential liability £'000	1986 Provision made £'000	1986 Full potential liability £'000
Accelerated capital allowances	x	x	x	x
Revalued properties	–	x	–	x
ACT recoverable	(x)	(x)	(x)	(x)
	x	x	x	x

No provision has been made for deferred taxation in respect of the tax that would be payable if revalued properties were sold at their revalued amounts because there is no intention currently to dispose of the properties.

8.37 SSAP 15 requires that the total amount of any unprovided deferred tax should be disclosed in a note, analysed into its major components. Many companies use the above presentation where they disclose the amount provided in the accounts and full potential liability. The difference between the full potential liability and the amount provided in the accounts would give the amount unprovided.

UNDERSTANDING ACCOUNTING STANDARDS

Combined effect of timing differences

8.38 Appendix to SSAP 15: 'The combined effect of timing differences should be considered when attempting to assess whether a tax liability will crystallise, rather than looking at each timing difference separately'.
EXAMPLE
A PLC which has a year end of 31 December shows the following position as at 31 December 1987.

	£
Excess of capital allowances over depreciation	100,000
Interest receivable	5,000
Total timing difference as at 31/12/87	105,000

There were no timing differences as at 1/1/1987 and therefore, no deferred tax provision was required at that date.

When attempting to assess whether a tax liability will crystallise on £105,000 of timing differences, reasonable assumptions, by reference to suitable financial plan or projections covering a period of years, will be required. Projections covering the next five years show the following:

	1988	1989	1990	1991	1992
Capital allowances	180,000	170,000	50,000	40,000	190,000
Depreciation	100,000	100,000	100,000	100,000	100,000
Originating/(Reversal)	80,000	70,000	(50,000)	(60,000)	90,000

	1988	1989	1990	1991	1992
Interest receivable	2,000	8,000	4,000	7,000	15,000
Originating/(Reversal)	(3,000)	6,000	(4,000)	3,000	8,000

Year ended 31/12	Excess of capital allowances over depreciation originating/ (Reversing) £	Interest receivable originating/ (Reversing) £	Cumulative Total – Originating/ (Reversing) Timing Difference £
1988	80,000	(£3,000)	77,000
1989	70,000	£6,000	157,000
1990	(50,000)	(£4,000)	99,000
1991	(60,000)	£3,000	42,000
1992	90,000	£8,000	140,000
1993 onwards	Always originating	Always originating	Always originating

No deferred tax provision will be required at 31 December 1987 as no cumulative reversals are foreseen.

Assuming that the 1988 and 1989 budgeted figures become actual, the following would be the situation:

SSAP 15: ACCOUNTING FOR DEFERRED TAXATION

Total originating timing difference @ 31/12/88 will equal £182,000 [£105,000 + £77,000 = £182,000]. The projections from 1989 show as follows:

	Originating/(Reversing) £	Cumulative Originating/ (Reversing) £
1989	76,000	76,000
1990	(54,000)	22,000
1991	(57,000)	(35,000)
1992	98,000	63,000
1993 onwards	Originating	Originating

At first glance, it appears that no deferred tax provision will be required at 31 December 1988. However, since there is a cumulative net reversal of £35,000 by the end of 1991, a deferred tax provision on this amount @ 35% will be required at 31 December 1988.

Therefore, the deferred tax provision required at 31 December 1988 = 35% × £35,000 = £12,250. Since no deferred tax provision was brought forward on 1 January 1988, the charge to the profit and loss account for the year ended 31 December 1988 will equal £12,250.

Year ended 31 December 1989:

Total originating timing difference @ 31/12/89 = £258,000 (£182,000 + £76,000)

The projections for the year 1990 will show as follows (assuming no revision is required to the projections prepared at the end of 1987):

	Originating/(Reversing) £	Cumulative Originating/ (Reversing) £
1990	(54,000)	(54,000)
1991	(57,000)	(111,000)
1992	98,000	(13,000)
1993 onwards	Originating	Originating

At first glance once again it appears that no deferred tax provision will be required as at 31 December 1989 since the projections from 1990 onwards show a total cumulative originating timing difference. However, on examining the 1990 and 1991 figures closely, there is a cumulative reversal of £111,000 by the end of 1991. Since a deferred tax provision has already been made on a timing difference of £35,000 as at 31 December 1988, a further deferred provision as at 31/12/1989 will be required on the difference of £111,000 less £35,000 = £76,000 @ 35% giving £26,600. The charge in the profit and loss account for the year ended 31 December 1989 = £26,600 − £12,250 = £14,350.

The projections from 1992 show cumulative originating timing difference. The provision for deferred tax as at 31/12/1989 will be written back in 1990 and 1991 as follows:

UNDERSTANDING ACCOUNTING STANDARDS

Transfer from deferred tax
1990: 35% × £54,000 =   18,900
1991: 35% × £57,000 =   <u>19,950</u>
                        <u>38,850</u>

No further provision will be required from 1992 onwards.

DETAILED EXAMPLE

Camel plc is the holding company for a number of UK subsidiaries. An overseas subsidiary, Zebra, was acquired on 31 March 1987 and accounted for under the acquisition method. Zebra needs to retain all its profits to finance working capital requirements. The group makes a substantial taxable profit each year and expects to continue doing so. All intra-group trading ceased on 1 April 1986.

The following consolidated information, excluding any amounts in respect of Zebra, is relevant to Camel plc:

	Actual		Estimated		
Years to 31 March	1986	1987	1988	1989	1990
Depreciation £'000	140	180	220	240	200
Capital allowances £'000	200	220	300	150	150
Assumed corporation tax rate	40%	40%	35%	35%	35%

	At 31 March	
	1986	1987
	£'000	£'000
Fixed assets eligible for capital allowances		
— Net book amounts	950	880
— Tax written down values	780	720
Short-term timing differences (gross)		
— Patent royalties receivable	70	—
— Consolidation provision for unrealised profit in stock	60	—
— Provision for loss on closure of material business segment	—	100

In addition to the above, deferred tax of £45,000 was fully provided in the accounts of Zebra at the date of acquisition. Retained earnings of Zebra at 31 March 1987 were £75,000.

At 31 March 1986, the advance corporation tax rate was 30% and unutilised tax at that date amounted to £90,000. All such tax had been fully utilised against mainstream liabilities by 31 March 1987.

Requirements:

(a) Calculate the group deferred tax charge for the year ended 31 March

SSAP 15: ACCOUNTING FOR DEFERRED TAXATION

1987 and the balance sheet provision at that date. Present all related information in a form suitable for publication in the consolidated financial statements of Camel plc at 31 March 1987. Comparatives are required for balance sheet, but not for profit and loss information.

NOTE: A three year timespan may be regarded as the minimum period for the anticipation of timing differences but a four year timespan should be used where information is available.

(b) Outline the practical problems associated with accounting for deferred taxation and their particular relevance to the recognition of deferred tax debit balances.

SOLUTION
(a) Balance sheet

	1987 £	1986 £
Provision for liabilities and charges		
Deferred tax	31,000	1,500
Debtors		
ACT recoverable (90,000 − 9,000)	—	81,000

Balance sheet notes

Movement in deferred tax

	£
At 1/4/86	1,500
ACT recovered against 86/87	
Corporation tax	9,000
Charge in P/L a/c	
— ordinary (21,000 − 10,500)	10,500
— extraordinary	(35,000)
Deferred tax on acquisition of Zebra	45,000
At 31/3/87	£31,000

Amounts provided and unprovided

	1987 provided £	1987 unprovided £	1986 provided £	1986 unprovided £
Accelerated CAs	21,000	35,000	7,000	52,500
Miscellaneous	(35,000)	—	3,500	500
Zebra	45,000	—	—	—
	31,000	35,000	10,500	53,000
ACT recoverable	—	—	9,000	—
	£31,000	£35,000	£1,500	£53,000

UNDERSTANDING ACCOUNTING STANDARDS

Profit and Loss Account

	£
Tax on profits on ordinary activities	10,500
Deferred tax (21,000 − 10,500)	
Tax on extraordinary loss	(35,000)
Deferred tax	

Accounting policy note
Deferred tax is provided for, using the liability method, to the extent that a liability is expected to crystallise in the foreseeable future. The provision is made at the rates of tax which are expected to apply when the liabilities crystallise.

WORKINGS

Full provision at 31/3/86

	£		£
Depreciation / CAs			
NBV	950,000		
Tax WDV	780,000		
	£170,000	@ 35%	59,500

Short–term timing differences reversing in Y/E 31/3/87

Royalties	70,000		
Provision for unrealised profit	(60,000)		
	10,000	@ 40%	4,000
			£63,500

Partial provision at 31/3/86

	1987 £	1988 £	1989 £	1990 £
Depreciation / CAs				
Depreciation	180,000	220,000	240,000	200,000
CAs	220,000	300,000	150,000	150,000
Originating/(Reversing) timing differences	40,000	80,000	(90,000)	(50,000)
Royalties	(70,000)			
Provision for unrealised profit	60,000			
	£ 30,000	£ 80,000	£(90,000)	£ 50,000

Maximum cumulative reversal = £(30,000)

SSAP 15: ACCOUNTING FOR DEFERRED TAXATION

Provision required:

	£			£
Short–term timing differences				
(70,000 − 60,000)	10,000	@ 35%	=	3,500
Accelerated CAs	20,000	@ 35%	=	7,000
	£30,000			£10,500

Amount unprovided @ 31/3/86 £
Depreciation / CAs
59,500 − 7,000 =   52,500
Short–term timing
differences 4,000 −
3,500   500
                          £53,000

WORKINGS

Full provision at 31/3/87

	£		£
Depreciation / CAs			
NBV	880,000		
Tax WDV	720,000		
	160,000	@ 35%	56,000
Extraordinary items	(100,000)	@ 35%	(35,000)
Zebra			45,000
			£66,000

Partial provision @ 31/3/87

	1988 £	1989 £	1990 £
Depreciation / CAs			
Depreciation	220,000	240,000	200,000
CAs	300,000	150,000	150,000
Originating/(Reversing) timing differences	£ 80,000	£(90,000)	£(50,000)

Maximum cumulative reversal = £(60,000)
Provision for loss on closure
  Reversal in 1988   £100,000
  Deferred tax provision   £
  Depreciation / CAs   60,000 @ 35%   21,000
  Extraordinary item   (100,000) @ 35%   (35,000)
  Zebra   45,000
                                                                £31,000

Amount unprovided @ 31/3/87
Depreciation / CAs   56,000 – 21,000 =   £35,000

ACT Recoverable at 31/3/86   £

Offset against deferred tax provision
Limited to 30,000 @ 30% =   9,000
Balance C/F as debtor   81,000
    £90,000

(b) SSAP 15 requires that deferred tax should be provided to the extent that it is probable that a liability or asset will crystallise but not where it will not crystallise. This results in a partial provision. A partial provision requires forecasts of future timing differences, unlike the full provision which is purely based on past timing differences which can be determined with complete accuracy. The major problem with the partial provision is obtaining reliable forecasts relating to capital expenditure, finance leases, interest payable and receivable, asset sales and other sources of miscellaneous timing differences. Management plans change over time and may in many cases be only tentative and subject to revision in the future. The reliability of such forecasts may be checked through comparisons of previous years figures with budgets. However the forecasts can only be estimates and therefore the resulting partial provision is largely subjective.

If forecasts are thought not to be sufficiently reliable then a full provision may be justified considering the prudence concept; however, SSAP 15 emphasises that the lack of forecasts does not itself justify a full provision.

A timing difference gives rise to a deferred tax asset or debit balance when in the year the timing difference originates it results in accounting profits being less than taxable profits. The most common timing differences which cause deferred tax assets are interest payable, provisions and finance leases. The same criteria are applied to deferred tax assets as to liabilities concerning their recognition, namely, provision if it is probable the asset will crystallise. Such debit balances are offset against other credit balances when determining the net liability or asset. Where, however, a net deferred tax asset results such an asset should be carried forward only where it crystallises without replacement by an equivalent debit balance.

Deferred tax net debit balances can also be caused by tax losses. However, SSAP 15 gives specific guidance concerning the recognition of an asset in such cases. This ensures that an asset is recognised only when the tax losses are reasonably certain to produce tax savings in a future period.

SSAP 15: ACCOUNTING FOR DEFERRED TAXATION

Question

1. The 1985 revision of SSAP 15: Accounting for Deferred Tax has made some changes in the criteria for making the relevant provisions in company accounts.
Required:
(a) Discuss the new criteria for determining the amount of the charge or credit for deferred tax in the profit and loss account, and of the provision for it in the balance sheet.
(b) Comment on the problems which SSAP 15 poses for the company accountant.

Chapter Nine
Accounting for investments (1)

Methods of recognising investments

9.1 There is a wide variety of methods by which the results of an investment may be recognised, and the investment valued, in the accounts of an investor. Each method is appropriate in certain circumstances and inappropriate in others. Depending on the method used, a widely divergent set of results will be produced.

(1) Cost method

Balance sheet
9.2 The investment is carried in the investing company's balance sheet at its historical cost to the investing company. Where there is a permanent diminution in value, the investment is written down to its realisable amount. Any dividends received by the investing company from pre-acquisition profits (i.e. out of profits earned by the investee company prior to the investment being acquired by the investing company) will be used to reduce the cost of the investment. The investing company parted with capital to acquire this investment and any dividend out of pre-acquisition profits represents a return of this capital.

Profit and loss account
9.3 The income from these investments will be recognised by the investing company on the basis of dividends receivable.

(2) Valuation method

Balance sheet
9.4 The investment is carried in the investing company's balance sheet at a valuation which is generally intended to be an approximation of the fair market value of the investment. The surplus or deficit arising on valuation will either be recorded as a movement on reserves or taken through the profit and loss for the year. The treatment will depend on the type of organisation involved and the legal requirements to which it is subject.

Profit and loss account
9.5 The income from these investments will be recognised by the investing company on the basis of dividends receivable.

(3) The equity method

Balance sheet
9.6 Under the Equity Method of accounting, the balance sheet carrying value of the investment is:
(a) the cost of the investment; plus
(b) the investing company's share of post-acquisition retained profits and reserves of the company in which the investment is made; less
(c) any amounts written off in respect of (a) and (b) above.

Profit and loss account
9.7 The amount included in the profit and loss account is:
(a) the investor's share of current year's profit or loss before tax brought in as a single figure; and
(b) attributable share of the tax charge on the share of profit or loss.

(4) Consolidation
9.8 The accounts are prepared under the assumption that the investing company and each of the investments are part of a single business unit. The only transactions recorded in the consolidated accounts are transactions between the outsiders and the single business unit. Any transactions between the investing company and investee company and between the investee companies are cancelled. Similar items in the accounts of each of the companies concerned are aggregated to give one figure in the profit and loss account and balance sheet. Any outside shareholders in the investee companies will be treated in the same way as any other 'creditors' and are called minority interest and will be shown separately as a single figure.

9.9 There are two different methods of consolidation – acquisition method and merger method.

Circumstances under which each method is appropriate

9.10 As stated earlier, each method is appropriate in certain circumstances and inappropriate in others.

(1) Trade investment

9.11 Where the investment is simply a trade investment, i.e. it was acquired with the purpose of receiving a regular cash flow in form of dividends and an element of capital growth, the investment should be recorded using the cost or valuation method. The valuation method is not commonly used in the UK as it would recognise an unrealised surplus.

(2) Associated company

9.12 The definition of an associated company is discussed on pages 185–89. In the investing company's own accounts, the investment in the associated company would be recorded using the cost method. If the investing company is required to prepare group accounts in the form of consolidated accounts, the investment in the associated company would be recorded using the equity method. The investing company is required to prepare group accounts if it has a subsidiary company or companies on the date of the balance sheet (S229 CA 1985).

(3) Subsidiary company

9.13 The definition of a subsidiary company is discussed on pages 201–03. Where the investing company has at the end of its financial year a subsidiary company or companies, S229 of the CA 1985 requires that it should also prepare group accounts.

9.14 S229 also lists possible reasons for exclusion of a subsidiary company from group accounts and these reasons are discussed later. The CA 1985 requires that a holding company's group accounts shall be consolidated accounts comprising:

(a) a consolidated balance sheet dealing with the state of affairs of the company and all the subsidiaries to be dealt with in group accounts; and
(b) a consolidated profit and loss account dealing with the profit or loss of the company and those subsidiaries.

9.15 However, if the directors are of the opinion that the purpose of presenting the same or equivalent information about the state of affairs and profit or loss of the company and those subsidiaries will be better served by some other form of group accounts which may be readily appreciated by the company's members, the group accounts so prepared may consist of:

(a) more than one set of consolidated accounts dealing respectively with

the company and one group of subsidiaries and with other groups of subsidiaries; or
(b) separate accounts dealing with each of the subsidiaries; or
(c) statements expanding the information about the subsidiaries in the company's individual accounts; or
(d) any combination of (a), (b) and (c).

9.16   SSAP 14 requires that a holding company should prepare group accounts in the form of a *single* set of consolidated financial statements covering the holding company and its subsidiary companies, at home and overseas. It also lists exceptions to the above which are discussed in Chapter 10.

9.17   SSAP 23 describes the two methods which can be used to prepare consolidated accounts: acquisition method and merger method, which are discussed in Chapter 12.

SSAP 1: Accounting for associated companies

Definition

9.18   An associated company is a company not being a subsidiary of the investing group or company in which:
(a) the investor of the investing group or company is effectively that of a *partner in a joint venture or consortium* and the investing group or company is *in a position to exercise a significant influence* over the company in which the investment is made; *or*
(b) the interest of the investing group or company is for the *long term* and is *substantial* and, having regard to the disposition of the other shareholdings, the investing group or company is *in a position to exercise a significant influence* over the company in which the investment is made.

9.19   SSAP 1 explains that 'significant influence over a company essentially involves participation in the financial and operating policy decisions of that company (including dividend policy) but not necessarily control of those policies. Representation on the board of directors is indicative of such participation, but will neither give conclusive evidence of it nor be the only method by which the investing company may participate in policy decisions'.

UNDERSTANDING ACCOUNTING STANDARDS

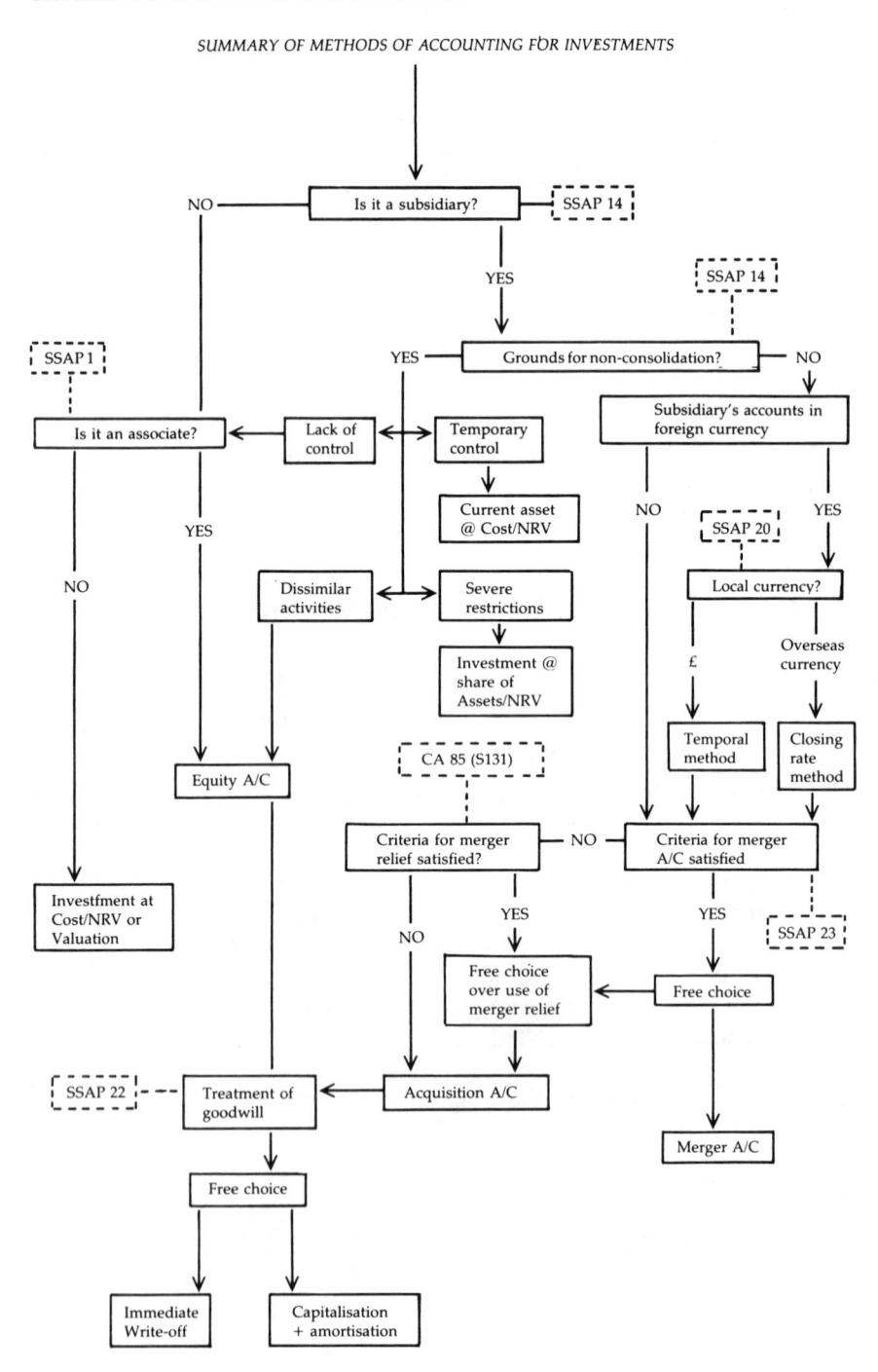

SUMMARY OF METHODS OF ACCOUNTING FOR INVESTMENTS

[Flowchart]

- Is it a subsidiary? — SSAP 14
  - NO → Is it an associate? — SSAP 1
    - YES → Equity A/C
    - NO → Investment at Cost/NRV or Valuation
  - YES → Grounds for non-consolidation? — SSAP 14
    - YES:
      - Lack of control → Is it an associate?
      - Temporary control → Current asset @ Cost/NRV
      - Dissimilar activities / Severe restrictions → Investment @ share of Assets/NRV
    - NO → Subsidiary's accounts in foreign currency
      - NO → Criteria for merger A/C satisfied
      - YES → Local currency? — SSAP 20
        - £ → Temporal method
        - Overseas currency → Closing rate method
        - → Criteria for merger A/C satisfied — SSAP 23
          - YES → Free choice → Merger A/C
          - NO → Criteria for merger relief satisfied? — CA 85 (S131)
            - YES → Free choice over use of merger relief
            - NO → Acquisition A/C → Treatment of goodwill — SSAP 22
              - Free choice
                - Immediate Write-off
                - Capitalisation + amortisation

186

Joint ventures

9.20 An example of this would be where three or more companies get together and set up another company to carry out a particular project, each investing company having an equal holding in the new company with board representation. None of the investing companies will have a controlling interest in this new company but each will have a significant influence over the investee, i.e. they will have a say in, and will influence, the management policy of the joint venture. The new company will be an associate of each of the investing companies.

Other companies

9.21 There are three important terms introduced in the definition:

The investment must be of a long-term nature

9.22 Whether an investment is held for long term or not depends on a number of factors:

(a) *Reasons for which that investment was acquired*
A relationship between the investor and investee will have to be examined and where there is a trading relationship between the two, the investment in the investee is an extension of the trade of the investor, the investment can be assumed to be long term provided there is no intention to dispose of it.

(b) *Future intentions of the investor*
The investment can not be treated as being for long term if it was made mainly for the purpose of achieving an element of capital growth, and that investment will be sold when such growth is achieved or the decision to hold it or dispose of it depends on the performance of the investment.

9.23 An investment which was considered to be long term in the past does not cease to be such purely because the investor decides to dispose of it. The change in status will depend on the circumstances that surround the decision and whether the relationship between the two companies has changed. The accounting treatment of the investment will not change for the period during which the legal formalities to dispose of the investment are being finalised. However, if a decision is taken to dispose of the investment and there is a change in the relationship between the investing company and investee, i.e. there is no longer a trading relationship between the two companies but the investor retains the shares until he can sell at a good price, the investment can no longer be considered to be of a long-term nature.

The holding must be substantial

9.24 This must be in context of the size of holding in the investee company and not in relation to the accounts of the investor. SSAP 1 does not specifically define what the size of this holding should be. However, there is an argument that a substantial holding must be considered in the context of the net assets of the investor, i.e. by comparing the cost of investment with the net assets of the investor. Since the standard does not apply to immaterial items, an investment which is not material in relation to the net assets of the investor is specifically excluded from the scope of the standard.

The investing group or company is in a position to exercise a significant influence

9.25 'Significant influence' is a term which is very difficult to define. Whether an investor exercises a significant influence or not is very subjective because such influence may be exerted in any one of many ways. Control over the company or policies of the company in which the investment is held is not the same as having a significant influence over that company. If control is exercised over the other company or its policies, then it becomes a subsidiary company. SSAP 1 states that 'significant influence over a company essentially involves participation in the financial and operating policy decisions of that company (including dividend policy) but not necessarily control of those policies'. Whether a significant influence exists or not will depend on the relationship between the two companies and any one or more of the following factors will have to be considered:

(a) *Representation on the board*
    This is indicative of significant influence over the company's financial and operating policy decisions (including dividend policy) but does not give conclusive evidence of it.
(b) *Trading relationship*
    Whether the investor is a major supplier or customer to the company in which the investment is made.
(c) *Other relationships*
    Whether there is a joint participation in research and development projects.
    Whether there is a regular interchange of staff.
    Whether there are any other joint participations.
(d) *Size of the holding*
    SSAP 1 states that where the investing group or company has a holding of '20 per cent or more of the equity voting rights of a company, it should be presumed that the investing group or company has the ability to exercise significant influence over that

company unless it can be clearly demonstrated otherwise'. For example, a single holding of 80 per cent may prevent somebody with a holding of 20 per cent from exercising a significant influence.

9.26 SSAP 1 also states that where the investing group or company has a holding of 'less than 20 per cent of the equity voting rights of a company it should be presumed that the investing group or company does not have the ability to exercise significant influence unless it can be clearly demonstrated otherwise'.

9.27 For the purposes of the above, the size of the investment should be related to the aggregate of the holding company and its subsidiaries, but excluding its associates. This is because the investing company controls the subsidiaries but only exercises a significant influence over its associates.

Bases of accounting for associated companies

9.28 SSAP 1 specifies different treatments for associated companies in the accounts of the investing company itself and in the consolidated accounts of the group of which the investing company is the holding company.

1. Accounts of the individual company

Profit and Loss Account
9.29 Income from investments in the associated companies should be recognised on the basis of dividends received and receivable.

Balance sheet
9.30 Cost or valuation methods (explained above).

2. Consolidated accounts

Profit and Loss Account
9.31 Income from investments in associated companies should be recognised on the basis of the equity method as follows:

(a) *The investing group's share of the profits less losses before tax*
9.32 These should be brought into consolidated profit and loss account as a single item and included as part of consolidated profit on

ordinary activities before taxation. It should be separately shown on the face of the profit and loss account and suitably described as share of profits less losses of associated companies.

(b) *Taxation*
9.33 The investing group's share of tax attributed to the share of profits of associated companies should be disclosed separately as part of the group tax charge in the consolidated profit and loss account.

(c) *Extraordinary items*
9.34 The group's share of extraordinary items in the associated companies will be classified as extraordinary items in the consolidated profit and loss account to the extent that they are extraordinary in the context of group accounts. If the group's share is material, it should be disclosed separately from extraordinary items arising from companies belonging to the group. To the extent that these items are not classified as extraordinary in the group's accounts, the group's share of these items will be included as part of the group's share of the profits before tax of the associated companies.

(d) *Other items*
9.35 The investing group should not include its share of associated companies' items such as turnover and depreciation in the aggregate of these items disclosed in its consolidated financial statement because to do so would be inconsistent with the equity accounting treatment which brings in the results of the associated companies as one item.

Balance Sheet
9.36 The amount at which the investment is recorded in the consolidated balance sheet should be determined on the basis of the equity method as follows:

(i) Cost of the investment		x
Less (ii) Any amounts written off		(x)
		x
Plus/(minus) (iii) the investing group's share of post-acquisition retained profits or losses and reserves		x
		x

9.37 SSAP 1 requires that this amount should be analysed into three separate elements as follows:
(i) the investing group's share of net assets (other than goodwill) of the associated companies stated, where possible, after attri-

buting fair values to the net assets at the time of acquisition of the interest in the associated companies, and   x
(ii) the investing group's share of any goodwill in the associated companies' own financial statements, together with   x
(iii) the premium (or discount) on the acquisition of the interests in the associated companies insofar as it has not already been written off or amortised.   x
    x

9.38 The items (ii) and (iii) may be combined but item (i) must be shown separately.

9.39 SSAP 1 does not specify an accounting treatment for the premium/(discount) which may arise on the acquisition of an interest in an associated company. The recommendation on this is given in SSAP 22: *Accounting for goodwill* which is discussed in detail in Chapter 11. The summary of the requirements in SSAP 22 is as follows:

Purchased positive goodwill
9.40 There is a choice of treatments:
(i) immediate write-off against reserves; or
(ii) capitalise and amortise.

Negative goodwill
9.41 Credit reserves.

Other items
SSAP 1 requires that the following should be disclosed separately by way of note:

- Loans to associated companies.
- Loans from associated companies.
- Balances in current account if material (which would normally be included as part of current assets or liabilities, as appropriate).

9.42 The cost of the investment comprises two elements:
1. The goodwill or premium paid when the investment is acquired; and
2. The underlying net assets.

9.43 The value of either one or both of these may be impaired and the following is the treatment proposed by SSAP 1:
(a) Where there is a permanent impairment in value of the goodwill element, this should be written down and the amount written off in the accounting period should be separately disclosed.

UNDERSTANDING ACCOUNTING STANDARDS

(b) Where there is an impairment in value of underlying net assets, no additional provision will be required in consolidated accounts as provision will already have been made in the accounts of the associated company, and its results will then have been incorporated in the consolidated accounts. A situation may arise where the impairment in the value of the assets is such as to reduce their value to less than the fair value recorded in the consolidated accounts but more than their book value in the accounts of the associated company. In this case, a provision for loss of value will be required in the consolidated accounts.

Deficiency of net assets in associated company

9.44 A deficiency of net assets may arise because the associated company has continually made losses. Since the investing company's liability is restricted to any amounts unpaid on the shares it holds, a question arises as to whether the equity method should be applicable when the associated company is making losses. SSAP 1 states that where the investing company regards this investment as being a long-term investment, it will usually support the associated company by way of loans or by way of an agreement, either formal or informal. In such cases, the investing company should continue to use the equity method and reflect its share of the deficiency of net assets in its consolidated financial statements.

EXAMPLE

H plc acquired 40 per cent of the share capital of A plc many years ago at a cost of £60,000 when A plc's reserves amounted to £30,000.

A plc's balance sheet at 31 December 19X7 and profit and loss account for the year ended 31 December 19X7 are as follows:

	£'000	£'000
Balance sheet (summary)		
Fixed Assets		240
Current Assets		230
		470
CREDITORS (Amounts faling due within one year)		
Trade Creditors	120	
Current account with H plc	30	
Dividends payable	60	
		(210)
		260
Share capital		100
Reserves		160
		260

Profit and loss account

Profit on ordinary activities before tax	200
Taxation	100
Profit on ordinary activities after tax	100
Proposed dividends	60
Retained profit	40
Balance brought forward	120
Balance carried forward	160

H PLC – *Individual company accounts*
Balance Sheet as at 31 December 19X7
1. *Fixed Assets*
    Investments – Shares in associated company
    Investment in A plc   60

2. *Current Assets*
    Dividends receivable from associated company*   24
    Amounts owed by associated company   30

Profit and Loss Account for the year ended 31 December 19X7

Turnover	x
Income from shares in associated company	24*
Profit on ordinary activities before taxation	x

*This would normally be grossed up in accordance with SSAP 8.

H PLC – *Consolidated accounts*
Consolidated Balance Sheet as at 31 December 19X7   £'000
1. *Fixed Assets*
    Investments
    Shares in associated company   112
    (i) proportion of net assets (40% × £260)   104
    (ii) premium paid on acquisition*   8
                                                                              112

* premium paid on acquisition:
Cost of investment   60
Less: 40% × (share capital and preacquisition reserve)
i.e. 40% (100 + 30)   (52)
premium paid on acquisition   8

2. *Current Assets*
    Dividends receivable from associated company   24
    Amounts owed by associated company   30

A note to group reserves would indicate that the investing group's share of the post-acquisition accumulated reserves amounted to £52,000 (40% × (160,000–30,000)).

Consolidated Profit and Loss Account for the year ended 31 December 19X7

	£'000	£'000
Turnover		x
Share of profits of associated company (40% × £200,000)		80
Profit on ordinary activities before taxation		x
Taxation		
Group	x	
Share of tax of associated company (40% × £100,000)	40	
		x
Profit on ordinary activities after taxation		x
Retained profit for the year		x
Retained in Holding company		x
Retained in Subsidiary companies		x
Retained in Associated company (40% × £40,000)		16
		x

Other points

1. Coterminous dates and consistent accounting policies

9.45 The amounts included in an investor's consolidated accounts for its associated companies should be extracted from accounts of the associated company which are, as far as possible, drawn up for the same period and to the same date as those of the investing group, and in which the same accounting policies as those applied by the investing group have been adopted.

2. Unrealised profits

9.46 Adjustments should be made to exclude from the investing group's accounts such items as unrealised profits on stocks transferred to or from associated companies.

3. Restrictions on distributions

9.47 If there are significant restrictions on the ability of an associated company to distribute its retained profits (other than those shown as non-distributable) because of statutory, contractual or exchange control restrictions, the extent of the restrictions should be indicated.

4. Minority interests

9.48 Where the investment in an associated company is held by a subsidiary in which there are minority interests, the minority interests shown in the consolidated financial statements of the group should include the minority share of the subsidiary's interest in the results and net assets of the associated company.

5. Investments by associated companies

9.49 Where an associated company itself has subsidiary or associated companies, the results and net assets to be dealt with in the investing group's consolidated financial statements are its attributable proportion of the results and net assets of the group (including the appropriate proportion of the results and net assets of its associated companies) of which the associated company is the holding company.

6. Loss of status as associated company

9.50 When an investment in a company ceases to fall within the definition of an associated company, it should be stated in the consolidated balance sheet of the investing group at the carrying amount under the equity method at that date. However, the carrying value should be adjusted if dividends are subsequently paid out of profits earned prior to the change of status. Provision should be made against the investment if there has been an impairment in value.

7. Effective date of acquisition or disposal

9.51 The effective date for both acquisition and disposal of an interest, or any portion of an interest, in an associated company should be the earlier of:
(a) the date on which consideration passes; or
(b) the date on which an offer becomes unconditional.

This applies even if the acquiring company has the right under the agreement to share in the profits of the acquired business from an earlier date.

8. Disclosure of particulars of associated companies

9.52 The names of the principal associated companies should be disclosed in the financial statements of the investing group showing for each of these associated companies:

(a) the proportion of the number of the issued shares of each class held by the investing group; and
(b) an indication of the nature of its business.

Arguments for and against the use of equity method for associated companies

Arguments for

9.53 In the past, the investments in associated companies were accounted on the basis of the cost method. SSAP 1 in its explanatory note states that where a company conducts an important part of its business through the medium of other companies, the mere disclosure of dividend income (or mere inclusion of dividend income alone) from these companies is unlikely to give adequate information regarding the sources of their income and the manner in which their funds are being employed. The equity method is generally advocated today as an intermediate method between full consolidation of subsidiaries under the effective control of the holding company's board of directors (so that they are effectively extensions of the holding company's business), and the cost method (where it is treated as a pure income producing investment). Neither the consolidation method nor the cost method are appropriate for an associated company because of the investing company's relationship with it. Since the investing company exercises a significant influence over financial and operating policy decisions (including dividend policy) but does not control them the equity method seems to be most appropriate in accordance with the rule of substance over form. The economic reality is that the investing company can exercise a significant influence. However, to be able to convert these profits into dividends, the investing company would need control over the associated company.

9.54 Because the investing company is in a position to exercise significant influence over the associated company, income from the associated company should be accounted for on an earnings, instead of dividend, basis. The investing company is in a position to influence the level of dividend, and it may have some effect on its earnings. Hence, its proportion of those earnings is a more realistic measure of its income from the investment than is the dividend only. The case is even stronger when the associated company makes a loss, since the mere absence of a dividend does not constitute adequate disclosure of impairment of the investing company's interest, for which it may bear some responsibility.

9.55 The importance today of earnings per share as an item of financial information (especially as a component of the price/earnings ratio) makes it essential to include in the calculation the relevant portion of the earnings of associated companies.

9.56 The equity method of valuing the investment in the consolidated balance sheet is helpful to the user of the financial statements, as conveying an idea of the underlying net assets of the associated company, including revaluations and goodwill.

Arguments against

9.57 The accounts should be prepared in accordance with the legal form rather than the substance. The investment should be recorded at cost and income should be recognised on dividends received and receivable basis. The investing company does not control the earnings or net assets.

9.58 Since whether or not the investing company exercises a significant influence is subjective, it could lead to manipulation of results – especially earnings per share.

9.59 Since the amount stated on the balance sheet of the investing company for an associated company is neither cost nor market value, it is a meaningless figure.

9.60 The equity method, which requires investing company's share of earnings to be recognised in the consolidated profit and loss account, may give the impression that these earnings are realised.

9.61 The equity method information ought to be given in the notes, leaving the accounts themselves to treat the investment on a dividend/cost basis.

Absence of consolidated accounts

9.62 When the investing company is itself a wholly owned subsidiary, there is no requirement to prepare consolidated accounts. SSAP 1 in this

UNDERSTANDING ACCOUNTING STANDARDS

case gives the investing company a specific exemption from the use of the equity method in respect of its associated company as this will normally be given in the consolidated accounts of the ultimate holding company.

9.63 A company which does not have a subsidiary company but has an associate will not prepare consolidated accounts. In such a case, SSAP 1 gives two alternatives in respect of both the profit and loss account and the balance sheet:

(a) The equity method information would be incorporated in additional statements which should be headed in such a way that they clearly indicate that they include the associated companies on the basis of equity accounting.
(b) The equity method information may be given by adding it in supplementary form to the company's profit and loss account and balance sheet in such a way that the company's share of profits of the associated companies is not treated as realised for the purposes of the CA 1985.

CA 1985 and the Equity Method

9.64 In British law, the equity method is recognised in the CA 1985 (Schedule 4 para. 65). However, the CA does not define the equity method. Notwithstanding the general obligation to consolidate subsidiaries, the consolidated accounts prepared by a holding company may deal with an investment of any member of the group in the shares of any other body corporate by way of the equity method of accounting in any case where it appears to the holding company's directors that the body corporate is so closely associated with any member of the group as to justify the use of that method in dealing with investments by that or any other member of the group in the shares of that body corporate.

9.65 The CA 1985 calls for certain separate disclosures in respect of what it terms 'related companies'. 'Related companies' are defined in the Act as follows:

1. 'Any body corporate (other than one which is a group company in relation to that company) in which that company holds on a long-term basis a qualifying capital interest for the purpose of securing a contribution to that company's own activities by the exercise of any control or influence arising from that interest.'
2. 'Qualifying capital interest' means an interest in shares comprised in the equity share capital of that company of a class carrying rights to vote in

all circumstances at general meetings of the company and 'equity share capital' has the meaning given by Section 744 of the Act.

3. Where —

(a) a company holds a qualifying capital interest in the other company; and
(b) the nominal value of any relevant shares in the other company held by the company is 20 per cent or more of the nominal value of all relevant shares in the other company.

9.66 The definition of a related company is wider than that of an associated company. The definition of the related company does not specify the degree of influence required. Consequently, a company may be a related company without being an associated company, but if it is an associated company it will almost always be a related company. The items which should be separately disclosed in respect of related companies under the formats given in the CA 1985 are:

Profit and Loss Account
Income from shares in related companies.
Balance Sheet

(a) shares in related companies;
(b) loans to related companies;
(c) amounts owed by related companies;
(d) amounts owed to related companies.

Notes: Disclosure of

(a) the aggregate capital and reserves; and
(b) the profit or loss for the year.

This requirement does not apply where the investment is included in the accounts by way of the equity method.

Questions

1. The accountancy profession has developed a range of techniques to measure and present the effect on one company owning shares in another company.
Required:
Briefly describe each of these techniques and how the resulting information may best be presented.
2. The equity method of valuing certain forms of investment made by one company in another has been in common use since the early 1970s.

Required:
(a) Define concisely the term 'equity method' and outline the accounting procedures by which it is applied.
(b) Describe the present position regarding the use of the method, as referred to in the law and in SSAPs 1 and 14.
(c) Assess the validity of the equity method as an alternative to other modes of accounting for the relevant investments.

Chapter Ten

Accounting for Investments (2): SSAP 14: Group accounts

SSAP 14 requirements

10.1 SSAP 14 requires that 'a holding company should prepare group accounts in the form of a single set of consolidated financial statements covering the holding company and its subsidiary companies, at home and overseas'.

10.2 As discussed in Chapter 9, S229 of the CA 1985 states that the investing company is required to prepare group accounts if it has at the end of its financial year a subsidiary company or companies. Group accounts are the financial statements of the group. The difference between the legal requirements and the SSAP 14 requirement is that the Act requires the investing company with a subsidiary company or companies to prepare group accounts, allowing a variety of methods of so doing (see Chapter 9), whereas SSAP 14 requires that the investing company should prepare consolidated statements, which is only one way of preparing group accounts, and which presents the information contained in the separate financial statements of a holding company and its subsidiaries as if they were the financial statements of a single entity.

Definitions

10.3 Holding company and subsidiary company have statutory definitions and are as follows:

Subsidiary company: A company shall be deemed to be a subsidiary company if, but only if,
(a) that other either:
  (i) is a member of it and controls the composition of its Board of Directors; or
  (ii) holds more than half in nominal value if its equity share capital; or
(b) the first mentioned company is a subsidiary of any company which is that other's subsidiary (S229 CA 1985).

Holding company: A company is a holding company of another if, but only if, that other is its subsidiary as defined above.

Group is a holding company and its subsidiaries.

UNDERSTANDING ACCOUNTING STANDARDS

Consolidated financial statements: One form of group accounts which presents the information contained in the separate financial statements of a holding company and its subsidiaries as if they were the financial statements of a single entity.

10.4 The definition of a subsidiary company has three parts to it and these are explained below:

1. One company (H) holds more than half (in nominal value) of the equity share capital of another (S):

$$H \\ | \\ S$$

S is a subsidiary of H (its holding company). Since the term equity share capital may include non-voting ordinary shares, it is possible for H to own more than half the equity capital of S and yet not be able to control S. S is legally a subsidiary of H. However, in such circumstances it may be necessary to present the group accounts in an alternative form from the single consolidated balance sheet and consolidated profit and loss account.

2. One company T is a subsidiary of another company S which in turn is a subsidiary of H. T is referred to as a sub-subsidiary. A possible situation falling within the definition is:

$$H \\ |\ 60\% \\ S \\ |\ 70\% \\ T$$

T is a subsidiary of H even though H's effective stake is only 42 per cent (60 per cent of 70 per cent). In this case, the CA requires two sets of group accounts:

(i) H group comprising H, S and T;
(ii) S group comprising S and T.

If, however, H owns 100 per cent of S (i.e. S is a wholly-owned subsidiary of H), then the CA 1985 states that group accounts are not required for S group.

3. One company H is a member of, and controls the composition of the board of directors of another company S.

Two examples may illustrate this point:

EXAMPLE 1

H owns 20% of S and 60% of K
K owns 35% of S

H → 20% to S, 60% to K; K → 35% to S

ACCOUNTING FOR INVESTMENTS (2)

H is a member of S by virtue of its 20 per cent shareholding. H can control the composition of the board of directors by virtue of its 20 per cent holding in S and the 35 per cent of the votes of S held through a partly owned subsidiary K. S is a subsidiary even though H's effective equity share is only 41 per cent [20 per cent + (60 per cent × 35 per cent)].

EXAMPLE 2
The share capital of S Ltd consists of:

	£
1,000 £1 voting ordinary shares	1,000
1,000 £1 non-voting ordinary shares	1,000
	2,000

H owns 600 £1 voting ordinary shares and 100 £1 non-voting ordinary shares. Therefore H owns 35 per cent of the total equity share capital of S (which is less than 50 per cent of the total equity share capital of S). But H is a member of S and does control the composition of the board of directors of S (by virtue of owning more than 50 per cent of the voting ordinary shares). Therefore, S is a subsidiary of H and S should be consolidated in the usual way.

10.5 Reasons for preparing consolidated accounts

1. Each company within the group is a separate legal entity. As far as the investing company is concerned all it has is shares in the subsidiary or subsidiaries. However, consolidated financial statements, which present financial information concerning the group as if it is a single enterprise without regard for the legal boundaries of the separate legal entities, are required when the investing company controls the subsidiary company or companies. This is in accordance with the principle of substance taking precedence over form. The commercial or economic reality is that the investing company *controls* the net assets of the subsidiary or subsidiaries even though legally it does not *own* them.

2. The present and potential shareholders, employees, customers and, in the same circumstances, creditors of the parent company are concerned with the fortunes of the entire group and this information can best be provided by preparing consolidated financial statements which give the results of operations and the financial position of the group as a whole.

10.6 Arguments against preparing consolidated financial statements

1. The financial statements should be prepared in accordance with the legal form (rather than perceived commercial or economic reality) in order to avoid subjective and inconsistent judgments on the nature of such 'reality'.
2. As discussed earlier, legally one company may be a subsidiary of another but this other company may not necessarily control this subsidiary company.
3. Where the group is very large it may be difficult to determine whether a company is a subsidiary or not.
4. The aggregation of accounting information in the form of consolidated accounts of the investing company and its subsidiaries may allow management to hide information that it does not want published. For example, management may wish to hide the fact that certain companies within the group are being operated at a loss, or are insolvent, for fear that they will be criticised by the shareholders for managerial inefficiency. This could be concealed by using profitable or solvent companies within the group to cover up the results of loss-making or insolvent companies within the group.
5. The creditors of an insolvent subsidiary may believe that they will be compensated by the holding company if the insolvent subsidiary is allowed to go into liquidation.

Exclusion from consolidation

1. CA 1985

10.7 (a) Section 229(2) of the CA 1985 states that group accounts are not required 'if at the end of the financial year, the holding company is the wholly-owned subsidiary of another body corporate in Great Britain'.

(b) Section 229(3) of the CA 1985 states that group accounts need not deal with a subsidiary if the company's directors are of the opinion that:
  (i) it is *impracticable*, or would be of *no real value* to the company's members, in view of the *insignificant amounts involved*, or
  (ii) it would *involve expense or delay out of proportion* to the value to members, or
  (iii) the result would be *misleading*, or *harmful* to the business of the company or any of its subsidiaries, or
  (iv) the *business of the holding company and that of the subsidiary are so*

different that they cannot reasonably be treated as a single undertaking; and, if the directors are of that opinion about each of the company's subsidiaries, group accounts are not required.
(c) Section 229(4) of the CA 1985 states that the approval of the Secretary of State is required for not dealing in group accounts with a subsidiary on the ground that the result would be harmful or on the ground of the difference between the business of the holding company and that of the subsidiary.

10.8 The reasons for exclusion stated in the Act can be explained as follows:

Consolidation of a subsidiary at an early stage of development would be 'of no real value'. The same would apply to dormant or inactive subsidiary. A subsidiary in a distant country might be left out because of 'disproportionate expense or delay' in obtaining the latest accounts. Consolidation of 'dissimilar businesses' might be meaningless, and thus 'misleading', if their asset structures are incompatible (as with an exempt insurance company in a trading group). Consolidation and disclosure of a subsidiary based in a country which is at war with the country of domicile could be 'harmful to the business'.

2. SSAP 14

10.9 Whilst the CA refers to exclusion from group accounts, SSAP 14 refers only to exclusion from consolidation. The reasons stated in the CA for exclusion from group accounts are subjective and have often led to variety in accounting practices among companies accounting for similar situations. SSAP 14 remedies this situation by defining more closely the reasons that would justify exclusion of a subsidiary from consolidation.

Reasons and accounting treatment for a subsidiary excluded from consolidation

(a) 'Dissimilar activities'

10.10 SSAP 14: 'A subsidiary should be excluded from consolidation if its activities are so dissimilar from those of other companies within the group that consolidated financial statements would be misleading and that information for the holding company's shareholders and other users of the statements would be better provided by presenting separate financial statements for such a subsidiary.'

10.11 This is also one of the exclusions listed in the CA. Consolidation of a subsidiary company which computes its profits and prepares its accounts on a fundamentally different basis ('dissimilar business') from those of other companies within the group might be meaningless, and thus misleading. The main examples of this are 'exempt' banks or insurance companies which are part of a trading group.

10.12 Where companies within the group carry on a wide range of very diverse activities, it is relatively unusual for subsidiary or subsidiaries not to be consolidated. The CA 1985 requires the accounts to disclose an analysis of turnover and pre-tax profit by different classes of business.

Accounting treatment

10.13 The subsidiary company excluded from consolidation on the above grounds should be included in the consolidated financial statements under the equity method of accounting. The use of equity method would give the same group earnings per share as would the consolidation method. In addition, SSAP 14 requires that the group accounts should include separate financial statements of the subsidiary which has been excluded from consolidation.

10.14 The requirement to include the separate financial statements of the subsidiary which has been excluded from consolidation is in accordance with the provision in the CA 1985 (S229) which deals with alternative ways of preparing group accounts (see p. 184). The separate statements may be combined with the financial statements of other subsidiaries with similar operations, if appropriate.

(b) 'Lack of control'

10.15 SSAP 14: 'The holding company, although owning directly or through other subsidiaries more than half the equity share capital of the subsidiary, either:
 (i) does not own share capital carrying more than half the votes; or
 (ii) has contractual or other restrictions imposed on its ability to appoint the majority of the Board of Directors.'

This is best illustrated as follows.
EXAMPLE
S has the following equity shares in issue:
 100,000 ordinary voting NV £1 shares; and
 100,000 ordinary non-voting NV £1 shares.
H has acquired 45,000 ordinary voting shares and 65,000 ordinary non-voting shares. Therefore H holds 55 per cent of the issued ordinary shares. Legally, S is a subsidiary of H but H does not control S. In this type

of situation it would be misleading to consolidate S as it does not fit into the traditional concept of a group as a single economic unit.

Accounting treatment

10.16 Where a subsidiary is excluded from consolidation on the grounds of lack of effective control, it should be dealt with in the consolidated financial statements:

either:
(i) under the equity method of accounting if in all other respects it satisfies the criteria for treatment as an associated company under SSAP 1 (see Chapter 9)
or, if these conditions are not met,
(ii) as an investment at cost or valuation less any provision required.

(c) 'Severe restrictions'

10.17 SSAP 14: 'The subsidiary operates under severe restrictions which significantly impair control by the holding company over the subsidiary's assets and operations for the foreseeable future'.

10.18 This is another example of 'misleading effect'. This type of a situation may arise if an overseas subsidiary's management is severely constrained or interfered with by the overseas government, or its business is disrupted by serious disorders in the country concerned. To justify the exclusion of a subsidiary the restrictions must be 'severe' and expected to persist for the foreseeable future.

Accounting treatment

10.19 The subsidiary concerned would have been consolidated prior to the severe restrictions coming into existence. SSAP 14 requires that the amount of the group's investment in the subsidiary should be stated in the balance sheet at the amount at which it would have been included under the equity method of accounting at the date the restrictions came into force. The group's share of post-acquisition reserves of the subsidiary company recognised up to the date the restrictions came into force will be unaffected by this treatment. SSAP 14 also requires that no further accruals should be made for the profits or losses of the subsidiary company excluded from consolidation and where there is a permanent loss in value of investment, a provision for loss should be made through the consolidated profit and loss account.

(d) 'Temporary control'

10.20 SSAP 14: 'Control is intended to be temporary'.
This is another example where consolidation would be 'misleading'. Where the control is temporary, the subsidiary company concerned cannot be treated as part of a single economic unit. The exclusion depends on the intention of the investing company at the time of acquisition and it must be clear from the start that the control will only be temporary. Consolidation should not cease where a decision has been taken to sell or dispose of a subsidiary already held for some time.

Accounting treatment

10.21 The temporary investment in the subsidiary should be stated in the consolidated balance sheet at the lower of cost and net realisable value.

Disclosure in respect of subsidiaries excluded from consolidation

1. Companies Act 1985

10.22 The CA refers to exclusion from group accounts. The following should be disclosed for the subsidiaries excluded from group accounts:
(a) reasons for exclusion;
(b) a statement showing any audit report qualifications;
(c) the amount of the investment in subsidiaries calculated by way of the equity method of valuation.

2. SSAP 14

10.23 In addition to the CA requirements, SSAP 14 requires that in respect of subsidiaries excluded from consolidation, the following information should be disclosed in the group accounts:
(a) the names of the principal subsidiaries excluded;
(b) any premium or discount on the acquisition (by comparison with the fair value of assets acquired) to the extent not written off.

Other disclosures under SSAP 14

1. 'Dissimilar activities'

10.24 Where a subsidiary is excluded from consolidation on the grounds of 'dissimilar activities', the group accounts should include separate financial statements of the subsidiary. The separate financial statements should include the information:

(a) a note of the holding company's interest;
(b) particulars of intra-group balances;
(c) the nature of transactions with the rest of the group;
(d) a reconciliation with the amount included in the consolidated financial statements for the group's investment in the subsidiary which should be stated under the equity method of accounting.

2. 'Severe restrictions'

10.25 Where a subsidiary is excluded from consolidation on the grounds of severe restrictions, the following should be disclosed:

(a) the net assets of the excluded subsidiary;
(b) the subsidiary's profits or losses for the period;
(c) any amounts included in the consolidated profit and loss account as regards:
   (i) dividends received;
   (ii) writing-down of the investment.

3. 'Lack of control' and 'temporary control'

10.26 There are no additional disclosures specifically required in these situations.

Mechanics of consolidation

10.27 This chapter is only concerned with the particular aspects of group accounts covered by SSAP 14 and does not deal with the mechanics of consolidation.

Accounting policies and periods

Accounting policies

10.28 Consolidated financial statements should be prepared on the basis of consistent accounting policies.

10.29 It will not always be possible for all companies in the group to adopt the same policies (e.g. foreign subsidiaries subject to local regulations). In these cases, appropriate consolidation adjustments should be made.

10.30 In very rare cases, it may not be practicable to make the appropriate adjustments and consequently the consolidated accounts will be based on different policies. SSAP 14 then requires disclosure of:

(a) the different accounting policies used (these policies must be generally acceptable),
(b) an indication of the amounts of the assets and liabilities involved and, where practicable, an indication of the effect on results and net assets of the adoption of policies different from those of the group, and
(c) the reasons for the different treatment.

Accounting periods and dates

10.31 Wherever practicable, the financial statements of all subsidiaries should be prepared to the same accounting date and for identical accounting periods as the holding company.

10.32 If this is not practicable, two alternative possibilities are:

(a) *Special financial statements.* Provided Department of Trade and Industry consent is obtained, it may be possible to use special financial statements drawn up to the same date as the holding company.

EXAMPLE

Holding company accounts cover the year ended 31 December 19X4. The audited accounts of a particular subsidiary cover the year ended 30 September 19X4. The holding company could require the subsidiary to prepare special statements – essentially a profit and loss account for the three months ended 31 December 19X4 and a balance sheet at that date. These statements need not be audited, but they must be sufficiently reliable for inclusion in the group accounts.

(b) *Consolidate to different year-ends.* In the above example this would involve consolidating a 30 September balance sheet for the subsidiary with a 31 December balance sheet for the rest of the group. Similar considerations would apply to the profit and loss accounts.

10.33 In the case of (b), it is necessary to consider (1) accounting adjustments and (2) disclosures.

1. *Accounting adjustments.* SSAP 14 requires that 'appropriate adjustments should be made to the consolidated financial statements for any abnormal transactions in the intervening period'. Forms requiring particular attention include:
    (i) inter-company transactions (particularly loans)
    (ii) major trading losses of the subsidiary
    (iii) disposals of significant fixed assets or parts of the business of the subsidiary.
2. *Disclosures.* SSAP 14 requires the following information to be disclosed for each principal subsidiary with a different accounting date:

(i) its name
(ii) its accounting date
(iii) the reason for using a different accounting date.

10.34 In addition, SSAP 14 requires disclosure of the length of the accounting period of a subsidiary where this differs from that of the holding company.

10.35 Reasons for having non-coterminous dates

1. The most common reason is to avoid undue delay in the presentation of the group accounts. The investing company may have subsidiaries which are based overseas and it may take time to obtain the accounts of these subsidiaries.
2. The different accounting date may be chosen by a particular subsidiary to correspond with its natural trading cycle. Where a subsidiary is involved in agricultural activities and is in a different climatical zone, the investing company may wish this subsidiary to have a different year end in order to avoid peak trading periods.

Changes in the composition of the group

1. Acquisitions

10.36 SSAP 14 states that 'the effective date for accounting for both the acquisition and disposal of a subsidiary should be the earlier of:

(a) the date on which the consideration passes; or
(b) the date on which an offer becomes, or is declared, unconditional'.

SSAP 14 makes it clear that the above principle applies even if the acquiring company has the right under the agreement to share in the profits of the acquired business from an earlier date. The above requirement means that the acquisition of a subsidiary company cannot be backdated (as was the practice before SSAP 14 was issued).

10.37 The acquisition can be deemed to be effective from 'the date on which an offer becomes or is declared unconditional' even though the consideration may not be formally passed until a later date.

10.38 SSAP 14 requires that 'when subsidiaries are purchased, the purchase consideration should be allocated between the underlying net tangible and intangible assets other than goodwill on the basis of the fair value to the acquiring company. If this is not done by means of adjusting the values in the books of the acquired company, it should be done on consolidation. Any difference between the purchase consideration and the value ascribed to net tangible assets and identifiable assets such as trade marks, patents or development expenditure, will represent premium or discount on acquisition'.

10.39 In the investing company's books, the investment in the subsidiary should be recorded at the cost to the investing company, which is the fair value of the consideration given. If the consideration is in the form of an issue of shares by the acquiring company, the cost will be the market value of the shares issued. If the acquiring company is a quoted company, the market value may be easy to ascertain. However, if it is a private company, market value will have to be determined by reference to earnings or dividends. Section 130 of CA 1985 requires that where the value ascribed to shares issued exceeds their nominal value, the excess should be recorded as share premium.

10.40 The purchase consideration is made up of two components:

(a) net tangible and intangible assets other than goodwill, and
(b) premium or (discount) on acquisition.

SSAP 14 requires that on the date of acquisition fair values should be ascribed to net tangible and intangible assets.

10.41 The reason for this is that fair value is the cost to the group and the treatment is consistent with the historical cost convention. The difference between the fair value of purchase consideration and the fair value of net tangible and identifiable intangible assets, like trade marks, patents or development costs, will represent premium or discount on acquisition. If the original book values were used, this would distort the consolidated balance sheet by stating group assets at less than their true cost to the group. Also the goodwill element of the purchase consideration would be overstated. In addition, any profits arising on the sale of these assets would be available for distribution to the shareholders of the acquiring company, even though some of these profits may be pre-acquisition profits.

10.42 The consolidation will begin from the date of acquisition and, in the year of acquisition of a subsidiary, will include only those profits (or losses) of the subsidiary earned after the effective date of acquisition. The pre-acquisition reserves will be capitalised.

Disclosure

10.43 SSAP 14 simply states that 'in the case of material additions to ... the group, the consolidated financial statements should contain sufficient information about the results of subsidiaries acquired ... to enable shareholders to appreciate the effect on the consolidated results'.

10.44 This rather vague requirement of SSAP 14 leaves it to each company to decide how much information to disclose.

EXAMPLE

Holt Ltd. acquired 90 per cent of the ordinary share capital of Stop Ltd. on 31 March 19X4. The purchase consideration consisted of 300,000 £1 shares in Holt, issued at 150p per share.

The following information relates to the two companies. For simplicity, certain of the information is summarised, and information regarding other subsidiaries has been excluded. All assets of Stop are considered to be at fair value as regards Holt.

Draft profit and loss accounts for the year ended 31 December 19X4	Holt £	Stop £
Turnover	2,000,000	600,000
Cost of sales	(960,000)	(240,000)
Distribution costs	(103,000)	(30,000)
Administrative expenses	(205,000)	(90,000)
Dividends from Stop	72,000	–
Taxation	(410,000)	(100,000)
Dividends proposed	(250,000)	(80,000)
Retained profit	144,000	60,000
Balance at 1/1/X4	974,000	305,000
	1,118,000	365,000

Draft balance sheets as at 31 December 19X4	£	£
Ordinary share capital	800,000	100,000
Share premium	150,000	–
Profit and loss account	1,118,000	365,000
10% debenture stock	350,000	–
Current liabilities	432,000	133,000
Proposed dividends	250,000	80,000
	3,100,000	678,000

	£	£
Tangible fixed assets	2,014,000	473,000
Investment in Stop	450,000	–
Current assets	564,000	205,000
Divided receivable	72,000	–
	3,100,000	678,000

Treatment of proposed dividend of Stop
In the draft profit and loss account of Holt, Holt's share (90% × £80,000 = £72,000) of the dividend has been treated as post-acquisition. Clearly, this is not the case. The holding company's separate legal accounts must apportion the dividend receivable between:

	£
Post-acquisition 9/12 × £72,000	54,000
Pre-acquisition 3/12 × £72,000	18,000
	72,000

The correct treatment in the separate (as opposed to consolidated) accounts of Holt is:

	£
Dr dividend receivable	72,000
Cr profit and loss account	54,000
Cr investment in subsidiary	18,000

So the correcting journal entry required is:

	£
Dr profit and loss account	18,000
Cr investment in subsidiary	18,000

Consolidated balance sheet workings

Adjustment (Consolidation Goodwill) Account

	£		£
Cost of investment	450,000	Ordinary share capital	90,000
less pre-acquisition dividend	(18,000)	Profit & loss reserves (see working)	288,000
		Goodwill on consolidation	54,000
	432,000		432,000

ACCOUNTING FOR INVESTMENTS (2)

Calculation of reserves at acquisition

	£
Balance at 1/1/X4	305,000
Profit after tax 1/1/X4–31/3/X4 (3/12 × 140,000)	35,000
Pre-acquisition part of proposed dividend (3/12 × 80,000)	(20,000)
Adjusted reserves at acquisition	320,000

Group share 90% × £320,000 = £288,000

Profit and Loss Account (reserves) of Stop

	£		£
Pre-acquisition (adjustment)	288,000	Balance	365,000
MI (10% × 365,000)	36,500		
Consol. res. (balance)	40,500		
	365,000		365,000

Minority Shareholders' Interest (MI)

	£		£
Balance c/d	46,500	Ordinary share capital	10,000
		Reserves	36,500
	46,500		46,500

Consolidated Reserves

	£		£
Balance c/d	1,140,500	Holt (1,118,000 – 18,000)	1,100,000
		Stop	40,500
	1,140,500		1,140,500

Dividend Receivable

	£		£
Balance	72,000	Contra	72,000

Dividend Payable

	£		£
Contra	72,000	Balance	80,000
Balance c/d			
(= minority interest)	8,000		
	80,000		80,000

215

UNDERSTANDING ACCOUNTING STANDARDS

Consolidated balance sheet as at 31 December 19X4

	£	£	£
Fixed assets			
* Intangible assets – Goodwill on consolidation			54,000
Tangible assets			2,487,000
			2,541,000
Current assets		769,000	
Current liabilities	565,000		
Proposed dividends			
Holt	250,000		
Minority shareholders	8,000		
		823,000	
Net current liabilities			(54,000)
Total assets less current liabilities			2,487,000
10% debenture stock			(350,000)
Minority shareholders' interest			(46,500)
			2,090,500
		£	£
Capital and reserves			
Called-up share capital			800,000
Share premium account		150,000	
Profit and loss account		1,140,500	
			1,290,500
			2,090,500

* Note: There are two alternative treatments for Goodwill under SSAP 22:
(i) 'Immediate write-off against reserves', or
(ii) 'Capitalise and amortise.'
A detailed discussion on this is in Chapter 11.

Consolidated profit and loss workings

		£
(i) Turnover	2,000,000 + 9/12 × 600,000 =	2,450,000
(ii) Cost of sales	960,000 + 9/12 × 240,000 =	1,140,000
(iii) Distribution costs	103,000 + 9/12 × 30,000 =	125,500
(iv) Administrative expenses	205,000 + 9/12 × 90,000 =	272,500
(v) Tax	410,000 + 9/12 × 100,000 =	485,000
(vi) Minority interest	10% × 9/12 × 140,000 =	10,500
(vii) Profit retained:		
Holding company	144,000 − 18,000 =	126,000
Subsidiary	90% × 9/12 × 60,000 =	40,500

ACCOUNTING FOR INVESTMENTS (2)

Consolidated profit and loss account for the year ended 31 December 19X4

	£	£
Turnover		2,450,000
Cost of sales		1,140,000
Gross profit		1,310,000
Distribution costs	125,500	
Administrative expenses	272,500	
		398,000
Profit on ordinary activities before taxation		912,000
Tax on profit on ordinary activities		485,000
Profit on ordinary activities after taxation		427,000
Minority interests		10,500
Profit for the financial year		416,500
Dividends proposed		250,000
Retained profit		166,500
By holding company	126,000	
By subsidiary	40,500	
	166,500	
Profit and loss account brought forward		974,000
Profit and loss account carried forward		1,140,500

Accounting policy note
Turnover and profits of subsidiaries acquired during the financial year are included from the date of acquisition.

Note to the financial statements
The following amounts are included within the respective consolidated profit and loss account headings in respect of newly acquired subsidiary, Stop Ltd.:

	£
Turnover	450,000
Profit on ordinary activities before tax	180,000
Taxation	75,000
Profit on ordinary activities after tax	105,000

2. Disposals

10.45 Where there is a material disposal, the consolidated profit and loss account should include:

(a) the subsidiary's results up to the date of disposal; and
(b) the gain or loss on the sale of the investment, being the difference at the time of the sale between:
  (i) the proceeds of the sale and
  (ii) the holding company's share of its net assets together with any premium (less any amounts written off) or discount on acquisition.

Holding company profit and loss account:

	£
Sale proceeds	X
Less: Cost of investment	(X)
Extraordinary gain or loss	X

Consolidated profit and loss account:

	£	£
Sale proceeds		X
Less:		
(i) Holding company's share of net assets per last balance sheet	X	
(ii) Holding company's share of after tax profits (less any dividends paid) of current year attributable to the group up to the date of sale	X	
		(X)
Extraordinary gain or loss		X

EXAMPLE

H Co. sold its investments in wholly-owned subsidiary S Co. (cost £400,000) for £750,000. The net assets of S Co. on the last balance sheet date were £520,000 and its profit after tax up to the date of sale was £50,000. S Co. did not pay any dividends in the year in which H Co. sold its shares in S Co.

Holding company profit and loss account

	£
Sale proceeds	750,000
Less: cost of investment	(400,000)
Extraordinary gain	350,000

Consolidated profit and loss account

	£	£
Sale proceeds		750,000
Less:		
(i) Holding company's share of net assets per last balance sheet	520,000	
(ii) Holding company's share of after tax profits of current year attributable to the group up to the date of sale	50,000	(570,000)
Extraordinary gain		180,000

Further considerations

1. Tax on sale of the shares

10.46 The tax would be based on the holding company (as opposed to group) gain. This would be deducted from the extraordinary gain or loss in the consolidated accounts.

2. Accounting policy note

10.47 Turnover and profits of subsidiaries disposed of during the financial year are included up to the date of disposal.

3. Material additions or disposals

10.48 In the case of material additions or disposals from the group, the consolidated financial statements should contain sufficient information about the results of the subsidiaries acquired or sold to enable shareholders to appreciate the effect on the consolidated results.

An example of this is as follows:

The following amounts are included within the respective consolidated profit and loss account headings in respect of the subsidiary disposed of during the year:

	£
Turnover	X
Profit on ordinary activities before tax	X
Taxation	X
Profit on ordinary activities after tax	X

4. Analysis of gain on sale of shares

10.49 It is important to distinguish between:
(i) the holding company profit and loss account which, prior to the date of sale, takes account of only dividends received, and

UNDERSTANDING ACCOUNTING STANDARDS

(ii) the consolidated profit and loss account which takes account of post-acquisition retained profit.

The extraordinary gain in the consolidated profit and loss account and the holding company's gain may be reconciled as follows:

	£
Extraordinary gain/(loss) Group	X
Plus:	
Holding company's share of post-acquisition retained profits of subsidiary at the start of the year	X
Plus:	
Holding company's share of current years profit after tax included in consolidated profit and loss account less dividends received by holding company	X
Extraordinary gain/(loss) – holding company	X

5. Analysis of retained profit and reserves (for disclosure purposes)

10.50

(a) Retained profit for the year:

	£	£
(i) Holding company		
– per its own accounts (excluding profit/(loss) on sale of shares)	X	
– profit/(loss) on sale of shares	X	
– Holding company's share of current year's profit after tax of subsidiary company sold included in the consolidated profit and loss account less dividends received by holding company	X	
		X
(ii) Other subsidiaries at the year end		X
(iii) Associated companies		X
		X

(b) Detailed analysis of reserves. Although not 'mandatory', it may be used in practice.

	Total	Holding company	Subsidiaries
	£	£	£
Balance at the start of the year	X	X	X
Retained for the year (see (a) above)	X	X	X
Change in composition of the group	—	X	(X)
Balance at the end of the year	X	X	X

Notes
1. The analysis of retained profit and reserves is on the assumption that the entire holding in the subsidiary company is sold. See the detailed example on later pages for partial disposal.
2. The adjustment for change in composition of the group relates to the holding company's share of post-acquisition reserves at the start of the year of the subsidiary company sold. These reserves were retained in the subsidiary company at the start of the year but are now included in the holding company's profit and loss account, i.e. as part of profit on sale of profits, therefore, a transfer is made in respect of subsidiary sold between reserves retained in subsidiaries and reserves retained in the holding company.

Comment on SSAP 14 requirement for the treatment of disposals of shares in a subsidiary company:

(a) Goodwill

10.51 The group policy regarding the treatment of the premium or discount on acquisition will also affect the profit or loss to the group.

(i) If the goodwill was carried as an asset in the consolidated balance sheet and amortised over its useful life, the unamortised amount will need to be eliminated on the disposal of the related investment. In the earlier example on p. 218, if the unamortised goodwill was £110,000, the group profit on disposal would be reduced to £70,000.
(ii) If the goodwill had been previously written off, the profit on sale by the group would be £180,000.

(b) Treatment of subsidiary company disposed of during the year

10.52 (a) Results up to the date of disposal will be included as part pre-tax profits and will therefore affect earnings per share (EPS).
(b) The gain or loss on sale will be an extraordinary item (and consequently excluded from EPS).

10.53 Before SSAP 14, it was reasonably common for the consolidated results to include the results of companies which were subsidiaries at the end of the accounting period, with the results of subsidiaries disposed of during the accounting period being excluded apart from any dividends receivable declared out of profits of the period to the date of sale. This distorted the group results in some cases – if the results of a subsidiary which had incurred material losses during a year, but which had been sold just before the year-end, were excluded from the trading results of the group for the year it could be argued that the accounts were not showing a true and fair view as the directors of a holding company were responsible for the companies under their control until a sale is agreed and they should account for the results of that stewardship in the consolidated profit and loss account.

10.54 Three main arguments have been put forward for not accounting for the results of subsidiaries after the date of disposal:
(a) It is impracticable, because once the ownership of a company has been transferred, the vendor is no longer in a position to obtain information on the results up to the date of sale.
(b) The disposal may be negotiated on the basis of the last published results, and in such cases the accounting treatment should reflect this.
(c) The consolidated profit and loss account should only include the results of the companies which will continue.

EXAMPLE 1: **Disposal of an entire shareholding in a subsidiary company**

10.55 Hook Ltd has two subsidiaries, Line Ltd and Sinker Ltd. Details of the original acquisitions are as follows:

	Date of Acquisition	Cost of Acquisition	Reserves at Acquisition	Percentage of Ordinary Shares held
		£	£	
Line Ltd	19W3	370,000	230,000	90%
Sinker Ltd	19W7	122,000	56,000	70%

It is Hook Ltd's policy to write off any consolidation goodwill direct to reserves immediately on acquisition. All profits and losses accrue evenly on a time basis.

The draft financial statements for the three companies for the year 19X4 are as opposite:

ACCOUNTING FOR INVESTMENTS (2)

Draft Profit and Loss Account for the year ended 31 December 19X4

	Hook Ltd £	Line Ltd £	Sinker Ltd £
Turnover	2,400,000	890,000	720,000
Cost of sales and other expenses	(1,300,000)	(503,000)	(480,000)
Operating profit	1,100,000	387,000	240,000
Dividends received/receivable:			
Line	126,000	—	—
Sinker	21,000	—	—
	1,247,000	387,000	240,000
Taxation	(520,000)	(130,000)	(108,000)
	727,000	257,000	132,000
Dividends – paid (31/7/X4)	—	—	(30,000)
proposed	(500,000)	(140,000)	(60,000)
Retained profit	227,000	117,000	42,000
Balance b/fwd	935,000	700,000	370,000
Balance c/fwd	£1,162,000	£817,000	£412,000

Draft Balance Sheets at 31 December 19X4

	Hook Ltd £	Line Ltd £	Sinker Ltd £
Ordinary share capital (£1 shares)	500,000	150,000	100,000
Profit and loss account	1,162,000	817,000	412,000
Proceeds – Sale of Shares	450,000	—	—
Proposed dividend	500,000	140,000	60,000
Sundry liabilities	842,000	232,000	187,000
	3,454,000	1,339,000	759,000
Investment in Line	370,000	—	—
Investment in Sinker	122,000	—	—
Dividends receivable	126,000	—	—
Sundry assets	2,836,000	1,339,000	759,000
	3,454,000	1,339,000	759,000

Required:
(a) Consolidated profit and loss account for the year 31/12/19X4 and consolidated balance sheet on 31/12/19X4 on the assumption that £450,000 proceeds on sale of shares were for the disposal of Hooks entire shareholding in Sinker Ltd on 30/9/X4;

UNDERSTANDING ACCOUNTING STANDARDS

(b) Reconciliation between the gain or loss on the sale of shares in Sinker Ltd reported in the Consolidated profit and loss account and holding company profit and loss account;
(c) Analysis of retained profit for the year; and analysis of consolidated reserves on 31 December 19X4.

WORKINGS:
(i) Goodwill

Line Ltd.:	£	£
Cost of Shares		370,000
Less:		
90% ordinary share capital	135,000	
90% pre-acquisition reserves	207,000	342,000
Goodwill		28,000

Sinker Ltd.:	£	£
Cost of shares		122,000
Less:		
70% ordinary share capital	70,000	
70% pre-acquisition reserves	39,200	109,200
Goodwill		£12,800

(ii) Consolidated reserves brought forward on 1/1/19X4

	£	£
Hook Ltd		935,000
Line Ltd	700,000	
Less: pre-acquisition reserves	(230,000)	
	470,000	
Holding company's share	90%	423,000
Sinker Ltd	370,000	
Less: pre-acquisition reserves	(56,000)	
	314,000	
Holding company's share	70%	219,800
		1,577,800
Less: Goodwill written off:		
Line	28,000	
Sinker	12,800	(40,800)
Balance on 1/1/19X4		1,537,000

224

ACCOUNTING FOR INVESTMENTS (2)

(iii) Workings for the consolidated profit and loss account
(a) The disposal of entire shareholding in Sinker took place on 30/9/19X4. Therefore the results of Sinker up to 30/9/19X4 will be consolidated.
(b) Gain/Loss on disposal of shares in Sinker Ltd.

	£	£
Proceeds		450,000
Less: Group's share of net assets of Sinker on 30/9/X4 computed as follows:		
(i) Net assets on 1/1/19X4 (= ordinary share capital plus reserves on 1/1/19X4)	470,000	
(ii) Profit after tax to 30/9/X4 = 9/12 × £132,000	99,000	
(iii) Less: Dividends paid by Sinker on 31/7/X4	(30,000)	
	539,000	
Group's share	70%	(377,300)
Gain		72,700

(c) Minority interest in Profit and Loss account:
Line Ltd: 10% × Profit after Tax
= 10% × £257,000   25,700
Sinker Ltd: 30% × profit after tax to
30/9/19X4 = 30% × (9/12 × £132,000)   29,700
  55,400

(iv) Workings for the consolidated balance sheet:
(a) Since the entire shareholding in Sinker was disposed of on 30/9/19X4, Sinker will not be consolidated on 31/12/19X4.
(b) The dividends proposed by Sinker do not affect the group. Therefore ignore them.

	£
(c) Line: Proposed dividend	140,000
Less: Payable to minority interest (10%)	(14,000)
Group share	126,000
Already provided in Hooks' books	126,000
(d) Minority interest in Line:	£
10% × Ordinary share capital	15,000
10% × Reserves	81,700
	96,700

UNDERSTANDING ACCOUNTING STANDARDS

SOLUTION
(a) *Consolidated profit and loss account*

	£
Turnover (2,400,000 + 890,000 + 9/12 × 720,000)	3,830,000
Less: Cost of sales, etc. (1,300,000 + 503,000 + 9/12 × 480,000)	(2,163,000)
	1,667,000
Tax (520,000 + 130,000 + 9/12 × 108,000)	(731,000)
	936,000
Minority interest (see Working (iii)(c))	(55,400)
	880,600
Extraordinary gain (see Working (iii)(b)) (Tax ignored)	72,700
	953,300
Proposed dividends	(500,000)
Retained profit for the year	453,300
Balance b/fwd (see Working (ii))	1,537,000
Balance c/fwd	£1,990,300

Analysis of retained profit for the year:

	£	£
Retained in holding company:		
Per draft accounts	227,000	
Profit on sale of shares	72,700	
Profit from 1/1/X4–30/9/X4	48,300	
[70% × (9/12 × (132,000) − 30,000)]		348,000
Retained in subsidiary company:		
Line (90% × 117,000)		105,300
		£453,300

Disposal at 30/9/X4:

	£
Holding Company books:	
Proceeds	450,000
Less: Cost of shares	(122,000)
Gain	£328,000

226

ACCOUNTING FOR INVESTMENTS (2)

Reconciliation between the gain in the consolidated profit and loss account and holding company profit and loss account

	£	£
Gain – Group		72,700
Add: Share of post-acquisition retained profits of Sinker Ltd on 1/1/X4:		
70% (370,000 – 56,000)	219,800	
Less: Goodwill written off	(12,800)	207,000
Add: Share of profits of Sinker Ltd from 1/1/X4–30/9/X4 included in consolidated P&L A/c less dividends received:		
70% (⁹⁄₁₂ × £132,000 – 30,000)		48,300
HOLDING COMPANY – GAIN		£328,000

Note:
Throughout the period of ownership of shares in Sinker, the holding company has been accounting for income from Sinker on the basis of dividends received and receivable. The group accounts, by contrast, consolidate the results as a whole.

When the holding company disposes of its shares in the subsidiary part of the proceeds will relate to the holding company's share of post acquisition profits retained in the subsidiary, but which belong to the holding company. On disposal, therefore, this share of the subsidiary's undistributed profits become part of the holding company's realized profits.

(b) CONSOLIDATED BALANCE SHEET

	£	£
Sundry assets (2,836,000 + 1,339,000)		4,175,000
Less: Sundry liabilities		
(842,000 + 232,000)	1,074,000	
Dividends payable to Minority interest	14,000	
Proposed dividends	500,000	(1,588,000)
		2,587,000
Less: Minority interest (Working (iv) (d))		(96,700)
		£2,490,300
Ordinary share capital		500,000
Profit and loss account		1,990,300
		£2,490,300

(c) ANALYSIS OF RESERVES

	Total £	Holding company £	Subsidiaries £
Balance 1/1/X4	1,537,000	935,000	*602,000
Retained profit for year	453,300	**348,000	**105,300
Change in composition of group		***207,000	(207,000)
Balance 31/12/X4	£1,990,300	£1,490,000	£500,300

	£
* Line: 90% (700,000 − 230,000)	423,000
Sinker: 70% (370,000 − 56,000)	219,800
	642,800
Less: Goodwill	(40,800)
Brought forward	£602,000

** See analysis of retained profit for the year
*** See reconciliation between the gain in the consolidated profit and loss account and holding company profit and loss account.

CHECK:

		£
Holding Co.	Per draft accounts	1,162,000
	Profit on sale of shares	328,000
		£1,490,000
Line:	Per draft accounts	817,000
	Less: Pre-acquisition	(230,000)
	Post-acquisition	£587,000
	Group share (90%)	528,300
	Less: Goodwill	(28,000)
		£500,300

EXAMPLE 2: **Disposal of a part shareholding in a subsidiary company but the control is retained**

10.56 In the previous example, assume Hook sold part of its shareholding in Sinker, so that after the sale, the group interest was 60 per cent.
The proceeds of sale were £50,000.
The profit and loss account of Hook would show:

ACCOUNTING FOR INVESTMENTS (2)

	£	£
Operating profit		1,100,000
Dividends received/receivable:		
Line	126,000	
Sinker (interim)	21,000	
Sinker (final)	36,000	
(60% × £60,000)		183,000
		1,283,000
Taxation		(520,000)
Proposed dividend		(500,000)
		263,000
Balance at 1/1/X4		935,000
Balance at 31/12/X4		1,198,000

BALANCE SHEET	£
Ordinary share capital	500,000
Profit and loss account (1,162,000 + 36,000)	1,198,000
Proceeds of sale of shares	50,000
Proposed dividends	500,000
Sundry liabilities	842,000
	3,090,000
Investment in Line	370,000
Investment in Sinker	122,000
Dividends receivable (126,000 + 36,000)	162,000
Sundry assets [2,836,000 − 400,000]	2,436,000
	3,090,000

WORKINGS
(i) Goodwill (same as in EXAMPLE 1)

	£
Line	28,000
Sinker	12,800

(ii) Consolidated reserves brought forward on 1/1/19X4 (same as in EXAMPLE 1)   1,537,000

(iii) Workings for the consolidated profit and loss account:
(a) The holding in Sinker is reduced from 70% to 60% on 30/9/19X4. As

Sinker remains a subsidiary at the end of the year, full years' results of Sinker will be consolidated.

(b) Gain/Loss on disposal of shares in Sinker Ltd.

	£	£
Proceeds on disposal of 10% holding in Sinker		50,000
Less: Share of net assets of Sinker disposed of on 30/9/19X4 computed as follows:		
(i) Net assets on 1/1/19X4 (= Ordinary share capital plus reserves on 1/1/19X4)	470,000	
(ii) Profit after tax to 30/9/19X4 = 9/12 × £132,000	99,000	
(iii) Less: Dividends paid by Sinker on 31/7/19X4	(30,000)	
	539,000	
Group's share 10%		53,900
Loss		(3,900)

(c) Minority interest in Profit and loss account:

	£	£
Line: 10% × £257,000		25,700
Sinker: 30% × 9/12 × £132,000	29,700	
40% × 3/12 × £132,000	13,200	
		42,900
		68,600

(iv) Workings for the consolidated balance sheet:
(a) Sinker will be included in the consolidated balance sheet at the end of the year as Hook still has a 60% holding in it.
(b) Dividends

	£	£	Minority Interest £
Line: Proposed dividend	140,000		
Less: Payable to MI – 10%	(14,000)		14,000
Group share – 90%		126,000	
Sinker: Proposed dividend	60,000		
Less: Payable to MI – 40%	(24,000)		24,000
Group share – 60%		36,000	
Provided in Hook's accounts		162,000	
			38,000

ACCOUNTING FOR INVESTMENTS (2)

	£	£
(c) Minority interest:		
Line – (as in example 1)		96,700
Sinker: 40% × ordinary share capital	40,000	
40% × Reserves	164,800	
		204,800
		301,500

Consolidated profit and loss account

	£
Turnover (2,400,000 + 890,000 + 720,000)	4,010,000
Less: Cost of sales, etc. (1,300,000 + 503,000 + 480,000)	(2,283,000)
	1,727,000
Taxation (520,000 + 130,000 + 108,000)	(758,000)
	969,000
Minority interest (Workings (ii)(c))	(68,600)
	900,400
Extraordinary loss (ignore tax) (Workings (iii)(b))	(3,900)
	896,500
Proposed dividends	(500,000)
Retained profit for the year	396,500
Brought forward (Workings (ii)(d))	1,537,000
Carried forward	1,933,500

Analysis of retained profit for the year:

	£	£
Holding company		
Per draft accounts	263,000	
Loss on sale of shares	(3,900)	
Share of Sinker profit re 10% holding disposed of — 10% ×[(9/12 × 132,000) − 30,000]	6,900	
		266,000
Subsidiaries:		
Line: 90% × £117,000	105,300	
Sinker: 60% × £42,000	25,200	
		130,500
		396,500

Disposal at 30/9/X4
(a) Holding company books:

	£
Proceeds	50,000
Less: Cost of shares (10/70 × £122,000)	(17,429)
Gain	32,571

UNDERSTANDING ACCOUNTING STANDARDS

Reconciliation between the loss in the consolidated P&L A/c and gain in the holding company P&L A/c

	£	£
Loss – in Group accounts		(3,900)
Add: Share of post-acquisition reserves on 1/1/X4:		
10% (370,000 – 56,000)	31,400	
Less: Goodwill written off		
($^{10}/_{70}$ × £12,800)	(1,829)	
		29,571
Add: Share of profits from 1/1/X4–30/9/X4:		
10% [($^9/_{12}$ × £132,000) – 30,000]		6,900
Holding company gain		32,571

Consolidated balance sheet

	£	£
Sundry assets (2,436,000 + 1,339,000 + 759,000)		4,534,000
Sundry liabilities (842,000 + 232,000 + 187,000)	1,261,000	
Dividends to Minority interests	38,000	
Proposed dividends	500,000	
		(1,799,000)
		2,735,000
Less: Minority interest		(301,500)
		2,433,500
Ordinary share capital		500,000
Profit and Loss Account		1,933,500
		2,433,500

Analysis of reserves

	Total	Holding company	Subsidiaries
	£	£	£
Balance 1/1/X4	1,537,000	935,000	602,000
Retained profit	*396,500	266,000	130,500
Change in status of group companies	—	** 29,571	(29,571)
	1,933,500	1,230,571	702,929

232

ACCOUNTING FOR INVESTMENTS (2)

CHECK:		£
Holding company	per draft accounts	1,198,000
	+ Extra-ordinary item	32,571
subsidiaries		1,230,571

* See analysis of retained profit
** See reconciliation between the loss in the consolidated profit and loss account and gain in the holding company profit and loss account.

	£
Line: 90% (817,000 − 230,000) =	528,300
Sinker: 60% (412,000 − 56,000) =	213,600
	741,900
Less: Goodwill:	
Line	(28,000)
Sinker (12,800 − 1,829)	(10,971)
	702,929

EXAMPLE 3: Disposal of a part shareholding in a subsidiary company but associated company holding is retained

10.57 In the example 1, assume that Hook sells half of its holding for proceeds of £200,000. The remaining holding (= 35 per cent of total issued share capital of Sinker) is accounted for as an associated company.

HOOK LIMITED
Draft Profit and Loss account for the year ended 31/12/19X4

	£	£
Operating profit		1,100,000
Dividends		
Line	126,000	
Sinker (interim)	21,000	
Sinker (final)		
35% × £60,000	21,000	168,000
		1,268,000
Taxation		(520,000)
Proposed dividend		(500,000)
		248,000
Balance at 1/1/X4		935,000
Balance at 31/12/X4		1,183,000

233

UNDERSTANDING ACCOUNTING STANDARDS

Balance sheet on 31/12/19X4

	£
Ordinary share capital	500,000
Profit and Loss account	1,183,000
Proceeds of sale of shares	200,000
Proposed dividends	500,000
Sundry liabilities	842,000
	3,225,000

	£
Investments: Line	370,000
Sinker	122,000
Dividends receivable (126,000 + 21,000)	147,000
Sundry assets [2,836,000 − 250,000]	2,586,000
	3,225,000

SOLUTION
Workings:
(i) Goodwill (same as in example 1)

	£
Line	28,000
Sinker	12,800

(ii) Consolidated reserves brought forward on 1/1/19X4 (same as in example 1)   1,537,000

(iii) Workings for the consolidated profit and loss account:
(a) The remaining holding in Sinker from 1/10/19X4 = 35%. The results of Sinker will be consolidated up to 30/9/X4 and accounted for using the equity method as from 1/10/19X4.
(b) Gain/loss on disposal:

	£
Proceeds	200,000
Less: Share of net assets disposed:	
35% × £539,000 (see example 1)	(188,650)
Gain	£11,350

(c) Equity method from 1/10/X4 for Sinker:
Share of profits before tax: 35% × 3/12 × £240,000 = £21,000
Share of tax on share of profits: 35% × 3/12 × £108,000 = £ 9,450
(d) Turnover, cost of sales and minority interest – same as example 1 consolidated profit and loss account.
(iv) Workings for the consolidated balance sheet:

ACCOUNTING FOR INVESTMENTS (2)

(a) Minority interest in Line – same as example 1   £96,700
(b) Dividends payable to MI – same as example 1   £14,000
(c) Sinker Ltd will be recorded on the consolidated balance sheet as at 31/12/19X4 using the equity method.

Equity method at 31/12/19X4.
Proportion of net assets = 35% (759,000 – 60,000 – 187,000) = £179,200
OR

	£	£
Cost of 35% holding		61,000
Plus: Share of post-acquisition reserves:		
35% (412,000 – 56,000)	124,600	
Less: Goodwill written off		
($35/70 \times 12,800$)	(6,400)	
		118,200
		179,200

Consolidated profit and loss account

	£	£
Turnover		3,830,000
Cost of sales, etc.		(2,163,000)
		1,667,000
Share of profits of associated company		21,000
		1,688,000
Taxation:		
Group	731,000	
Associated company	9,450	
		740,450
		947,550
Minority interest		55,400
		892,150
Extraordinary gain on sales of shares		11,350
		903,500
Proposed dividends		500,000
Retained profit		403,500
Balance b/fwd		1,537,000
Balance c/fwd		1,940,500

Analysis of retained profit:

	£	£
Holding company:		
Per draft accounts	248,000	
Profit on sale of shares	11,350	
Sinker – share of profits to 30/9/X4		
35% × [(132,000 × 9/12) − 30,000]	24,150	
		283,500
Subsidiary company:		
90% × £117,000		105,300
Associated company:		
35% × £42,000		14,700
		403,500

Disposal at 30/9/X4:

	£
Holding company	
Proceeds	200,000
Less: Cost of shares (½ × £122,000)	(61,000)
Gain	£139,000

Reconciliation:	£	£
Extraordinary profit (group)		11,350
Add: Share of post-acquisition reserves on 1/1/X4		
35% × (370,000 − 56,000)	109,900	
Less: Goodwill written off		
35/70 × £12,800	(6,400)	
		103,500
Add: Share of profits from 1/1/X4–30/9/X4:		
35% [(9/12 × 132,000) − 30,000]		24,150
Extraordinary profit (Holding company).		139,000

ACCOUNTING FOR INVESTMENTS (2)

Consolidated balance sheet

	£	£
Sundry assets (2,586,000 + 1,339,000)		3,925,000
Shares in associated company – share of net assets		179,200
Sundry debtor – dividend receivable from Associated company (35% × £60,000)		21,000
		4,125,200
Sundry liabilities (842,000 + 232,000)	1,074,000	
Dividends payable to Minority interest	14,000	
Proposed dividend	500,000	(1,588,000)
		2,537,200
Less: Minority interest		(96,700)
		2,440,500
Ordinary share capital		500,000
Profit and Loss Account		1,940,500
		2,440,500

Analysis of reserves

	Total	H Co.	S Co.	A Co.
	£	£	£	£
Balance 1/1/X4	1,537,000	935,000	602,000	—
Retained profit*	403,500	283,500	105,300	14,700
Change in status of group companies**		103,500	(207,000)	103,500
Balance 31/12/X4	£1,940,500	£1,322,000	£500,300	£118,200

* See Consolidated Profit and Loss Account – Analysis of retained profit.
** See reconciliation between gain in the consolidated profit and loss account and Holding Company profit and loss account.

UNDERSTANDING ACCOUNTING STANDARDS

		£	£
Check:			
Holding company:	Per draft accounts	1,183,000	
	Plus profit on sale	139,000	1,322,000
Subsidiary company:	Per draft accounts	817,000	
	Less: Pre-acquisition reserves	(230,000)	
		587,000	
	Group share – 90%	528,300	
	Less: Goodwill	(28,000)	500,300
Associated company:	Per draft accounts	412,000	
	Less: Pre-acquisition reserves	(56,000)	
		356,000	
	Group share – 35%	124,600	
	Less: Goodwill	(6,400)	118,200

EXAMPLE 4: **Disposal of a part shareholding in a subsidiary company but a trade investment is retained**.
In the example 1, assume that Hook sells its holding in Sinker Limited so as to retain only 10%. The proceeds on disposal were £400,000. The remaining holding [= 10 per cent of total issued share capital of Sinker] is accounted for as a trade investment.

HOOK LIMITED
Draft Profit and Loss account for the year ended 31/12/19X4

	£	£
Operating profit		1,100,000
Dividends:		
Line	126,000	
Sinker (interim)	21,000	
Sinker (final) 10% × £60,000	6,000	
		153,000
		1,253,000
Taxation		(520,000)
Proposed dividend		(500,000)
		233,000
Balance 1/1/19X4		935,000
Balance 31/12/19X4		1,168,000

ACCOUNTING FOR INVESTMENTS (2)

Balance Sheet on 31/12/19X4

	£
Ordinary share capital	500,000
Profit and loss account	1,168,000
Proceeds of sale of shares	400,000
Proposed dividends	500,000
Sundry liabilities	842,000
	£3,410,000
Investments: Line	370,000
Sinker	122,000
Dividends receivable (126,000 + 6,000)	132,000
Sundry assets [2,836,000 − 50,000]	2,786,000
	£3,410,000

SOLUTION

Workings:

(i) Goodwill and consolidated reserves brought forward on 1/1/19X4 same as in example 1.

(ii) Workings for the consolidated profit and loss account:

(a) The remaining holding in Sinker from 1/10/19X4 = 10%. The results of Sinker will be consolidated up to 30/9/X4 and accounted for as a trade investment as from 1/10/19X4.

(b) Gain/loss on disposal

	£
Proceeds	400,000
Less: Share of net assets disposed 60% × £539,000 (see example 1)	(323,400)
	£76,600

(c) Turnover, cost of sales and minority interest same as example 1.

(iii) Workings for the consolidated balance sheet:

(a) Minority interest and dividends same as example 1.

(b) As from 1/10/19X4, the 10% investment in Sinker Ltd. will be recorded at cost plus share of post-acquisition reserves as at 30/9/X4, i.e. the investment will be recorded at 'equitised' amount which equals 10% × £539,000 = £53,900. The 'equitised' amount becomes the new cost.

Consolidated profit and loss account

	£	£
Turnover		3,830,000
Cost of sales, etc.		(2,163,000)
		1,667,000
Investment income		6,000
		1,673,000
Taxation		731,000
		942,000
Minority interest		55,400
		886,600
Extraordinary gain on sale of shares		76,600
		963,200
Proposed dividends		500,000
Retained profit		463,200
Balance brought forward		1,537,000
Balance carried forward		2,000,200

Consolidated balance sheet

	£	£
Sundry assets [2,786,000 + 1,339,000]		4,125,000
Investment in Sinker Ltd.		53,900
Sundry debtor – dividend receivable from a trade investment		6,000
		4,184,900
Sundry liabilities [842,000 + 232,000]	1,074,000	
Dividends payable to MI	14,000	
Proposed dividend	500,000	(1,588,000)
		2,596,900
Less: minority interest		(96,700)
		2,500,200
Ordinary share capital		500,000
Profit and loss a/c		2,000,200
		2,500,200

Other Considerations (SSAP 14)

Disclosure of principal subsidiaries

10.58 As regards *principal* subsidiaries, SSAP 14 requires disclosure of:
(a) name,
(b) proportion of nominal value of the issued shares of each class held by the group, and
(c) an indication of the nature of its business.

Minority (outside) interests

10.59 (a) General considerations
(i) In the consolidated balance sheet, minority interest in share capital and reserves should be disclosed as a separate amount. Minority interest should not be shown as part of shareholders' funds.
(ii) In the consolidated profit and loss account, profits or losses attributable to minority interests should be shown separately. Minority interests should be shown *after* profits on ordinary activities after taxation but *before* extraordinary items. Extraordinary items should be shown net of minority interest.

10.60 (b) Loss-making subsidiaries
(i) *Solvent subsidiaries.* Where such subsidiaries are solvent, the minority interest in the profit and loss account will take up the minority share of the losses. The minority interest in the balance sheet will thus decrease in size.

EXAMPLE
10.61 The balance sheets of Sub. Ltd. at various dates are as follows:

	31st December			
	19X1 £	19X2 £	19X3 £	19X4 £
Ordinary share capital	5,000	5,000	5,000	5,000
Profit and loss account	1,200	700	(100)	(2,600)
Net assets	6,200	5,700	4,900	2,400
Profits (losses) for the year	100	(500)	(800)	(2,500)

The subsidiary is 80% owned by H. Ltd.

Relevant minority interest figures in the consolidated financial statements are:

	£	£	£	£
Consolidated profit and loss account	20	(100)	(160)	(500)
Consolidated balance sheet	1,240	1,140	980	480

(ii) *Subsidiaries which are 'technically' insolvent.* SSAP 14 states that 'debit balances should be recognised only if there is a binding obligation on minority shareholders to make good losses incurred which they are able to meet'.

This is an extremely unlikely situation. Obligations of minority shareholders are unlikely to extend beyond amounts unpaid on share capital.

EXAMPLE

10.62 Continuing the above example, suppose S incurred a loss in 19X5 amounting to £4,200. This would mean that the balance sheet of S at 31/12/X5 would appear:

	£
Ordinary share capital	5,000
Profit and loss account	(6,800)
Deficiency of assets	(1,800)

It is quite possible that the company would go into liquidation before this stage is reached. If the company continued trading it would probably be because the holding company had given various guarantees to banks, creditors and so on, as well as providing inter-company loans.

In most situations it is unlikely that individual minority shareholders would be involved in guarantees, etc. (An exception may be where one substantial minority shareholder had a major investment in the company.) Assuming no 'binding obligation' on the part of minority shareholders, the effect on the consolidated financial statements for 19X5 would be:

(1) Minority interest in profit and loss account restricted to 20% × £2,400 = £480
(2) Minority interest in balance sheet = NIL
(3) Losses taken up by group in the consolidated P/L:

	£
Losses of S	4,200
Minority share 20% × 4,200 = 840, but restricted to	480
Losses taken up by group	3,720

Note that in the event of subsequent profits, the allocation of these would have to take account of the above, i.e. subsequent profits would be shared:

First £1,800: H
Remainder: 80% H, 20% to MI

(iii) *IAS 3*. Para. 17 of IAS 3 is more explicit than SSAP 14:

The losses applicable to the minority interest in a consolidated subsidiary may exceed the minority interest in the shareholders' equity of the subsidiary. The excess and any further losses applicable to the minority interest are charged against the majority interest except to the extent that the minority interest has a binding obligation to make good the losses. If future profits are reported by the subsidiary, the majority interest is credited with all such profits until the minority's share of losses previously absorbed by the majority has been recovered.

Restrictions on distributions

10.63 SSAP 14 states that if there are significant restrictions on the ability of the holding company to distribute the retained profit of the group (other than those shown as non-distributable) because of statutory, contractual or exchange control restrictions, the extent of the restrictions should be indicated. Below is an illustration of a note which appeared in the accounts of one particular company.

10.64 'The profit for the year retained in subsidiaries includes £0.3 million (1978 – £3.4 million) retained in countries from which remittances are deferred because of exchange control restrictions. The total retentions at 29 December 1987 subject to these restrictions are £1.3 million (1986 – £2.5 million).'

Questions

1. In relation to group accounting, there has been over a period of time a gradual shift from 'ownership' to 'control' as the attribute for identifying subsidiaries to be included in the consolidated accounts.

Required:
Discuss, in the light of this change, the approach now adopted to the exclusion of subsidiaries from consolidation, and their treatment in group accounts.

2. In the early days of group accounting, the consolidation and equity methods were regarded as alternative accounting treatments for investments in subsidiaries and for the profit/losses generated by them. Since then the consolidation method has prevailed in this field.

Required:

(a) to outline the similarities and differences between the two methods;
(b) to explain the conventional present-day uses of the two methods; and
(c) to argue FOR and AGAINST the general use of the equity method, in accounting for investments in subsidiaries.

3. JP Stevens plc (JPS) is the holding company of a group which at 30 June 1986 had the following direct or indirect investments:

	Effective Group Holding	Cost £'000	Activity
Stevenhold Ltd	100%	—	investment
Engineering Ltd	90%	90	engineering
Transport Ltd	100%	45	haulage
Electrical Ltd	75%	150	electrical contractor
Jacobson Ltd	70%	30	research
Manufacturing Ltd	40%	60	furniture
Selbyco Ltd	5%	10	retail
McDermot Ltd	22%	30	food
Sunshine plc	1%	25	travel

For the year ended 30 June 1987 the following transactions and information may be relevant:

(a) JPS directly owned all the investments other than the holdings in Engineering Ltd and in Transport Ltd both of which were owned by Stevenhold Ltd The group's 70% holding in Jacobson Ltd was owned by Transport Ltd
(b) At 30 June 1986 JPS was the largest shareholder in Manufacturing Ltd which had an equity share capital of 60,000 ordinary shares of £1 each and reserves of £140,000. JPS purchased a further 12,000 ordinary shares in the company for £65,000 on 1 July 1986. It made profits of £20,000 during the year ended 30 June 1987 and paid a dividend of £5,000.
(c) A loan of £60,000 was made during the year to Transport Ltd by JPS.
(d) McDermot Ltd was initially established by a number of shareholders each holding less than 10%. The board of directors of McDermot Ltd has three members from JPS and five members from other companies not otherwise related to JPS or each other. McDermot Ltd had profits in the current year of £30,000, paid a dividend of £10,000 and at 30 June 1987 had a share capital of £200,000 and retained reserves of £300,000.
(e) Negotiations started in March 1986 for the sale of the holding in Selbyco Ltd and are expected to be finalised shortly.

(f) The net assets of certain companies mentioned above are set out in the following table:

	30 June 1986 £	30 June 1987 £
Stevenhold Ltd	210,000	240,000
Engineering Ltd	80,000	70,000
Transport Ltd	50,000	60,000
Electrical Ltd	100,000	80,000
Jacobson Ltd	60,000	68,000
Manufacturing Ltd	200,000	215,000
Selbyco Ltd	250,000	260,000

(g) All group companies were profitable in the year ended 30 June 1987 except for Engineering Ltd and Electrical Ltd, where losses are expected to continue.
(h) The market value of the holding in Sunshine plc at 30 June 1987 was £50,000 (30 June 1986 £40,000).
(i) All holdings are of ordinary shares and there are no other classes of share capital.

Requirements
(a) Prepare the notes relating to fixed asset investments in a form suitable for publication in the parent company and consolidated financial statements of JPS for the year ended 30 June 1987.
(b) Describe the circumstances in which subsidiary companies should or may be excluded from group accounts and consolidation.

4. Greater Combinations Ltd, and its subsidiary Cooperative Ltd, have produced the following summarized balance sheets as on 30 November 19X5 and profit and loss accounts for the year ended on that date.

Summarized Balance Sheets as on 30 November 19X5

	Greater Combinations £'000	Cooperative £'000
Issued share capital ordinary shares of £1	500	100
Reserves and unappropriated profits	800	260
Deferred taxation	100	90
	1,400	450

	Greater Combinations £'000	Cooperative £'000
Fixed assets	600	100
Shares in subsidiary 75,000 shares of £1	25	—
Patents and trade marks	75	20
Net current assets	700	330
	1,400	450

Summarized Profit and Loss Accounts for year ended 30 November 19X5

	Greater Combinations £'000	Cooperative £'000
Trading profit	300	80
Taxation at 55%	165	44
	135	36
Proposed dividend	75	20
Retained	60	16

You have ascertained that:

(a) The entire issued share capital of Cooperative Ltd was acquired on 1 August 19X6 at £1 per share. At this date total reserves and unappropriated profits of Cooperative Ltd were equivalent to £0.80 per share. There have not been any changes in the issued share capital since that date.
(b) On 31 May 19X5 25,000 shares of Cooperative Ltd were sold at £3 per share.
(c) The sale had been recorded in the books of Greater Combinations Ltd by crediting the receipt against the cost of purchase.
(d) Trading and profit of Cooperative Ltd arise evenly throughout the year.
(e) Greater Combinations Ltd sells to Cooperative Ltd on the normal trade terms of cost plus 25%, goods to the value of £100,000 per month. Stock held by Cooperative Ltd at the end of the year represents one month's purchases.
(f) Both companies maintain the deferred taxation account under the liability method.
(g) Greater Combinations Ltd does not take credit in its own accounts for dividends until they have been received.

You are required to:

(a) prepare a consolidated balance sheet at 30 November 19X5 which complies with the best current practice in so far as the information provided will allow,
(b) prepare a detailed analysis of the movements in the group 'reserves and unappropriated profits', and
(c) write a *brief* note with numerical illustration comparing the alternatives available to reflect in the group accounts the trading between parent and subsidiary.

Chapter Eleven

Accounting for investments (3): SSAP 22: Accounting for goodwill

11.1 Over the years, several methods of accounting for goodwill have been put forward and adopted by various companies. These methods have included:

(a) Treatment as fixed asset without amortisation;
(b) Fixed asset subject to amortisation over its economic life;
(c) Immediate write-off or elimination as it arises, either
 — through the profit and loss account, or
 — through reserves (without an entry in P/L);
(d) Carried forward each year in the balance sheet as a deduction from reserves (the 'dangling debit' method).

11.2 The arguments for and against each approach are discussed below.

Fixed asset without amortisation

Arguments for	*Arguments against*
(a) In a profitable business, the value of goodwill is always likely to exceed its historical cost. On a going concern basis, the value of goodwill is maintained by the normal operations of the business.	(a) *Purchased* goodwill does not maintain its value. Over a period of time, the value of purchased goodwill falls and is replaced by internally generated goodwill (and the latter is not usually recognised in financial statements).
(b) Expenditure charged to P/L (advertising, wages and salaries, etc.) helps to maintain the value of goodwill.	(b) The charge for expenditure incurred and any amortisation of goodwill charge are unrelated items.

Arguments for	Arguments against
(c) If the residual value of goodwill is expected to exceed cost, no amortisation of goodwill is necessary.	(c) The residual value of purchased goodwill is actually nil (this should not be confused with the internally generated goodwill).
(d) In some businesses, it is difficult to distinguish between the value of tangible fixed assets and the value of goodwill.	(d) The treatment is not permitted by the CA 1985 as regards goodwill in the balance sheet of a single company.

Fixed asset subject to amortisation

Arguments for	Arguments against
(a) Purchased goodwill is a cost incurred in anticipation of future earnings. Under the accruals concept, such costs should be amortised and matched against the revenues of the periods which benefit from the expenditure.	(a) Possible double-charge to P/L (i) Amortisation charge (ii) Expenditures incurred in building up internally generated goodwill.
(b) Over a period of time, purchased goodwill declines in value and is replaced by internally generated goodwill.	(b) Any amortisation period is arbitrary.
(c) The method favoured by EEC 4th Directive and the CA 1985.	(c) Conflicts with going concern assumption since goodwill (in total) is likely to maintain its value.

Immediate write off to profit and loss account

11.3 Some companies write off the full amount of goodwill as an extraordinary item. This treatment should be used only where the goodwill has suffered a permanent fall in value due to an extraordinary event, when it should be written down to a lower amount.

11.4 The method suffers from the disadvantages referred to below.

Immediate write off to reserves

Arguments for	Arguments against
(a) Goodwill is unlike any other asset and should not be recognised in financial statements.	(a) The method ignores the existence of purchased goodwill and disregards the accruals concept.
(b) Purchased and internally generated goodwill should be treated consistently – under this approach neither type of goodwill is recognised in financial statements.	(b) The method is inconsistent in that expenditure incurred building up internally generated goodwill is charged to P/L, but purchased goodwill itself is charged direct to reserves.
(c) The P/L account is unaffected by what is an arbitrary write-off under method referred to above. (Fixed asset subject to amortisation.)	

Carry-forward as a deduction from reserves

11.5 This method, sometimes known as the dangling debit method, reflects the view of investment analysts who effectively disregard goodwill when considering a company's assets. However, the method has little theoretical support and is effectively prohibited by the CA 1985.

SSAP 22: Accounting for goodwill

11.6 SSAP 22 defines goodwill as being the difference between the value of a business as a whole and the aggregate of the fair values of its separable net assets. Separable net assets are those assets (and liabilities) which can be identified and sold (or discharged) separately without necessarily disposing of the business as a whole. They include identifiable intangibles. SSAP 22 also states that purchased goodwill is that which is established as a result of the purchase of a business accounted for as an acquisition, and goodwill arising on consolidation is one form of purchased goodwill. Non-purchased goodwill is any goodwill other than purchased goodwill.

11.7 1. Both SSAP 22 and the CA 1985 require that:
No amount should be attributed to non-purchased goodwill in the balance sheet of companies or groups.
2. SSAP 22 also requires that:
The amount attributed to purchased goodwill should be the difference between the fair value of purchase consideration given and the aggregate of the fair values of the separable net assets acquired.
3. The amount attributed to purchased goodwill should not include any value for separable intangibles. The amount of these, if material, should be included under the appropriate heading within the intangible fixed assets in the balance sheet.
4. Purchased goodwill (other than negative goodwill) should normally be eliminated from the accounts immediately on acquisition against reserves ('immediate write-off').
5. Any excess of the aggregate of the fair values of the separable net assets acquired over the fair value of the consideration given (negative goodwill) should be credited directly to reserves.
6. Purchased goodwill (other than negative goodwill) may be eliminated from the accounts by amortisation through the profit and loss account in arriving at profit or loss on ordinary activities on a systematic basis over its useful economic life ('amortisation').

Measurement of goodwill

11.8 The definition of goodwill in SSAP 22 includes purchased and non-purchased goodwill. Since SSAP 22 requires that the latter should not be recognised in the balance sheet, the discussion here is based on purchased goodwill. For the measurement of goodwill, a number of elements will have to be considered.

Fair value of the consideration given

11.9 The assets received by the holding company are the shares in the new subsidiary. Since the shares are recorded at cost, no goodwill will appear in the books of the holding company. The assets received by the group are the net assets plus goodwill of the subsidiary company. The fair value of the consideration given by the holding company depends on the nature of the consideration. If the shares are acquired for cash, the fair value of the consideration given will equal the face value of the cash. If the consideration is in the form of shares or loan stock, the market-value of these shares or loan stock will have to be determined.

Identification of separable net assets

11.10 The consolidated balance sheet will include the separable net assets of the subsidiary company at fair value. The identification of these separable net assets will involve a detailed analysis. The separable net assets will include identifiable intangibles like 'concessions, patents, licences, trade marks and similar rights and assets'.

11.11 Some of these intangible assets may have been created by the company itself and will have to be identified. Equally important is to consider the existence of, and amounts to be ascribed to, liabilities. The acquired company may have underprovided or overprovided for some of its liabilities like deferred taxation, pension costs. A provision may also be required for warranty or maintenance costs.

Ascription of fair values to separable net assets

11.12 SSAP 22 defines fair value as the amount for which an asset (or liability) could be exchanged in an arm's length transaction. There is no explanation of how this would be arrived at, although the Technical Release issued with SSAP 22 indicates that a separate working party is developing guidance on the question. It may be appropriate to use the principles stated in SSAP 16: *Current Cost Accounting* (now withdrawn) where the basis of valuation was 'value to the business' or 'deprival value'. Deprival value has been defined as the minimum amount that would compensate the owner of the asset being valued in the event of its hypothetical loss. This can be expressed as the lower of:

(a) the net replacement cost, and
(b) the recoverable amount.

The recoverable amount = Higher of economic value and net realisable value.

ACCOUNTING FOR INVESTMENTS (3)

(Economic value will approximate the Net Relevant Cash Flow derived from the future use of the asset.)

Purchased goodwill

11.13 As stated earlier SSAP 22 recommends that purchased goodwill (other than negative goodwill) be eliminated from the accounts immediately on acquisition against reserves ('immediate write-off'). It also states that purchased goodwill (other than negative goodwill) may be eliminated from the accounts by amortisation through the profit and loss account in arriving at profit or loss on ordinary activities on a systematic basis over its useful economic life ('amortisation').

11.14 The choice between 'immediate write-off' and 'amortisation' means that there is no requirement for consistency and will lead to lack of inter-firm and intra-firm comparisons. SSAP 22 contains no requirement for a company to select one method of elimination of goodwill and apply it consistently to the goodwill arising on all acquisitions. A company may decide to eliminate goodwill immediately on one acquisition, whilst goodwill on another may be eliminated by amortisation. This flexibility gives considerable scope for inconsistent treatment.

11.15 The Technical Release issued with SSAP 22 envisages that 'immediate write-off' will continue to be the more common method, and that amortisation in future will be used only in special cases:
1. The company is a subsidiary of a company based overseas where amortisation is mandatory. The application of a consistent accounting policy within the group would reduce the number of consolidation adjustments.
2. 'In certain service industries which are typically acquired at prices that are high in relation to their net assets', i.e. where goodwill comprises most of the purchase price. The Technical Release notes that 'in these ... cases, amortisation may be necessary because of the effect which immediate write-off would have on reserves'. In the above case where the company has low reserves, the immediate write-off could give rise to two problems.
    (a) It may deplete the distributable reserves of an individual company. The write-off of goodwill arising on consolidation against the consolidated reserves has no impact on the reserves of the individual company as it is the reserves of individual companies from which distributions are made.
    (b) It may lead to lack of confidence in the company or group. A

depletion of reserves may give the impression that the position of the company or group is weak.

Immediate write-off

11.16 The immediate write-off is advocated on the grounds that this is consistent with the accepted practice of not including non-purchased goodwill in accounts. If the purchased goodwill is treated as an asset and non-purchased goodwill is not, then only part of the goodwill of the company or group has been recognised, that is, goodwill of the acquired company has been recognised but not that of the acquiring company. This will lead to lack of consistency between the treatment of purchased and non-purchased goodwill on the balance sheet. Some companies expand through internal growth, whilst others do so through acquisitions. If the purchased goodwill is recognised as an asset, then there will be a lack of comparisons between the companies which have expanded through internal growth (whose non-purchased goodwill is not recognised) and companies which have grown through acquisitions (where purchased goodwill is recognised as an asset).

11.17 Other arguments in favour of this treatment are:

1. Goodwill is not an asset in the normal sense of the word because it cannot be realised separately from other assets, and
2. purchased goodwill, as a premium paid on acquisition, is considered to be a one-off payment associated with the acquisition, and not an asset which is acquired, maintained and 'used in the business'.

11.18 The immediate write-off of goodwill should be against reserves. The write-off should not be charged in the profit and loss account for the year and SSAP 22 gives the following reasons for this:

1. purchased goodwill is written off as a matter of accounting policy, that is, in order to achieve consistency of treatment with non-purchased goodwill, rather than because it has suffered a permanent diminution of value, and
2. the write-off is not related to the results of the year in which the acquisition was made.

11.19 SSAP 22 does not specify the reserves against which purchased goodwill should be written off. The question that arises is whether the immediate write-off constitutes a reduction of realised reserves. The question of what is realised is relevant only in the case of an individual company and not in the case of a group. Distributions are made from the

ACCOUNTING FOR INVESTMENTS (3)

profits of individual companies, not by groups, and hence the elimination of consolidation goodwill has no effect on the distributable profits.

11.20 The view taken in ED 30: *Accounting for Goodwill* was that write-off was a reduction of realised reserves. However, the Appendix to SSAP 22 takes a different view. This is:

'To the extent that the goodwill is considered to have suffered an actual diminution in value, the write-off should be charged against reserves. In other cases, where goodwill is written off on acquisition as a matter of accounting policy, rather than because of an actual diminution in value, realised reserves should not be reduced immediately ... However, the standard is based on the concept in the CA 1985 that purchased goodwill has a limited useful life so that ultimately its elimination must constitute a realised loss. It may in some circumstances (e.g. where a company lacks sufficient distributable reserves to cover the purchase cost of the goodwill) be appropriate to charge the elimination of goodwill initially to a 'suitable' unrealised reserve, thereby spreading the effect of the elimination of goodwill on realised reserves over its useful life rather than impairing realised reserves immediately'.

11.21 As can be seen from the above paragraph, taken from the Appendix to SSAP 22, immediate write-off will be a reduction of realised reserves only if there is a permanent diminution in value and not if it is a matter of accounting policy.

11.22 However, purchased goodwill has a limited useful life and ultimately its elimination will constitute a realised loss. The Appendix to SSAP 22 suggests that it may in some circumstances be appropriate to charge the elimination of goodwill initially to a suitable unrealised reserve and then make transfers to realised reserves. A suitable unrealised reserve may be negative goodwill or merger reserve (discussed in the chapter on SSAP 23). This means that the purchased goodwill will be amortised but without affecting the profit and loss account for the year.

EXAMPLE
A LIMITED   Y/E 31/12/86
Purchased Goodwill £100,000   Useful Life = 5 years
Balance b/fwd: Realised reserves   £500,000
                       Negative Goodwill (unrealised)   £400,000

Reserves	Realised £	Negative goodwill £
B/forward	500,000	400,000
Goodwill – immediate write off		(100,000)
	500,000	300,000
Y/E 31/12/86	(20,000)	20,000
87	(20,000)	20,000
88	(20,000)	20,000
89	(20,000)	20,000
90	(20,000)	20,000

11.23 If a suitable unrealised reserve is not available, immediate write-off will have to be against realised reserves. The Department of Trade and Industry issued a Consultative Note in May 1986 specifically disapproving of the use of Revaluation Reserves for the purpose of immediate write-off of goodwill, a practice adopted by several companies. The DTI intends to introduce statutory changes to this effect in the next CA, as part of the Seventh Directive implementation.

11.24 It is now apparent that a situation may arise where the immediate write-off of consolidation goodwill will have the effect of reducing the consolidated reserves to an amount below that of the holding company's reserves. There may even be cases where the holding company's reserves are positive but the consolidated reserves are negative. This is because there is no requirement in SSAP 22 to make an adjustment in the holding company's books to reduce the carrying value of the investment when, and to the extent that, consolidation goodwill is written off in the consolidated accounts.

Amortisation

11.25 This is not the preferred method and, as discussed earlier, SSAP 22 envisages that this treatment will be used in special circumstances only. When this treatment is selected, the following points apply:
1. Purchased goodwill should be capitalised as a fixed asset and amortised over its economic life. The charge should be made on a systematic basis and should be debited in arriving at profit or loss on ordinary activities. That is, it should not be charged as an extraordinary item nor taken directly to the reserves.
2. Purchased goodwill should not be revalued. If there is a permanent

diminution in value of purchased goodwill, it should be written down immediately through the profit and loss account to its estimated recoverable amount.
3. The useful economic life should be estimated at the time of acquisition. It should not include any allowance for the effects of subsequent expenditure or other circumstances subsequently affecting the company since these would have the effect of creating non-purchased goodwill.
4. The estimated useful economic life over which purchases goodwill is being amortised may be shortened but may not be increased.

11.26 The above treatment is based on the view that when a business is purchased, the price paid includes an amount attributable to purchased goodwill. This price paid for purchased goodwill is in anticipation of future earnings. Therefore, the matching principle requires that purchased goodwill should be recognised and amortised over its economic life.

11.27 One of the problems that arises under this method is the determination of the useful economic life as it cannot be carried out with scientific accuracy. Useful economic life of purchased goodwill is the period over which benefits may reasonably be expected to accrue from that goodwill by the acquired company, as identified at the time of acquisition.

Negative goodwill

11.28 SSAP 22 requires negative goodwill (defined earlier) to be credited directly to reserves at the time of acquisition. Yet again there is an inconsistency in the recommendations of SSAP 22. There is a choice of treatment allowed for purchased positive goodwill but not for negative goodwill. Amortisation of negative goodwill to income is not permitted.

11.29 The other problems with SSAP 22 are that it does not specify to which reserves it should be credited and under which heading it should be disclosed.

11.30 The Appendix to SSAP 22 gives guidance which applies in the case of negative goodwill within the accounts of an individual company. The Appendix indicates that it should be credited initially to an unrealised reserve, from which it may be transferred to realised reserves (as movement on reserves) in line with depreciation or realisation of the assets acquired in the business combination which gave rise to the negative goodwill in question.

11.31 Since the negative goodwill cannot be disclosed under the headings of capital redemption reserve or share premium account or revaluation reserve or retained profits, it seems that it may be most appropriate to disclose it under the heading of other reserves.

Purchased goodwill

Some current practices

Write-off against revaluation reserve
11.32 Since SSAP 22 gives no specific guidance on the reserves against which goodwill may be written off, some companies have written off goodwill against revaluation reserves. This practice raises the question of whether revaluation reserve should be available for goodwill write-off. The revaluation reserve, like share premium, is designed to be used for certain restricted purposes – capitalisation by way of share issues or to deal with a surplus or deficit arising on a revaluation of tangible assets. The next CA may reduce the availability of revaluation reserves for such write-offs in accordance with the EC Seventh Directive.

Creating a negative reserve by goodwill write-off
11.33 The purchased goodwill is written off to a 'non-existent reserve', giving rise to a negative reserve balance on the 'goodwill write-off reserve' account. When the DTI was asked to comment on this treatment, they stated that even though they agreed that it was artificial, they found nothing intrinsically illegal about the practice.

Use of share premium account to write-off goodwill
11.34 S130, CA 1985 restricts the use to which the share premium account can be put. It cannot be used for writing off goodwill. A number of companies (which are in good financial health) have, however, applied to the courts for a reorganisation of capital and sought court approval for the cancellation of their share premium account in order to create a reserve which can be used for writing off goodwill.

11.35 The courts have allowed this type of arrangement because they accept the argument put forward by accounting experts that SSAP 22 favours the writing off of goodwill against reserves and the court is merely being asked to provide the necessary reserve to enable the

ACCOUNTING FOR INVESTMENTS (3)

standard to be complied with. In the past such capital reconstruction schemes, petitioning the courts for permission to cancel share premium account and share capital, have been used by financially troubled companies where the write-off reflects lost capital. It is not known, however, whether the courts will continue to allow this in all cases. For example, at the time of writing, Thorn EMI have applied in relation to a share premium account of several hundred million pounds – unprecedented by comparison with the size of earlier applications.

Giving different name to goodwill

11.36 Different names are given to goodwill paid when a business is acquired, particularly in service companies. Since it is not categorised as goodwill, it is argued that no write-down is required. Examples of alternative names include 'newspaper/magazine titles', 'shop fronts', 'milkrounds', etc.

Writing off part of the goodwill to reserves and amortising the remaining portion through the profit and loss account

11.37 Since both the CA 1985 and SSAP 22 allow the choice of methods, there can be no objection to this treatment, but it makes comparisons between companies more difficult.

Question

The treatment of goodwill in published company and group accounts has been a highly controversial topic for several decades.

Required:
(a) Discuss critically the methods of goodwill accounting that are in common use in companies and groups, with reference to both positive and negative goodwill.
(b) Give your views on the methods of goodwill accounting that are most suitable for general use by companies and groups.
(c) Discuss critically whether the entire basis of SSAP 22 is conceptually sound.

Chapter Twelve

Accounting for investments (4): Accounting for business combinations

12.1 There are two different methods of accounting for business combinations.

Acquisition accounting

Holding company accounts

12.2 The investment in the subsidiary company is normally recorded at the cost to the investing company.

12.3 When the subsidiary is acquired through a share exchange, the difference between the fair value of the investment and the nominal value of shares issued by the acquiring company is transferred to a share premium account (S130 CA 1985). For this purpose 'fair' value is that which is based on an arm's length transaction. Any dividends received by the investing company from preacquisition reserves are credited to the cost of the investment, i.e. will reduce the cost of the investment in its own accounts.

Consolidated accounts

12.4 The consolidated accounts will reflect the results of the acquired company from the date of the acquisition only.

12.5 The acquiring group accounts for the net assets acquired at the cost to the group. The acquiring group determines cost by attributing a fair value to the assets and liabilities which it acquires. These fair values of assets are likely to be greater than the amounts recorded in the books of the combining companies. This will in turn lead to higher depreciation charges in the consolidated accounts.

12.6 Any difference between the fair value of the consideration given to former shareholders and the aggregate of fair values of the separable net assets acquired (including identifiable intangibles such as patents, licences and trade marks) will represent *goodwill*.

12.7 The effect of recording the transactions in this way is to freeze the pre-acquisition reserves of the subsidiary company just acquired. This prevents the investing company or group from paying dividends to its own shareholders out of preacquisition reserves of the subsidiary company. The investing company or group is effectively acquiring the capital of the subsidiary (which for this purpose includes reserves) and no dividends can be paid from capital. The recording of the assets at fair values is consistent with the historic cost rules and, until 1981, with company law.

12.8 However, acquisition accounting produces unsatisfactory results when two companies or groups combine by means of a share-for-share exchange. There are the following disadvantages:
(a) The pre-acquisition reserves of the acquired company are frozen even though the shareholders before and after combination may be the same.
(b) The investing company may have to create a share premium account which inhibits distributions.
(c) The combined group may have to recognise goodwill arising on consolidation. This is equivalent to recognising non-purchased goodwill even though there is no change in 'ownership'.
(d) Fair values will have to be attributed to the net assets acquired which may result in increased depreciation charges in the profit and loss account of the combined companies.
(e) The effect of (c) and (d) will be to reduce the return on capital employed (ROCE).

Merger accounting

12.9 The merger method was evolved in response to the specific criticisms of acquisition accounting.

Holding company accounts

12.10 The investment in the subsidiary company is recorded in the holding company's accounts at the nominal value of the shares which it issued; where there is additional consideration in some form other than equity shares, the fair value of such additional consideration is added to the nominal value of the shares to arrive at the cost of investment.

12.11 No share premium account is created, leaving preacquisition reserves of the subsidiary company as 'free' reserves (i.e. free for distribution).

12.12 Any dividends received by the investing company from the pre-acquisition reserves of the subsidiary company will be credited to the investing company's profit and loss account for the year.

Consolidated accounts

12.13 The consolidated accounts for the period in which the business combination takes place will include the results of the subsidiary for the entire period. No apportionment is necessary since the companies' respective results are simply aggregated.

12.14 The group does not need to incorporate in its consolidated accounts the fair values of assets and liabilities of the subsidiary and goodwill therefore does not arise under this method. The difference between the value at which the holding company carries its investment in the subsidiary and the nominal value of the shares acquired by the holding company will be adjusted against consolidated reserves.

12.15 Since no goodwill has been recognised and no fair values have been ascribed to the net assets of the subsidiary company, this method will not result in an increased depreciation charge and will produce a higher return on capital employed than the acquisition method.

12.16 However, there are a number of criticisms of this method:

Creation of instant earnings
The profit and loss account for the year includes the full year's results of both the companies, although the merger may have taken place towards the end of the year. This may boost the earnings (but not necessarily earnings per share) of the combined group in the year of the merger, to a misleading degree.

Creation of instant distributable reserves
By applying the merger method of accounting, the investing company may instantly acquire distributable reserves of the subsidiary company, which it may then pay to its own shareholders as a dividend.

Size test
There are arguments concerning the applicability of merger accounting in different circumstances. One view is that merger accounting is appropriate only in circumstances where there is a genuine pooling of resources by shareholders of two similar sized concerns which results in common ownership of the combined entity.

An alternative viewpoint is that provided a business combination is effected by a share-for-share exchange with no significant resources leaving the companies, the companies are essentially the same and so merger accounting is appropriate.

ED 3 (since withdrawn) was based on the former approach, whilst SSAP 23 is based on the latter.

Assets understated

The assets of the acquired company are not necessarily brought into the consolidated balance sheet of the acquiring group at a fair value.

The effect of this is to have unrealistic depreciation charges on the assets of the subsidiary company 'acquired' by the group, and a higher return on capital employed than would arise under the acquisition method.

Holding company profitability

Any dividends paid by the 'acquired' company out of its pre-acquisition profits will be credited to the holding company's profit and loss account. This could give a misleading view of the holding company's profitability.

Mechanics of accounting for acquisitions and mergers

12.17 Large PLC and Medium PLC decide to amalgamate by means of an exchange of voting ordinary shares.

12.18 Large PLC issues 700,000 £1 ordinary shares (with market value of 175 pence per share) in exchange for all shares of Medium PLC. The fair value of the fixed assets of Medium PLC is estimated @ £750,000.

Balance sheet (Extract)

	Large PLC £'000	Medium PLC £'000
Fixed Assets	820	560
Net Current Assets	330	270
	£1,150	£830
Ordinary share capital	800	600
P&L A/c	350	230
	£1,150	£830

Acquisition accounting

	£'000	£'000
Cost of Investment		1,225 (700,000 @ 175 pence per share)
Less:		
Ordinary share capital	600	
Profit & Loss A/c	230	
Revaluation (750–560)	190	
		1,020*
Goodwill		205

* Obviously the same result is achieved if net assets at fair value (i.e. including the revaluation) is used.

Large PLC holding company balance sheet

	£'000	
Fixed Assets	820	
Investment in M PLC	1,225	recorded at a fair value
Net Current Assets	330	
	2,375	

Ordinary Share Capital (800 + 700)	1,500	
Share Premium A/c (1225–700)	525	Difference between the fair value and nominal value of shares issued
P&L A/c	350	
	2,375	

Any dividends out of preacquisition reserves of Medium PLC will reduce the cost of investment.

Large PLC – consolidated balance sheet

	£'000	
Fixed Assets (820 + 750)	1,570	Subsidiary company's fixed assets at fair value. Depreciation charge will be based on fair value.
Goodwill – on consolidation	205	
Net Current Assets (330 + 270)	600	
	2,375	

Ordinary Share Capital	1,500	
Share Premium A/c	525	
Profit & Loss A/c	350	
	2,375	

Medium PLC's preacquisition reserves are 'frozen'.

Reconciliation of share premium account

	£'000	£'000
Balance per Large PLC Balance Sheet		525
Profit & Loss A/c of Medium PLC	230	
Revaluation of fixed assets of Medium PLC	190	
	420	
Goodwill	205	
	625	
Less Difference between nominal value of shares issued by Large PLC and issued share capital of Medium PLC	(100)	
		525

Merger method of accounting

Large PLC – holding company balance sheet

	£'000	
Fixed Assets	820	
Investment in Medium PLC	700	recorded at nominal value of shares issued by Large PLC
Net Current Assets	330	
	£1,850	
Ordinary Share Capital (800 + 700)	1,500	new issue recorded at nominal value. NOTE: No share premium a/c.
P & L A/c	350	
	£1,850	

Any dividends received from preacquisition reserves of Medium PLC will be included as part of P & L a/c of Large PLC and will therefore be distributable.

Large PLC – consolidated balance sheet

	£'000	
Fixed Assets (820 + 560)	1,380	NOTE: No revaluation of fixed assets of Medium PLC. No Goodwill
Net Curent Assets	600	
	1,980	
Ordinary Share Capital	1,500	
Profit & Loss A/c		
(350 + 230 − 100)*	480	
	1,980	

* NV of shares issued by Large PLC	700
Less NV of issued share capital of Medium PLC	(600)
	100

12.19 On consolidation, the difference between the value at which the investment is recorded in the holding company's books and the nominal value of the share capital of the subsidiary company acquired by Large PLC will be recorded as a movement on reserves. If the value at which the investment is recorded is greater than the issued share capital of the subsidiary company, reserves will be capitalised. If it is less than the issued share capital of the subsidiary company, there will be a 'consolidation' reserve.

Profit and loss account

12.20 In the accounts for the period in which a merger takes place, the results of subsidiaries brought in for the first time should be included for the whole of the current year.
(Compare: Acquisition method – from the date of control only.)

12.21 Corresponding amounts should be restated, although the company may not have been a subsidiary in the prior year or in part of the current year.

12.22 An analysis of results between pre- and post-merger and between the parties to the merger should be disclosed.

Background to the merger method

ED 3 (issued in 1971)
12.23 ED 3, which never became a Standard, stated that both acquisition accounting and merger accounting were acceptable methods of accounting for business combinations. However, ED 3 said that acquisition accounting and merger accounting should not be alternatives in accounting for the same business combination. If a particular business combination met all of certain conditions, it should be accounted for as a merger. If the business combination did not meet all of those conditions, it should be accounted for as an acquisition.

12.24 Under ED 3, the conditions which had to be met in order for merger accounting to apply were as follows:
1. the substance of the main businesses of the constituent companies continued in the amalgamated undertaking;
2. the equity voting rights of the amalgamated undertaking to be held by the shareholders of any one of the constituent companies were not more than three times the equity voting rights to be held by the shareholders of any of the other constituent companies;
3. the amalgamation resulted from an offer to equity voting shareholders and not less than 90 per cent in value of the offer was in the form of equity capital with rights indentical to the equity voting capital rights of the offeree company or companies already in issue; for this purpose convertible loan stock or equity voting capital which could be converted into cash through an underwriting agreement was not to be regarded as equity voting capital; and
4. the offer was approved by the voting shareholders of the company making the offer and it was accepted by shareholders representing at least 90 per cent of the total equity capital (voting and non-voting) of the company or companies receiving the offer.

12.25 ED 3 viewed a merger as the joining together of two companies which resulted in very little change, e.g. the substance of the main businesses was to continue; and the shareholders were to receive shares with 'rights identical' to those which they previously enjoyed. However, the legal opinion at the time was that merger accounting might be in contravention of S56 of the CA 1948 (now S130 CA 1985) and the ASC decided not to grant ED 3 the status of an accounting standard. The above legal opinion was later confirmed in the case of *Shearer* v *Bercain Ltd.* in 1980.

Shearer v Bercain Ltd. (1980)

12.26 The judgement in the case appeared to confirm the following points:

1. the investment in a subsidiary company by the investing company should be recorded in the investing company's balance sheet at fair value rather than the nominal value of shares issued and the excess of fair value over the nominal value of shares issued should be credited to the share premium account; and
2. the pre-acquisition profits of acquired subsidiaries were not available for distribution by the holding company; and any dividends paid by a subsidiary company to its holding company out of pre-acquisition profits should be applied by the holding company to reduce the cost of the investment in that subsidiary.

Companies Act 1981

12.27 Following the judgement in *Shearer v Bercain Ltd*, the law was changed. Sections 36 to 41 of the CA 1981 (now S131 to 134 CA 1985) give relief in certain circumstances from S56, CA 1948 (now S130 CA 1985). Such relief allows companies to dispense with the requirement to create a share premium account on the issue of shares if the conditions described below are met.

12.28 Sections 36 to 41, CA 1981 (S131 to 134 CA 1985) deal with the merger relief provisions and apply only to individual companies, not to groups.

Conditions for merger relief

12.29 The conditions that an issuing company must satisfy in order to utilise the merger relief provisions are as follows:

1. The issuing company must have secured a 90 per cent equity holding in the other company in pursuance of an arrangement.
2. The consideration that the issuing company receives for the shares it issues must be provided either by the issue or the transfer to the issuing company of equity shares in that other company, or by the cancellation of any such shares that the issuing company does not hold.
3. Where the equity share capital of the other company consists of different classes of shares, the issuing company must secure at least 90 per cent of each class.

12.30 The relief applies only to premiums on the shares that the holding company issues in the transaction that take its holding to at least

90 per cent. The relief does not apply to shares that the holding company issued before the transaction. So if a holding company acquires 70 per cent of another company by means of a share-for-share exchange, and subsequently acquires the remaining 30 per cent in a separate transaction, then the merger relief provisions apply only to the shares that the holding company issues in the second transaction.

12.31 When the relevant clauses were being debated in Standing Committee, the Government indicated that it would be for a future accounting standard to prescribe the accounting treatment to be adopted in circumstances that fall within the scope of this part of the Act.

There are important differences between the SSAP 23 merger conditions and the conditions for merger relief in S36 in CA 1981 (now S131 CA 1985). These are discussed in Section 12.51.

ED 31

12.32 This was issued in October 1982 in response to the comments referred to above.

12.33 ED 31 proposed that the two methods should not be alternatives in accounting for the same business combination. The conditions which must be met in order for a business combination to be accounted for as a merger are as follows:
1. the business combination should result from an offer to the holders of all equity shares and the holders of all voting shares which are not already held by the offeror; the offer should be approved by the holders of the voting shares of the company making the offer; and
2. the offer should be accepted by holders of at least 90 per cent of all equity shares and of the shares carrying at least 90 per cent of all votes of the offeree company; for this purpose, any convertible stock is not to be regarded as equity except to the extent that it is converted into equity as a result of the business combination; and
3. not less than 90 per cent of the fair value of the total consideration given for the equity share capital (including that given for shares already held) should be in the form of equity capital; and not less than 90 per cent of the fair value of the consideration given for voting non-equity share capital (including that given for shares already held) should be in the form of equity and/or voting non-equity share capital.

12.34 ED 31 did not stipulate that the substance of the businesses of the constituent companies should continue in the amalgamated undertaking. It said this is because rationalisation is a common feature of the operations of many companies and such rationalisation should not invalidate the merger concept. Neither did it have a size test similar to that in ED 3. ED 31 saw merger as a combining of interests of two (or more) groups of shareholders in such a way that no material resources left the group. Further, any size test which was introduced would by definition be arbitrary.

12.35 Condition 1 in ED 31 required that the offer should be approved by the holders of the voting shares of the company making the offer. This was based on the view that if two companies were merging, both groups of shareholders should approve the merger.

12.36 Condition 2 in ED 31 required that the offer should be accepted by holders of at least 90 per cent of all equity shares and of the shares carrying at least 90 per cent of all votes of the offeree company for merger accounting to apply. This would then have permitted the compulsory acquisition by a company of the remaining 10 per cent of the shares (S209 CA 1948. Now S428 CA 1985).

12.37 Condition 3 in ED 31 restricted the maximum cash content to 10 per cent of purchase consideration.

Statement of intent (SOI)

12.38 This was issued in 1984 and confirmed the ASC's views in ED 31 that merger accounting and acquisition accounting should not be alternative methods of accounting for a particular business combination. The statement restricted the maximum cash content to 20 per cent of purchase consideration. The SOI also proposed that maximum prior holdings be restricted to 20 per cent (ED 31 – 10 per cent). A further change was that the SOI prescribed the accounting treatment to be used only on consolidation.

SSAP 23: Accounting for acquisitions and mergers

12.39 There are four merger conditions in the standard. If the business combination satisfied *all* of these conditions, then the group *may* use either merger accounting or acquisition accounting to account for the business combination. If the business combination does not satisfy all the conditions, then the group must use acquisition accounting to account for the business combination.

ACCOUNTING FOR INVESTMENTS (4)

12.40 SSAP 23 does not deal with the treatment to be used in the parent's own accounts.

12.41 SSAP 23 makes merger accounting optional rather than mandatory. The following reasons were given by the working party:
1. Few people are strongly in favour of merger accounting being mandatory.
2. Merger accounting is relatively new in the UK.
3. Sections 36 to 41 of the CA 1981 (CA 1985 S131 to S134) are permissive rather than prescriptive. Also, in the EC 7th Directive on consolidated accounts merger accounting is permitted but is not required.
4. Some companies perceive themselves to be acquisitive, whether they are making offers in cash or in shares. Such a company may wish to account for its business combinations as acquisitions even though they satisfy the conditions for merger accounting.
5. Many consider acquisition accounting to be the benchmark, with merger accounting being the exception. Consequently, a standard should not prohibit acquisition accounting.

12.42 SSAP 23 has been criticised for making the merger method optional. The fact that the fulfilment of certain conditions does not lead to the mandatory use of merger accounting but allows either approach is a retrograde step. Such a decree does not help the user of financial statements who wishes to analyse a company's performance over time or who wishes to compare the published results of one company with those of another. Such an option also allows the company to use the acquisition method for one combination and the merger method for another even though all the merger conditions have been satisfied in both cases.

12.43 SSAP 23 has also been criticised for not prescribing the treatment to be used in the parent company's own accounts. The situation may arise whereby the parent company may record the investment in a subsidiary company at a fair value but prepare consolidated accounts on a merger basis if all the merger conditions are satisfied. Also a parent company that does not qualify for merger treatment under SSAP 23 can make use of the merger relief provisions of S131 to S134 of CA 1985 in its individual accounts. The consistency principle suggests that the holding company's accounts and the consolidated accounts should be prepared on the same basis.

12.44 If acquisition accounting is used in the group's accounts, the individual accounts of a holding company, which can make use of S131 to 134 of CA 1985, will need to record shares acquired at fair value and show a corresponding non-statutory 'merger reserve account' in respect of the difference between the fair value of purchase consideration and the nominal value of shares issued. Any dividends received out of pre-acquisition reserves will then have to be offset against the fair value. There is no legal ruling as to whether the merger reserve can be regarded as realised and so available for distribution.

SSAP 23 merger conditions

12.45 Condition 1: The business combination results from an offer to the holders of all equity shares and the holders of all voting shares which are not already held by the offeror.

This means that the business combination must arise from a single offer. One exception to this would be where the first few offers acquired less than 20 per cent of the offeree's share capital (see condition 3).

ED 31 required that the offer should be approved by the holders of the voting shares of the company making the offer. This has been deleted from SSAP 23 because the approval procedure would be expensive and time consuming.

12.46 Condition 2: The offeror has secured, as a result of the offer, a holding of

(i) at least 90 per cent of all equity shares (taking each class of equity separately) and
(ii) the shares carrying at least 90 per cent of the votes of the offeree.

The offeror must acquire at least 90 per cent of each class of equity share. An offer which secures 90 per cent of the total equity share capital may not necessarily satisfy the SSAP 23 merger conditions. Suppose the offeree has two classes of equity shares.
CLASS A: 100 NV £1 ordinary shares
CLASS B: 1 million NV £1 ordinary shares
(NB: NV = Nominal value)
If the offeror acquires 100 per cent of Class B and none of Class A, he will have acquired more than 90 per cent of equity share. However, this will not satisfy SSAP 23 merger conditions. To satisfy the merger conditions, the offeror will have to acquire at least 90 per cent of Class A and 90 per cent of Class B.

Condition 2 also requires the offeror to acquire shares carrying at least 90 per cent of the votes of the offeree. Suppose the offeree has two classes of equity shares and voting preference shares.
Equity shares
Class A 100 NV £1 ordinary shares
Class B 1 million NV £1 ordinary shares

ACCOUNTING FOR INVESTMENTS (4)

Voting non-equity shares
100,000 ORDINARY NV £1 voting preference shares.
To satisfy the merger conditions in SSAP 23, the offeror would have to acquire:

(i) 90 per cent of Class A; *and*
(ii) 90 per cent of Class B; *and*
(iii) 90 per cent of 1,100,100 shares.

12.47 Condition 3: Immediately prior to the offer, the offeror does not hold

(i) 20 per cent or more of all equity shares of the offeree (taking each class of equity separately), or
(ii) shares carrying 20 per cent or more of the votes of the offeree.

In ED 31, the prior holding was restricted to 10 per cent. This was found to be very restrictive as many companies undertake business combinations on the basis of prior holdings that exceed 10 per cent. Also there was a belief that a prior holding acquired some years earlier was irrelevant. SSAP 23 therefore relaxed this condition and selected a 20 per cent limit on prior holdings as the offeror would normally have accounted for a higher holding in the offeree as an associated company. SSAP 1 (Associated Companies) requires fair values to be ascribed to the relevant shares of assets and the ASC considers that to ascribe fair values is inconsistent with merger accounting.

12.48 Condition 4: Not less than 90 per cent of the fair value of the total consideration given for the equity share capital (including that given for the shares already held) is in the form of equity share capital; not less than 90 per cent of the fair value of the total consideration given for voting non-equity share capital (including that given for shares already held) is in the form of equity and/or voting non-equity share capital. This means that the cash element is restricted to 10 per cent of the purchase consideration (including that for prior holdings). Suppose that the offeree has 100,000 ordinary NV £1 shares in issue and the offeror has already acquired 12,000 ordinary shares for £15,000 cash. Suppose the offeror then secures the remainder of 88,000 ordinary shares by means of a share-for-share exchange and the fair value of this consideration is £100,000.

		Fair value £	Settlement
1st	12 per cent – Prior Holding	15,000	CASH
2nd	88 per cent	100,000	SHARES
	100 per cent	115,000	

The cash content in the purchase consideration = 15/115 = 13 per cent. The 4th merger condition says that not less than 90 per cent of the fair value of the total consideration must be equity shares. The above business combination would not satisfy the 4th SSAP 23 merger condition as the fair value of shares issued is only 87 per cent of the total purchase consideration.

12.49 There is a conflict between the 4th Condition in SSAP 23 and the EC 7th Directive. The 7th Directive requires that, for merger accounting to be available, the cash element of the consideration should not exceed 10 per cent of the nominal value of shares issued.

12.50 For the purposes of the merger conditions, any convertible stock outstanding at the time of the offer is not to be regarded as equity except to the extent it is converted into equity as a result of and at the time of the business combination. The 'offeror' includes the offeror's holding company or subsidiary or fellow subsidiary or its or their nominee.

Say Company A has a subsidiary B which in turn has a holding of 3 per cent in another company C. If A combines with C through a share-for-share exchange deal, it will not have to make an offer for shares held by B in C. A will treat the 3 per cent as if it were owned by A itself, not by B, as A has effective control over B.

12.51 SSAP 23 and CA conditions for merger relief

SSAP 23	Companies Act
1. Group Accounts only.	1. Individual company only.
2. The offeror must secure a holding of at least 90 per cent of each class of equity shares, and must also acquire shares carrying at least 90 per cent of the offeree's votes.	2. The issuing company must secure a holding of at least 90 per cent of each class of equity shares.
3. At least 90 per cent of the fair value of the total consideration that the issuing company gives for equity shares must be in the form of equity shares.	3. No such condition.
4. The offeror's maximum prior holding restricted to 20 per cent.	4. No such condition.

12.52 The conditions for merger accounting in SSAP 23 are more restrictive than the conditions in the Act. If a business combination satisfies SSAP 23 conditions, then it will automatically satisfy the conditions in the Act. However, a situation may arise whereby the combination does not satisfy the SSAP 23 conditions but does satisfy the merger relief conditions in the Act. On such occasions, the law allows the company to record its investment in a subsidiary at nominal value, but SSAP 23 requires the group to use the acquisition method on consolidation.

12.53 The holding company may record the investment at its fair value to be consistent with the treatment to be used in the consolidated accounts but at the same time use the merger relief provisions. The difference between the fair value of the investment and the nominal value of shares issued will be credited to a non statutory 'merger reserve account'.

12.54 This merger reserve is unrealised at the time it is recognised. However, there is no legal ruling as to whether it will become realised as and when the holding company receives dividends out of pre-acquisition reserves of the subsidiary company. The merger reserve may also be used to write off purchased goodwill.

Summary

12.55 Merger accounting principles:
1. It is not necessary to adjust carrying values of the assets and liabilities of the subsidiary to fair value either in its own books or on consolidation.
2. Appropriate adjustments should be made to achieve uniformity of accounting policies between the combining companies.
3. In the group accounts for the period in which the merger takes place, the profits or losses of subsidiaries brought in for the first time should be included for the entire period without any adjustment in respect of the pre-merger period.
4. Corresponding amounts should be presented as if the companies had been combined throughout the previous period and at the previous balance sheet date.
5. On consolidation, a difference between the carrying value of the investment in the subsidiary and the nominal value of the shares transferred to the issuing company will be recorded as a movement on reserves.
   Where the carrying value of the investment is less than the nominal value of shares transferred, the difference will be treated as a capital reserve arising on consolidation.

Where the carrying value of the investment is greater than the nominal value of shares transferred, the difference will be treated on consolidation as a reduction of reserves.

Disclosure

12.56 The following information should be disclosed in respect of all material business combinations, whether accounted for as acquisitions or mergers, in the financial statements of the acquiring or issuing company which deal with the year in which the combination takes place:
(a) the names of the combining companies;
(b) the number and class of the securities issued in respect of the combination, and details of any other consideration given;
(c) the accounting treatment adopted for the business combination (i.e. whether it has been accounted for as an acquisition or a merger); and
(d) the nature and amount of significant accounting adjustments by the combining companies to achieve consistency of accounting policies.

12.57 As required by SSAP 14, in respect of all material acquisitions during the year, the consolidated financial statements should contain sufficient information about the results of subsidiaries acquired to enable shareholders to appreciate the effect on the consolidated results. In addition, disclosure should be made of the date from which the results of major acquisitions have been brought into the accounts (that is, the effective date of those acquisitions).

12.58 In respect of all material mergers, the following information should be disclosed in the financial statements of the issuing company for the year in which the merger takes place:
(a) the fair value of the consideration given by the issuing company;
(b) an analysis of the current year's attributable profit before extraordinary items both before and after the effective date of the merger;
(c) an analysis of the attributable profit before extraordinary items of the current year up to the effective date of the merger and of the previous year between that of the issuing company and that of the subsidiary; and
(d) an analysis of extraordinary items so as to indicate whether each individual extraordinary item relates to pre- or post-merger events, and to which party to the merger the item relates.

Accounts of the holding company

12.59 SSAP 23 deals only with the method of accounting to be used in group accounts. It does not deal with the form of accounting to be used in the offeror's own accounts. As discussed earlier, a situation may arise whereby the offeror satisfies the merger relief conditions (CA 1985 S131 to 134) but does not satisfy the SSAP 23 conditions. This means that the consolidated accounts will have to be prepared using the acquisition method. However, the holding company may record part of the investment in the subsidiary company at the nominal value of shares issued. If the holding company records the investment in the subsidiary company at fair value, any difference between the fair value of purchase consideration and the nominal value of shares issued will be transferred to a non-statutory merger reserve. This merger reserve would also appear in the consolidated accounts. The above is based on the guidance given in the appendix to SSAP 23. The appendix does not specifically comment on whether this merger reserve is realised or unrealised. It implies that the merger reserve is unrealised, as it is equivalent to the share premium which would have arisen under the acquisition method.

12.60 If the fair value of any shares that the offeror company includes in the consideration exceeds their nominal value, and if merger relief is not available under S131 to 134 CA 1985, then the offeror should credit the excess of fair value over nominal value to a share premium account.

Conclusion

12.61 Doubts have been raised as to the effectiveness of SSAP 23 safeguards against abuses of merger accounting. The problem has arisen partly because of two contrived methods of financing acquisitions, known as 'vendor rights' and 'vendor placings'. The standard is defective because it does not prevent the use of merger accounting in these situations.

Vendor placing

12.62 This is a situation where the acquiring company may wish to use merger accounting on consolidation but some of or all of the shareholders may prefer to receive cash, rather than to receive shares in the acquiring company. The acquiring company will offer shares to the target company shareholders in exchange for their shares in that company. The acquiring company will arrange for a merchant bank to buy shares for cash from those target company shareholders who do not wish to receive shares in the acquiring company. The merchant bank will then exchange these shares in the target company for the shares in the acquiring company. The acquiring company will have complied with the SSAP 23 conditions and will be able to use the merger accounting on consolidation. The merchant bank which owns the shares in the acquiring company will place these shares in the market and sell them.

Vendor rights

12.63 Under this technique, the acquiring company's shares are offered to the shareholders of the target company. Once the share-for-share exchange deal has been concluded, the former shareholders of the target company offer the shares back to the acquiring company's shareholders for cash. The shareholders of the acquiring company will take up these shares on a pro rata basis. So after the vendor rights method is completed, cash will have been transferred from the shareholders of the acquiring company to some or all of the shareholders of the target company. If all the shareholders in the acquiring company take up their rights, then their share in the company will be in the same proportion as it was before the business combination. The acquiring company will have acquired the shares in the target company paying cash and therefore can use merger accounting on consolidation.

12.64 There is an argument that both vendor placings and vendor rights do not comply with the spirit of SSAP 23 (i.e. no significant change in ownership and no significant resources leaving the group), and that therefore the acquiring company should account for the business combination as an acquisition, not as a merger.

Other contrivances

(a) 20 per cent rule
12.65 In order to use merger accounting, SSAP 23 requires that immediately prior to the offer, the offeror does not hold more than 20 per cent of the target company's equity. To overcome this constraint, some companies have sold their shareholding in the market to reduce the holding to less than 20 per cent.

(b) 90 per cent of the purchase consideration for equity shares must be in equity shares
12.66 Some schemes reduce the amount of equity to be issued by capitalising reserves of the target company as non-voting preference shares, and then acquiring these by agreement in advance. The acquiring company pays cash for these preference shares, leaving only a small amount of equity to be issued.

ACCOUNTING FOR INVESTMENTS (4)

(c) Exploitation of merger relief provisions

12.67 The rules in SSAP 22, 23 and the merger relief provisions are used in such a way as to achieve, as far as they permit, the results desired by the acquiring company.

EXAMPLE

Company A, whose market value per share was 455p, acquires shares in company B in the following way:

	£million
Payment of cash	182
Issue of loan stock	31
Issue of 91 million ordinary nominal value 50 pence per share @ 455p per share	414
Therefore total purchase consideration for shares in B	627

Since company A (issuing company) has secured a 90 per cent equity holding in company B, company A is entitled to merger relief and records shares it has issued at their nominal value (S131–134 CA 1985). In the books of A, the investment in company B is recorded as follows:

	£million
1. Nominal value of shares issued = 91 million ordinary shares at 50p each	46
2. Cash	182
3. Loan stock	31
Investment in B	259

Since the shares issued by A are recorded at their nominal value, no share premium account is recognised. If the shares had been recorded at their fair value, a share premium of £368 million would have been recognised (£414 million − £46 million). Therefore, the investment in B is understated by £368 million.

The net assets of B are valued at £340 million. SSAP 14 requires that on the date of acquisition fair values should be ascribed to net tangible and intangible assets. A recorded these assets in its consolidated account at £259 million – the result is that the value at which the investment in B is recorded in A's books exactly matches the value at which the net assets of B were incorporated in the consolidated accounts. Therefore, no goodwill arises on consolidation. If goodwill of £285 million (difference between fair value of purchase consideration of £625 million and fair value of identifiable separate net assets of £340 million) had been recognised, it may have affected the earnings per share of A.

A treated the difference between the fair value of separable net assets acquired and the value at which they were recorded in the consolidated accounts as follows:

	£million
(i) Immediate write-off to the profit and loss account	40.5
(ii) Provision for reorganisation costs	40.5
Differences £340 million − £259 million =	81.0

A used the provision for reorganisation of £40.5 in the next year to absorb costs of £40.5 million – thus earnings per share is not affected.

There are two objectives which A managed to achieve by means of the above method:

1. By creating a reorganisation provision, A succeeded in insulating its profit and loss account from the effects of one year's costs of reorganising and restructuring its acquisition.

Because the provision is created at the point at acquisition in respect of reorganisation costs flowing therefrom, it is not charged against profits but rather as part of the acquisition costs themselves. The inflation of acquisition costs in this way (by their nature subjectively judged) can in some cases create a substantial goodwill element which, as explained in the chapter on SSAP 22, is then written off against reserves. The overall result either way is that charges, normally shown against profits on the face of the profit and loss account, are transferred to reserves – the very type of accounting treatment that SSAPs in general (and SSAP 6 in particular) are designed to avoid!

If B had remained independent and its management had taken the necessary steps now being taken by A to rehabilitate the group, the costs of so doing would have appeared on the face of the profit and loss account and would have probably been charged as an exceptional item in accordance with SSAP 6, thus affecting the earnings per share figure.

2. A, by perfectly legitimate means, also managed to avoid creating goodwill without the need for merger accounting.

Questions

1. Accountants in the United Kingdom/Ireland have been trying for some 20 years to determine the appropriate respective uses of the acquisition and merger methods of preparing group accounts.

Required:

(a) Explain the objectives of the two methods, and the way in which the said objectives are attained.

(b) Give your opinion of the success or otherwise of SSAP 23: Accounting for acquisitions and mergers (1985) in assigning each of the two methods of group accounting to its proper sphere.

2. **Required:**
(a) Using the information in appendices 1– 4: prepare a consolidated balance sheet as at 31 December 1986 for Watersports Limited, Roadsports Limited and Propulsion Limited.
N.B. The consolidation is to be carried out (i) using the merger method for Roadsports Limited and (ii) treating Propulsion Limited as an associate.
(b) Show the effects on:
   (i) the balance sheet of Watersports Ltd, and
   (ii) the consolidated balance sheet
if the directors of Watersports Limited had decided to include the investment in Roadsports Ltd in the parent company's own accounts at the fair value of the shares issued.

3. **Required:**
(a) Translate the balance sheet and profit and loss account of Speedsports Limited using the closing rate method. It is group policy to translate the profit and loss account using the closing rate.
(b) In accordance with the 'net investment' concept as per SSAP 20 for consolidated financial statements:
   (i) calculate the translation difference, and
   (ii) state how any such difference should be treated in the accounts of the holding company.
(c) Calculate the profits for inclusion in the consolidated balance sheet of Watersports Limited and subsidiaries for the year ended 31 December 1986 if Speedsports Ltd's profit and loss account is translated using:
   (i) the average rate
   (ii) the closing rate.
(d) Calculate the goodwill or reserve arising on consolidation that will be entered in the consolidated balance sheet as at 31 December 1986 in respect of the investment in Speedsports Ltd.

Information for questions 2 and 3 above:
The following appendices are attached:
Appendix
1 General introduction to Watersports Limited.
2 Draft balance sheet and profit and loss account of Watersports Limited.
3 Draft balance sheet and profit and loss account of Roadsports Limited.
4 Draft balance sheet and profit and loss account of Propulsion Limited.
5 Draft balance sheet and profit and loss account of Speedsports Limited.

UNDERSTANDING ACCOUNTING STANDARDS

Appendix 1: General introduction to Watersports Limited
Watersports Limited was incorporated in 1975 to carry on business as a wholesaler of sports equipment.
The company has decided to pursue a policy of growth by acquisition and made the following investments:

Date of purchase	Shares acquired	Consideration provided by Watersports Ltd	Carrying value of the investment in the Balance Sheet £
31/12/86	945,000 ordinary shares in Roadsports Limited	700,000 ordinary shares in Watersports Limited	350,000
1/1/86	441,000 ordinary shares in Propulsion Limited	Cash	332,500
1/1/86	1,050,000 ordinary shares in Speedsports Limited, a wholesaler operating in Germany	Cash	400,000

Note
(i) It is the group policy to write off goodwill at the rate of 20% per annum commencing in the year of acquisition.
(ii) A recent valuation of the ordinary shares of Watersports Limited carried out by the company's auditors places a value of 75p per share on each ordinary share.

Appendix 2: Draft balance sheet and profit and loss account of Watersports Limited for the year ended 31 December 1986

Balance Sheet as at 31 December 1986

	£	£
Fixed assets		
Tangible assets (net book value)		550,000
Investments		1,082,500
Current assets		
Stock	259,000	
Debtors	238,000	
Cash	7,000	
	504,000	

ACCOUNTING FOR INVESTMENTS (4)

	£	£
Creditors (due within one year)		
Trade and other creditors	246,200	
Bank overdraft	227,000	
Proposed dividends	21,000	
	494,200	
Net current assets		9,800
Total assets less current liabilities		1,642,300
Creditors (due after one year)		
9% Debentures	245,000	
Deferred tax	52,500	297,500
Net assets		1,344,800
Capital and reserves		
Ordinary shares of 50p each		
(fully paid up)	700,000	
Share premium account	320,000	
Revaluation reserve	225,000	
Other reserves	30,000	
Profit and loss account	69,800	1,344,800
		1,344,800

Profit and Loss Account of Watersports Limited
for the year ended 31 December 1986

	£	£
Sales		605,850
Cost of sales		245,000
Gross profit		360,850
Administration expenses	160,200	
Selling expenses	96,350	256,550
Trading profit		104,300
Interest payable		25,200
		79,100
Taxation		27,000
		52,100
Dividends		28,000
Retained profit		24,100

Reserve movement
Profit brought forward	45,700
Profit retained	24,100
Profit carried forward	69,800

Note
Dividends receivable for 1986 have not been taken into account in the profit and loss account.

Appendix 3: Draft balance sheet and profit and loss account of Roadsports Limited for the year ended 31 December 1986

Balance Sheet as at 31 December 1986

	£	£
Fixed assets		
Tangible assets (net book value)		1,100,000
Current assets		
Stock	175,250	
Debtors	132,500	
Cash	74,750	
	382,500	
Creditors (due within one year)		
Trade and other creditors	236,000	
Bank overdraft	283,300	
Proposed dividends	14,000	
	533,300	
Net current assets		(150,800)
Total assets less current liabilities		949,200
Creditors (due after one year)		
10% Debentures	106,750	
Deferred tax	23,450	130,200
Net assets		819,000
Capital and reserves		
Ordinary shares of 50p each (fully paid up)	525,000	
Reserves	140,000	
Profit and loss account	154,000	
		819,000
		819,000

ACCOUNTING FOR INVESTMENTS (4)

*Profit and Loss Account of Roadsports Limited
for the year ended 31 December 1986*

	£	£
Sales		565,000
Cost of sales		232,500
		332,500
Administration expenses	110,300	
Selling expenses	130,400	240,700
Trading profit		91,800
Interest payable		20,950
		70,850
Taxation		24,000
		46,850
Dividends		14,000
Retained profit		32,850
Reserve movement		
Profit brought forward		121,150
Profit retained		32,850
Profit carried forward		154,000

Note

(i) During 1986 Watersports Limited had sold goods to Roadsports Limited with an invoiced value of £80,500.

At 31 December 1986 Roadsports Limited still held in stock such goods with an invoiced value of £21,500.

Watersports Limited invoiced goods to Roadsports Limited at 25% on cost.

(ii) The fair value of the tangible fixed assets in Roadsports Limited was £1,250,000.

Appendix 4: Draft balance sheet and profit and loss account of Propulsion Limited for the year ended 31 December 1986

Balance Sheet as at 31 December 1986

	£	£
Fixed assets		
Tangible assets		2,090,000
Current assets		
Stock	300,250	
Debtors	160,200	
Cash	11,000	
	471,450	

Creditors (due within one year)
  Trade and other creditors   491,130
  Bank overdraft   68,950
                                      560,080
Net current liabilities   (88,630)
Total assets less current liabilities   2,001,370
Creditors (due after one year)
  10% Debentures   350,000
  Deferred tax   103,250
                                                     453,250
Net assets   1,548,120

Capital and reserves
Ordinary shares of 50p each   1,050,000
Share premium account   70,000
Revaluation reserve   300,000
Profit and loss account   128,120
                                                   1,548,120
                                                   1,548,120

Profit and Loss Account of Propulsion Limited
for the year ended 31 December 1986

	£	£
Sales		524,790
Cost of sales		215,130
		309,660
Administration expenses	138,400	
Selling expenses	78,720	
		217,120
Trading profit		92,540
Interest payable		36,000
		56,540
Taxation		35,000
Retained		21,540

Note
(i) Propulsion Limited revalued its assets on 31 December 1985 and created a revaluation reserve of £250,000 in order to show its assets at fair value at that date.
(ii) During 1986 Propulsion Limited increased the revaluation reserve by £50,000 which represented an increase in asset valuation that occurred during 1986.

ACCOUNTING FOR INVESTMENTS (4)

Appendix 5: Draft balance sheet and profit and loss account of Speedsports Limited for the year ended 31 December 1986

Balance Sheet as at 31 December 1986

	DM	DM
Fixed assets		
Tangible assets (net book value)		1,950,000
Current assets		
Stock	320,800	
Debtors	224,950	
Cash	17,600	
	563,350	
Creditors (due within one year)		
Trade and other creditors	361,450	
Dividends	70,000	
	431,450	
Net current assets		131,900
Total assets less current liabilities		2,081,900
Creditors (due after one year)		
7% Debentures		450,000
Net assets		1,631,900
Capital and reserves		
Ordinary shares of 1DM each	1,400,000	
Revaluation reserve	170,000	
Profit and loss account	61,900	
		1,631,900
		1,631,900

Profit and Loss Account for the year ended 31 December 1986

	DM	DM
Sales		475,000
Cost of sales		135,500
Gross profit		339,500
Administration expenses	82,900	
Selling expenses	61,600	144,500
Trading profit		195,000
Interest paid		4,500
		190,500
Taxation		69,240
		121,260
Dividends proposed		70,000
Retained profit		51,260
Reserve movement		
Profit brought forward		10,640
Profit retained		51,260
		61,900

Note
 (i) The revaluation reserve was credited on 1 January 1986 and the assets were accepted as being at fair value when Watersports Limited acquired their holding.
 (ii) The exchange rates for DMs to the £ were:
  1 January 1986   3.20
  31 December 1986 3.25
  Average for 1986 3.22

4. Consolidated Furniture Group plc wishes to adopt the merger accounting principles in SSAP 23: *Accounting for Acquisitions and Mergers*, in respect of its combination with Tables & Chairs Ltd on 30 September 19X3.

On 1 August 19X3 Consolidated Furniture Group plc acquired 5% of the issued share capital of Tables & Chairs Ltd for a consideration of 80 000 shares of 25p each at an agreed value of 125p each.

The terms of the merger on 30 September 19X3, which were accepted by all shareholders and declared unconditional on the same day, were that for every 8 shares held in Tables & Chairs Ltd, a holder received 20 shares of 25p each at an agreed value of 135p each in Consolidated Furniture Group plc plus £3 nominal of 13% Unsecured Loan Stock 2002.

ACCOUNTING FOR INVESTMENTS (4)

All the shares issued were credited as fully paid and ranked *pari passu* with existing shares in issue except that those issued on 30 September 19X3 were not to rank for the final dividend in respect of the year ended 30 November 19X3.

The draft summarized balance sheet and profit and loss account of the companies for the year ended 30 November 19X3, the accounting reference date for Consolidated Furniture Group plc, were:

	Consolidated Furniture Group plc	Tables & Chairs Ltd
Balance sheet	£'000	£'000
Fixed assets	4563	3092
Goodwill at cost	—	800
Investments	175	—
Current assets	2369	3626
Current liabilities	(2286)	(4207)
	4821	3311
Share capital	3000	1600
Reserves	1821	1711
	4821	3311

	£'000	£'000
Profit and loss account		
Turnover	36873	25003
Profit before tax	1151	127
Taxation	260	—
Profit after tax	891	127
Dividends paid	288	—
Profits retained	603	127

Additional information is given as follows:

(1) The reserves of Consolidated Furniture Group plc at 30 November 19X3 consisted of a share premium account of £140,000 and revenue reserves of £1,681,000. The reserves in Tables & Chairs Ltd are undistributed revenue reserves.
(2) The issue of the shares made on 1 August 19X3 is reflected in the draft financial statements.
(3) It is the policy of Consolidated Furniture Group plc to write off goodwill in equal instalments over 5 years.
(4) It is considered that the market value of the 13% loan stock issued is par.

(5) The share capitals of the companies are:
Consolidated Furniture Group plc – ordinary 25p each
Tables & Chairs Ltd – ordinary £1 each
(6) The directors of Consolidated Furniture Group plc propose a final dividend of 1p per share. This is not yet reflected in the draft financial statements.

You are required to:

(a) prepare a consolidated balance sheet and profit and loss account, in summary form, of Consolidated Furniture Group plc at 30 November 19X3
(b) give the revised analysis of reserves of Consolidated Furniture Group plc at 30 November 19X3 suitable for inclusion in the published financial statements, and
(c) comment whether you consider merger accounting to be appropriate in the above example giving an indication of advantages which may arise.

Note: Make calculations to nearest £'000 and ignore the costs of the merger and Advance Corporation Tax.

Chapter Thirteen

Accounting for Investments (5): SSAP 20: Accounting for Foreign Currency Translations

Accounting Procedures

13.1 SSAP 20 considers the accounting procedures for foreign currency operations in two stages:
(a) the individual company stage – direct transactions by an individual company in foreign currencies;
(b) the consolidated financial statements stage – where foreign operations are carried out through an intermediary, which could be a subsidiary, associated company or branch.

The individual company stage

13.2 SSAP 20 outlines the following general requirements:
(a) all transactions in a foreign currency should be translated at the exchange rate ruling on the date on which the transaction occurred (i.e. actual rate);
(b) at the balance sheet date there will be no retranslation of non-monetary items (i.e. fixed assets and stocks). Thus, non-monetary items acquired in foreign currency will always be translated at the actual rate ruling on the date of transaction and there will therefore be no exchange gain or loss;
(c) at the balance sheet date, all monetary items should be translated at the rate ruling on the balance sheet date (i.e. closing rate);
(d) as stated in (b) above, there will be no exchange gain or loss on non-monetary items. Therefore an exchange gain or loss will arise only when:
  (i) at the balance sheet date, monetary items originally translated at the rate ruling on the date of transaction are now being re-translated at the closing rate;
  (ii) the rate ruling on the date of settlement of a transaction is different from the actual rate in existence when the transaction was recorded.

13.3 The only exception to the rule in (a) above occurs when foreign equity investments are financed by foreign currency borrowings. This is fully explained in a later section.

13.4 SSAP 20 requires all exchange gains and losses on settled and unsettled transactions to be taken to the profit and loss account as part of the profit or loss from ordinary activities unless they arise from events which themselves would fall to be treated as extraordinary items, in which case they should be included as part of such items. SSAP 20 states 'Exchange gains or losses arising on settled transactions in the context of an individual company's operations have already been reflected in cash flows, since a change in the exchange rate increases or decreases the local currency equivalents of amounts paid or received in cash settlement. Similarly, it is reasonably certain that exchange gains or losses on unsettled short-term monetary items will soon be reflected in cash flows'. Since these gains or losses have a direct impact on the cash flows of the company, SSAP 20 requires them to be included as part of the profit and loss account for the year.

13.5 Any long-term monetary items will be translated at the year-end rate (i.e. closing rate) as this gives the best estimate of the liability or asset in terms of the reporting currency. SSAP 20 requires that 'in order to give a true and fair view of results, exchange gains and losses on long-term monetary items should normally be reported as part of the profit or loss for the period in accordance with the accruals concept of accounting; ...'

13.6 The treatment of long-term monetary items on a simple cash movement basis, as in the case of short-term monetary items, would be inconsistent with the accruals concept. The Technical Release issued with SSAP 20 states 'the application of the above rule may result in unrealised exchange gains on unsettled long-term monetary items being taken to the profit and loss account. The ASC considers that there is a need for symmetry in the treatment of exchange gains and losses; this treatment acknowledges that exchange gains can be determined no less objectively than exchange losses at the balance sheet date and that it would be illogical to deny that favourable movements in exchange rates had occurred whilst accounting for adverse movements'.

13.7 The foregoing explains the necessity for departing from the requirement in Sch 4, CA 1985 (the 'prudence' principle) that only *realised* profits shall be included in the profit and loss account.

13.8 The following example illustrates the general requirements of the standard outlined above:

ACCOUNTING FOR INVESTMENTS (5)

A Ltd, a UK company whose accounting year ends on 31 December 1986, carried out the following transactions in foreign currencies during the year:

Rate of Exchange

(a) Purchases goods from a German company on
1 July 1986 for DM 105,000   £1 = DM 3.5
Pays amount due to German company on
1 October 1986   £1 = DM 3
Goods remain in stock until after 31 December 1986

(b) Sells other goods to a French company on
1 December 1986 for FF 550,000   £1 = FF 11
No cash received in payment until 31 January 1987

(c) Takes out a long-term loan on 31 March 1986 for
US $1,500,000   £1 = US $1.5

(d) Purchases plant and machinery from a Swiss
company for SWF 500,000 on 1 September 1986   £1 = SWF 2.5
Pays Swiss company on 30 November 1986   £1 = SWF 2
Exchange rates at balance sheet date   £1 = DM 3.1
  £1 = FF 9.9
  £1 = US $1.25
  £1 = SWF 2.00

13.9 Under the requirements of SSAP 20 these transactions will be treated as follows in the accounts of A Ltd:

(a) The purchases will be recorded at the ruling rate on the transactions date:
$$\frac{DM\ 105{,}000}{3.5} = £30{,}000.$$
The charge to cost of sales will therefore be £30,000. On the date of settlement of the creditor, the amount of pounds sterling required will be $\frac{DM\ 105{,}000}{3} = £35{,}000$. This will give rise to an exchange loss of £5000 which will be debited to profit and loss account for the year as part of profit or loss on ordinary activities. The stock held at the balance sheet date is a non-monetary item and is therefore translated at the transaction rate of DM 3.5 = £30,000.

(b) The sales will be translated at the rate ruling on the transaction date:
$$\frac{FF\ 550{,}000}{11} = £50{,}000.$$
At the year end the debtor, which is a monetary item, will need to be translated at the closing rate: $\frac{FF\ 550{,}000}{9.9} = £55{,}555.$

UNDERSTANDING ACCOUNTING STANDARDS

This will give rise to an exchange gain of £5,555 which will be credited to profit and loss account for the year as part of profit or loss on ordinary activities.

(c) The loan will initially be recorded in the books at the rate ruling on the transaction date: $\dfrac{US \$ 1,500,000}{1.5} = £1,000,000$.

At the balance sheet date the loan will be translated at the closing rate: $\dfrac{US \$ 1,500,000}{1.25} = £1,200,000$.

The resulting loss of £200,000 will be charged to the profit and loss account as part of profit or loss on ordinary activities.

(d) The fixed assets will be capitalised at the transaction rate of £1 = SWF 2.5 as $\dfrac{SWF\ 500,000}{2.5} = £200,000$ and no subsequent translations will need to be made. Depreciation charges will be based on this amount.

The payment to the Swiss company is made when the exchange rate is £1 = SWF 2.0 requiring a pound sterling payment of £250,000 giving rise to an exchange loss of £50,000. This loss will be debited to profit and loss account for the year as part of profit or loss on ordinary activities.

Forward contracts

13.10 As already stated, the general requirement in SSAP 20 is that all transactions in foreign currency should be translated at the exchange rate in operation on the date on which the transaction occurred and at the balance sheet date all monetary items should be translated at the closing rate. It is, however, acknowledged in SSAP 20 that a rate specified in a forward hedging contract *may* be used for the translation of trading transactions denominated in a foreign currency (and for any monetary assets or liabilities arising from such transactions) where these have been covered by a related or matching forward contract. This treatment recognises the fact that such contracts are used to hedge any exchange risks involved in foreign currency operations, and that no economic gain or loss will therefore arise.

EXAMPLE

A Ltd purchases goods from a German company on 1 July 1986 for DM 105,000 when the rate of exchange is £1 = DM 3.5. A Ltd buys on 1 July 1986 DM 105,000 for forward three month delivery on 1 October 1986 at £1 = DM 3.3. The initial transaction could be recorded at the forward rate of DM 3.3 giving $\dfrac{DM\ 105,000}{3.3} = £31,818$ which would match the amount paid to purchase the currency. No exchange gain or loss would therefore arise on the transaction. This treatment under SSAP 20 is optional.

Circumstances under which exchange gains arising on translation of long-term monetary items would not be recognised in the profit and loss account.

13.11 As stated earlier, the long-term monetary items should be translated at the year-end rate and exchange gains and losses on long-term monetary items should normally be reported as part of the profit or loss for the period in accordance with the accruals concept. SSAP 20 recognises that there may be exceptional circumstances when this treatment may not be prudent. To quote SSAP 20: 'it is necessary to consider on the grounds of prudence whether the amount of the gain, or the amount by which exchange gains exceed part exchange losses on the same items, to be recognised in the profit and loss account should be restricted in the exceptional cases where there are doubts as to convertibility or marketability of the currency in question'.

13.12 These considerations may be appropriate in the following circumstances:
(a) where a country is subject to stringent exchange control regulations and unauthorised foreign remittances are banned;
(b) where there is a severe political upheaval in the country and all assets are frozen.

13.13 The recognition of any exchange gains in the profit and loss account under these circumstances may be imprudent and the implication in SSAP 20 is that the extent to which these gains exceed past exchange losses on the same items should be taken to the reserves.

Consolidated financial statements

1. The closing rate method (net investment method)

Mechanics
13.14
(a) All amounts in the balance sheet of a foreign enterprise should be translated at the rate of exchange ruling at the balance sheet date.
(b) Amounts in the profit and loss account of the foreign enterprise should be translated using either the closing rate or an average rate for the period.

13.15 SSAP 20 allows the choice of the closing rate or an average rate for translation of profit and loss account, but the method selected must be applied consistently from period to period. The use of closing rate is more likely to achieve the objective of translation – i.e. recognition that the investment is in the net worth of its foreign enterprise rather than a direct investment in the individual assets and liabilities of that enterprise. However, it can be argued that an average rate reflects more fairly the profits and losses and cash flows, since they accrue to the group throughout the accounting period.

13.16 Exchange differences will arise when:

1. The closing rate differs from that ruling at the previous balance sheet date. The net assets of a foreign subsidiary which at the start of the year were translated at the rate ruling at that date are now being translated at the closing rate.
2. An average rate is used to translate the profit and loss account items. This is because all the items on the balance sheet are at closing rate.

SSAP 20 requires that when foreign subsidiaries are translated using the closing rate method, **exchange differences should be recorded as movements on reserves and not taken to the profit and loss account**. This is because exchange gains and losses resulting from foreign exchange rate changes may have no impact on cash flows to and from the investing group.

EXAMPLE *The closing rate method*
London PLC

(a) London PLC acquired 80 per cent of the share capital of Ohio Inc in 19W3 when the reserves of Ohio were $2,500. The cost of the investment was £2,450.
(b) Ohio Inc raises its finances locally and the company is semi-independent as most decisions are made by its local board of directors.
(c) The draft financial statements for the year ended 30/11/19X4 are shown below.
(d) During the year, Ohio purchased fixed assets at a cost of $2,800.
(e) Relevant exchange rates were:

At acquisition	$2.20 = £1
At 30/11/X3	$2.40 = £1
At 30/11/X4	$2.50 = £1
Average for 19X4	$2.45 = £1
At the date of dividend payment	$2.47 = £1

(f) Operating profit is arrived at after charging depreciation of:
London £4,730
Ohio $2,260

ACCOUNTING FOR INVESTMENTS (5)

Profit and loss account for the year ended 30/11/19X4

	London £	Ohio $
Operating profit	29,392	10,600
Dividends Received	259	—
Dividends Receivable	384	—
	30,035	10,600
Taxation	12,650	4,200
Profit after tax	17,385	6,400
Extraordinary items (redundancy costs on closure of business segment.)	—	(2,500)
	17,385	3,900
Dividends – Paid	(4,000)	(800)
– Proposed	(8,000)	(1,200)
Retained Profit	5,385	1,900
Balance at 1/12/X3	17,966	7,500
Balance at 30/11/X4	23,351	9,400

Balance Sheet at 30 November 19X4

	London £	Ohio $
Fixed assets – cost	47,300	22,600
– depreciation	11,400	6,600
	35,900	16,000
Investment in Ohio Inc	2,450	—
Stocks	18,200	4,100
Debtors	5,960	2,350
Dividends receivable	384	—
Cash at bank	907	2,000
	63,801	24,450
Long-term loans	6,000	3,000
Creditors	16,450	6,850
Dividends payable	8,000	1,200
Ordinary share capital	10,000	4,000
Profit and Loss account	23,351	9,400
	63,801	24,450

Required: (i) Consolidated Balance Sheet
(ii) Consolidated Profit and Loss Account
(iii) Relevant extracts from the fixed asset schedule as regards the fixed assets of Ohio.

Profit and Loss Account to be translated at average rate.

UNDERSTANDING ACCOUNTING STANDARDS

Workings and solution

(a) *Translation of balance sheet of Ohio Inc*

	$	Rate	£
Fixed assets – cost	22,600	2.5	9,040
– depreciation	(6,600)	2.5	(2,640)
	16,000		6,400
Stocks	4,100	2.5	1,640
Debtors	2,350	2.5	940
Cash at bank	2,000	2.5	800
Long-term loans	(3,000)	2.5	(1,200)
Creditors	(6,850)	2.5	(2,740)
Dividends payable	(1,200)	2.5	(480)
	13,400		5,360
Equity interest			
Ordinary share capital	4,000	2.2	1,818
Profit & loss A/C	9,400	Balance	3,542
	13,400		5,360

Note: All assets and liabilities must be translated at the closing rate. However, the equity interest of $13,400 is eliminated on consolidation so this rule does not have to be applied to the constituent part of shareholders' funds. For convenience of workings (particularly in calculating goodwill on consolidation) share capital is translated at the rate of exchange corresponding with that prevailing when the shares were acquired, and the accumulated profit and loss account is a balancing figure.

(b) *Consolidation workings*

	£
(i) Cost of Investment	2,450
Less 80% ordinary share capital (4/5 × 1818)	(1,454)
Less Pre-acquisition reserves 80% × $2,500 / 2.2	(909)
Goodwill on consolidation	87

	£
(ii) Reserves	
Ohio – Balance	3,542
Less Pre-acquisition 80% × 2500 / 2.2	(909)
Less Minority Interest 20% × 3,542	(708)
To consolidated balance sheet	1,925

ACCOUNTING FOR INVESTMENTS (5)

	£
(iii) Minority Interest	
Ordinary Share Capital 20% × 1,818	364
Reserves	708
Consolidated Balance Sheet	1,072
Dividends payable – Ohio	480
Minority Interest – 20%	(96)
Contra	384

(c) *Consolidated balance sheet at 30 November 19X4*

	£	£
Fixed assets		
Intangible assets – goodwill		87
Tangible assets (35,900 + 6,400)		42,300
		42,387
Current assets		
Stocks (18,200 + 1,640)	19,840	
Debtors (5,960 + 940)	6,900	
Cash at bank (907 + 800)	1,707	
	28,477	
Creditors (amounts falling due within one year)		
Creditors (16,450 + 2,740)	19,190	
Dividends payable – Holding company	8,000	
– Minority interest	96	
	27,286	
		1,161
		43,548
Debenture loans		(7,200)
		36,348
Minority interest		(1,072)
		35,276
Ordinary share capital		10,000
Profit and Loss Account (23,351 + 1,925)		25,276
		35,276

UNDERSTANDING ACCOUNTING STANDARDS

(d) *Fixed asset note (items relating to Ohio only)*

	£	$	@	£
			Translation workings	
Balance @ 31/12/X3	8,250	19,800	2.4	8,250
Therefore Exchange Adjustment	(330)			
Additions	1,120	2,800	2.5	1,120
Balance @ 30/11/X4	9,040	22,600	2.5	9,040
Depreciation provision				
Balance @ 31/12/X3	1,808	4,340	2.4	1,808
Charge	922	2,260	2.45	922
Therefore Exchange Adjustment	(90)			
Balance @ 30/11/X4	2,640	6,600	2.5	2,640
Net book value 30/11/X4	6,400	16,000	2.5	6,400
Net book value 30/11/X3	6,442	15,460	2.4	6,442

(e) *Translation of profit and loss account for Ohio*

	$	@	£
Operating Profit	10,600	2.45	4,326
Taxation	4,200	2.45	1,714
	6,400		2,612
Extraordinary items	(2,500)	2.45	(1,020)
	3,900		1,592
Dividends – paid	(800)	2.47	(324)
– proposed	(1,200)	2.5	(480)
Retained profit	1,900		788

(f) *Calculation of Exchange Difference*

	£
Total exchange difference	
Equity interest @ 30/11/X4 @ closing rate (see balance sheet)	5,360
Equity interest @ 30/11/X3 @ last year's closing rate:	

Ordinary share capital $ 4,000
+ Reserves $ 7,500
= Net Assets $11,500
                  ÷ 2.4   4,792
Increase during the year   568
Retained profit per P & L A/C   788
Therefore total exchange loss   (220)
Proportion charged direct to reserves 80% × 220   (176)

ACCOUNTING FOR INVESTMENTS (5)

(g) *Analysis of exchange difference*

	Equity interest 100%	Rate	Equity interest 100%	Net investment 80%
	$		£	£
Balance at 31/12/X3	11,500	2.4	4,792	3,834
Therefore loss on retranslaton of opening net investment	—	—	(192)	(154)
Opening net investment retranslated @ closing rate	11,500	2.5	4,600	3,680
Retained profit	1,900	Various	788	630
Therefore difference between P/L translated at average and closing rates	—	—	(28)	(22)
Closing net investment @ closing rate	13,400	2.5	5,360	4,288

Exchange loss taken to reserves = £154 + £22 = £176.

(h) *Consolidated profit and loss account workings*

	£
1. Profit on ordinary activities before tax (29,392 + 4,326)	33,718
2. Tax (12,650 + 1,714)	14,364
3. Minority interest (20% × 2,612)	522
4. Extraordinary items (80% × 1020)	(816)
5. Profit and account balance at 1/12/X3:	
Equity interest at acquisition $6,500 ÷ 2.2	2,954
Equity interest at 1/12/X3 $11,500 ÷ 2.2	4,792
Increase (100%)	1,838
Ohio (80% × 1,838)	1,470
London	17,966
	19,436

(i) *Consolidated profit and loss account for the year ended 30 November 19X4*

	£	£
Profit on ordinary activities before taxation		33,718
Tax on profit on ordinary activities		14,364
		19,354
Minority shareholders interest		(522)
		18,832
Extraordinary charges		(816)
		18,016
Dividends – paid	4,000	
– proposed	8,000	
		(12,000)
Retained profit		6,016
Reserves:		
Profit and loss account at 1/12/19X3		19,436
Retained profit		6,016
Exchange loss		(176)
Profit and loss account at 30/11/19X4		25,276

The temporal method

Mechanics

13.17 SSAP 20 contains no details as to how the temporal method is to be operated and merely states that 'the mechanics of this method are identical with those used in preparing the accounts of an individual company'. This implies that the following treatment is appropriate:

(a) all transactions should be translated at the rate ruling on the transaction date or at an average rate for a period if this is not materially different;
(b) non-monetary assets should not normally be retranslated at the balance sheet date;
(c) monetary assets and liabilities should be retranslated at the closing rate; and
(d) all exchange gains and losses should be taken to the profit and loss account as part of the profit or loss from ordinary activities.

EXAMPLE

The same facts are used as for the London/Ohio example. The following additional information is required:

(a) Exchange rates at acquisition of fixed assets:
    Assets acquired prior to 19X4 $ 2.31 = £1
    Assets acquired in 19X4 $ 2.48 = £1
(b) Depreciation charge
    Pre-19X4 assets $ 1,980
    19X4 assets $ 280
                                         $ 2,260
(c) Extraordinary item – assume this relates to charges incurred when the exchange rate was $ 2.45 = £1.

Workings and solution
(a) *Translation of balance sheet at 30 November 19X4*

	$	@	£
Fixed assets – cost (pre 19X4)	19,800	2.31	8,571
– cost (19X4)	2,800	2.48	1,129
– depreciation (pre 19X4 assets)	(6,320)	2.31	(2,736)
– depreciation (19X4 assets)	(280)	2.48	(113)
Stocks	4,100	2.5	1,640
Debtors	2,350	2.5	940
Cash at bank	2,000	2.5	800
Long-term loans	(3,000)	2.5	(1,200)
Creditors	(6,850)	2.5	(2,740)
Dividends payable	(1,200)	2.5	(480)
	13,400		5,811
Equity interest			
Ordinary share capital	4,000	2.2	1,818
Reserves (P & L A/C)	9,400	Balance	3,993
	13,400		5,811

(b) *Consolidated workings*

	£
Reserves (P & L a/c) of Ohio:	
Per Balance Sheet	3,993
Less Pre-acquisition 80% × 2,500 / 2.2	(909)
Less Minority interest 20% × 3,993	(799)
To consolidated balance sheet	2,285
Minority Interest	
Ordinary share capital 20% × 1,818	364
Reserves	799
Consolidated balance sheet	1,163

UNDERSTANDING ACCOUNTING STANDARDS

Goodwill
Cost of Investment	2,450
Less 80% ordinary share capital	(1,454)
Less pre-acquisition reserves	(909)
	87

(c) *Consolidated balance sheet at 30 November 19X4*

	£	£
Fixed assets		
Intangible assets – goodwill		87
Tangible assets (35,900+(8571+1129−2736−113))		42,751
		42,838
Current assets		
Stocks (18,200+1,640)	19,840	
Debtors (5,960+940)	6,900	
Cash @ bank (907+800)	1,707	
	28,447	
Creditors (Amounts falling due within one year)		
Creditors (16,450 + 2,740)	19,190	
Dividends payable – Holding company	8,000	
– Minority interest	96	
	27,286	
		1,161
		43,999
Debenture loans (6,000 + 1,200)		(7,200)
Minority interest		(1,163)
		35,636
Capital and reserves		
Called up share capital		10,000
Profit and loss account (23,351 + 2,285)		25,636
		35,636

ACCOUNTING FOR INVESTMENTS (5)

(d) *Translation of profit and loss account of Ohio*

	$	@	£
Profit before depreciation (10,600 + 2,260)	12,860	2.45	5,249
Depreciation – pre 19X4 assets	(1,980)	2.31	(857)
– 19X4 addition	(280)	2.48	(113)
Operating profit	10,600		4,279
Taxation	(4,200)	2.45	(1,714)
	6,400		2,565
Extraordinary items	(2,500)	2.45	(1,020)
	3,900		1,545
Dividends – paid	(800)	2.47	(324)
– proposed	(1,200)	2.5	(480)
	1,900		741

(e) *Calculation of total exchange difference*
1. Equity interest @ 30/11/X4 = £5,811 from Balance Sheet
2. Retained profit for the year = £741 from Profit and Loss Account
3. Equity interest @ 30/11/X3 – unknown in £
   Equity interest @ 31/11/X3 in $:

	$
Ordinary share capital	4000
Reserves	7500
	11500

Under the temporal method, the different parts of this figure are translated at different exchange rates:

	$	@	£
Fixed assets (19800–4340)	15,460	2.31	6,693
Loan (assume no change during year)	(3,000)	2.4	(1,250)
Therefore net current liability	(960)	2.4	(400)
	11,500		5,043
Equity interest @ 30/11/X4			5,811
Equity interest @ 30/11/X3			(5,043)
Increase during year			768
Retained profit			(741)
Therefore EXCHANGE GAIN			27

Therefore the whole of this exchange gain is treated as part of the profit for the year from ordinary operations.

(f) *Consolidated profit and loss account workings*

	£
1. Profit on ordinary activities before tax	
(29,392 + 4279)	33,671
Exchange gain	27
	33,698
2. Tax (12,650 + 1714)	14,364
3. Minority interest:	
20% × £2565 + 20% × £27	519
4. Extraordinary items (80% × 1020)	816
5. Profit and loss account balance at 30/11/19X3:	
Equity interest at acquisition $6500 ÷ 2.2	2,954
Equity interest at 30/11/19X3 (see (e) above)	5,043
Increase	2,089
Ohio 80% × £2089	1,671
London	17,966
	19,637

(g) *Consolidated profit and loss account for the year ended 30 November 19X4*

	£	£
Profit on ordinary activities before tax		33,698
Taxation		14,364
Profit on ordinary activities after tax		19,334
Minority interest		519
		18,815
Extraordinary items		816
		17,999
Dividends – paid	4000	
– proposed	8000	
		12,000
Retained profit		5,999
Note – reserves		
Profit and Loss a/c @ 30/11/X3		19,637
Retained Profit		5,999
Profit and Loss a/c @ 30/11/X4		25,636

Choice of method

13.18 The choice of method is not left to the investing company to determine but depends on the relationship between the investing company and the foreign enterprise.

(a) The closing rate method (also called the net investment method)

13.19 SSAP 20 recognises that this method will probably be used in the majority of cases. This method is most suitable when an investing company regards its foreign enterprises as separate businesses which are independent of the business of the investing company. SSAP 20 states that 'this method recognises that the investment of a company is in the net worth of its foreign enterprise rather than direct investment in the individual assets and liabilities of that enterprise. The foreign enterprise will normally have net current assets and fixed assets which may be financed partly by local currency borrowings. In its day-to-day operations the foreign enterprise is not normally dependent on the reporting currency of the investing company. The investing company may look forward to a stream of dividends but the net investment will remain until the business is liquidated or the investment disposed of'.

13.20 The exchange differences under this method are recorded as part of reserve movements as they do not have any direct impact on cash flows to and from the investing company. This treatment also prevents the trading operations of the foreign enterprises being distorted by factors unrelated to their trading performance.

(b) The temporal method

13.21 SSAP 20 states that there may be cases in which the affairs of a foreign enterprise are so closely interlinked with those of the investing company that its results may be regarded as being more dependent on the economic environment of the investing company's currency than on its own reporting currency. In these cases the temporal method must be used to restate the foreign enterprise's assets and liabilities for incorporation in the consolidated accounts. The effect of this will be as if the transactions of the foreign enterprise had been entered into by the investing company itself in its own currency.

13.22 SSAP 20 states that it is not possible to select one factor which of itself will lead to a company to conclude that the temporal method should be adopted. All the available evidence should be considered in determining whether the currency of the investing company is the dominant currency in the economic environment in which the foreign enterprise operates. SSAP 20 requires some of the following factors to be taken into account:

(a) the extent to which the cash flows of the foreign enterprise have a direct impact upon those of the investing company;
(b) the extent to which the functioning of the foreign enterprise is dependent directly upon the investing company;
(c) the currency in which the majority of the trading transactions are denominated; and
(d) the major currency movements to which the operation is exposed in its financing structure.

13.23 SSAP 20 gives the following examples of situations where the temporal method may be appropriate:

The foreign enterprise A acts as a selling agency receiving stocks of goods from the investing company and remitting the proceeds of sale back to the company;

B produces a raw material or manufactures parts or sub-assemblies which are then shipped to the investing company for inclusion in its own products;

C is located overseas for tax, exchange control or similar reasons to act as a means of raising finance for other companies in the group.

13.24 SSAP 20 requires that when foreign subsidiaries are translated using the temporal method, **exchange differences should be taken to the profit and loss account as part of the profit or loss from ordinary activities** as they have an impact on cash flows of the investing company.

The special case of equity investment financed by foreign borrowings

The individual company stage

13.25 As previously stated, the general rule is that there will be NO retranslation on non-monetary items acquired in foreign currency once they have been translated at the actual rate ruling on the date of transaction. There is one exception to this rule which relates to the treatment of foreign equity investments financed by foreign currency borrowings.

13.26 A foreign equity investment denominated in foreign currency would normally be translated at the rate ruling on the transaction date as

ACCOUNTING FOR INVESTMENTS (5)

it would be regarded as non-monetary asset. Since it would not be retranslated at a later date, no exchange gain or loss would arise. The loan would initially be translated at the rate ruling on the transaction date and then retranslated at the closing rate. An exchange gain or loss would arise which would be included as part of the company's profit or loss from ordinary activities. Where the purpose of such foreign borrowing was to provide a hedge against the exchange risk associated with existing equity investments, an unmatched gain or loss would arise when the exchange rate fluctuates.

13.27 A provision is included in the standard whereby an individual company which has used borrowings in currencies other than its own to finance foreign equity investments, *may* opt to treat the foreign currency investment as a monetary asset subject to certain conditions being met (outlined below). Where foreign equity investments are treated as monetary assets, any resulting exchange gains or losses *should be taken directly to reserves*. The exchange gains or losses on the borrowings *should be offset against exchange losses or gains arising on foreign equity investments as a reserve movement*.

13.28 This treatment is regarded as appropriate as in economic terms the company probably regards the foreign currency loan as a hedge against the exchange risk associated with the equity investment and therefore no economic gain or loss would be deemed to arise when there is a movement in exchange rates.

13.29 The conditions which must apply are as follows:
(a) in any accounting period, exchange gains or losses arising on the borrowings may be offset *only to the extent* of exchange differences arising on the equity investments;
(b) the foreign borrowings, whose exchange gains or losses are used in the offset process, should not exceed, in the aggregate, the total amount of cash that the investments are expected to be able to generate from profits or otherwise; and
(c) the accounting treatment adopted should be applied consistently from period to period.

Comments on the three conditions

Condition (a) restricts the total gains or losses on the loans which can be taken to the reserves to the gains or losses on foreign equity investments. Any gains or losses on loans in excess of gains or losses on foreign equity investments will be reported as part of the company's profit or loss from ordinary activities.

Condition (b) is intended to ensure that the hedge is a genuine one. This condition would ensure that the net realisable value or the economic value of the investment is equal to or greater than its original cost. The hedge need *not* be in the same currency as the investment and the offsetting process would be carried out on an aggregable basis. This condition is consistent with the general principle that net relevant cash flows should be considered in determining the economic value of an asset.

Condition (c) is intended to ensure that once this treatment is selected, it is applied consistently to all foreign equity investments financed by foreign loans.

EXAMPLE

A Ltd, a UK company whose accounting year ends on 31 December 1986 takes out a long-term loan on 31 March 1986 for US $1,500,000. A Ltd uses this loan to finance the acquisition of two equity investments on 31 March 1986.

A Ltd uses this loan to finance the acquisition of two equity investments on 31 March 1986.

(a) 100 per cent of the share capital of X SA, a Swiss company, at SWF 3,000,000; and
(b) a 5 per cent equity interest in D GmbH, a German company, for DM 875,000.

13.30   The relevant rates at 31 March 1986 are £1 = US $1.20 = SWF 3.0 = DM 3.5.
The relevant rates at 31 December 1986 are £1 = US $1.0 = SWF 2.4 = DM 2.8.
The following steps should be taken to comply with SSAP 20:
(a) Translate the investments at the rate ruling on the date of acquisition:
   (i) Swiss investment   = £1,000,000
   (ii) German investment = £250,000
(b) At the year end, the net realisable value or the economic value of the investments must equal or be greater than the carrying amount of the investments in the books of A Ltd.
(c) Translate the investments at closing rates:
   (i) SWF 3,000,000 at 2.4 = £1,250,000
   (ii) DM 875,000 at 2.8   = £312,500
(d) Calculate the net profit/loss on translation
   (i) £1,250,000 − £1,000,000   = £250,000 (GAIN)
   (ii) £312,500 − £250,000   = £ 62,500 (GAIN)
   Net exchange gain on investments   £312,500
(e) Translate the US $ loan at the rate ruling on the transaction date.
   US $ 1,500,000 @ 1.20 = £1,250,000
(f) Translate the US $ loan at the closing rate:

US $ 1,500,000 @ 1.00 = £1,500,000
(g) Calculate the net profit/loss on the translation:
£1,250,000 − £1,500,000 = £250,000 (LOSS)

	£
(h) Net exchange gain on investments – to reserves	312,500
Less Net exchange loss on foreign loan – to reserves	(250,000)
Net movement to reserves	62,500
Effect on Profit and Loss Account	NIL

13.31 However, if the loss on the loan was greater than £312,500, the amount to be offset would be limited to £312,500 and anything in excess should be charged against profit/loss from ordinary activities.

The consolidation stage

13.32 A similar provision to that for an individual company is also allowed in consolidated financial statements. SSAP 20 states 'within a group, foreign borrowings may have been used to finance group investments in foreign enterprises or to provide a hedge against the exchange risk associated with similar existing investments. Any increase or decrease in the amount outstanding on the borrowings arising from exchange movements will probably be covered by corresponding changes in the carrying amount of the net assets underlying the net investments (which would be reflected in reserves). Since in this case the group will be covered in economic terms against any movement in exchange rates, it would be inappropriate to record an accounting profit or loss when exchange rates change'.

13.33 Subject to certain conditions (listed below), the exchange gains or losses on foreign currency borrowings, which would otherwise have been taken to the group profit and loss account, may be offset as reserve movements against exchange differences on the retranslation of the net investments. The conditions which must apply are as follows:
(a) the relationship between the investing company and the foreign enterprises concerned should be such as to justify the use of the closing rate method for consolidation purposes;
(b) in any accounting period, exchange gains or losses arising on foreign currency borrowings may be offset only to the extent of the exchange differences arising on the net investments in foreign enterprises;
(c) the foreign currency borrowings, whose exchange gains or losses are used in the offset process, should not exceed, in the aggregate, the total amount of cash that the net investments are expected to be able to generate from profits or otherwise; and

(d) the accounting treatment adopted should be applied consistently from period to period.

13.34 The last three conditions are the same as those specified in the case of individual companies. The first condition that the relationship between the investing company and the foreign enterprises concerned justify the use of the closing rate method for consolidation purposes is new. The use of the temporal method is based on the premise that the foreign subsidiary is an extension of the investing company and the investment is in the individual assets and liabilities. Under this method, only monetary items give rise to exchange difference and therefore only these items can be hedged by any foreign loans taken out by the group. The offset takes place in the profit and loss account. The use of the closing rate method is based on the premise that their is a 'net investment' and the exchange differences are taken to the reserves.

13.35 Differences between the offset allowed on consolidation and that allowed in the individual company's accounts

INDIVIDUAL COMPANY	CONSOLIDATION
1. Offset relate to all equity investments regardless of the size of the holding and the relationship between the investing company and each individual investment.	1. On consolidation, the offset only applies to foreign enterprises translated using the closing rate method. However, where the offset procedure has been applied in the investing company's financial statements to a foreign equity investment which is neither a subsidiary nor an associated company, the same offset procedure may be applied in the consolidated accounts.
2. The amount available for offset is limited to the exchange difference arising each year on the carrying value of the investment (and which, therefore, may include goodwill) translated at closing rates.	2. The amount against which exchange gains and losses on the borrowings may be offset is the exchange difference arising on the retranslation of the opening net investment (which excludes goodwill) at closing rates.
3. Only loans raised by the company itself will be available for offset.	3. Loans raised by any group company may be included in the amount available for offset against the net investment in any foreign enterprise.

ACCOUNTING FOR INVESTMENTS (5)

EXAMPLE

A Ltd, a UK company whose accounting period ends on 31 December 1986, has two subsidiaries:
USA Corp, a US subsidiary acquired in 1979 for US $ 1,000,000
FR SA, a French subsidiary acquired on 1 January 1986 for FF 2,000,000.
At 1 January 1986, the net assets of USA Corp. = US $ 900,000
FR SA = FF 1,600,000.
At 31 December 1986 A Ltd has a loan outstanding of US $ 1,000,000 which is intended as a hedge against any exchange risk arising on its investment in USA Corp.

On 1 January 1986 USA Corp takes out a loan of FF 400,000, which A Ltd regards as a partial hedge against the acquisition of FR SA. A Ltd finances the acquisition partly by means of another US $ loan of US $ 100,000 and partly by a sterling bank loan.

The relevant exchange rates are as follows:

1 January 1986	£1 = US $1.6
	£1 = FF 10
	US $1 = FF 5
31 December 1986	£1 = US $1.25
	£1 = FF 11
	US $1 = FF 6.4

SOLUTION

(a) *Individual company accounts*
  (i) A Ltd has two loans of US $ 1,000,000 and US $ 100,000 which are intended as a hedge against any exchange risks arising on its investments in USA Corp and FR SA.

Exchange loss on US $ loan

	£
($1,000,000 ÷ 1.6) − ($1,000,000 ÷ 1.25) =	(175,000)
($100,000 ÷ 1.6) − ($100,000 ÷ 1.25) =	(17,500)
Exchange Loss on foreign borrowings	(192,500)

Exchange difference on equity investments

USA Corp ($1,000,000 ÷ 1.6) − ($1,000,000 ÷ 1.25)	175,000	GAIN
FR SA (FF 2,000,000 ÷ 10) − (FF 2,000,000 ÷ 11)	(18,189)	LOSS
Amount available in reserve for offset	156,811	GAIN

Exchange loss on foreign borrowings	192,500
To reserves − to be offset against gain on equity investments	(156,811)
Profit and Loss account charge	35,689

313

(ii) USA Corp takes out a loan of FF 400,000.

	US $
Exchange gain on FF loan	
(FF 400,000 ÷ 5) − (FF 400,000 ÷ 6.4) =	17,500

Since USA Corp does not own any foreign equity investments, the whole of this gain of US $ 17,500 will be credited to the Profit and Loss account in the USA Corp books.

Consolidated accounts
Exchange movements on group foreign borrowings

	£
US $ loans of $1,100,000	(192,500) LOSS
Exchange gains on FF loan of	
US $ 17,500 ÷ 1.25	14,000 GAIN
Net exchange loss available for offset	(178,500)

Exchange differences available on opening net investments

USA Corp ($900,000 ÷ 1.6) − ($900,000	
÷ 1.25) =	157,000 GAIN
FR SA (1,600,000 ÷ 10) − (1,600,000 ÷ 11) =	(14,545) LOSS
	142,955

Net exchange loss arising on foreign currency borrowings	178,500
Less amount offset in reserves against opening net investments	(142,955)
Net amount charged to P&L a/c	35,545
Exchange differences arising on opening net investment	142,955
Exchange losses on foreign currency borrowings offset in reserves	(142,955)
Net movement on reserves	—

Associated companies − Closing rate/net investment method

13.36 The requirements for the closing rate/net investment of translation apply equally to translation of investments in associated companies.

Foreign branches

13.37 A foreign branch can be either a legally constituted enterprise located overseas or a group of assets and liabilities which are accounted for in foreign currencies. This wide definition allows companies considerable flexibility in their approach to translation. Since the branch is normally an extension of the investing company, the temporal method should be used. However, there are situations in which a foreign branch may be accounted for under the closing rate/net investment method.

SSAP 20 and distributable profits

13.38 SSAP 20 specifically excludes the question of distributable profits from its scope and it makes the following statement in its introductory foreword:

'This statement sets out the standard accounting practice for foreign currency translation, but does not deal with the method of calculating profits or losses arising from a company's normal currency dealing operations; neither does it deal specifically with the determination of distributable profits.'

13.39 The question of what is realised and hence distributable is relevant only in the case of an individual company and not in the case of a group, since only an individual company can make distributions.

13.40 A number of problems may arise in the determination of realised and distributable profits in the case of an individual company when translating transactions denominated in foreign currency.

1. Exchange gains arising on settled transactions

13.41 These exchange gains are realised in cash terms and therefore can be included in the profit and loss account.

2. Exchange gains arising on short-term monetary items

13.42 These are not realised in cash terms but their ultimate cash realisation can be assessed with reasonable certainty and therefore, in accordance with the prudence principle in the Companies Act and SSAP 2, they are realised. The closing rate at which they are translated represents the best possible estimate of the amount receivable or payable in the foreseeable future.

3. Exchange gains arising on long-term monetary items

13.43 SSAP 20 requires these gains to be taken to the profit and loss account on the ground that the profit and loss account for the period gives a true measurement of the company's performance in the period. This treatment is justified on the basis that there is a need for a symmetry in the treatment of exchange gains and losses. Since the exchange losses are taken to the profit and loss account, exchange gains should not be excluded from the profit and loss account. However, these exchange gains will be unrealised at the balance sheet date and this is therefore a departure from the accounting principles stated in the Act. The reason for the departure can be justified on the grounds of the necessity to show a true and fair view of the results (Section 228, CA 1985).

4. The application of the cover concept to the individual company's financial statements

13.44 As explained earlier, this will result in exchange gains or losses on foreign currency borrowings being taken to reserves for offset against exchange gains or losses on foreign equity investments. It can be argued that exchange loss on foreign borrowings should be considered a provision and therefore treated as a realised loss for purposes of determining profits available for distribution. This means that the loss should either be taken to the profit and loss account for the period or be deducted before arriving at distributable profits. If this treatment is adopted, the exchange gain on investment is unrealised and would remain on the balance sheet.

13.45 SSAP 20's reason for this treatment is that the two transactions are linked and therefore that an offset should be available.

Disclosure

13.46 The methods used in the translation of the financial statements of foreign enterprises and the treatment accorded to exchange differences should be disclosed in the financial statements.

13.47 The following information should also be disclosed in the financial statements:
(a) for all companies, or groups of companies, which are not exempt companies, the net amount of exchange gains and losses on foreign currency borrowings less deposits, identifying separately:
 (i) the amount offset in reserves; and
 (ii) the net amount charged/credited to the profit and loss account;
(b) for all companies, or groups of companies, the net movement on reserves arising from exchange differences.

ACCOUNTING FOR INVESTMENTS (5)

DETAILED EXAMPLE

Hatch PLC operates in the UK, and its subsidiary Match Ltd operates in the country of Utopia, whose currency is the ducat. Their profit and loss accounts and balance sheets (simplified) are given below. Translation of ducats (D) to pounds sterling (£) is effected by the closing rate/net investment method, with use of the average rate for the year in the case of profit and loss account items.

Required

Prepare a consolidated profit and loss account and consolidated balance sheet from the accounts given below and the notes which follow them. No analysis of consolidated retained earnings, or earnings per share figure, is required.

Profit and loss accounts for the year ended 31 December 1985

	Hatch PLC £'000	Hatch PLC £'000	Match Ltd D'000	Match Ltd D'000
Turnover		7,000		22,000
Cost of sales		(5,600)		(16,500)
Gross profit		1,400		5,500
Distribution costs	(200)		(600)	
Administrative expenses	(600)	(800)	(2,000)	(2,600)
		600		2,900
Income from shares in group company	68		—	
Income from shares in related company	30		—	
	—	98	—	—
		698		2,900
Interest payable		(150)		—
Profit on ordinary activities before taxation		548		2,900
Tax on profit on ordinary activities		(240)		(1,000)
Profit on ordinary activities after taxation		308		1,900
Extraordinary profit (loss)	100		(250)	
Tax on extraordinary loss (profit)	(45)		75	
		55		(175)
Profit for the financial year		363		1,725
Dividends		(250)		(1,000)
Retained profit for the financial year		113		725

Balance sheets as at 31 December 1985

	Hatch PLC £'000	Hatch PLC £'000	Match Ltd D'000	Match Ltd D'000
Fixed assets				
Tangible (net)		1,700		4,000
Investments:				
Shares in group company (cost)	900		—	
Shares in related company (cost)	300	1,200	—	—
		2,900		4,000
Current assets				
Stocks	1,500		5,000	
Debtors:				
Trade debtors	900		4,000	
Amount owed by group company	—		1,000	
	900		5,000	
Cash at bank and in hand	214		425	
	2,614		10,425	
Creditors: amounts falling due within one year				
Trade creditors	(600)		(2,000)	
Amount owed to group company	(100)		—	
Other creditors including taxation and social security	(100)		(925)	
Proposed dividend	(150)		(500)	
ACT on proposed dividend	(64)		—	
	(1,014)		(3,425)	
Net current assets		1,600		7,000
Total assets less current liabilities		4,500		11,000

ACCOUNTING FOR INVESTMENTS (5)

	Hatch PLC £'000	Hatch PLC £'000	Match Ltd D'000	Match Ltd D'000
Financed by				
Creditors: amounts falling due after more than one year				
Debenture loans		1,000		—
Provisions for liabilities and charges				
Taxation, including deferred taxation		136		—
Capital and reserves				
Called up share capital:				
Ordinary shares	2,000		8,000	
Revaluation reserve	500		—	
Profit and loss account	864	3,364	3,000	11,000
		4,500		11,000

Notes

(1) Rates of exchange (ducats to the pound sterling):
   31 December 1984   10.00
   Average for year 1985 11.00
   31 December 1985   12.00

(2) Hatch PLC acquired 600,000 of the D10 (10 ducats) ordinary shares of Match Ltd (no more have been issued since), at a time when Match's profit and loss account showed a credit balance of D1,000,000. At that time the exchange rate was D9.00 to the £.

(3) 'Shares in related company' consist of 200,000 £1 ordinary shares in Despatch PLC (i.e. 40% of its issued equity capital), acquired when Despatch's reserves were £125,000. Hatch has a seat on Despatch's board of directors. During the year ended 31 December 1985, Despatch had pre-tax profits of £200,000, taxation thereon £80,000, and no extraordinary items. As at 31 December 1985, Despatch's reserves were £300,000.

(4) The dividends from Despatch PLC have been grossed up on the basis of the income tax basic rate of 30%. The dividends from Match Ltd (an overseas company) have not been grossed up; they have been converted to sterling at the average rate of exchange for the year. The proposed dividend of Match Ltd as at 31 December 1985 has not been taken into Hatch PLC's accounts.

(5) Goods invoiced in sterling at £500,000 have been sold by Hatch PLC to Match Ltd over the year. Of these goods, £100,000 were in Match Ltd's hands at 31 December 1985; they had cost Hatch £80,000. At 31 December 1984 the corresponding amounts were £80,000 and £64,000, respectively. (Ignore deferred taxation in respect of these items.)

UNDERSTANDING ACCOUNTING STANDARDS

(6) Hatch PLC's policy is to write off all purchased goodwill (positive or negative) to reserves in the consolidated accounts.

SOLUTION

Hatch plc
Consolidated Profit and Loss account for the Year ended 31 December 1985

	£000	£000
Turnover		8,500
Cost of sales		(6,604)
Gross profit		1,896
Distribution costs [200 + 55]	(255)	
Administrative expenses [600 + 182]	(782)	
Exchange gain	17	
		(1,020)
		876
Income from shares in related company		80
		956
Interest payable		(150)
Profit on ordinary activities before taxation		806
Tax on profit on ordinary activities:		
Group	322	
Related company	32	
		(354)
Profit on ordinary activities after taxation		452
(Of which £308,000 has been dealt with in the accounts of Hatch PLC)		
Minority interest in profit of subsidiary company		(43)
		409
Extraordinary income	100	
Less: Extraordinary charges	(23)	
	77	
Tax on extraordinary profit (45 – 7)	(38)	
	39	
Minority interest's share of loss	4	
		43
Profit for the financial year		452
Dividends of Hatch PLC		(250)
Retained earning for the financial year		202

Consolidated Balance Sheet on 31 December 1985

	£000	£000
Fixed assets:		
Tangible (net) (1,700 + 333)		2,033
Investments:		
Shares in related company on equity method basis		320
		2,353
Current assets:		
Stocks	1,897	
Trade debtors (900 + 333)	1,233	
Cash (214 + 36)	250	
	3,380	
Creditors (Amounts falling due within one year)		
Trade creditors (600 + 167)	767	
Taxation (100 + 77)	177	
Proposed dividend of Hatch plc	150	
ACT on proposed dividend	64	
Dividends payable to minority interest	11	
	1,169	
		2,211
		4,564
Financed by:		
Creditors (Amounts falling due after more than one year):		
Debenture loans		1,000
Provision for liabilities and charges		
Taxation including deferred taxation		136
Minority interest		229
Capital and reserves:		
Called up share capital:		
Ordinary shares	2,000	
Reserves:		
Revaluation reserves	500	
Profit and loss account	629	
Group's proportion of reserves of related company accrued since acquisition	70	
		3,199
		4,564

UNDERSTANDING ACCOUNTING STANDARDS

Workings:

(1) Match Limited:

(a) Translation of Profit and Loss Account:

	D000	Rate	£000
Turnover	22,000	11	2,000
Cost of sales	(16,500)	11	(1,500)
	5,500		500
Distribution costs	(600)	11	(55)
Administrative expenses	(2,000)	11	(182)
	2,900		263
Tax	(1,000)	11	(91)
	1,900		172
Extraordinary loss	(250)	11	(23)
Tax	75	11	7
	1,725		156
Dividends:			
Paid	(500)	11	(45)
Proposed	(500)	12	(42)
Retained profit	D725		£69

(b) Translation of Balance sheet:

	D000	Rate	£000
Tangible fixed assets	4,000	12	333
Stocks	5,000	12	417
Trade debtors	4,000	12	333
Group Co.	1,000	12	83
Cash	425	12	36
Trade creditors	(2,000)	12	(167)
Taxation etc.	(925)	12	(77)
Proposed dividend	(500)	12	(42)
	D11,000		£916
Ordinary share capital	8,000	9	889
Profit and loss account	3,000	Balancing figure	27
	D11,000		£916

322

ACCOUNTING FOR INVESTMENTS (5)

(c) Goodwill paid by Hatch plc.

	£000
Cost of shares	900
Less: 75% × (Ordinary share capital plus pre-acquisition reserves translated at the rate ruling on the date of acquisition)	
$= 75\% \times \dfrac{(8,000,000 + 1,000,000)}{9}$	(750)
Goodwill	£150

(d) *Minority interest's shares*:

(i) Profit and loss account:

Share of profit on ordinary activities after tax

$= 25\% \times £172,000$ = £43,000

Share of extraordinary loss

$= 25\% \times (23,000 - 7,000)$ = £4,000

(ii) Balance sheet:

Share of ordinary share capital plus reserves

$= 25\% \times £916,000$ = £229,000

Share of proposed dividends

$= 25\% \times £42,000$ = £11,000

(2) Shares in Despatch PLC (an Associated Company)

(a) Goodwill:

	£	£
Cost of shares		300,000
Less:		
£1 shares held	200,000	
Share of pre-acquisition reserves (40% × £125,000)	50,000	
		(250,000)
Goodwill		£50,000

323

(b) Profit and loss account using the equity method:

Share of profit on ordinary activities before tax
= 40% × £200,000 = £80,000

Share of tax on share of profits
= 40% × £80,000 = £32,000

(c) Balance sheet using the equity method:

Share of net assets = £1 shares plus share of reserves at 31/12/1985
= 200,000 + 40% × £300,000 = £320,000

OR

	£
Cost of shares	300,000
plus: share of post-acquisition reserves	
= 40% (300,000 − 125,000)	70,000
	370,000
Less: Goodwill write off	(50,000)
	£320,000

(3) *Other adjustments*

(a) Turnover:

	£000
Hatch plc	7,000
Match Ltd	2,000
	9,000
Less: Inter-company sales	(500)
Consolidated P & L A/c	£8,500

(b) Cost of sales

	£000
Hatch plc	5,600
Match Ltd	1,500
	7,100
Less:	
Inter-company sales	(500)
Provision for unrealised profits (20 − 16)	4
	£6,604

(c) Exchange differences on inter-group balances:

	£000
Hatch plc – Amounts due to Match Ltd	100
Match Ltd – Amounts due from Hatch plc	83
Exchange gain in the books of Hatch PLC – taken to the P & L A/c	£17

(d) Tax profit on ordinary activities:

	£000
Hatch plc	240
less: tax credit on dividends received from Despatch plc	(9)
	231
Match Ltd	91
Group	322
Related company	32
	£354

(e) Stocks:

	£000
Hatch plc	1,500
Match Ltd	417
	1,917
Less: Provisions for unrealised profits	(20)
	£1,897

UNDERSTANDING ACCOUNTING STANDARDS

(4) *Consolidated retained profit:*

	£000	£000
Hatch plc:		
Per accounts		864
Less: Provisions for unrealised profits		(20)
Add: Exchange gain on inter-group balances		17
		861
Match Ltd:		
Per accounts	27	
Less: Pre-acquisition (75% × $\frac{1,000,000}{9}$)	(83)	
Minority interest (25% × 27)	(7)	
Group's share of proposed dividends		
Add:		
(75% × $\frac{500,000}{12}$)	31	
		(32)
		829
Less: Goodwill write off:		
Match Ltd	150	
Despatch plc	50	
		(200)
		£629

Question

1. SSAP 20: Foreign currency translation constitutes the first definitive statement of practice in this area.

Required

(a) define concisely the two methods of currency translation specified in SSAP 20;
(b) explain the precise circumstances in which the use of each method is mandatory under SSAP 20; and
(c) justify the treatment prescribed in SSAP 20 for overseas investment financed by overseas borrowings.

Chapter Fourteen

Accounting for leases and hire purchase contracts

14.1 Leases and hire purchase contracts are the means by which companies obtain the right to use or purchase asset. Under a lease contract, the legal title does not pass to the lessee. A hire purchase contract has similar features to a lease except that the hirer acquires legal title on payment of the final instalment.

14.2 Leases may be classified between finance leases and operating leases and the distinction between the two will usually be evident from the terms of the contract between the lessor and the lessee.

Finance lease

14.3 This is a lease that transfers substantially all the risks and rewards of ownership of an asset to the lessee. It is a lease of a long-term nature, i.e. it is intended that the lessee will have the use of the asset for the greater part of the asset's useful life.

14.4 The lease term is normally divided into a primary period and a secondary period. The lessee guarantees to pay rent in the primary period and this part of the contract is legally binding and non-cancellable. The lessor earns the bulk of his profits in the primary period. In the secondary period, the lessee has an option to continue with the use of the asset for which he will pay a nominal rent to the lessor. The transfer of the risks and rewards of ownership to the lessee means that whilst the lessee earns revenue from the use of the asset, he will also pay all the costs of upkeep and maintenance of the asset.

14.5 SSAP 21, in its explanatory note, states that 'the effect of a lease is to create a set of rights and obligations related to the use and enjoyment by the lessee of a leased asset for the term of the lease. Such rights constitute the rewards of ownership transferred under the lease to the lessee whilst the obligations, including in particular the obligation to continue paying rent for the period specified in the lease, constitute the risks of ownership so transferred. Where the rights and obligations of the lessee are such that his corresponding rewards and risks are, despite the absence of the ability to obtain legal title, substantially similar to those of an outright purchaser of the asset in question, the lease will be a finance lease'.

SSAP 21 definition

14.6 A finance lease is a lease that transfers substantially all the risks and rewards of ownership of an asset to the lessee.

14.7 It should be presumed that such a transfer of risks and rewards occurs if, at the inception of a lease, the present value of minimum lease payments, including any initial payment, amounts to substantially all (normally 90 per cent or more) of the fair value of the asset. The present value should be calculated by using the interest rate implicit in the lease. If the fair value of the asset is not determinable, an estimate thereof should be used.

14.8 Fair value is the price at which an asset could be exchanged in an arm's length transaction less, where applicable, any grants receivable towards the purchase or use of the asset.

14.9 The inception of a lease is the earlier of the time the asset is brought into use and the date from which rentals first accrue.

14.10 The lease term is the period for which the lessee has contracted to lease the asset and any further terms for which the lessee has an option to continue to lease the asset, with or without further payment, which option it is reasonably certain at the inception of the lease that the lessee will exercise.

14.11 The minimum lease payments are the minimum payments over the remaining part of the lease term (excluding charges for services and taxes to be paid by the lessor) and:
(a) in the case of the lessee, any residual amounts guaranteed by him or by a party relating to him; or
(b) in the case of the lessor, any residual amounts guaranteed by the lessee or by an independent third party.

14.12 The interest rate implicit in a lease is the discount rate that, at the inception of a lease, when applied to the amounts which the lessor expects to receive and retain produces an amount (the present value) equal to the fair value of the leased asset. The amounts which the lessor expects to receive and retain comprise:

ACCOUNTING FOR LEASES AND HIRE PURCHASE CONTRACTS

(a) the minimum lease payments to the lessor, plus
(b) any unguaranteed residual value, less
(c) any part of (a) and (b) for which the lessor will be accountable to the lessee.

14.13 If the interest rate implicit in the lease is not determinable it should be estimated by reference to the rate which a lessee would be expected to pay on a similar lease.

14.14 Even though the definition of the finance lease in SSAP 21 is brief, a number of terms have been introduced in this definition which need to be explained.

(a) 'A transfer of risks and rewards'
14.15 This term is subjective, and it means essentially that the 'owner' has a right to use the asset for a large part of its useful life and earn benefits in return for which he will pay 'rent' to the lessor and will bear the cost of upkeep and maintenance.

14.16 The appendix to SSAP 21 states that in practice there are a number of arrangements which may in substance be leases even though different terms are used to describe them. Whether such arrangements fall within the definition of a lease will have to be decided in the light of the facts of each case. The appendix gives an example of an arrangement which would not normally be classified as a lease contract (although in exceptional cases they could in substance be leases).

14.17 Company A builds a plant on the basis that Company B is obliged to buy sufficient of the output of the plant (whether or not B requires it) in order to give A a full payout on the cost of the assets involved, together with a normal profit margin (such arrangements are sometimes called take-or-pay contracts or through-put agreements). In many cases such arrangements will in substance be more in the nature of long-term purchase/supply contracts and *not* contracts 'for the hire of specific asset ... '.

(b) '... if at the inception of a lease the present value of minimum lease payments, including any initial payments, amount substantially all (normally 90 per cent or more) of the fair value of the asset'

14.18 To classify the lease, the present value of minimum lease payments will have to be computed. If this present value equals the fair

UNDERSTANDING ACCOUNTING STANDARDS

value of the asset (or 90 per cent or more), it will be a finance lease. This can be illustrated as follows:

14.19 A lessee leases an asset on a non-cancellable lease contract with a primary term of five years from 1/1/19X7. The rental is £2,500 per annum payable in advance. The lessee has the right to continue to lease the asset after the end of a primary period of five years for as long as he wishes at a peppercorn rent. In addition, the lessee is required to pay all maintenance and insurance costs as they arise. The lessor has used a discount rate of 10 per cent to calculate the rental payments. The lessee estimates that the asset will have a useful life of eight years and no residual value thereafter. Present value of minimum lease payments=

$$C_1 + \frac{C_2}{1+i} + \frac{C_3}{(1+i)^2} + \frac{C_4}{(1+i)^3} + \frac{C_5}{(1+i)^4} \text{ (Where first payment is in advance)}$$

C_1 = Rental in Year 1
i = discount rate or 'rate implicit' in the lease

$$= 2500 + \frac{2500}{1.1} + \frac{2500}{(1.1)^2} + \frac{2500}{(1.1)^3} + \frac{2500}{(1.1)^4}$$

= £10,425

If this present value equals the fair value or is 90 per cent or more of fair value, then this is a finance lease.

14.20 Alternatively, the present value can be computed by use of annuity tables. From tables, for four years (ignore first year as the payments are in advance) with discount rate of 10 per cent, annuity factor = 3.170

Annuity factor = $\frac{\text{Present value} - 2500}{2500}$

Therefore present value = £2500 × 3.17 + £2500
= £10,425

14.21 There may be some marginal cases where the classification of leases will be difficult. In these cases the role of residual values is important. Some or whole of the residual value of a leased assset
(a) may be guaranteed by the lessee to the lessor or
(b) may be guaranteed to the lessor by a third party (i.e. residual values may be insured) or
(c) may be unguaranteed.

14.22 The part of residual value which is guaranteed by the lessee will be included in his minimum lease payments. The lessor will include in his minimum lease payments any residual values guaranteed by the lessee *or* by an independent third party. Thus the amounts which a lessor expects to receive in relation to a lease may exceed the minimum lease payments which a lessee expects to make, to the extent of

(a) residual amounts guaranteed by a third party and/or
(b) unguaranteed residual amounts.

14.23 The Appendix to SSAP 21 gives an example where classification of a lease may be difficult. Consider a lease of an asset which has a fair value of £3,900. The lessee is required to make three annual payments of £1,000 in advance. The lessor estimates that the asset will have a residual value of £1,500 at the end of the three years, the manufacturer guarantees to buy it back for £1,200.

Lessee

14.24 The minimum lease payments, as far as the lessee is concerned, are £3,000. The lessee will treat this as an operating lease because, even with a zero rate of interest, the minimum lease payments are less than 90 per cent of the fair value (3000/3900 or 77 per cent).

Lessor

14.25 Since the unguaranteed residual value is less than 10 per cent of the fair value (300/3900 = 7.7 per cent), the lessor will treat it as a finance lease.

In the above example, the two parties to the lease will classify it in different ways and this is recognised in SSAP 21.

(c) Fair value

14.26 Once again, the definition of fair value is subjective. There are no guidelines in the standard or Appendix to the Standard as to how one would determine this fair value. The ASC is currently considering the subject of fair values and we should have some guidance on it in the near future.

(d) Minimum lease payments

14.27 From the lessee's viewpoint, there are minimum payments which he is legally obliged to pay to the lessor. Any residual values guaranteed by the lessee (or related party to the lessee) to the lessor would be included in this amount.

14.28 From the lessor's viewpoint, there are minimum payments which the lessee is legally obliged to pay plus
  (i) any residual values guaranteed by the lessee or
  (ii) any residual values guaranteed by an independent third party.

UNDERSTANDING ACCOUNTING STANDARDS

(e) The interest rate implicit in a lease
14.29 This is simply the rate which the lessor would use to compute the minimum lease payments. If it is difficult for a lessee to determine this rate, he should estimate it by reference to the rate which he would be expected to pay on a similar lease.

Operating lease

14.30 Under such a lease the lessor retains all the risks and rewards of ownership of an asset. SSAP 21 defines it as any lease other than a finance lease.

Accounting treatment
Finance Leases in Lessee's Books
1. *Capitalisation*
14.31 SSAP 21 requires that '**A finance lease should be recorded in the balance sheet of a lessee as an asset and as an obligation to pay future rentals**'. At the inception of the lease the sum to be recorded both as an asset and as a liability should be the present value of the minimum lease payments, derived by discounting them at the rate implicit in the lease. The fair value of the asset less any grants is usually a reasonable approximation of the present value.

2. *Rental*
14.32 The rental which the lessee pays should be apportioned between the finance charge and a reduction of the outstanding obligation for future amounts payable.

3. *Finance Charge*
14.33 The total finance charge under a finance lease should be allocated to accounting periods during the lease term so as to produce a **constant periodic rate of charge** on the remaining balance of the obligation for each accounting period, or a reasonable approximation thereto.

14.34 Three methods of writing off finance charges to the profit and loss account are discussed in the Appendix to SSAP 21. These are:
(a) the actuarial method;
(b) the 'Rule of 78' (or 'Sum of the Digits') method; and
(c) the straight-line method.

4. *Depreciation*
14.35 An asset leased under a finance lease should be depreciated over the shorter of:
(a) the lease term (as defined earlier), and
(b) its useful life.

ACCOUNTING FOR LEASES AND HIRE PURCHASE CONTRACTS

EXAMPLE

Lessee plc leases an asset under a non-cancellable lease contract with a primary term of five years from 1 1 19X7. The rental is £2,500 per annum payable in advance. The lessee has the right to continue to lease the asset after the end of the primary period for as long as he wishes at a nominal rent. In addition, the lessee is required to pay all maintenance and insurance costs as they arise.

The leased asset could have been purchased for cash at the start of the lease for £10,425. The lessee estimates that the asset will have a useful life of eight years and no residual value.

Stages

1. *Present value of minimum lease payments*

Since the rate implicit in the lease is not available, assume the present value of minimum lease payments will equal the fair value of asset (i.e. £10,425).

2. *Capitalise present value of minimum lease payments*

	£	£
DR leased asset	10,425	
CR lease obligations		10,425

with the present value of minimum lease payments.

3. *Finance Charge*

Total rental = 5 × £2,500 per annum =		12,500
Less present value of minimum lease payments		(10,425)
Total finance charge		£ 2,075
DR Finance Charge Suspense Account	2,075	
CR Lease Obligations		2,075

with total finance charge.

4. *Lease Obligations*

The balance in this account at the start of lease will equal:

Present value of minimum lease payments	10,425
plus total finance charge	2,075
= Total rental payable	£12,500

This balance will be reduced by annual rental payments of £2,500

DR Lease Obligation	2,500	
CR Cash		2,500

with rental payments.

5. *Depreciation*

Leased Asset: Present value of minimum lease payments = £10,425
Depreciate assets over 8 years = £10,425 ÷ 8 years = £1,303 per annum

6. Allocation of finance charge to Profit and Loss Account
(a) Actuarial method
(i) Identification of rate of discount

This may be estimated using annuity tables. Since the payments are in advance, the initial payment of £2,500 must be deducted from £10,425. This then leaves four payments of £2,500 each payable at the end of a year.

Annuity factor = $\dfrac{£10{,}425 - £2{,}500}{£2{,}500}$ = 3.17. From tables, for four years, rate of discounting is 10 per cent.

(ii)

Period	Capital sum at start period	Rental paid	Capital sum during period	Finance charge at 10%	Capital sum at end of period
	£	£	£	£	£
19X7	10,425	(2,500)	7,925	792	8,717
19X8	8,717	(2,500)	6,217	622	6,839
19X9	6,839	(2,500)	4,339	434	4,773
19Y0	4,773	(2,500)	2,273	227	2,500
19Y1	2,500	(2,500)	—	—	—
		£12,500		£2,075	

DR Profit and Loss Account   x
CR Finance Charge   x

with the amount charged in the profit and loss account each year. In the year 19X7, it will be £792.

(b) Sum of the digits method (rule of 78)

This method is intended to be a reasonable approximation of the actuarial method. Finance charges will be allocated to four years, i.e. 19X7, 19X8, 19X9, 19Y0. No part of the finance charge will be allocated to 19Y1 because the final payment is made on 1/1/19Y1. The sum of the digits = 4 + 3 + 2 + 1 = 10 (i.e. the charge is allocated to four periods). Alternatively, the sum of the digits may be calculated using the formula:

Sum of the digits = $\dfrac{n(n+1)}{2}$ where n = 4

$= \dfrac{4(5)}{2} = 10$

The finance charge would be allocated as follows:

		£
19X7	$\frac{4}{10}$ × £2,075 =	830
19X8	$\frac{3}{10}$ × £2,075 =	622
19X9	$\frac{2}{10}$ × £2,075 =	416
19Y0	$\frac{1}{10}$ × £2,075 =	207
		£2,075

The table may be reconstructed as follows:

Period	Capital sum at start period	Rental paid	Capital sum during period	Finance charge	Capital sum at end of period
	£	£	£	£	£
19X7	10,425	(2,500)	7,925	830	8,755
19X8	8,755	(2,500)	6,255	622	6,877
19X9	6,877	(2,500)	4,377	416	4,793
19Y0	4,793	(2,500)	2,293	207	2,500
19Y1	2,500	(2,500)	—	—	—
		£12,500		£2,075	

If the payments had been in arrears, sum of the digits would equal 5 + 4 + 3 + 2 + 1 = 15 or $\frac{n(n+1)}{2}$ (where n = 5) = $\frac{5(6)}{2}$ = 15. The finance charges would have been allocated over five years.

(c) *Straight line method*

Under this method, $\frac{£2,075}{4}$, i.e. £519, would be allocated to each of the years from 19X7 to 19Y0 inclusive. This method is not usually regarded as acceptable, as it fails to allocate to accounting periods a finance charge which produces a constant periodic rate of charge on the remaining balance of the liability for each period.

Disclosures in financial statements (based on actuarial method)

Profit and Loss Account

Profit on ordinary activities before taxation has been arrived at after charging (see overleaf):

UNDERSTANDING ACCOUNTING STANDARDS

	19X7 £	19X8 £	19X9 £	19Y0 £	19Y1 £
*Depreciation	1,303	1,303	1,303	1,303	1,303
Interest payable – Finance charges under finance leases	792	622	434	227	—

* Should be disclosed for each major class of asset

Balance Sheet

Fixed Assets	19X7 £	19X8 £	19X9 £	19Y0 £	19Y1 £
Tangible Assets					
Plant and Machinery					
Leased property under finance leases	10,425	10,425	10,425	10,425	10,425
Less accumulated depreciation	(1,303)	(2,606)	(3,909)	(5,212)	(6,515)
	£9,122	£7,819	£6,516	£5,213	£3,910
Creditors (Amounts falling due within one year)					
Current obligations under finance leases	1,878	2,066	2,273	2,500	—
Creditors (Amounts falling due after more than one year)					
Non-current obligations under finance leases	6,839	4,773	2,500	—	—
	£8,717	£6,839	£4,773	£2,500	£—

Deferred taxation

14.36 If a company capitalises its financial leases, as required by SSAP 21, this creates timing differences. The reported accounting profit of is charged each year with depreciation plus finance charge, whereas the tax-adjusted profits are charged with rentals actually paid. For leased assets, the comparison to be made each year is between:
1. Depreciation plus finance charge as provided in the accounts and
2. Rentals paid charged against taxable income.

14.37 SSAP 21 requires that tax deferred or accelerated by the effect of timing differences should be accounted for to the extent that it is probable that a liability or asset will crystallise. Tax deferred or accelerated by the effect of timing differences should not be accounted for to the extent that it is probable that a liability or asset will not crystallise. Criteria similar to depreciation and capital allowances will have to be considered and a full discussion of this appears in the chapter on deferred taxation.

What are the issues in recognising a finance lease as a fixed asset?

1. The substance over form argument
14.38 SSAP 21 requires accounting recognition for a finance lease according to its economic substance rather than its legal form. The rule of substance over form requires that transactions and other events should be accounted for and presented in accordance with their substance and commercial reality and not merely with their legal form. In the case of finance leases the substance and commercial reality are that the lessee acquires the economic benefits of the use of the leased asset for the major part of its useful life in return for entering into an obligation to pay for that right an amount approximating the fair value of the asset and the related finance charge.

14.39 The lessee's asset is not the physical property itself, but an 'equity' in it, lasting for the lease term and expiring at the end of it, irrespective of the condition of the property. The lessor retains the legal title and the 'equity of redemption' (right to repossess at the end), but parts with possession and control for a term of years in return for a series of periodic payments by the lessee. The lessor regards the present value of these as initially equal to the fair value of the asset to himself.

14.40 This concept has been applied to hire purchase transactions. Hire purchase assets, and the related obligations to the finance company, are recognised in the accounts from the very start of the agreement. This is so even though the legal ownership is not transferred until the final instalment has been paid.

2. Ratio analysis
14.41 If such lease transactions are not reflected in the lessee's balance sheet, the economic resources and the level of obligations of the enterprise are understated, thereby distorting financial ratios like earnings per share, return on capital employed (ROCE), and debt/equity ratio (gearing).

14.42 The traditional treatment of finance leases (i.e. exclusion from balance sheet) has been referred to as 'off balance sheet finance'. Such treatment distorts comparisons between a company which leases an asset

Problems in proposed recognition of a finance lease as a fixed asset in lessee's books

14.43 In relation to physical property, ownership by the accounting entity is deemed to be of the essence of an asset. Thus it is difficult to accept, at first sight, that an asset owned by some other entity can be an asset of the company in possession of it, or can legitimately appear on its balance sheet especially as in the event of default it would be repossessed by the lessor. Therefore, it must be the legal form rather than the economic substance that should prevail when recording transactions. This is certainly the view adopted by the legal profession.

14.44 It is questionable accounting to treat as the cost of an asset a sum derived from an artificial computation of its 'fair value', or of the present value of minimum lease payments which, at the end of the lease, will not normally result in the acquisition of any property of lasting value – as in the case of an asset bought on hire purchase.

14.45 As discussed earlier, there may some marginal cases where the classification of leases will be difficult, and may even result in inconsistent treatment as between lessor and lessee.

14.46 At one stage, there was a fear that if the finance leases were capitalised in the lessee's books, the tax legislation may be changed to allow the lessee the benefit of capital allowances, with detrimental consequences for the leasing industry.

Operating leases in lessee's books

14.47 Since the lessor retains most of the risks and rewards of ownership of an asset in the case of an operating lease, the asset should not be capitalised in the lessee's books.

14.48 The rental under an operating lease should be charged on a straight-line basis over the lease term. The amount charged in the profit and loss account should be disclosed and analysed between (i) amounts payable in respect of hire of plant and machinery and (ii) amounts payable in respect of other operating leases.

ACCOUNTING FOR LEASES AND HIRE PURCHASE CONTRACTS

Lessor's Books

Finance Leases

1. Balance Sheet
14.49 SSAP 21 requires that the lessor must record the amount due from a lessee in its balance sheet as a debtor at the amount of net investment in the lease after making provisions for items such as bad and doubtful rentals receivable.

(a) 'The net investment in a lease at a point in time comprises:
  (i) the gross investment in a lease; less
  (ii) gross earnings allocated to future periods.'
(b) 'The gross investment in a lease at a point in time is the total of the minimum lease payments and any unguaranteed residual value accruing to the lessor.'

2. Profit and Loss Account
Allocation of gross earnings to the Profit and Loss Account

14.50 'The total gross earnings under a finance lease should normally be allocated to accounting periods to give **a constant periodic rate of return on the lessor's net cash investment** in the lease in each period.'

14.51 The net cash investment in a lease at a point in time is the amount of funds invested in a lease by a lessor, and comprises the cost of the asset plus or minus the following related payments or receipts:

(a) government or other grants receivable towards the purchase or use of the asset;
(b) rentals received;
(c) taxation payments and receipts, including the effect of capital allowances;
(d) residual values, if any, at the end of the lease term;
(e) interest payments (where applicable);
(f) interest received on cash surplus;
(g) profit taken out of the lease (= finance charge after interest and tax).

14.52 The two methods which would give a constant periodic rate of return (or a reasonable approximation thereof) on the lessor's net cash investment (NCI) in the lease in each period are:

(a) the actuarial method after tax; or
(b) the investment period method (IPM).

14.53 There are also other methods which may yield acceptable results. Both (a) and (b) are known as 'after-tax' methods. This means that

UNDERSTANDING ACCOUNTING STANDARDS

the gross earnings are being allocated on a basis which takes account of the tax effect on cash flows.

14.54 The treatment proposed by SSAP 21 for finance leases in the lessor's books is consistent with the rule of substance over form. Under a finance lease the lessor retains legal title to an asset but passes substantially all risks and rewards of ownership to the lessee in return for a stream of rentals. In substance, under a finance lease, the lessor provides finance and expects a return thereon. The lessor, therefore, should account for leases in accordance with their economic substance. Hence, a finance lease should be accounted for on a similar basis to that of a loan, rather than as a fixed asset subject to depreciation.

EXAMPLE

Lessor plc leases plant (cost £50,000) to Lessee Ltd for four years from 1 January 19X7 at a rental of £8000 per half year, payable in advance. Corporation tax is 35 per cent, and capital allowances on the plant are 25 per cent per annum, reducing balance basis. The rate of return (post-tax) on the lessor's net cash investment is 5.4 per cent per half year. The plant is assumed to have no residual value at the end of the lease term. Corporation tax is payable 12 months after the year-end.

1. *At the start of the lease*
   (a) The lessor's net investment in the lease = £50,000
   (b) The total minimum lease payments due = 2 × £8000 × 4 years = £64,000
   (c) Gross earning due (or finance charge due) = £14,000
2. *During the term of the lease*
   (a) Rental received by the lessor is made up of two components:
      (i) capital repayment which will go towards reduction of the lessor's net investment in the lease; and
      (ii) finance charge which will be credited to the profit and loss account as earned.
   (b) Allocation of gross earning or finance charge to the profit and loss account using the actuarial method after tax:

   The allocation must be at a constant periodic rate of return on the lessor's net cash investment in the lease. This means that average net cash investment in each period has to be identified. The lessor will have to pay corporation tax on the rental he receives and is entitled to the capital allowances on the cost of the asset. Both the corporation tax and capital allowances affect the net cash investment and the first stage will be to identify tax payments or receipts due in each period.

(i) *Tax Computations*

	£
Capital Allowances	
1/1/19X7 Capital Cost	50,000
Year ended 31/12/X7 *WDA @ 25 per cent	(12,500)
at 31/12/X7 **WDV	37,500
Year ended 31/12/X8 WDA @ 25 per cent	(9,375)
at 31/12/X8 WDV	28,125
Year ended 31/12/X9 WDA @ 25 per cent	(7,031)
at 31/12/X9 WDV	21,094
Year ended 31/12/Y0 WDA @ 25 per cent	(5,274)
at 31/12/Y0 WDV	15,920

* WDA – Writing down allowance
** WDV – Written down value

The lease term is for four years. By the end of the fourth year, the lessor will have received minimum lease payments of £64,000 which includes his gross earnings of £14,000. There is a written down value of £15,820 left at the end of the fourth year. There are two things that could happen at this stage:

(1) The lessor sells the asset for its tax written down value (£15,820) and passes the proceeds to the lessee as a rebate of rentals; or
(2) The lessor continues to hold the asset and the tax written down value of £15,820 will remain part of a pool and will continue to attract a stream of allowances totalling £15,820. The rental income is not material after this date (i.e. a 'peppercorn' rent in the secondary period).

Corporation Tax

Year ended	Corporation Tax		Due date
	£		
31/12/X7	35% (16,000 – 12,500)	= £1225	1/1/X9
31/12/X8	35% (16,000 – 9375)	= £2319	1/1/Y0
31/12/X9	35% (16,000 – 7031)	= £3139	1/1/Y1
31/12/Y0	35% (16,000–5274–15,820)	=(£1783)	1/1/Y2

In the year ended 31/12/Y0, the lessor will sell the asset for its tax written down value of £15,820 and pass the proceeds to the lessee as a rent rebate.

UNDERSTANDING ACCOUNTING STANDARDS

	£
Therefore, rental due	16,000
less: Rebate to the lessee	(15,820)
	180
less: WDA	(5,274)
Tax loss	(5,094)
Tax relief at 35%	1,783

(ii) *Net cash investment*

A table will have to be compiled showing the effect of all significant cash flows which affect the lease. In the above example, the post-tax rate of return on the lessor's net cash investment is 5.4 per cent per half year. This is the rate at which the profit will be taken out of the lease to pay indirect costs and dividends. The calculations made to arrive at 5.4 per cent will normally be carried out by financial institutions by computer program, but it can also be obtained by trial and error.

Cash flow profile:

Period (six months)	Net cash investment at start of period	Cash flows (out) (i)	Cash flows (in) (ii)	Average net cash investment in period	Profit taken out of lease (5.4%)	Net cash investment at end of period
	£	£	£	£	£	£
1/X7	—	(50,000)	8,000	(42,000)	(2,268)	(44,268)
2/X7	(44,268)	—	8,000	(36,268)	(1,958)	(38,226)
			16,000		(4,226)	
1/X8	(38,226)	—	8,000	(30,226)	(1,632)	(31,858)
2/X8	(31,858)	—	8,000	(23,858)	(1,288)	(25,146)
			16,000		(2,920)	
1/X9	(25,146)	(1,225)**	8,000	(18,371)	(992)	(19,363)
2/X9	(19,363)	—	8,000	(11,363)	(614)	(11,977)
			16,000		(1,606)	
1/Y0	(11,977)	(2,319)**	8,000	(6,296)	(304)	(6,636)
2/Y0	(6,636)	—	8,000	1,364	74	1,438
			16,000		(266)	
1/Y1	1,438	(3,139)**	—	(1,701)	(92)	(1,793)
2/Y1	(1,793)	—	—	(1,793)	(97)	(1,890)
1/Y2	(1,890)	1,783 **		(107)	107*	—
					82	
Total		Cost (50,000) Tax (4,900)	64,000		9,100	

* rounding error
** from tax computation

RENTAL	CAPITAL COST	TAX	PROFIT AFTER TAX
64,000 =	50,000 +	4,900 +	9,100

Gross earnings = £14,000

PUBLISHED ACCOUNTS OF LESSOR PLC

Profit and loss account for the year ended:

	31/12/X7 £	31/12/X8 £	31/12/X9 £	31/12/Y0 £	31/12/Y1/2 £	Total £
1. Rental	16,000	16,000	16,000	16,000	—	64,000
2. Less: Capital repayment (balancing figure)	(9,498)	(11,508)	(13,529)	(15,591)	126	(50,000)
3. Profit before tax (= gross earnings)	6,502	4,492	2,471	409	126	14,000
Less: *Taxation*						
4. Corporation tax (from tax computation)	(1,225)	(2,319)	(3,139)	1,783	—	(4,900)
5. Transfer to/from deferred tax (balancing figure)	(1,051)	747	2,274	(1,926)	(44)	
	(2,276)	(1,572)	865	143	44	4,900
6. Profit after tax (= profit taken out of lease)	£4,226	£2,920	£1,606	£266	£82	£9,100

Average net cash investment in period =
$\dfrac{42,000 + 36,268}{2} = 39,134$
$\dfrac{30,226 + 23,858}{2} = 27,042$
$\dfrac{18,371 + 11,363}{2} = 14,867$
$\dfrac{6,296 - 1,364}{2} = 2,466$

Gross earnings / Average net cash investment = 16.6% 16.6% 16.6% 16.6%

Note:
Items 1 and 6 from cash flow profile.
Item 4 from corporation tax computation.
Item 3 Profit after tax grossed up at 35% (e.g. Y/E 31/12/X7 – £4,226 × (100 ÷ 65) = £6,502).
Item 2 is a balancing figure.
Item 5 is a balancing figure i.e. Total tax charge = Profit before tax – Profit after tax. Therefore Deferred tax = Total tax charge – Corporation tax

UNDERSTANDING ACCOUNTING STANDARDS

Balance Sheets for year ended:

	19X7 £	19X8 £	19X9 £	19Y0 £
Fixed assets	X	X	X	X
Current assets				
Other debtors:				
Net investment in a finance lease:				
Amounts due within 1 year **	11,508	13,529	15,465	—
Amounts due after 1 year	28,994	15,465	—	—
	*£40,502	£28,994	£15,465	—

* Y/E 19X7: £50,000 − capital repayment of £9,498 = £40,502.
Or future rental of £48,000 less gross earnings allocated to future periods of £7,498 = £40,502
** Capital repayment of £11,508 in 19X8.
* Y/E 19X8: £40,502 − £11,508 = £28,994.
Or future rental of £32,000 less gross earnings allocated to future period of £3,006 = £28,994.
** Capital repayment of £13,529 in 19X9.

The transfers to or from deferred tax can be confirmed as follows:

Year ended	Accounting profit	Tax profit	Timing difference	Transfer to/from deferred tax @ 35%
	£	£	£	£
31/12/X7	6,502	3,500	3,002	1,051
31/12/X8	4,492	6,625	(2,133)	(747)
31/12/X9	2,471	8,969	(6,498)	(2,274)
31/12/Y0	409	(5,094)	5,503	1,926
31/12/Y1 + 2	126	—	126	44
	14,000	14,000	—	—

(d) **Allocation of gross earnings or finance charge to the profit and loss account using the Investment Period Method (IPM)**

This method allocates the gross earnings over that part of the lease in which the lessor has a net cash investment in proportion to the net cash investment at each interval. Using the cash flows set out in the Table on page 342, the allocation of gross earnings becomes:

Allocation of gross earnings under IPM

Period	Net cash investment at end of period £	Gross earnings allocation £	Total gross earnings for year – to P&L A/C £	£
1/X7	44,268	$44,268 \times 14,000 = $ 181,157	3,421	
2/X7	38,226	$38,226 \times 14,000 = $ 181,157	2,954	6,375
1/X8	31,858	$31,858 \times 14,000 = $ 181,157	2,462	
2/X8	25,146	$25,146 \times 14,000 = $ 181,157	1,943	4,405
1/X9	19,363	$19,363 \times 14,000 = $ 181,157	1,496	
2/X9	11,977	$11,977 \times 14,000 = $ 181,157	926	2,422
1/Y0	6,636	$6,636 \times 14,000 = $ 181,157	513	
2/Y0	*(1,438)	—	—	513
1/Y1	1,793	$1,793 \times 14,000 = $ 181,157	139	
2/Y1	1,890	$1,890 \times 14,000 = $ 181,157	146	285
1/Y2	* —			
	181,157			£14,000

* Ignore positive cash flows – it is more prudent.

(e) Profit and Loss Accounts – Investment Period Method

Year ended	31/12/X7 £	31/12/X8 £	31/12/X9 £	31/12/Y0 £	31/12/Y1+2 £	Total £
1. Rental	16,000	16,000	16,000	16,000	—	64,000
2. Less capital repayment	(9,625)	(11,595)	(13,578)	(15,487)	285	(50,000)
3. Gross earnings	6,375	4,405	2,422	513	285	14,000
Taxation						
4. Corporation Tax	(1,225)	(2,319)	(3,139)	1,783	—	(4,900)
5. Deferred tax	(1,005)	777	2,291	1,963	100	—
6. Total tax charge	(2,230)	(1,542)	(848)	(180)	(100)	(4,900)
7. Net profit after tax	4,145	2,863	1,574	333	185	9,100

1. Rental due in the year
2. Capital repayment – balancing figure
3. Gross earnings calculated as shown in the Table on page 345
4. Corporation tax – from tax computation
5. Deferred tax – balancing figure
6. Total tax charge – 35% of gross earnings
7. Net profit – 65% of gross earnings

Interest payments

14.55 Where a lessor borrows funds to finance his leases a more realistic reflection of his cash flows may be obtained by building into cash flows payments of interest on his borrowings. The tax charges will alter, as will the amount required to finance the lease in each period.

Hire purchase

14.56 The appendix to SSAP 21 states 'in the case of hire purchase, profit recognition should also be based on net cash investment. However, since the capital allowances under a hire purchase contract accrue to the lessee, the finance company's net investment is often not significantly different from its net cash investment; hence the allocation of gross earnings (i.e. finance charges) based on net investment will in most cases be a suitable approximation of the allocation based on net cash investment'. The two methods which may be used:

ACCOUNTING FOR LEASES AND HIRE PURCHASE CONTRACTS

(i) the actuarial method before tax;
(ii) the rule of 78.

14.57 Both these are pre-tax methods as they ignore the tax effect on cash flows when allocating gross earnings to the profit and loss account.

The Actuarial Method before tax

14.58 Same example as before:

Annuity factor = $\dfrac{50,000 - 8,000}{8,000}$ = 5.25 from tables, where n = 7, annuity factor = 5.25, i = 7.75% per six months.

Period	Net investment at start of the period	Rental	Net investment during the period	Finance charge @ 7.75%	Net investment at the end of the period
	£	£	£	£	£
1/X7	(50,000)	8,000	(42,000)	(3,255)	(45,255)
2/X7	(45,255)	8,000	(37,255)	(2,887)	(40,142)
		16,000		6,142	
1/X8	(40,142)	8,000	(32,142)	(2,491)	(34,633)
2/X8	(34,633)	8,000	(26,633)	(2,064)	(28,697)
		16,000		4,555	
1/X9	(28,697)	8,000	(20,697)	(1,604)	(22,301)
2/X9	(22,301)	8,000	(14,301)	(1,108)	(15,409)
		16,000		2,712	
1/Y0	(15,409)	8,000	(7,409)	(574)	(7,983)
2/Y0	(7,983)	8,000 *	17	(17)	—
		16,000		591	

* rounding error

347

UNDERSTANDING ACCOUNTING STANDARDS

Profit and Loss Account – Actuarial Method before tax

	19X7 £	19X8 £	19X9 £	19Y0 £	Total £
Rental receivable	16,000	16,000	16,000	16,000	64,000
Less capital repayments	(9,858)	(11,445)	(13,288)	(15,409)	(50,000)
Finance charges	6,142	4,555	2,712	591	14,000

The rule of 78

14.59   Sum of the digits = 7 + 6 + 5 + 4 + 3 + 2 + 1 = 28

or $\frac{n}{2}(n+1) = \frac{7}{2}(8) = 28$

Period	Basis of allocation	P&L A/C £
19X7: 1	$\frac{7}{28} \times £14,000$	3,500
2	$\frac{6}{28} \times £14,000$	3,000
		6,500
19X8: 1	$\frac{5}{28} \times £14,000$	2,500
2	$\frac{4}{28} \times £14,000$	2,000
		4,500
19X9: 1	$\frac{3}{28} \times £14,000$	1,500
2	$\frac{2}{28} \times £14,000$	1,000
		2,500
19Y0: 1	$\frac{1}{28} \times £14,000$	500
2	—	—
		500

ACCOUNTING FOR LEASES AND HIRE PURCHASE CONTRACTS

Comparison of methods

	19X7 £	19X8 £	19X9 £	19Y0 £	19Y1/2 £	Total £
Actuarial method after tax	6,502	4,492	2,471	409	126	14,000
IPM	6,426	4,441	2,441	405	287	14,000
Actuarial method before tax	6,142	4,555	2,712	591	—	14,000
Rule of 78	6,500	4,500	2,500	500	—	14,000

14.60 The two after tax methods give very similar results. Depending on the materiality of amounts involved, it may be appropriate under assumptions such as those used in the above numerical examples to use the actuarial method before tax and the rule of 78 to allocate gross earnings from finance leases, although these methods are primarily intended for use in allocating finance charges for hire purchase contracts.

Operating leases in lessor's books

14.61 SSAP 21 requires that an asset held for use in operating leases by a lessor should be recorded as a fixed asset and depreciated over its useful life. Rental income from an operating lease should be recognised on a straight-line basis over the period of the lease.

14.62 The gross amounts of assets held for use in operating leases, and the related accumulated depreciation charges, should be disclosed.

Questions

1. The following information was obtained about the computer equipment shown in the draft profit and loss account of FACT PLC.

Yearly rental payable in advance	£6,000
Term of lease	5 years
Date agreement was signed	1 January 1984
Anticipated residual value on disposal at the end of the lease term	£2,500
Lessees interest in the residual proceeds	95%
Anticipated life of the equipment	7 years

A trainee accountant has produced the following notes:

(i) Because the lessor has less than 10% interest in the residual value, the lease should be classified as a financial lease.

(ii) The typical implicit interest rate for a lease of this type of computer equipment is 10%.
(iii) The practice of charging the rental of £6,000 to the profit and loss account is incorrect and should not be followed in the accounts for future years.

Required:
Summarise the effect on the profit and loss accounts and balance sheets of FACT PLC for each of the years ending 31 December 1984 to December 1988 if the company decides to treat the above computer transaction as a finance lease.

Note: Discount factors are set out below:

Year	8%	10%	12%
1	.9259	.9090	.8930
2	.8573	.8264	.7972
3	.7938	.7513	.7118
4	.7350	.6830	.6355
5	.6806	.6209	.5674
6	.6302	.5645	.5066

2. Data: Asset cost = £40,000
   Lease period = 4 years
   Lease payments half yearly in advance = £6,000
   Expected residual value = £5,000
   Interest rate implicit in the lease = 6.83% per half year
   Depreciation method = straight line
   Residual value to be split 50:50 lessor and lessee
   Actual sale proceeds in year 4 = £6,200
   Corporation tax = 35%

Required:
(a) Show the accounting entries in the lessee's books in respect of this lease for each year, assuming the lease is taken out at the start of an accounting period and that finance charges are allocated using the actuarial method. Also assume that the lease is recorded using an interest suspense account.
(b) Calculate the charge or credit in respect of deferred tax each year for the lease, assuming a full provision is made.

3. *Lessor PLC*
Actuarial method after tax:

Data:
Asset cost	£20,000
Primary lease period	4 years
Lease payments ½ yearly in advance	£3100
Estimated residual value	Zero
Post-tax return on lessors net cash investment	4.54% per ½ year
Tax rate	35%
Writing down allowances (reducing balance	25%
Tax payable 12 months after end of accounting period	
Lease commences at start of an accounting period.	

Required:
Summarise the effect on the profit and loss accounts and balance sheets of Lessor PLC for each of the years ending 1–4.

Chapter Fifteen
Earnings per Share

15.1 SSAP 3, the accounting standard on earnings per share, applies only to those companies listed on a recognised Stock Exchange for any class of equity. SSAP 3 defines earnings per share as the profit in pence attributable to each equity share where:

(a) Profit = consolidated profit for the period after (i) tax, (ii) minority interests, and (iii) preference dividends, but before taking into account extraordinary items. These profits are also called earnings.
(b) Equity shares must be in issue and ranking for dividend in respect of the period. Equity share capital is defined by the CA 1985 as being issued share capital of a company excluding any part thereof which, neither as respects dividends nor as respects capital, carries any right to participate beyond a specified amount in a distribution.

Therefore

$$\text{EARNINGS PER SHARE} = \frac{\text{Earnings}}{\text{Number of equity shares in issue and ranking for dividend in the period}}$$

Taxation charge in the Profit and Loss Account

15.2 The taxation charge in the profit and loss account comprises two elements

(a) *Constant elements.* These elements do not vary with the company's dividend policy. They arise due to trading and are taxes on profits. Examples of constant element of taxes are:

   (i) Corporation tax on income;
   (ii) Tax attributable to dividends received;
   (iii) Overseas tax unrelieved because the rate of overseas tax exceeds the rate of UK Corporation Tax.

(b) *Variable elements.* These vary according to the amount of profits distributed and which would be absent if no distribution were made, i.e. they are dependent on the dividend policy of the company. Examples of variable elements of taxes are:

(i) Irrecoverable ACT;
(ii) Overseas tax unrelieved because dividend payments restrict the double tax credit available.

Earnings

15.3 There are two alternative methods of computing earnings:
(a) *NET BASIS*. The earnings figure is net of all elements (i.e. both constant and variable) of taxation. This is the actual position.
(b) *NIL BASIS*. The earnings figure is arrived at after deducting only the constant elements of taxation. The assumption is that there were nil distributions and therefore, no variable elements of taxation.

Preference dividends

15.4 The cash amount declared and payable to the shareholder should be deducted from the profit after tax in calculating earnings per share. That is, they should not be grossed up.

15.5 Where the preference shares are cumulative, the dividend for the period should be taken into account, whether or not it has been earned or declared. In the case of a non-cumulative dividend the deduction should be the amount of preferential dividend paid or proposed.

A plc
Group Profit and Loss Account for year ended . . .

	£	£
Turnover		x
Profit on ordinary activities before tax		a
Taxation		
Constant elements	b	
Variable elements	c	
		(x)
Profit on ordinary activities after tax		d
Minority share		(e)
		f
Extraordinary income	x	
Less extraordinary charges	(x)	
	x	
Less taxation	(x)	

	£	£
	x	
Less minority interest	(x)	
		g
Profit for the year		h
Dividends		
Preference	i	
Ordinary	j	
		k
Retained profit for the year		£x

(i) Earnings on net basis =
a − b − c − e − i

(ii) Earnings on nil basis =
a − b − e − i

OR

Earnings on Net Basis	x
Plus: Add back variable element of tax	x
Earnings on nil basis	x

SSAP 3 requirement

15.6 The earnings per share should be shown on the face of the profit and loss account on the net basis both for the period under review and for the corresponding period. Where, however, there is a material difference between earnings per share calculated on the net basis and on the nil basis, the nil basis should also be disclosed.

15.7 The basis of calculating earnings per share should be disclosed.

15.8 SSAP 3 requires the net basis always to be disclosed in the published accounts because it takes into account all the relevant facts, including any additional tax liabilities inherent in the dividend policy followed by the company. However, the nil basis facilitates comparisons between companies because it produces an earnings figure which is not dependent on the dividend policy of the company.

Equity share capital

15.9 Where there is only one class of equity share capital ranking for dividend, the calculation of earnings per share should be based on the number of such shares in issue during the period. Where there is more than one class of equity shares or where some of the shares are not fully paid, the earnings should be apportioned over the different classes of

EARNINGS PER SHARE

shares in accordance with their dividend rights or other right to participate in profits. Any changes in equity share capital during the financial year will affect the method of determining the earnings per share. The ways in which the equity share capital may change during the financial year are as follows:

(a) fresh issue at full market price;
(b) purchase of own shares in the market;
(c) capitalisation or bonus issue;
(d) rights issues at less than full market price; and
(e) acquisition of a subsidiary company by exchange of shares.

Calculation of earnings per share when there is a change in equity share capital during the financial year

15.10 Fresh issue at full market price
(a) Earnings – no adjustment
(b) Shares – time-apportion the new issue

15.11 Purchase of own shares
(a) Earnings – no adjustment
(b) Shares – time-apportion the shares purchased

15.12 Capitalisation or Bonus Issue
(a) Earnings – no adjustment
(b) Shares – the earnings should be apportioned over the number of shares ranking for dividend after the bonus
(c) The corresponding figure for all earlier periods should be adjusted accordingly

EXAMPLE
A plc

Year ended	31/12/X7	31/12/X6
	£	£
Earnings	1,000,000	800,000

On 1/1/19X6, there were 4 million ordinary nominal value £1 shares fully paid in issue.
On 1/4/19X7, the company made fresh issue of 1 million ordinary shares at market price.
On 1/7/19X7, a bonus issue of 1:5 was made.
19X7
(a) No adjustment is required to the earnings figure.
(b) Bonus issue is based on:
  (i) 4 million shares at the start and
  (ii) 1 million shares issued on 1/4/19X7

355

Therefore the bonus issue will have to be apportioned over (i) and (ii).
(c) The number of shares in issue at the start of the year, plus* the bonus issue based on these shares, will be brought in for the full year.
(d) The fresh issue on 1/4/19X7, plus* the bonus issue based on the fresh issue, will be time-apportioned from 1/4/19X7 to 31/12/19X7.
 * to adjust for the bonus issue which took place on 1/7/19X7, the number of shares prior to the issue are multiplied by 1 ÷ factor (f).

$$f = \frac{\text{Number of shares before the bonus issue}}{\text{Number of shares after the bonus issue}} = \frac{5}{6}$$

Shares	Actual		Weighted average
1/1/19X7 Number of shares	4,000,000	× *6/5 × 12/12	4,800,000
1/4/19X7 Fresh issue	1,000,000	× *6/5 × 9/12	900,000
	5,000,000		
1/7/19X7 Bonus issue 1:5	1,000,000		—
31/12/19X7 Number of shares	6,000,000		5,700,000

19X7: Basic earnings per share = $\frac{£1{,}000{,}000}{5{,}700{,}000}$ = 17.54 pence/share

19X6
Basic earnings per share reported in 19X6 accounts = $\frac{£800{,}000}{4{,}000{,}000 \text{ shares}}$
= 20 pence/share.

This figure will have to be restated in 19X7 comparative figures to adjust for the bonus issue in 19X7, as follows:

Revised 19X6 Basic earnings per share = earnings per share as reported in 19X6 × factor = 20p × $\frac{5}{6}$ = 16.66 pence per share.

15.13 Rights issue at less than full market price
(a) Earnings – no adjustment
(b) Shares – rights issue comprises two elements:
   (i) fresh issue at market value – this should be time-apportioned from the date of the rights issue;
   (ii) bonus issue – the earnings should be apportioned over the number of shares ranking for dividend after the bonus issue.
(c) The corresponding figures for all earlier periods should be adjusted for the bonus element in rights issue.

EARNINGS PER SHARE

EXAMPLE
A plc
Year ended   31/12/X7   31/12/X6
                                                   £   £
Earnings   100,000   80,000

On 1/1/19X6, there were 360,000 ordinary 25p nominal value fully paid shares in issue.
Market value per share on 30/6/19X7 was £1 (closing price on the last day of quotation of the share cum rights). On 1/7/19X7, there was a rights issue of 1:4 at 50p/share.

19X7: Shares
The rights issue on 1/7/19X7 can be split into:

(a) *Fresh issue at market value*
Total proceeds from rights issue = 90,000 shares @ 50p = £45,000.
Market price = £1 per share.
Fresh issue at market value = $\dfrac{£45,000}{£1}$ = 45,000 shares.

(b) *Bonus issue*
Total number of shares issued   = 90,000
Less: from (a) above, fresh issue at
market value   = (45,000)

Therefore bonus issue   = 45,000
Bonus issue of 45,000 shares is based on
  (i) 360,000 shares in issue on 1/1/19X7 and
  (ii) 45,000 shares (fresh issue) on 1/7/19X7
       405,000 total

Therefore bonus ratio = 45,000:405,000 = 1:9

Therefore factor = $\dfrac{9}{10}$

Shares	Actual		Weighted average
1/1/19X7 B/Fwd	360,000	× * $\dfrac{10}{9}$ × $\dfrac{6}{12}$	200,000
1/7/19X7 Fresh issue	45,000		
	405,000	× * $\dfrac{10}{9}$ × $\dfrac{6}{12}$	225,000
1/7/19X7 Bonus issue	45,000		—
31/12/19X7 C/Fwd	450,000		425,000

UNDERSTANDING ACCOUNTING STANDARDS

* Adjustment for bonus element in rights issue.

19X7 Basic EPS = $\dfrac{£100,000}{425,000}$ = 23.53 pence/share

19X6

Basic EPS as reported in 19X6 Accounts = $\dfrac{£80,000}{360,000}$ = 22.22 pence

19X6 Basic EPS – as revised in 19X7 Accounts = 22.22p × $\dfrac{9*}{10}$ = 20 pence
* Adjustment for bonus element in rights issue.

15.14 The Appendix to SSAP 3 requires that 'where equity shares are issued by way of rights during the period it is recommended that the factor for adjustment of past earnings per share after a rights issue be based on the closing price (the official middle market quotation published on the following day) on the last day of quotation of the shares cum rights. The factor is therefore:

$$\dfrac{\text{Theoretical EX RIGHTS price}}{\text{Actual CUM RIGHTS price on the last day of quotation cum rights}}$$

15.15 Where a rights issue is made during the year under review, the earnings per share for the previous year, and for earlier years, will need to be adjusted by the factor, calculated as above, to correct for the bonus element in the rights issue'.

Calculation of factor

	Number		£
Before rights issue:	4 shares @ CUM rights price of £1		4.00
Rights issue:	1 at 50p/share		0.50
After rights issue:	5 shares		£4.50

Therefore theoretical EX RIGHTS price = $\dfrac{£4.50}{5}$ = 90p/share.

Therefore factor = $\dfrac{90}{100}$ (same as the earlier calculation).

19X7 Shares	Actual	Average
1/1/19X7 B/Fwd	360,000 × $\dfrac{10}{9}$ × $\dfrac{6}{12}$	200,000
1/7/19X7 Rights issue 1:4	90,000	
31/12/19X7 C/Fwd	450,000 × $\dfrac{6}{12}$	225,000
		425,000

BASIC EPS = $\dfrac{£100,000}{425,000}$ = 23.53 pence per share

19X6

| 19X6 BASIC EPS revised in 19X7 accounts | BASIC EPS reported in = 19X6 accounts × f = 22.22 pence × $\frac{9}{10}$ = 20 pence per share |

15.16 Acquisition of a subsidiary company by exchange of shares

(a) *Acquisition method of accounting*

The consolidation will begin with effect from the date of acquired control or the date of acquisition. Any earnings of the subsidiary company from the date of control will be treated as being the post-acquisition earnings of the group. All pre-acquisition earnings will be capitalised. If the date on which the shares are issued to acquire the subsidiary company is different from the date of gaining control, an assumption should be made that these shares were issued on the control date, and time-apportioned from that date.

EXAMPLE

The earnings of H plc and S Ltd for the year ended 31/12/X7 are as follows:

	H plc Year ended 31/12/19X7	S Ltd
	£	£
Earnings	1,000,000	500,000 (full year)

On 1/1/19X7, H plc had in issue 4 million ordinary NV 25p shares fully paid. On 1/10/19X7, H plc issued 1 million ordinary NV 25p shares to acquire 100 per cent equity in S Ltd. However, H plc had taken control of S Ltd as from 1/7/19X7.

H plc

$$\text{Basic earnings per share} = \frac{£1,000,000 + \frac{6}{12}(£500,000)}{4,000,000 + \frac{6}{12}(1,000,000)}$$

= 27.78 pence per share

(b) *Merger Method of Accounting*

15.17 Since the consolidation will begin from the first day of the year, assume that shares were issued on that day. In the earlier example, basic earnings per share = $\frac{£1,000,000 + £500,000}{4,000,000 + 1,000,000}$

= 30 pence/share

UNDERSTANDING ACCOUNTING STANDARDS

15.18 There is also a requirement in SSAP 23 to restate the comparative figure on the assumption that the merger took place on the first day of the previous year.

Fully diluted earnings per share

15.19 Where a listed company has outstanding:
(a) A separate class of equity shares which do not rank for dividend in the period, but will do so in the future; or
(b) Debentures or loan stock (or preference shares) convertible into equity share of the company; or
(c) Options or warrants to subscribe for equity share of the company.
SSAP 3 requires that in these circumstances, in addition to the basic earnings per share, the fully diluted earnings per share should be calculated and shown on the face of the profit and loss account if materially (5 per cent or more) different from basic earnings per share.

15.20 To be able to compute fully diluted earnings per share, *assume* a full conversion of the above three items into equity shares during the current year at the later of:
(a) first day of accounting period; and
(b) date of issue of the above three items (if in the current year).

15.21 If the above assumption results in increasing the earnings per share to above the basic figure, it should not be disclosed as it is unlikely that the conversion rights or options would be exercised. The fully diluted earnings per share should take into account only those 'convertibles', shares, options or warrants which would have a diluting effect on the earnings per share, and should disregard those which have no such diluting effect, i.e. a separate calculation will have to be made for each item to discover whether they cause a dilution on their own (see detailed example).

15.22 Since the fully diluted earnings per share is concerned with future dilution, a corresponding amount for the previous period should not be disclosed unless the assumptions on which it was based are still applicable.

EXAMPLES
1. *Another class of equity share ranking for dividend in the future*
A plc
Year ended 31/12/19X7
Earnings   £1,000,000

EARNINGS PER SHARE

On 1/1/19X7, A plc had 4 million ordinary NV 25p shares in issue (all ranking for dividends).
On 1/10/19X7, A plc issued 1 million ordinary NV 25p shares. These shares will start ranking for a dividend as from 1/1/19X8.

Basic earnings per share = $\dfrac{£1,000,000}{4 \text{ million}}$ = 25p/share

Fully diluted earnings per share
(a) Earnings – no adjustment required
(b) New shares – treat them as equity shares as from 1/10/19X7

Therefore fully diluted earnings per share = $\dfrac{£1,000,000}{4 \text{ million} + 3/12 \,(1 \text{ million})}$ = 23.53 pence

95% of Basic EPS = 95% × 25p = 23.75 pence
Since fully diluted earnings per share is less than 23.75 pence, it should be disclosed.

2. *Convertible loan stock*
A plc
Year ended 31/12/19X7

	£
Earnings	1,000,000

on 1/1/19X7, A plc had in issue
(a) 4 million ordinary NV 25p fully paid shares
(b) £1 million 10 per cent Convertible Loan Stock
    Terms of conversion

On 31/12/19X9: 100 ordinary NV 25p fully paid shares for every £100 loan stock
    31/12/19Y0: 95 ordinary NV 25p fully paid shares for every £100 loan stock
    31/12/19Y1: 90 ordinary NV 25p fully paid shares for every £100 loan stock (Final date)

Basic earnings per share = $\dfrac{£1,000,000}{4 \text{ million}}$ = 25p/share

Fully diluted earnings per share
1. *Shares* Assume that the maximum number of new equity shares had been issued on conversion and that this conversion had taken place on the first day of the period (or on the date of issue of the convertible loan stock if later).

361

UNDERSTANDING ACCOUNTING STANDARDS

	Actual	Average
1/1/19X7 Number of ordinary shares in issue	4,000,000	
1/1/19X7 Assume a full conversion of convertible loan stock into equity shares. Select a term which gives a maximum number of shares: £1,000,000 × $\frac{100}{£100}$	1,000,000	
	5,000,000 × $\frac{12}{12}$	5,000,000

2. Earnings

The earnings for the period should be adjusted by adding back the assumed saving of interest on the stock so converted, net of corporation tax.

	£	£
Earnings as per basic earnings per share		1,000,000
Add back assumed saving of interest:		
10% × £1 million	100,000	
Less corporation tax @ 35 per cent	(35,000)	
Saving net of tax		65,000
		£1,065,000

Fully diluted earnings per share = $\frac{£1,065,000}{5,000,000}$ = 21.3 pence

Since this is less than 95 per cent × 25 pence = 23.75 pence, it should be disclosed.

3. Options or Warrants to subscribe

A plc
Year ended 31/12/19X7

	£
Earnings	1,000,000

On 1/1/19X7, A plc had in issue 4 million ordinary NV 25p fully paid shares. On 1/10/19X7, the directors of A plc took up options to acquire 1 million ordinary NV 25p fully paid shares at a price of £1.20 per share. The option is to be exercised by 31/12/19X9.
On 1/10/19X7, the yield on 2½ per cent consolidated stock is 10 per cent.

Basic earnings per share = $\frac{£1,000,000}{4\text{ million}}$ = 25 pence/share

EARNINGS PER SHARE

Fully diluted earnings per share:
1. *Shares* Assume that the option had been exercised on the first day of the period *or* the date of issue if later.

	Actual	Average
1/1/19X7 – Ordinary shares in issue	4,000,000 × 12/12	4,000,000
1/10/19X7 – Assume options are exercised on this date	1,000,000 × 3/12	250,000
	5,000,000	4,250,000

2. *Earnings*
Assume that proceeds from options had been invested in 2½ per cent consolidated stock.

	£	£
Earnings – as per Basic Earnings per share		1,000,000
Add: Return on 2½ per cent consolidated stock as from 1/10/19X7:		
10 per cent × £1,200,000 × 3/12	30,000	
Less tax @ 35 per cent	(10,500)	
		19,500
		£1,019,500

Fully diluted earnings per share = $\dfrac{£1,019,500}{4,250,000}$ = 23.99 pence

Since this is not less than 95 per cent × 25 pence = 23.75 pence, it should not be disclosed.

A detailed example

You are required to compute from the information below the group's basic and fully diluted earnings per share for the year to 31 December 19X7, and the corresponding Basic Earnings per share for the year to 31 December 19X6 (as shown in the 19X7 accounts). The information provided is as follows:

FACT plc, as at 31 December 19X5 (its accounting date) had in issue 10 per cent cumulative preference shares of £1 each (all fully called), together with £1,000,000 of 7 per cent convertible debentures, convertible into 50 ordinary shares per £100 debentures (ranking for dividend immediately), with adjustment for subsequent bonus and rights issue.

UNDERSTANDING ACCOUNTING STANDARDS

On 1 April 19X6, £250,000 of the debentures were converted. On 1 October 19X6, the company made a rights issue of ordinary shares of 50p each, 1 for 4, at a price of £1.25 per share. The market price before the rights issue was £1.50 per share. The shares ranked for dividend as from 1 October 19X6.

On 1 April 19X7, £400,000 debentures were converted. On 1 July 19X7 a bonus issue 1 for 5 was made. On 1 September 19X7 the company issued options to executives to subscribe for 200,000 ordinary shares at £1.80 each; none had been taken up by 31 December 19X7. At 1 September 19X7, the price of 2½ per cent consols was 25.

Corporation tax 35 per cent

Income tax basic rate 25 per cent

FACT plc's Consolidated Profit and Loss Account for the years to 31 December 19X6 and 19X7 were as follows:

FACT plc and subsidiaries
Consolidated Profit and Loss Account (extracts) for the years to 31 December 19X6 and 19X7

	19X6		19X7	
	£	£	£	£
Profit on ordinary activities before taxation		1,060,000		1,500,000
Tax on profit on ordinary activities (see p. 365)		(560,000)		(707,000)
		500,000		793,000
Extraordinary income	25,000		10,000	
Extraordinary charges	(60,000)		—	
Extraordinary profit/loss	(35,000)		10,000	
Tax on extraordinary loss/profit	18,200		(5,200)	
		(16,800)		4,800
Profit for the financial year		483,200		797,800
Dividends paid and proposed		(356,250)		(523,221)
Retained profits transferred to reserves		£126,950		£274,579

EARNINGS PER SHARE

Note	19X6 £	19X7 £
Tax on profit on ordinary activities		
Corporation tax on current year's profits:		
UK	360,000	650,000
Overseas	55,000	70,000
(of which £10,000 in 19X6 and £12,000 in 19X7 was unrelieved because dividend payments restrict double taxation relief)		
Transfer to (from) deferred taxation	140,000	(20,000)
Tax credits on dividends received	15,000	12,000
Corporation tax overprovided in previous year	(10,000)	(5,000)
	560,000	707,000

SOLUTION
Basic earnings per share
1. Earnings

	19X6	19X7
Profit on ordinary activities after taxation	500,000	793,000
Less: Preference dividends	(50,000)	(50,000)
EARNINGS ON NET BASIS	450,000	743,000
Add back: variable element of tax – overseas tax unrelieved because dividend payments restrict double taxation relief	10,000	12,000
EARNINGS ON NIL BASIS	£460,000	£755,000

2. *Shares*
Year ended 31/12/19X6

	Actual		Average
1/1/19X6 Brought Forward	6,000,000 × $\frac{150}{145}$ × $\frac{9}{12}$		4,655,172
1/4/19X6 Conversion of Loan Stock:			
£250,000 × $\frac{50}{£100}$	$\frac{125,000}{6,125,000}$ × $\frac{150}{145}$ × $\frac{6}{12}$		64,655
1/10/19X6 Rights Issue of 1:4	1,531,250		
31/12/19X6 Carried Forward	7,656,250 × $\frac{3}{12}$		1,914,063
			6,633,890

UNDERSTANDING ACCOUNTING STANDARDS

Notes
Terms of conversion are 50 ordinary shares per £100 debentures, with adjustment for subsequent bonus and rights issue, Since no information is given regarding earlier years, assume that there were no rights or bonus issues since the loan stock was first issued.

2. *Bonus element in the rights issue*

	£
Before rights issue: 4 shares-market value £1.50 per share	6
Rights issue: 1 share at £1.25 per share	1.25
After rights issue: 5 shares	£7.25

Therefore theoretical ex-rights price $= \dfrac{£7.25}{5} = £1.45$

$$\text{Factor} = \dfrac{\text{Theoretical ex-rights price}}{\text{Actual cum rights price}} = \dfrac{145}{150}$$

Adjust all the shares prior to the rights issue for the bonus element in rights issue.

19X6 Basic earnings per share as reported in 19X6 accounts

Net basis $= \dfrac{£450,000}{6,633,890} = 6.78$ pence

Nil basis $= \dfrac{£460,000}{6,633,890} = 6.93$ pence

Nil basis should not be disclosed in this case as the difference between net basis and nil basis is not material.

Year ended 31/12/19X7

	Actual	Average
1/1/19X7 Brought forward	$7,656,250 \times \dfrac{6}{5} \times \dfrac{12}{12}$	9,187,500
1/4/19X7 Conversion of Loan Stock $£400,000 \times \dfrac{50}{£100} \times \dfrac{150}{145}$	$206,897 \times \dfrac{6}{5} \times \dfrac{9}{12}$	186,207
	7,863,147	
1/7/19X7 Bonus Issue 1:5	1,572,629	—
31/12/19X7	9,435,776	9,373,707

Notes
1. There is a conversion of loan stock on 1/4/19X7. Since there was a rights issue prior to the conversion, they will be entitled to the bonus element in the rights issue at the point of conversion. Since the term of conversion is 50 ordinary shares per £100 debentures, with adjustment for subsequent bonus and rights issue $-\dfrac{50}{£100}$ will be multiplied by $\dfrac{150}{145}$ to adjust for the bonus element in the rights issue.

EARNINGS PER SHARE

2. All the shares prior to the bonus issue will be multiplied by the factor of $\frac{6}{5}$ as the earnings should be apportioned over the number of shares ranking for dividend after the bonus.

19X7 Basic earnings per share
NET BASIS = $\frac{£743,000}{9,373,707}$ = 7.93 pence

NIL BASIS = $\frac{£755,000}{9,373,707}$ = 8.05 pence

Since the difference between the net basis and the nil basis is not material, the nil basis would not be disclosed.

Restatement of 19X6 basic earnings per share in 19X7 accounts
Since there was a bonus issue in 19X7, 19X6 earnings will have to be apportioned over the number of shares ranking after the bonus.
Revised 19X6 basic earnings per share =
19X6 basic earnings per share as reported in 19X6 accounts × factor = 6.78 pence × $\frac{5}{6}$ = 5.65 pence/share.

Fully diluted earnings per share in 19X7 accounts
Consider the effect of convertible loan stock and options separately.
1. *Convertible Loan Stock*
Assume a full conversion of £750,000 of loan stock into equity shares on 1/1/19X7.

	Actual	Average
1/1/19X7 Brought forward	7,656,250 × $\frac{6}{5}$ × $\frac{12}{12}$	9,187,500
1/1/19X7 Full conversion of loan stock £750,000 × $\frac{50}{£100}$ × $\frac{150}{145}$	387,931 × $\frac{6}{5}$ × $\frac{12}{12}$	465,517
	8,044,181	
1/7/19X7 Bonus Issue 1:5	1,608,836	—
31/12/19X7	9,653,017	9,653,017

UNDERSTANDING ACCOUNTING STANDARDS

	£	£
Earnings		
As per basic earnings per share		743,000
Add: Assumed saving in interest		
7% × £400,000 × 3/12	7,000	
7% × £350,000 × 12/12	24,500	
	31,500	
Less tax at 35%	(11,025)	20,475
		£763,475

Therefore fully diluted earnings per share = £763,475 / 9,653,017

= 7.91 pence/share

(A small dilution)

2. OPTIONS

Assume a full conversion of options into equity shares as at 1/9/19X7.

	Actual	*Average*
As per basic earnings per share 1/9/19X7	9,435,776	9,373,707
Assume a full conversion of options into equity shares	200,000 × 4/12	66,667
	9,635,776	9,440,374

	£	£
Earnings as per basic earnings per share		743,000
1/9/19X7: assume proceeds from options are invested in 2½ per cent consols		
Therefore yield		
2½/25 × £360,000 × 4/12 =	12,000	
Tax at 35 per cent	(4,200)	
Post tax yield		7,800
		£750,800

Fully diluted earnings per share = £750,800 / 9,440,374

= 7.95 pence

There is an increase in earnings per share. Therefore ignore the effect of options on dilution.

If only the effect of convertible loan stock is considered, fully diluted earnings per share = 7.91 pence. Since the difference between basic earnings per share and fully diluted earnings per share is not material, fully diluted earnings per share should not be disclosed.

Usefulness of the earnings per share figures

15.23 The price earnings ratio (P/E ratio) is now used widely as a means of comparing similar companies. The P/E ratio is the share price divided by the earnings per share. It effectively represents the payback period of the shares, i.e. the number of years required for current earnings to recover the current share value.

15.24 Both earnings per share and P/E ratio are frequently used for share and business valuation. Earnings per share consists of the dividend paid to shareholders plus retained earnings and an historical analysis of earnings per share may well give a useful insight into how future earnings per share is likely to behave. This may then be 'capitalised' at the shareholders' required rate of return, or at the cost of equity capital to attain a share value.

15.25 The P/E ratio gives an indication of the capitalisation rate used by the market to value a particular share. When evaluating a particular unquoted company's share, a P/E ratio of an equivalent quoted company may be suitable.

15.26 By disclosing earnings per share figure, it enables shareholders to gain comparisons of the current year's results with the past results. Earnings per share represents the amount of earnings earned per each share held.

15.27 Earnings per share is also used to compute a ratio called 'dividend cover', which is:

= Earnings per share
  Dividend per share

This ratio indicates the number of times dividends are covered by earnings.

Problems that may arise in practice from the interpretation of earnings per share

15.28 SSAP 3 defines earnings per share as the profit in pence attributable to each equity share, based on the consolidated profit of the period after tax and after deducting minority interests and preference dividends, but before taking into account extraordinary items, divided by the number of equity shares in issue and ranking for dividend in respect of the period.

15.29 The exclusion of extraordinary items from the calculation of earnings means that earnings per share for a particular period is based only on a part of the performance of business. The distinction between exceptional items and extraordinary items is a subjective one and experience has shown that what has appeared as an exceptional item in one company has been treated as an extraordinary item in another and vice versa.

15.30 There are two elements of taxes which are charged in the profit and loss account for the year:
(a) a constant element which arises due to the trading, e.g. corporation tax, and
(b) a variable element which arises due to the dividend policy, e.g. irrecoverable ACT written off.

There are two ways of treating these elements of taxes when computing earnings:
(a) the earnings figure which is net of all the taxes is called earnings on net basis;
(b) the earnings figure which is computed on the basis of deducting only the constant element of tax is called the earnings on nil basis – i.e. it assumes *nil* distributions.

15.31 SSAP 3 requires that it should always be earnings per share on net basis which is disclosed. It also requires earnings per share on nil basis to be disclosed when there is a material difference between net basis and nil basis. One of the reasons the figure of earnings per share is required to be disclosed is to be able to make comparisons, and earnings per share on nil basis gives much better comparisons as it excludes the variable element of tax.

15.32 Earnings per share is based primarily upon historical information. Historic cost earnings are distorted from one year to another when there are price level changes. Historic cost earnings have been arrived at after matching revenue in terms of pounds of current purchasing power with costs expressed in terms of pounds of past and current purchasing power. Historic cost earnings are also a mixture of current operating profit and realised holding gains (specific price level changes). For these reasons, earnings per share based on historical information cannot be relied upon for making valid comparisons and investment decisions.

15.33 There are diverse accounting practices which also cause problems in interpreting earnings per share, of which the following are examples:

EARNINGS PER SHARE

(a)
- practice of revaluations on a partial basis;
- practice of providing 'suplementary' and 'split' depreciation (although now prohibited under revised SSAP 12);
- practice of underestimating useful life in times of inflation;
- treatment of sale of previously revalued assets.

(b) SSAP 13 states that development expenditure may be capitalised if certain conditions are satisfied. This means that SSAP 13 allows a choice between an 'immediate write-off' and capitalisation. Some companies will always write off this expenditure, whilst others may decide to capitalise and amortise it.

(c) The amount to be provided for deferred tax under SSAP 15 (revised) is subjective. The provision for deferred tax will depend on:
- budgets;
- company's intentions and circumstances; and
- tax legislation.

Under the original SSAP 15, some companies continued to provide deferred tax on a *full* provision basis and no justification was required for this basis of provision, while other companies, also following the requirements of the original SSAP 15, whereby deferred tax was provided on a *partial* provision basis, had to justify the amount provided. However, this flexibility has now been tightened up in the revised standard, which has firmly restated the principle of partial provision, specifying the use of the liability method.

(d) SSAP 20 allows a choice of the closing rate and temporal methods of foreign currency translations depending on the relationship with the foreign subsidiary. The treatment of exchange differences under these two methods is different. Under the temporal method, the exchange differences are taken to the profit and loss account, whilst under the closing rate method they are taken to the reserves.

(e) SSAP 22 allows a choice of treatment for accounting for purchased goodwill. It prefers the treatment of immediate write-off against reserves but it also allows the purchased goodwill to be treated as an intangible fixed asset with finite useful life, over which it should be systematically amortised.

(f) SSAP 23 allows a choice between the merger method and the acquisition method when certain conditions are satisfied.

Questions

1. The following information has been extracted from the profit and loss account of X Plc (a listed company) for the year ended 31 December 19X1.

UNDERSTANDING ACCOUNTING STANDARDS

	£m	£m
Profit before taxation		252
Taxation		(110)
		142
Minority interests		(21)
		121
Extraordinary items		17
		138
Dividends – Preference	(20)	
– Ordinary	(55)	
		(75)
		63

X Plc was financed at 1 January 19X1 by 250 million 8 per cent preference shares of £1 each and by 500 million ordinary shares of 25p each. The company's reported EPS for the year ended 31 December 19X0 was 18.9p and no changes in capital took place during that year. The rate of corporation tax is 35 per cent.

Calculate the figures for EPS which X Plc should disclose in its published accounts for the year ended 31 December 19X1 if:

(a) No changes in share capital took place during the year.
(b) A bonus issue of 1 for 2 was made on 31 March 19X1.
(c) An offer for sale by tender took place on 31 March. A total of 200 million shares were issued, the minimum tender price was 300p and the striking price was 360p. A placing was also made in the year on 1 December. Institutions were issued 70 million shares at a price of 390p.
(d) X Plc bought a subsidiary company on 1 July 19X1, the consideration being £80m of 12 per cent loan stock and 76m ordinary shares, issued at a time when the share price was 350p. A one for one bonus issue was subsequently made on 30 September 19X1.
(e) A one for five rights issue was made on 31 May at an issue price of 425p. The actual cum-rights price on the last day prior to the shares being quoted ex-rights was 495p.
(f) On 1 April 60 million shares were issued as part of the consideration in the acquisition of a subsidiary. Acquisition accounting was used on consolidation and the offer was declared unconditional on 1 March. On 1 July a one for five rights issue was made at a price of 270p. The actual cum-rights price on the last day of quotation cum-rights was 330p. On 1 December a one for three bonus issue was made.
(g) A one for three rights issue was made on 31 July 19X1 at a price of

EARNINGS PER SHARE

284p; the actual mid-market cum-rights price on the last day before the shares were quoted ex-rights was 316p. The new shares did not rank for the interim dividend payable on 9 September 19X1 but will rank for the final dividend payable in respect of that year. On 1 October 19X1 each 25p ordinary share was split into five 5p ordinary shares.

(h) On 1 May 50 million shares were repurchased and cancelled. A scrip issue of one for one was then made on 30 September.

(i) On 30 April 19X1 X Plc acquired another company by a share for share exchange, issuing 125m shares to the acquired company's shareholders. The acquisition is to be accounted for using the merger accounting rules and because of this the comparative figures in X Plc's 19X1 accounts have been restated to include an additional £11m profits after tax and minority interests. The new subsidiary had no extraordinary items that year. X Plc subsequently made a one for four rights issue on 30 November 19X1 which was priced at a discount of 60 per cent to the share price of 530p on the date of announcement. The shares lost 43p prior to going ex-rights.

(j) On 1 January 19X1 £150m of 6 per cent convertible loan stock was issued. Each £100 of loan stock may be converted into 31 shares anytime during 19X2 and 19X3, 27 shares during 19X4 and 25 shares during 19X5. Any loan stock unconverted at 31 December 19X5 will be redeemed at par on 30 June 19X9.

(k) On 30 June 19X1 X Plc issued £260m of 9 per cent loan stock together with attached warrants. An investor received 10 warrants per £100 nominal value of loan stock, each warrant enabling the holder to purchase 1 share for 550p any time before 31 December 19X5. Assume the yield on 2½ per cent consolidated stock is 8 per cent.

(l) On 1 January options to subscribe for a total of 67 million shares at a price of 256p each were granted. The price of 2.5 per cent consols on 1 December 19X0 was £32. On 30 June a one for two rights issue was made. The issue price was 290p and the actual cum-rights price was 355p. The terms of the options are fully protected for bonus issues and the bonus element of rights issues.

(m) On 1 July £100 million of 8 per cent convertible loan stock was issued with each £100 of loan stock being convertible into 47 ordinary shares. On 1 October a one for five rights issue was made, the issue price being 190p and the actual cum-rights price was 220p. The conversion terms of the convertible loan stock are protected for bonus issues and the scrip element of rights issues.

(n) On 1 March 19X1 X Plc made a one for one bonus issue. On 31 May 19X1 it made a one for five rights issue at a price of 150p. The cum-rights price on the last day of quotation cum-rights was 198p. On 1

July 19X1 a subsidiary company was acquired, the consideration being satisfied by the issue of 150m ordinary shares and £250m of 6 per cent convertible loan stock. The conversion terms for the loan stock are 75 shares per £100 of loan stock if conversion takes place before 30 June 19X3 and 85 shares per £100 of loan stock thereafter until the security is redeemed on 30 June 19X7.

(o) No changes in capital structure took place during the year. At the start of the year options were outstanding to subscribe for ordinary shares as follows:

20m shares at an option price of 200p
10m shares at an option price of 250p
12m shares at an option price of 360p
The yield on 2.5 per cent consols is 10 per cent.

(p) On 1 January £300 million or 6 per cent convertible loan stock was issued, each £100 of loan stock being convertible into 63 ordinary shares. On 30 June holders of £80 million of convertible loan stock exercised their option to convert. On 30 November 40 million shares were issued as part consideration in the acquisition of a subsidiary.

(q) On 1 January 19X1 X Plc instituted a share option scheme for its directors and senior management. Under this scheme eligible members will be allocated share options on each 1 January; the number of shares is to be based on the company's level of profitability. At the start of the scheme options to purchase, 25m shares were allocated. The exercise price for these options is 400p. On 1 March 19X1 X Plc issued £500m of 5 per cent convertible loan stock. Conversion may take place any time before 1 March 19X3, each £100 of loan stock being convertible into 34 ordinary shares until 1 March 19X4 and into 39 ordinary shares thereafter. Both the terms of the share option scheme and the convertible loan stock are fully protected for bonus issues, share splits and the scrip element of rights issues.

On 1 June 19X1 a one for two rights issue was made, the issue price being 300p and the cum-rights price on the last day before the shares were quoted ex-rights was 390p. On 1 November 19X1 options to subscribe for the 3 million shares were exercised. On 1 December 19X1 each 25p ordinary share was split into five 5p ordinary shares. At 31 December 19X0 the price of 2½ per cent consols was £28.

2. On 30 September 19X9, Purbeck Ltd had an issued share capital of £1,500,000 in ordinary shares of 25p each. On 31 March 19Y0 the company made a Rights Issue of 1:3 at 80p per share. The Rights Issue was fully taken up. The stock exchange quoted price of the existing shares on the day before the shares went ex rights was 140p per share. The new shares

EARNINGS PER SHARE

were not entitled to the 10 per cent dividends declared for the year ended 30 September 19Y0.

The consolidated profits of Purbeck Ltd and its subsidiaries for the year ended 30 September 19Y0 were £880,000 before deducting taxation £460,000 and profits attributable to minority interests in a subsidiary of £25,000. The earnings per share disclosed for the year ended 30 September 19X9 was 6.5p per share.

During the year ended 30 September 19Y1 Purbeck acquired the minority interest in the subsidiary by issuing 500,000 10 per cent cumulative preference shares. It also issued £1,000,000 8 per cent convertible debenture stock 19Z1. The debenture stock was convertible into ordinary shares as follows:

31 May 19Y2 200 ordinary shares per £100 of debenture stock
31 May 19Y3 180 ordinary shares per £100 of debenture stock
31 May 19Y4 160 ordinary shares per £100 of debenture stock

The terms of conversion included the clause that shares issued under the agreement would rank for dividend in the accounting year following the exercise of the conversion. Holders of £400,000 debenture stock exercised their conversion right on 31 May 19Y2. The profit and loss accounts for the years end 30 September 19Y1 and 19Y2 are as follows:

	19Y1 £	19Y1 £	19Y2 £	19Y2 £
Trading profit for the year		940,000		1,200,000
Less debenture interest		80,000		80,000
		860,000		1,120,000
Less taxation				
Corporation Tax		480,000		530,000
Transfer to (from) Deferred Tax		(30,000)		50,000
Profit after tax		410,000		540,000
Extraordinary items		(35,000)		20,000
		375,000		560,000
Less dividends				
Preference	50,000		50,000	
Ordinary	200,000	250,000	200,000	250,000
Profit retained		£125,000		£310,000

Assume Corporation Tax at 35 per cent.

Required:

(a) Calculate the earnings per share figures for disclosure in the profit and loss account of Purbeck Ltd for the year ended 30 September 19Y0 and the comparative figure for the year ended 30 September 19X9.

(b) Show the earnings per share calculation for disclosure in the profit and loss account of Purbeck plc (name changed from Purbeck Ltd in 19Y1) for the year ended 30 September 19Y2 and the comparative figure for 19Y1.

3. The computation and publication of earnings per share (EPS) figures by listed companies are governed by SSAP 3: *Earnings per share* (1972, revised 1974).

Required:

(a) On the basis of the facts given below, compute the group's EPS figures for the current AND previous years, stating your reasons for your treatment of items which may possibly affect the amount of EPS in the current year.
(b) Give your opinion as to the usefulness (to the user of financial statements) of the EPS figures that you have computed.

Nottingham Industries plc and its subsidiaries
Consolidated profit and loss account for the year ended 31 March 19Y6 (extract from draft unaudited accounts)

	£'000	£'000
Profit on ordinary activities before taxation		1,000
Tax on profit on ordinary activities		(420)
Profit on ordinary activities after taxation		580
Minority interests in profits of subsidiaries		(50)
Profit attributable to shareholders in Nottingham Industries plc (of which £415,000 is dealt with in the accounts of that company)		530
Extraordinary income	40	
Extraordinary charges	(550)	
Extraordinary loss	(510)	
Tax on extraordinary loss	220	
		(290)
Profit for the financial year		240
Dividends		(479)
Amount added to (deducted from) reserves for the financial year		(239)

Notes
(1) Called up share capital of Nottingham Industries plc:
 In issue at 1 April 19Y5:
 16,000,000 ordinary shares of 25p each;
 1,000,000 10% cumulative preference shares of £1 each.

1 July 19Y5: Bonus issue of ordinary shares, 1 for 5.

1 October 19Y5: Market purchase of 500,000 of own ordinary shares at a price of £1.00 per share.

1 January 19Y6: Executives of Nottingham Industries plc granted options to take up a total of 200,000 unissued ordinary shares at a price of £1.25 per share; no options had been exercised at 31 March 19Y6. (Assume that, at 1 January 19Y6, 2½% Consols stood at a price of 20; ignore transaction costs.)

(2) In the draft accounts for the year ended 31 March 19Y6, 'profit on ordinary activities before taxation' is arrived at after charging or crediting the following items:
   (i) accelerated depreciation on fixed assets, £80,000;
   (ii) book gain on disposal of a major subsidiary, £120,000.

(3) 'Extraordinary income' consists entirely of a write-back of deferred taxation (accounted for by the liability method), in consequence of a reduction in the rate of corporation tax from 45% in the financial year 19Y4 to 40% in the financial year 19Y5.

(4) 'Extraordinary charges' consist of:
   (i) provision for bad debts arising on the failure of a major customer, £150,000; other bad debts have been written off or provided for in the ordinary way; and
   (ii) provision for loss through expropriation of the business of an overseas subsidiary by a foreign government, £400,000.

(5) In the published accounts for the year ended 31 March 19Y5, the basic EPS was shown as 2.2p; fully diluted EPS was the same figure.

Chapter Sixteen

SSAP 10: Statements of source and application of funds

16.1 SSAP 10 applies to all financial statements intended to give a true and fair view of financial position and profit or loss other than those of enterprises whose turnover or gross income is less than £25,000.

16.2 The objective of a statement of source and application of funds ('funds statement') is 'to show the manner in which the operations of a company have been financed and in which its financial resources have been used'.

16.3 A major regular source of funds for companies will always be the profits it generates and SSAP 10 requires that the funds statement should show the profit or loss for the period together with the adjustments for items which do not involve movement in funds. Some examples of items which do not involve movement in funds are:

(a) depreciation;
(b) amortisation of goodwill;
(c) any profit or loss on sale of fixed assets included in proceeds shown as a source, and therefore needs to be eliminated from the trading profit.

16.4 SSAP 10 also requires that the following items should, where material, be shown separately in the funds statement:

(a) dividends paid;
(b) acquisitions and disposals of fixed and other non-current assets;
(c) funds raised by increasing, or expended in repaying or redeeming medium- or long-term loans or the issued capital of the company;
(d) increase or decrease in working capital sub-divided into its components, and movements in net liquid funds.

16.5 SSAP 10 does not prescribe a specific format.

16.6 Where a company prepares group accounts, the funds statement should be based on the group accounts. Any purchases or disposals of subsidiary companies during the year may be treated in the funds statement in one of the following ways:

SSAP 10: STATEMENTS OF SOURCE AND APPLICATION OF FUNDS

(a) as separate items; or
(b) by reflecting the effects on the separate assets and liabilities dealt with in the statement.

16.7 The above is illustrated later in a detailed example.

16.8 The appendix to SSAP 10 gives guidance on the formats and they are reproduced below:

Appendix

The appendix is for general guidance and does not form part of the statement of standard accounting practice.

The methods of presentation used are illustrative only and in no way prescriptive and other methods of presentation may equally comply with the accounting standard. The format used should be selected with a view to demonstrating clearly the manner in which the operations of the company have been financed and in which its financial resources have been utilised.

EXAMPLE 1
Company without subsidiaries Ltd
Statement of source and application of funds

	This Year			Last Year		
	£'000	£'000	£'000	£'000	£'000	£'000
Source of funds						
Profit before tax		1,430				440
Adjustments for iems not involving the movement of funds:						
Depreciation		380				325
Total generated from operations		1,810				765
Funds from other sources						
Issue of shares for cash		100				80
		1,910				845
Application of funds						
Dividends paid	(400)			(400)		
Tax paid	(690)			(230)		
Purchase of fixed assets	(460)	(1,550)		(236)	(866)	
		360			(21)	

379

Increase/decrease in working capital

Increase in stocks		80			114	
Increase in debtors		120			22	
(Increase) decrease in creditors – excluding taxation and proposed dividends		115			(107)	

Movement in net liquid funds:
Increase (decrease) in:

Cash balances	(5)			35		
Short-term investments	50			(85)		
	45		360	(50)		(21)

EXAMPLE 2
Groups Limited
Statement of source and application of funds
(based on the accounts of the group and showing the effects of acquiring a subsidiary on the separate assets and liabilities of the group)

	This Year			Last Year		
	£'000	£'000	£'000	£'000	£'000	£'000
Source of funds						
Profit before tax and extraordinary items, less minority interests		2,025			2,610	
Extraordinary items		450			(170)	
		2,475			2,440	
Adjustments for items not involving the movement of funds:						
Minority interests in the retained profits of the year		25			30	
Depreciation		345			295	
Profits retained in associated companies		(40)			—	
Total generated from operations		2,805			2,765	

SSAP 10: STATEMENTS OF SOURCE AND APPLICATION OF FUNDS

Funds from other sources
Shares issued in part consideration of the acquisition of subsidiary*   290   —
Capital raised under executive option scheme   100   80
                                                3,195   2,845

Application of funds
Dividends paid   (650)   (650)
Tax paid   (770)   (970)
Purchase of fixed assets*   (660)   (736)
Purchase of goodwill on
  acquisition of subsidiary*   (30)   —
Debentures redeemed   (890) (3,000) —   (2,356)
                                        195   489

Increase/decrease in working capital
Increase in stocks*   120   166
Increase in debtors*   100   122
Decrease in creditors – excluding taxation and
  proposed dividends*   75   17
Movement in net liquid funds
Increase (decrease) in cash
  balance*   (35)   10
Increase (decrease) in short-
  term investments   (65)   (100)   174   184   489
                                        195

* *Summary of the effects of the acquisition of Subsidiary Limited*

Net assets acquired		**Discharged by**	
Fixed assets	290	Shares issued	290
Goodwill	30	Cash paid	60
Stocks	40		
Debtors	30		
Creditors	(40)		
	350		350

EXAMPLE 3
Groups Limited
Statement of source and application of funds

(based on the accounts of the group and showing the acquisition of a subsidiary as a separate item)

	This Year £'000 £'000 £'000	Last Year £'000 £'000 £'000
Source of funds		
profit before tax and extraordinary items, less minority interests	2,025	2,610
Extraordinary items	450	(170)
	2,475	2,440
Adjustments for items not involving the movement of funds:		
Minority interests in the retained profits of the year	25	30
Depreciation	345	295
Profits retained in associated companies	(40)	—
Total generated from operations	2,805	2,765
Funds from other sources		
Shares issued in part consideration of the acquisition of subsidiary*	290	—
Capital raised under executive option scheme	100	80
	3,195	2,845
Application of funds		
Dividends paid	(650)	(650)
Tax paid	(770)	(970)
Purchase of fixed assets	(370)	(736)
Purchase of Subsidiary Ltd*	(350)	—
Debentures redeemed	(890) (3,030)	— (2,356)
	165	489

SSAP 10: STATEMENTS OF SOURCE AND APPLICATION OF FUNDS

Increase/decrease in working capital				
Increase in stocks	80		166	
Increase in debtors	70		122	
Decrease in creditors – excluding taxation and proposed dividends	115		17	
Movement in net liquid funds:				
Increase (decrease) in cash balance*	(35)		10	
Increase (decrease) in short-term investments	(65)	(100) 165	174	184 489

* *Analysis of the acquisition of Subsidiary Limited*

Net assets acquired		Discharged by	
Fixed assets	290	Shares issued	290
Goodwill	30	Cash paid	60
Stocks	40		
Debtors	30		
Creditors	(40)		
	350		350

DETAILED EXAMPLE

16.9 Below is the (historical cost) Consolidated Profit and Loss Account of the Alphabeta Group for the year ended 31 December, together with the (simplified) Consolidated Balance Sheets as at 31 December, and notes amplifying these accounts.

16.10 You are required:

(a) to prepare the Statement of Source and Application of Funds of the group for the year ended 31 December, in a form suitable for publication and complying with *SSAP 10: Statements of source and application of funds*.

Alphabeta plc and its Subsidiaries
Consolidated Profit and Loss Account for the year ended 31 December 19X2

	£'000s	£'000s	£'000s
Turnover			55,000
Change in stocks of finished goods and work in progress		4,700	
Own work capitalised		3,000	
Other operating income		2,000	
			9,700
			64,700
Raw materials and consumables	20,000		
Other external charges	1,000		
		21,000	
Staff costs		28,000	
Depreciation and amortisation of fixed assets (net of gains/losses on disposals)		4,482	
Other operating charges		2,500	
			55,982
Net Trading Profit			8,718
Group's proportion of pre-tax profits of related companies			100
Net Profit Before Interest			8,818
Interest payable and similar charges:			
On bank overdrafts		60	
On debenture loans of group companies (externally held)		1,050	
Amortisation of discount on above debenture loans		200	
			1,310
Net Profit Before Taxation			7,508
Tax on profit on ordinary activities:			
Of group companies		2,500	
Transfers to deferred taxation:			
Of group companies		1,000	
Group's proportion of tax on ordinary activities of related companies		50	
		3,550	

Less: Adjustment of previous year's tax charge		20	
			3,530
Profit on Ordinary Activities After Taxation			3,978
Minority interests therein			540
Attributable to Shareholders in Alphabeta plc			3,438
(of which £3,000,000 is dealt with in that company's accounts)			
Extraordinary income of group companies		46	
Extraordinary charges of related companies (group's proportion)		(10)	
Extraordinary profit before tax		36	
Less: Tax on extraordinary profit:			
Of group	24		
Of related companies (group's proportion)	(5)		
		19	
		17	
Less: Minority interest		(3)	14
Profit for the Financial Year			3,452
Dividends of Alphabeta plc:			
Preference – Paid		100	
Ordinary – Paid		600	
Ordinary – Proposed		1,440	
			2,140
Retained Earnings for the Financial Year:			
Of Alphabeta plc		870	
Of group companies (less minority interests)		422	
Of related companies (group's proportion)		20	
			1,312

Consolidated Balance Sheets, 31 December 19X1 and 19X2

	19X1 Gross £'000s	19X1 Depreciation £'000s	19X1 Net £'000s	19X2 Gross £'000s	19X2 Depreciation £'000s	19X2 Net £'000s
Net Assets						
Fixed Assets						
Intangible assets:						
Patents and trade marks	100	50	50	140	60	80
Goodwill	400	250	150	710	392	318
	500	300	200	850	452	398
Tangible assets:						
Land	1,000	—	1,000	2,700	—	2,700
Buildings	6,000	2,000	4,000	13,000	3,983	9,017
Plant and machinery	12,000	6,000	6,000	16,700	8,040	8,660
Fixtures and fittings	3,000	1,200	1,800	3,850	1,185	2,665
	22,000	9,200	12,800	36,250	13,208	23,042
Investments:						
Shares in related companies (on equity basis)	350	—	350	1,070	—	1,070
Total Fixed Assets	22,850	9,500	13,350	38,170	13,660	24,510
Current Assets						
Stocks:						
Raw materials and consumables	3,000			5,000		
Work in progress	1,000			1,700		
Finished goods	6,000			10,000		
		10,000			16,700	
Debtors:						
Trade debtors	4,700			5,654		
Prepayments	90			100		
		4,790			5,754	
Cash at bank and in hand		2,300			6,912	
			17,090			29,366

SSAP 10: STATEMENTS OF SOURCE AND APPLICATION OF FUNDS

	£'000s	£'000s	£'000s	£'000s	£'000s
B/Fwd		17,090			29,366
Creditors: Amounts Falling Due Within One Year					
Bank overdrafts	(600)			(1,014)	
Trade creditors	(2,500)			(3,000)	
Corporation tax – current year (*less* ACT)	(1,000)			(1,806)	
Accruals	(400)			(450)	
Proposed dividend	(1,000)			(1,440)	
ACT on proposed dividend	(429)			(617)	
		(5,929)			(8,327)
Net Current Assets		11,161			21,039
		24,511			45,549
Financed by:					
Creditors: Amounts Falling Due After One Year					
Debenture loans (externally held)	7,000			9,000	
Less: Unamortised discount	400			250	
		6,600			8,750
Provisions for Liabilities and Charges					
Deferred taxation		771			1,583
Minority Interests in Group Companies		1,200			1,497
Capital and Reserves					
Called up share capital:					
Preference (£1 shares)	1,000			1,000	
Ordinary (25p shares)	10,000			18,000	
		11,000			19,000

	£'000s	£'000s	£'000s	£'000s	£'000s
Reserves:					
Share premium account	1,500			6,300	
Revaluation reserve	—			3,667	
Profit and loss account	3,390			4,682	
Group's proportion of retained earnings of related companies since acquisition	50			70	
		4,940			14,719
		24,511			45,549

Notes

(1) The accounts were consolidated by the acquisition (purchase) method.
(2) Interests in related companies are accounted for by the equity method.
(3) During the year ended 31 December 19X2 a new wholly-owned subsidiary, Zeta Limited, was acquired by the issue, of 20,000,000 25p ordinary shares, whose fair market value was deemed to be 40p per share. Zeta Limited's identifiable assets (as revalued in its books before its acquisition by Alphabeta plc), and its liabilities, were:

	£
Land	300,000
Buildings (net)	1,500,000
Plant and machinery (net)	2,000,000
Fixtures and fittings (net)	500,000
Stocks: Raw materials and consumables	1,200,000
Stocks: Work in progress	400,000
Stocks: Finished goods	2,000,000
Debtors: Trade debtors	1,250,000
Debtors: Prepayments	20,000
Cash at bank and in hand	220,000
Creditors: Amounts falling due within one year:	
Trade creditors	800,000
Corporation tax – current year (*less* ACT)	450,000
Accruals	100,000
Provisions for liabilities and charges:	
Deferred taxation	350,000

SSAP 10: STATEMENTS OF SOURCE AND APPLICATION OF FUNDS

(4) During the year ended 31 December 19X2, Alphabeta plc purchased a 25% interest in the equity of Mu plc for £700,000 in cash.

(5) As at 1 January 19X2, the group's land was revalued in its books at market value, £2,000,000, and its buildings were revalued on the basis of gross replacement cost, £10,000,000. No deferred taxation adjustments were made in respect of these revaluations.

(6) During the year 19X2, £3,000,000 of plant and machinery was constructed by group companies, and £1,200,000 was purchased from outside the group. Plant valued at 1 January 19X2 at £1,500,000 gross, £200,000 net, was sold during 19X2 for £225,000, the difference being included in 'depreciation and amortisation', etc., in the Consolidated Profit and Loss Account.

(7) Corresponding movements on fixtures and fittings were: purchases, £800,000; disposals – gross, £450,000, net, £50,000, and proceeds, £70,000.

(8) All additions to land, buildings, and intangible assets were paid for in cash, unless otherwise accounted for.

(9) Minority interests in extraordinary income were £6,000 before taxation, and £3,000 after taxation.

(10) Corporation tax 35%, payable nine months after the year end. Basic rate of income tax 25%.

(11) All computations are to be made to the nearest £1,000.

SOLUTION TO DETAILED EXAMPLE – STUDENT GUIDE
Stages:

1. *Introduction*
16.11 Read through the question. A group statement of source and application of funds is required.

2. *Format*
16.12 Set up a format with just the main headings. We are going to use example 2 from the appendix to SSAP 10. In this example, the funds statement is prepared using the year end balance sheet which includes the separate assets and liabilities of the subsidiary company which was acquired during the year. The funds statement prepared on the basis of example 3 in the appendix to SSAP 10 is discussed later.

3. *Summary of the acquisition of a subsidiary company*
16.13 The information relating to the acquisition of the subsidiary is given in note 3 in the question. This can be inserted into the summary of the acquisition.

UNDERSTANDING ACCOUNTING STANDARDS

Summary of the effects of the acquisition of Zeta Limited

Net assets acquired		Discharged by	
	£'000		£'000
Land	300	Shares issued	8,000
Buildings	1,500		
.			
.			
.			
.			
.			
.			
Deferred taxation	(350)		
	7,690		
Goodwill	310		
(balancing figure)			
	8,000		8,000

4. Changes in working capital

16.14 The next stage is to move on to increase/decrease in working capital as it requires only a comparison of each component of working capital, and identify the difference. Please note that the dividends and tax paid must be shown separately as part of the application of funds. It is best to set up at this stage separate ledger accounts in workings for these two items.

		Balance Sheet	
	Year end	Opening	Difference
	£'000	£'000	£'000
Stocks	16,700	10,000	+6,700
Debtors and prepayments	5,754	4,790	+ 964
Cash at bank and in hand	6,912	2,300	+4,612
Bank overdraft	1,014	600	+ 414
Trade creditors	3,000	2,500	+ 500
Accruals	450	400	+ 50

5. Profit and loss account and balance sheet

16.15 Now that the easiest part of the funds statement is dealt with, it is best to work through the profit and loss account and the balance sheet in a systematic manner.

6. Profit before tax

16.16 The source of funds is sub-divided into (i) funds generated from operations and (ii) other sources. A major source of funds which a company generates from its operations is profit before tax. Example 2 in

SSAP 10: STATEMENTS OF SOURCE AND APPLICATION OF FUNDS

the appendix to SSAP 10 starts with profit before tax and extraordinary items, less minority interest, which in our example is £6,968,000 (£7,508,000 − £540,000). The extent to which £540,000 of profits belonging to the minority interest is retained within the group, it is a source of funds for the group and will be added back to £6,968,000 as part of the adjustments for items not involving the movement of funds. The alternative would have been to start with profit before tax and extraordinary items (which is £7,508,000) and show dividends paid to the minority interests separately as part of application of funds.

7. Extraordinary items
16.17 Since we started with profit before tax less the minority interest, we need to do the same thing with extraordinary items. Extraordinary items before tax less minority interest equals £33,000 (£36,000 − £3,000). Once again, to the extent that the minority interest i retained within the group, it will be added back as part of adjustments for items not involving the movement of funds. If the starting figure for profit had been inclusive of minority interest, the extraordinary items would have to be treated in a similar manner – i.e. extraordinary items before tax which equals £36,000. Dividends paid to the minority interest would then be shown as part of application of funds.

8. Adjustments for items not involving the movement of funds
16.18 The following items do not involve any movement in funds and will have to be adjusted to arrive at the total funds generated from operations:

(a) Depreciation   £4,482,000

No further adjustment is required for profit or loss on disposal as the above figure is already net of this.

(b) Minority interest to the extent that it is retained within the group. This is best calculated by comparing the year end figure with the opening figure on the balance sheet and the difference equals retained minority interest. Retained minority interest = £1,497,000 − £1,200,000 = £297,000.

Alternatively, it can be calculated by compiling a ledger account and identifying the dividends paid to the minority interest. The difference between the share of profits belonging to the minority interest and dividends paid to them will equal the retained minority interest.

UNDERSTANDING ACCOUNTING STANDARDS

Minority interest account

	£'000		£'000
		Balance b/fwd	1,000
		Share of profits	540
Therefore dividend paid		Share of	
(balancing figure)	246	extraordinary items	3
Balance c/fwd	1,497		
	£1,743		£1,743

	£'000
Share of profits	540
Share of extraordinary items	3
	543
Less dividends paid	(246)
Therefore retained within the group	£297

(c) Related company: Note 2 to the question states that the interests in related companies are accounted for by the equity method. The group's proportion of pre-tax profits of related company equals £100,000 and is included in the profit before tax less minority interests of £6,968,000. To the extent to which this profit is retained in the related companies, it is not a source of funds for the group and will, therefore, have to be deducted from the profit before tax figure. The extraordinary items will also have to be adjusted to the extent the profits or losses are retained within the related companies. This adjustment will be included as part of adjustments for items not involving the movement in funds. Therefore the amount that is left as part of the funds generated from operations will be the dividends received from the companies. The amounts retained in the related companies can be computed as follows:

The group's proportion of pre-tax profits of related companies less extraordinary items = £90,000 (£100,000 − £10,000)
Group's proportion of tax on these profits = £45,000 (£50,000 − £5,000)
Group's proportion of tax on these profits will be paid by the related companies and therefore this amount is retained in the related companies. In addition, included in the retained earnings for the financial year of £1,312,000 there is an amount of £20,000 which is retained in the related companies. Therefore, the total amount retained in the related companies equals £65,000 (£45,000 + £20,000).
If the summary of retained profits was not available, a ledger account would have been required to identify the dividends received.

SSAP 10: STATEMENTS OF SOURCE AND APPLICATION OF FUNDS

Related Companies

	£'000		£'000
Balance b/fwd	350		
Additions (Note 4)	700	Tax on share of profits	50
Share of profits	100	Share of extraordinary loss	10
Tax on share of extraordinary loss	5	Therefore dividends received	25
		Balance c/fwd	1,070
	£1,155		£1,155

	£'000
Thus, share of profits	100
Less share of extraordinary loss	(10)
	90
Less dividends received	(25)
Retained in related companies	65

A similar adjustment would be required for the associated companies which are accounted on the basis of the equity method.

(d) Amortisation of discount on debenture loans of £200,000 does not involve movement in funds and will have to be added back.

9. Taxation

16.19 We need to identify the amounts paid for tax during the financial year. This is best done by compiling a single ledger account for all the taxes.

Taxation

	£'000		£'000
		Balances b/fwd	
		Corporation tax	1,000
		ACT	429
		Deferred tax	771
Profit and Loss Account		*Profit and Loss Account*	
Adjustment of previous year's tax charge	20	Tax on profits	2,500
		Transfers to deferred tax	1,000
		Tax on extraordinary profit	24
Therefore cash paid	1,698		
Balances c/fwd			
Corporation tax	1,806		
ACT	617		
Deferred tax	1,583		
	£5,724		£5,724

UNDERSTANDING ACCOUNTING STANDARDS

Tax paid during the year was £1,698,000 and this will be shown as part of the application of funds.

10. Dividends
16.20 Dividends paid will be computed in the same way as tax.

Dividends

	£'000		£'000
		Balance b/fwd	1,000
Therefore cash paid	1,700	Profit and Loss A/c	2,140
Balance c/fwd	1,400		
	£3,140		£3,140

Dividends paid will be shown as part of the application of funds. All the items in the profit and loss account have now been dealt with and we can move onto the balance sheet.

11. Fixed assets
16.21 Any additions to fixed assets will be shown as part of the application of funds. The proceeds on disposal will be included as part of other sources and the profit before tax will have to be adjusted for profit or loss on disposal as it does not involve a movement in funds.

(a) Intangible assets
16.22 Since there is no additional information given on this in the question, we must assume that there were no disposals and the changes in gross amounts represent additions.

Patents and trademarks – Additions of £40,000 (£140,000 – £100,000)
Goodwill – Additions of £310,000 (£710,000 – £400,000)
Please note that the amount paid for goodwill is the same as the one in the summary of the acquisition.

(b) Tangible assets
(i) Land and Buildings
16.23 There appear to have been no disposals during the year. However, land and buildings were revalued at the start of the year and part of the increase in the gross amount must be due to the revaluation surplus. Revaluation surplus is taken straight to the reserves and does not involve any movement in funds. The land was revalued from £1,000,000 to £2,000,000 at the start of the year, giving a revaluation surplus of £1,000,000. Therefore, the additions to the land must be the difference between the gross amount at the year end and the revalued amount at the start of the year and which equals £700,000 (£2,700,000 – £2,000,000).

SSAP 10: STATEMENTS OF SOURCE AND APPLICATION OF FUNDS

16.24 Additions to the buildings equals the difference between the gross amount at the year end and the revalued amount at the start of the year, i.e. £3,000,000 (£13,000,000 − £10,000,000). The amount transferred to reserves will equal the gross revaluation reserve less the backlog depreciation.

	£'000
Gross surplus (10,000 − 6,000)	4,000
Less back-log depreciation	(1,333)
	£2,667

16.25 At the end of last year the historic cost was depreciated by one third. Therefore, the back-log depreciation will equal one third of the revaluation surplus. The total revaluation surplus on land and buildings amounts to £3,667,000 (1,000,000 + 2,667,000) and agrees with the balance sheet figure.

(ii) Plant and machinery and fixtures and fittings

16.26 All the information on additions to plant and machinery and fixture fittings is given in the question.

Additions	Plant and machinery £'000	Fixtures and fittings £'000
Constructed by group companies	3,000	
Purchased from outside the group	1,200	800
In the books of the subsidiary company at the point of acquisition	2,000	500
	£6,200	£1,300
Disposal proceeds – also given in the question	£225	£70

The profit of £25,000 on disposal of plant and machinery and £20,000 on disposal of fixtures and fittings has been deducted from the depreciation charge for the year, and therefore no further adjustment is required to the profit before tax.

The additions could have also been computed from ledger accounts as follows:

Plant and machinery (gross)

	£'000		£'000
Balance b/fwd	12,000	Disposals	1,500
Therefore additions	6,200	Balance c/fwd	16,700
	£18,200		£18,200

Fixtures and fittings (gross)

	£'000		£'000
Balance b/fwd	3,000		
		Disposals	450
Therefore additions	1,300	Balance c/fwd	3,850
	£4,300		£4,300

(c) *Investments*
16.27 £700,000 worth of shares were acquired in related companies.

12. *Creditors: Amounts falling due after one year*
16.28 The nominal value of new debenture loans issued during the year equals £2 million (£9 million less £7 million). The balance in the discount account at the start of the year was £400,000. The amount written off to the profit and loss equalled £200,000. The balance at the year end is £250,000. Therefore, the new debenture loans were issued at a discount of £50,000. The proceeds on issue of debenture loans, which will be included as part of other sources, equals £1,950,000.

13. *Called up share capital and share premium account*
16.29 No new preference shares were issued during the year. The change in the ordinary share capital equals £8,000,000 (£18,000,000 − £10,000,000) and share premium equals £4,800,000 (£6,300,000 − £1,500,000). Therefore the proceeds on new issue of ordinary shares equals £12,800,000. This new issue includes shares which were issued to acquire the new subsidiary company.

SSAP 10: STATEMENTS OF SOURCE AND APPLICATION OF FUNDS

SOLUTION
Alphabeta PLC
Statement of source and application of funds for the year ended 31 December 19X2

	£'000	£'000	Stage
Source of funds:			
Profit on ordinary activities before tax and extraordinary items, less minority interest		6,968	6
Extraordinary items before tax, less minority interest		33	7
		7,001	
Adjustments for items not involving the movement of funds:			
Retained minority interest	297		8b
Depreciation	4,482		8a
Amortisation of discount on debenture loans	200		8d
Profits retained in related companies	(65)	4,914	8c
Funds generated from operations		11,915	
Funds from other sources:			
Proceeds from sale of fixed assets	295		11b
Proceeds from issue of debentures	1,950		12
* Issue of shares	12,800		13
		15,045	
Total source of funds		26,960	
Less: *Application of funds:*			
Dividends paid	1,700		10
Tax paid	1,698		9
Purchase of shares in related companies	700		11c
Purchase of patents and trademarks	40		11a
* Purchase of goodwill on acquisition of a subsidiary	310		11a
* Purchase of land	700		11b
* Purchase of buildings	3,000		11b
* Purchase of plant and machinery	6,200		11b
* Purchase of fixtures and fittings	1,300		11b
		(15,648)	
Increase in working capital		11,312	

UNDERSTANDING ACCOUNTING STANDARDS

	£'000	£'000	Stage
Represented by:			
* Increase in stock	6,700		
* Increase in debtors and prepayments	964		
* Increase in creditors and accruals	(550)		
		7,114	4
Movement in net liquid funds:			
Increase in cash balance	4,612		
Increase in bank overdraft	(414)		
		4,198	
		11,312	

* *Summary of the effects of the acquisition of Zeta Limited*

Net assets acquired	£'000	Discharged by	£'000	Stage
Fixed assets:		Issue of shares	8,000	
Goodwill	310			3
Others	4,300			
Current assets:	5,090			
Creditors: Amounts falling due within one year	(1,350)			
Provision for liabilities and charges: Deferred taxation	(350)			
	£8,000		£8,000	

16.30 If the example 3 from the appendix to SSAP 10 had been used, a single figure of £8 million for purchase of shares in Zeta Limited would appear under the heading of application of funds. In example 2, this £8 million is broken up into separate assets and liabilities acquired. In example 3, since a single figure for £8 million would appear as part of the application of funds, the individual components of this will not be included as part of other items – i.e. there is no separate amount for goodwill; the amount shown for purchase of land will be reduced by £300,000 from the amount shown in example 2, and so on.

Other points
16.31 We started with a profit figure which was before tax, less minority interest. An alternative would be to start with a profit figure

inclusive of minority interests and show dividends paid to minority interests as an application.

Source of funds	£'000
Profit before tax	7,508
Extraordinary items before tax	36
	7,544
Application of funds	
Dividends paid to minority interest	(246)
	6,298

16.32 If there had been any minority interest at the point of acquisition, it would be shown as part of other sources.

Minority interest at the year end	x
Less minority interest at the start	(x)
Change in minority interest	x

16.33 There may be two reasons for this:
(a) They have been credited with their share of current year's profits and part of these are retained within the group. To the extent to which they are retained within the group, they form a source of funds for the group and will be added back as part of adjustments to the profits.
(b) There was a minority interest in the subsidiary company acquired during the year. This amount will be included as part of other sources as they are financing part of the net assets of the subsidiary company acquired during the year.

Question

1 Below are the profit and loss account (Format 2) of Thomas Manufacturing plc for the year ended 31 December 1985, and the balance sheets (Format 1) as at 31 December 1984 and 1985 (all simplified), with notes.
Required:
   (a) Prepare a statement of source and application of funds of Thomas Manufacturing plc for the year ended 31 December 1985, complying with SSAP 10 (1975) and showing dividends and taxes paid as applications.
   (b) Give your views on the utility of the funds statement to the user of published financial statements.

Thomas Manufacturing plc
Profit and loss account for the year ended 31 December 1985

	£'000	£'000
Turnover		5,000
Change in stocks of finished goods and work in progress		500
Own work capitalised		150
Other operating income		50
Raw materials and consumables	(2,000)	
Other external charges	(750)	
		(2,750)
Staff costs		(1,500)
Depreciation and other amounts written off tangible and intangible assets		(400)
Other operating charges		(100)
		950
Income from fixed asset investments (dividends)		20
Other interest receivable		5
		975
Interest payable and similar charges		(160)
Profit on ordinary activities before taxation		815
Tax on profit on ordinary activities		(325)
Profit on ordinary activities after taxation		490
Extraordinary income	70	
Extraordinary charges	(90)	
Extraordinary loss	(20)	
Tax on extraordinary loss	8	
		(12)
Profit for the financial year		478
Dividends:		
Paid	(100)	
Proposed	(150)	
		(250)
Retained profit for the financial year		228

SSAP 10: STATEMENTS OF SOURCE AND APPLICATION OF FUNDS

Balance sheet as at 31 December 1985

31/12/84						
Net £000	Cost £000		Cost £000	Depreciation etc. £000	Net £000	
		Fixed assets				
100	200	Intangible assets	350	200	150	
800	1,500	Tangible assets	2,500	775	1,725	
100	100	Investments	200	—	200	
1,000	1,800		3,050	975	2,075	
		Current assets				
	1,000	Stocks		1,600		
	1,000	Debtors		1,200		
	50	Investments		—		
	250	Cash at bank and in hand		30		
	2,300			2,830		
		Creditors: amounts falling due within one year				
	—	Bank loans and overdrafts		(257)		
	(500)	Trade creditors		(600)		
	(200)	Taxation		(210)		
	(100)	Proposed dividend		(150)		
	(43)	ACT on proposed dividend		(64)		
	(843)			(1,281)		
1,457		*Net current assets*			1,549	
2,457		*Total assets less current liabilities*			3,624	
		Financed by				
		Creditors: amounts falling due after more than one year				
980		Debenture loans			790	
		(Nominal value £800,000; 1984, £1,000,000)				
		Provisions for liabilities and charges				
100		Deferred tax			129	
		Capital and reserves				
		Called up share capital:				
	1,000	ordinary shares (£1)			1,500	
	200	Share premium account			300	
	—	Revaluation reserve			500	
	177	Profit and loss account			405	
1,377					2,705	
2,457					3,624	

401

Notes

(1) As at 1 January 1985, freehold land was revalued from £500,000 to £1,000,000.
(2) During the year ended 31 December 1985, plant and machinery costing £300,000, written down to £50,000 at 31 December 1984, was sold for £75,000. These book gains and losses were adjusted into the depreciation charge in the profit and loss account.
(3) 'Own work capitalised' refers to development work carried forward as an 'intangible asset'.
(4) Debentures with a nominal value of £200,000 (less unamortised discount, £4,000) were redeemed at par during the year.
(5) Ordinary shares were issued for cash during the year; there were no redemptions or purchases of the company's own shares.
(6) The investment shown as current assets at 31 December 1984 were realised during the year at £47,000.
(7) During 1985, the mainstream corporation tax charge for 1984 was settled and paid in the sum of £180,000.
(8) Corporation tax rate 35%; income tax basic rate 25%. Corporation tax payable 9 months after the year-end.

Appendix 1

The accounting treatment of government grants

(Issued April 1974)

The application of this statement is limited to grants made for the purchase of fixed assets in the United Kingdom and the Republic of Ireland.

Part 1 – Explanatory note

Introduction
The accounting treatment of government grants has varied as different grants schemes have been produced by successive governments. With the advent of regional development grants under the Industry Act 1972 it is desirable to standardise the accounting treatment of all capital-based grants.

1

Revenue-based grants
The Industry Act 1972 (and similar Acts in the Republic of Ireland and Northern Ireland) make provision for grants to be made by reference to specified categories of revenue expenditure. Such grants do not produce accounting problems as they clearly should be credited to revenue in the same period in which the revenue expenditure to which they relate is charged. If the amount receivable is not precisely ascertainable at the accounting date it is generally practicable to make a reasonable estimate.

2

Capital-based grants
The Industry Act 1972 (and similar Acts in the Republic of Ireland and Northern Ireland) also make provision for grants to be made by reference to certain types of capital expenditure. In the past, where expenditure on the acquisition of a fixed asset was eligible for a government grant, there have been different views about the choice of accounting treatments. Three principal treatments have been discussed:

3

(a) to credit to profit and loss account the total amount of the grant immediately;

(b) to credit the amount of the grant to a non-distributable reserve;

(c) to credit the amount of the grant to revenue over the useful life of the asset by:

    (i) reducing the cost of the acquisition of the fixed asset by the amount of the grant; or

    (ii) treating the amount of the grant as a deferred credit, a portion of which is transferred to revenue annually.

The effect of the grant on the company's reported earnings under the methods listed in paragraph 3 would be:

4

(a) immediate effect;

(b) no effect;

(c) progressive effect over the life of the asset.

403

5   Methods (a) and (b) provide no correlation between the accounting treatment of the grant and the accounting treatment of the expenditure to which the grant relates. Method (c) matches the application of the grant with the amortisation of the capital expenditure to which it relates and is therefore considered to be the most appropriate treatment.

6   Of the two ways in which (c) may be applied, the main argument in favour of the first alternative (reducing the cost of the fixed asset) is its simplicity. By crediting the grant to the cost of the asset the resulting reduced depreciation charge automatically credits the amount of the grant to revenue over the life of the asset.

7   The arguments in favour of the second alternative (crediting the amount of the grant to a deferred credit account, and releasing it to revenue over an extended period) are:

   (a) assets acquired at different times and locations are recorded on a uniform basis regardless of changes in government policy (such comparability is often important to management in establishing price structures and investment policies);

   (b) control over the ordering, construction and maintenance of assets is based on the gross value;

   (c) as capital allowances for tax purposes are normally calculated on the cost of an asset before deduction of the grant, adjustments of the depreciation charge shown in the accounts are avoided when computing the amount of deferred taxation.

Transitional arrangements

8   Where accounting practices other than those described in Part 2 of this statement have been adopted in respect of capital based grants received or receivable prior to its effective date, it is preferable but not a required standard accounting practice to restate them in a manner consistent with that afforded to grants to which the Statement applies.

Part 2 – Standard accounting practice

Accounting treatment and disclosure

9   Grants relating to fixed assets should be credited to revenue over the expected useful life of the asset. This may be achieved by:

   (a) reducing the cost of the acquisition of the fixed asset by the amount of the grant; or

   (b) treating the amount of the grant as a deferred credit, a portion of which is transferred to revenue annually.

   If method (b) is selected, the amount of the deferred credit should, if material, be shown separately in the balance sheet. It should not be shown as part of shareholders' funds.

Date from which effective

10 The accounting practices set out in this statement should be adopted as soon as possible and regarded as standard in respect of financial statements relating to accounting periods beginning on or after 1st January 1974.

Appendix 2

Accounting for value added tax

(*Issued April 1974*)

This statement seeks, by presenting a standard accounting practice, to achieve uniformity of accounting treatment of VAT in financial statements.

Part 1 – Explanatory note

General

VAT is a tax on the supply of goods and services which is eventually borne by the final consumer but collected at each stage of the production and distribution chain. As a general principle, therefore, the treatment of VAT in the accounts of a trader should reflect his role as a collector of the tax and VAT should not be included in income or in expenditure whether of a capital or of a revenue nature. There will however be circumstances, as noted below, in which a trader will himself bear VAT and in such circumstances the accounting treatment should reflect that fact.

Persons not accountable for VAT

Persons not accountable for VAT will suffer VAT on inputs. For them VAT will increase the cost of all goods and services to which it applies and should be included in such costs. In particular, the VAT on fixed assets should be added to the cost of the fixed assets concerned.

Accountable persons who also carry on exempted activities

In the case of persons who also carry on exempted activities there will be a residue of VAT, which will fall directly on the trader and which will normally be arrived at by division of his activities as between taxable outputs (including zero-rated) and those which are exempt. In such cases, the principle that such VAT will increase the costs to which it applies and should be included in such costs will be equally applicable. Hence the appropriate portion of the VAT allocable to fixed assets should, if irrecoverable, be added to the cost of the fixed assets concerned and the proportion allocable to other items should, if practicable and material, be included in such other items. In some cases, for example where financial and VAT accounting periods do not coincide, an estimate may be necessary.

Non-deductible inputs

All traders will bear tax in so far as it relates to non-deductible inputs (for example, motor-cars, other than for resale, and certain business entertaining expenses). Such tax should therefore be included as part of the cost of those items. A similar situation exists in the Republic of Ireland where traders dealing in products such as motor-cars, radios and television sets will bear some non-deductible VAT on the input cost of these items.

Amounts due to or from the revenue authorities

The net amount due to or from the revenue authorities in respect of VAT should be included as part of debtors or creditors and will not normally require separate disclosure.

Capital commitments

6 The estimated amount of capital commitments should include the appropriate amount, if any, of irrecoverable VAT.

Comparisons

7 Where it has been customary for purchase tax (or sales taxes in the Republic of Ireland) to be included in turnover, it may be desirable in the initial years of VAT to disclose the turnover of periods in which such tax applied both gross and net of tax so as to assist in comparisons. In some cases, for example retailers, it may not be possible to ascertain the amount of purchase tax (or sales taxes) included in turnover; in those cases an explanatory note will be desirable. Where customs or excise duties are included in turnover and such duties are reduced to take account of VAT, an explanatory note may be necessary.

Part 2 – Standard accounting practice

Turnover

8 Turnover shown in the profit and loss account should exclude VAT on taxable outputs. If it is desired to show also the gross turnover, the VAT relevant to that turnover should be shown as a deduction in arriving at the turnover exclusive of VAT.

Irrecoverable VAT

9 Irrecoverable VAT allocable to fixed assets and to other items disclosed separately in published accounts should be included in their cost where practicable and material.

Date from which effective

10 The accounting practices set out in this statement should be adopted as soon as possible and regarded as standard in respect of accounting periods starting on or after 1st January 1974.

Appendix 3

Accounting for pension costs

Contents

Paragraphs

Part 1 – Explanatory note	1–55
Part 2 – Definitions	56–72
Part 3 – Standard accounting practice	73–94
Scope	73–76
Pension cost	77
Defined contribution schemes	78
Defined benefit schemes	79–83
Ex gratia pensions and discretionary and *ex gratia* pension increases	84–85
Balance sheet	86
Disclosures	87–89
Group schemes	90
Foreign schemes	91
Transitional provisions	92
Date from which effective	93–94
Part 4 – Legal requirements in Great Britain and Northern Ireland	95–100
Part 5 – Legal requirements in the Republic of Ireland	101–104
Part 6 – Compliance with International Accounting Standard No. 19 'Accounting for Retirement Benefits in the Financial Statements of Employers'	105

Appendix 1 – Examples of disclosures

407

Accounting for pension costs
(Issued May 1988)

The provisions of this statement of standard accounting practice should be read in conjunction with the Explanatory Foreword to accounting standards *and need not be applied to immaterial items.*

Part 1 – Explanatory note

Importance of pension costs

1   The provision of a pension is part of the remuneration package of many employees. Pension costs form a significant proportion of total payroll costs and they give rise to special problems of estimation and of allocation between accounting periods. Accordingly, it is important that standard accounting practice exists concerning the recognition of such costs in the employers' financial statements. This statement deals with the accounting for, and the disclosure of, pension costs and commitments in the financial statements of enterprises that have pension arrangements for the provision of retirement benefits for their employees.

Types of pension schemes

2   Pension arrangements can take different forms. The employer may have a commitment arising from the contract of employment, the provision of pensions may have arisen from custom and practice or *ex gratia* arrangements may be made on a case by case basis. This Statement covers a scheme where an enterprise has entered into a commitment, whether legal, contractual or implicit in the employer's actions, to provide pensions for its employees. It also addresses situations where *ex gratia* or discretionary payments are made in the absence of such a commitment.

3   Pension schemes to which this Statement applies may basically be divided into defined contribution schemes and defined benefit schemes. In a defined contribution scheme, the employer will normally discharge his obligation by making agreed contributions to a pension scheme and the benefits paid will depend upon the funds available from these contributions and investment earnings thereon. The cost to the employer can, therefore, be measured with reasonable certainty. A number of pension schemes in the United Kingdom and Ireland, including many smaller ones, are defined contribution schemes.

4   In a defined benefit scheme, however, the benefits to be paid will usually depend upon either the average pay of the employee during his or her career or, more typically, the final pay of the employee. In these circumstances, it is impossible to be certain in advance that the contributions to the pension scheme, together with the investment return thereon, will equal the benefits to be paid. The employer may have a legal obligation to provide any unforeseen shortfall in funds or, if not, may find it necessary to meet the shortfall in the interests of maintaining good employee relations. Conversely, if a surplus arises the employer may be entitled to a refund of, or reduction in, contributions paid into the pension scheme. Thus, in this type of scheme the employer's commitment is generally more open than with defined contribution schemes and the final cost is subject to considerable uncertainty. The larger UK and Irish schemes are generally of the defined benefit kind and these cover the great majority of members of schemes.

Pension schemes may also be classified by the way in which they are financed, namely funded schemes or schemes where the benefits are paid directly by the employer. The same accounting principles apply to both types of scheme.

The trustees of a funded scheme may make use of the services of an insurance company — an approach that is particularly common amongst the smaller schemes. Insurance companies offer a wide variety of contracts, but, in the case of defined benefit schemes, these contracts are normally no more than investment management and administrative arrangements, possibly with life cover included, and do not relieve the employer of the responsibility to ensure that the scheme is adequately financed.

Actuarial considerations

In view of the very long-term nature of the pensions commitment, it is necessary to make use of actuarial calculations in determining the pension cost charge in respect of defined benefit schemes. In the case of defined contribution schemes there is no need for actuarial advice in order to establish the pension cost although such advice may be required for other purposes in connection with the operation of the scheme.

In defined benefit schemes, the choice of assumptions and the choice of valuation method can each have a major effect on the contribution rate calculated at each valuation. The choice of assumptions can be as significant as the choice of method.

The assumptions which the actuary must make in carrying out his valuation will be about matters such as future rates of inflation and pay increases, increases to pensions in payment, earnings on investments, the number of employees joining the scheme, the age profile of employees and the probability that employees will die or leave the company's employment before they reach retiring age. The actuary will view the assumptions as a whole; he will make assumptions which are mutually compatible, in the knowledge that, if experience departs from the assumptions made, the effects of such departures may well be offsetting, notably in the case of investment yields and increases in prices and earnings.

Most pension schemes undergo a formal actuarial valuation on a triennial basis. In such cases it is not intended that any special valuation exercise should be carried out by enterprises for the purpose of implementing this Statement for the first time.

The Councils of the Institute and Faculty of Actuaries published a paper in May 1986 entitled 'Pension Fund Terminology: specimen descriptions of commonly used valuation methods'. In addition, the Auditing Practices Committee has published an Audit Brief entitled 'The work of a pension scheme actuary'. This covers matters such as the valuation of defined benefit and defined contribution schemes, valuation assumptions and inter-professional co-operation. A glossary of pensions terminology for pension schemes has been published by The Pensions Management Institute and The Pensions Research Accountants Group.

The funding plan

The funding methods developed by actuaries are designed to build up assets in a prudent and controlled manner in advance of the retirement of the members of the scheme, in order that the obligations of the scheme may be met without undue distortion of the employer's cash flow. The actuary's main concern is that the present and estimated future contribution levels should be at least sufficient to provide security for the payment of the promised benefits.

13 A range of actuarial methods is available for determining the level of contributions needed to meet the liabilities of the pension scheme. Some methods will tend to lead to higher levels of funding in the scheme than others.

14 In practice, it is common for actuaries to aim at a level contribution rate, as a proportion of pensionable pay in respect of current service. The contribution rate thus determined depends on the particular actuarial method used and the assumptions made regarding new entrants to the scheme. In broad terms, in projecting a stable contribution rate, accrued benefits methods rely on the assumption that the flow of new entrants will be such as to preserve the existing average age of the work-force; prospective benefits methods, on the other hand, normally look only to the existing work-force and seek a contribution rate that will remain stable for that group despite its increasing age profile until the last member retires or leaves. In a mature scheme both types of method may in practice achieve stable contribution rates but the size of the fund under a prospective benefits method will tend to be larger than under an accrued benefits method because it is intended to cover the ageing of the existing work-force.

15 From time to time it may be necessary to improve the level of funding because of deficiencies (where these are not expected to be offset by future surpluses). This may be done by an increase in the ordinary annual rate of contribution or by additional special payments over a limited period. On occasion the employer may make additional lump sum contributions which have the effect of reducing his future liabilities, if to do so is convenient in the context of the financial policy of the employer's business. Conversely, a previously high level of funding may be lowered by reducing or interrupting the contributions if there is a surplus in the fund or in times of financial stringency for the company. However, whilst the financial position of the sponsoring employer may influence the pattern of funding it will not provide a satisfactory basis for determining the pension charge for the period.

The accounting objective

16 From the point of view of the employee a pension may be regarded as deferred remuneration; from the point of view of the employer it is part of the cost incurred in obtaining the employee's services. The accounting objective therefore requires the employer to recognise the cost of providing pensions on a systematic and rational basis over the period during which he benefits from the employees' services. Many companies have, until now, simply charged the contributions payable to the pension scheme as the pension cost in each accounting period. In future, in order to comply with this Statement, it will be necessary to consider whether the funding plan provides a satisfactory basis for allocating the pension cost to particular accounting periods.

Defined contribution schemes

17 In the case of a defined contribution scheme the employer's obligation at any point in time is restricted to the amount of the contributions payable to date. The pension cost is, therefore, the amount of the contributions payable in respect of the particular accounting period.

Defined benefit schemes
The selection of the actuarial method and assumptions to be used in assessing the pension cost of a defined benefit scheme is a matter of judgement for the actuary in consultation with his client, taking account of the circumstances of the specific company and its workforce. This Statement requires that the actuarial valuation method and assumptions used for accounting purposes should satisfy the accounting objective. In order that full provision may be made over the employees' service lives for the expected costs of their pensions, the effect of expected future increases in earnings, including merit increases, up to the assumed retirement date or earlier date of withdrawal or death in service, should be recognised. Account will also need to be taken of expected future increases in deferred pensions and pensions in payment where the employer has an express or implied commitment to grant such increases. The calculation of benefit levels should be based on the situation most likely to be experienced and not on a contingent event not likely to occur. The actuarial method selected should be used consistently and should be disclosed. If there is a change of method this fact should be disclosed and the effect quantified. The actuarial assumptions and the actuarial method taken as a whole should be compatible and should lead to the actuary's best estimate of the cost of providing the pension benefits promised. 18

If the funding plan does not provide a satisfactory basis for determining the pension cost charge, separate actuarial calculations will be required. 19

Regular pension cost and variations in cost
The total cost of pensions in a year can notionally be divided into the regular cost, which is the consistent ongoing cost recognised under the actuarial method used, and variations from the regular cost. Where a stable contribution rate for regular contributions, expressed as a percentage of pensionable earnings, has been determined, that rate will provide an acceptable basis for calculating the regular cost under the stated accounting objective so long as it makes full provision for the expected benefits over the anticipated service lives of employees. 20

Variations from the regular cost may arise from: 21
   (a) experience surpluses or deficiencies;
   (b) the effects on the actuarial value of accrued benefits of changes in assumptions or method;
   (c) retroactive changes in benefits or in conditions for membership;
   (d) increases to pensions in payment or to deferred pensions for which provision has not previously been made.

Spreading variations from regular cost
Experience deficiencies or surpluses are part of the ongoing process of revising the estimate of the ultimate liabilities which will fall on the employer. Any effect on the cost should normally be taken into account by adjusting the current and future costs charged in the accounts and should not be treated as a prior year adjustment. 22

In accordance with the accounting objective, the normal period over which the effect of material deficiencies or surpluses should be spread for accounting purposes is the expected 23 remaining service lives of the current employees in the scheme after making suitable allowances for future withdrawals. A period representing the average remaining service lives of the current membership may be used if desired. This period, which will vary from scheme to scheme and from time to time, should be determined by the actuary. It would not be appropriate to credit or charge the entire surplus or deficiency against profits in one accounting period, except as provided in paragraphs 81 to 83.

24 The only circumstances in which there may be a departure from the normal principle of spreading material surpluses or deficiencies as set out in paragraph 23 are summarised in this paragraph and in paragraph 29 below. The full conditions which must be satisfied before there may be a departure from the normal spreading requirements are set out in paragraphs 81 to 83. The circumstances referred to below represent situations that properly lie outside the actuarial assumptions and normal running of the scheme and, accordingly, are expected to arise infrequently. They are:

(a) where there is a significant reduction in the number of employees covered by the company's and/or group's pension scheme arrangements;

(b) where, in the circumstances set out in paragraph 82, prudence requires a material deficiency to be recognised over a shorter period.

25 In many companies, there have been reorganisation programmes in recent years that have involved significant redundancies. These have often led to large non-reversing surpluses building up in related pension schemes. This Statement recognises that in such instances it would not be appropriate to spread the effect of the refund of such surpluses over the remaining service lives of the current employees in the scheme.

26 In the circumstances set out in paragraph 24(a) a refund of a surplus, contributions holiday or reduction in contributions should be accounted for as it becomes receivable and should not be anticipated, that is, if it is agreed that contributions will be reduced for a period of years the reduction should be recognised on a year by year basis and not accumulated and reflected in the financial statements in the period the first reduction becomes effective. Where a reduction in the number of employees is related to an extraordinary event, such as the closure of a business segment, it is accepted that it may not be possible to apply the rule set out in this paragraph. This is because SSAP 6 (Revised) 'Extraordinary items and prior year adjustments' requires the individual elements of income and expenditure which derive from a single extraordinary event to be aggregated and so it may not be appropriate to defer recognition of an associated pension cost or credit.

27 The exemption from the normal spreading principle relating to significant reductions in the total number of employees covered by a group's or company's pension arrangements does not cover situations where employees are transferred from one group scheme to another one.

28 As stated in paragraph 24(b), in strictly limited circumstances prudence may require that a material deficiency should be recognised over a period shorter than the expected remaining service lives of current employees in the scheme. A precondition of invoking this section is that significant additional contributions have had to be paid into the pension scheme. Furthermore, the additional payments should have been made as stated in paragraph 24 in respect of a major transaction or event outside the actuarial assumptions and normal

running of the scheme. A possible example of such a situation would be where there had been a major mismanagement of a pension scheme's assets. However, it is emphasised that each situation must be judged on its particular merits.

Where a refund that is subject to deduction of tax in accordance with the provisions of the UK Finance Act 1986, or equivalent legislation, is made to the employer, the enterprise may depart from the normal spreading principle and instead recognise the refund in the period in which it occurs. The accounting treatment adopted in respect of such refunds should be disclosed.   29

Changes in assumptions, valuation method and benefits
The effect of changes in the assumptions or valuation method on the cost of providing for past service is analogous to an experience deficiency or surplus and should be accounted for in a similar way.   30

Retroactive changes in benefits and membership are decided upon currently and it is thus not appropriate to charge any part of the costs arising from these decisions as a prior year adjustment. Past service costs should normally be written off over the remaining service lives of the current employees.   31

Where a surplus in a pension fund is utilised to provide benefits for which the company had previously established a provision in its financial statements, the provision, to the extent that it is no longer required, should be released over the estimated remaining service lives of the current employees.   32

Increases to pensions in payment and deferred pensions
Increases to pensions in payment up to a certain level may be specified in the rules of the pension scheme. Other increases may be granted in response to pensioners' needs and in the interests of continuing good industrial relations. In the United Kingdom, increases to deferred pensions, that is the prospective pensions of early leavers, are required by law to be made up to a specified level.   33

Increases specified in the pension scheme rules or required by law will be taken into account in the actuarial assumptions. The cost will, therefore, be charged over the service lives of the employees. Any divergence between the assumptions and experience will be accounted for as an element of any overall experience deficiency or surplus.   34

Other increases are, at least in form, discretionary at the time they are awarded, whether they are paid through the scheme or directly by the employer. Discretionary increases may be granted on the basis that the rules require there to be an annual review or because the employer has announced an intention to grant increases but no previous commitment has been made. The preferred treatment is for such increases, where they are likely to be granted on a regular basis, to be allowed for in the actuarial assumptions. They will then be recognised as part of the pension cost over the working lives of the beneficiaries.   35

Once an increase has been awarded it is very unlikely that it will be withdrawn and so it should be regarded thereafter as part of the employer's commitments. Accordingly, this   36

Statement provides that, if provision has not been made for the increase in the actuarial assumptions, the capitalised amount of the increase should be provided for in the period in which it is granted to the extent that it is not covered by a surplus.

37 Where a non-recurring ('one-off') increase is granted which applies to the current period but will not affect pensions paid in future periods, it should be treated as purely *ex gratia* and its cost should be charged in the period in which it is granted to the extent that it is not covered by a surplus.

38 Employers may occasionally grant *ex gratia* pensions to employees at the time of their retirement. An example would be a pension granted to a long-serving employee who for some reason had not been a member of the company's scheme and for whom the company decided to make provision. As with discretionary pension increases, the capital cost of any such *ex gratia* pensions should be charged in the period in which they are granted to the extent that they are not covered by a surplus.

Hybrid schemes

39 A few schemes are hybrid in nature combining features of defined contribution and defined benefit schemes. In such instances the rules or trust deed should be carefully studied and the operation of the scheme in practice, or its proposed method of operation, taken into account when determining the appropriate accounting treatment. The accounting treatment adopted should be in accordance with the underlying substance of the scheme.

Discounting

40 By their nature actuarial valuations make allowance for interest so that future cash flows are discounted to their present value. Financial statements, however, normally include items at their face value without discounting them. The question of whether items should be discounted in financial statements is a general one and this Statement does not attempt to establish standard practice. Interest effects arising from short-term timing differences between the payment of contributions and the recognition of cost are not likely to be material and can be ignored. If the difference is long-term, the situation becomes akin to that arising in respect of an unfunded scheme. If a scheme is unfunded the provision for pension costs is assessed and reviewed on a discounted basis and adjusted each year by an amount comprising two elements: a charge for the year (equivalent to a contribution in a funded scheme) and interest on the unfunded liability.

Foreign schemes

41 In principle, the pension costs charged in respect of all pension schemes included in group accounts should conform to the accounting objective and a consolidation adjustment should be made where the cost charged in the individual accounts of a group company does not do so.

42 No adjustment would normally be necessary in respect of UK and Irish schemes as the pension cost in the individual company accounts should already conform to the requirements of this Statement. On the other hand, in the case of foreign schemes, the commitment of the employer regarding the provision of pensions may be very different from that which

is customary in the United Kingdom and Ireland so that it would be inappropriate to adjust the pension cost charged. In some cases, for example, the employer's obligation may be discharged by prescribed payments under a nationwide or industry-wide scheme with characteristics similar to those of the State scheme in the United Kingdom. In such cases charging the contributions payable will satisfy the requirements of this Statement.

In other instances the nature of the employer's commitment may be similar to that in the UK and Ireland and the different determination of the pension cost charge may be caused solely by different accounting policies. An adjustment to the charge would then be appropriate although it is recognised that it may sometimes be impractical to make such an adjustment because of the difficulties and cost of obtaining compatible actuarial valuations in order to be able to recalculate the pension charge in accordance with the full provisions of this Statement. In such circumstances while an adjustment to the charge is not mandatory it is encouraged and suitable disclosure should be made. 43

Deferred taxation
For many enterprises the pension cost charge for the period has in the past been equal to the contributions payable. Under the requirements of this Statement the charge in the financial statements could be different from the contributions payable if, for example, a deficiency on valuation is being spread forward in the financial statements over the estimated remaining service lives of current employees although an additional lump-sum payment has been paid into the pension fund. Since taxation relief is generally granted in respect of payments made to the pension fund, accounting for pension costs in the manner prescribed by this Statement may have deferred tax implications. Where these occur they should be accounted for in accordance with SSAP 15 (Revised) 'Accounting for Deferred Tax'. 44

Disclosures
Sufficient information should be disclosed to give the user of the financial statements a proper understanding of the impact of the pension arrangements on the group's and/or the company's financial statements. 45

For a defined contribution scheme it will usually suffice to indicate the nature of the scheme and the amounts included in the profit and loss account and balance sheet. 46

For a defined benefit scheme more extensive disclosures are needed because of the greater and more uncertain obligations of the employer. Disclosures required include the accounting policy, the actuarial valuation method and major actuarial assumptions adopted, the cost charged, with explanations of it, and certain actuarial valuation information. In view of the significant long-term variable commitment of the employer, the disclosures should not only relate to the amounts in the financial statements for the periods presented but should also give an indication of significant changes in future costs that are expected under the actuarial assumptions and method used. Examples of how a small company and a large group may satisfy the disclosure requirements are given in Appendix 1. 47

As explained in paragraph 14, the effect of aiming for a level contribution rate varies according to the actuarial method used and the assumption made regarding new entrants. It is therefore necessary to disclose what assumption has been made in this regard unless it is immediately apparent from the disclosure of the actuarial method used. 48

415

49 This Statement requires the disclosure of an outline of the results of the most recent formal actuarial valuation or later review of the pension scheme on an ongoing basis. Specific disclosures to be made include the market value of scheme assets at the date of their valuation or review and the level of funding expressed in percentage terms. In certain instances it may be necessary to provide further information in order that details on the level of funding may be seen in their proper context. The level of funding and/or market values of scheme assets at the date of valuation or review may, for example, have subsequently changed markedly as a result of changes in general stock market values or in the level of contributions paid into the pension scheme. In particular, it should be considered whether the figures disclosed relating to the last valuation or review need to be amplified by a discussion of changes that have occurred since that date.

50 Disclosure is also required of changes in the group and/or company's pension scheme arrangements where these have had, or will have, a material effect on the future cost of providing pensions.

51 Where a company or group has more than one scheme it will often be necessary to give information on a combined basis in order to keep the volume of disclosures within reasonable limits. However, it is important that the combined figures should provide a proper understanding of the impact of the pension arrangements on the group's and/or company's financial position.

Group schemes

52 It is quite common for a number of companies within the same group to contribute to a single group scheme. With such schemes it is normally accepted that the same contribution rate, expressed as a percentage of payroll, should apply to the different member companies even though, if calculated on an individual company basis, the rate payable may vary between the employers within a group. This Statement permits the use of a common group rate for contributions payable by sponsoring employers. If a group scheme is in operation it may not be possible to estimate the pension obligations for which a particular group company is responsible and it would not be meaningful to provide information relating to the group as a whole in the subsidiary's financial statements. Provision is therefore made for reduced disclosure in the financial statements of subsidiary companies that are members of group schemes. The full details relating to the pension scheme should be disclosed in the financial statements of the holding company.

Transitional provisions

53 When, on implementing this Statement for the first time, a cumulative adjustment arises in respect of prior years, this may either be dealt with in accordance with the other provisions of this Statement or accounted for in accordance with the provisions of SSAP 6 (Revised) 'Extraordinary items and prior year adjustments'. That is, the cumulative adjustment may, except as discussed below, be spread over the expected remaining service lives of current employees in the scheme or accounted for as a prior year adjustment. To the extent that the adjustment relates to a variation from regular cost that, in accordance with the provisions of paragraphs 81 and 82, would not be eligible to be spread over the remaining service lives it should be accounted for as a prior year item. (An example of such an adjustment would be one arising from a significant reduction in the number of employees

covered by a company's pension scheme arrangements.) Similar considerations may also arise in respect of paragraphs 84 and 85 which deal with discretionary and *ex gratia* pension increases and *ex gratia* pensions. The cumulative adjustment should be calculated, as at the beginning of the accounting period in which this Statement is first applied, as the actuarial value of the surplus or deficiency on an ongoing basis as adjusted by any existing provision for unfunded pension costs or any existing pensions prepayment. In order that enterprises do not have to undertake a special valuation exercise for the purposes of implementing this Statement, they may base the calculation of the cumulative adjustment on the results of the last actuarial valuation so long as it was carried out on a basis broadly consistent with the requirements of this Statement. In arriving at the adjustment any surplus or deficiency at the last valuation date should be adjusted to take account of any additional payments or reduced contributions made since that date as a consequence of it. It may also be necessary to make allowance for major changes affecting the pension scheme since the last valuation.

The Republic of Ireland

The Republic of Ireland, unlike the United Kingdom, currently does not have any legislative requirement for defined benefit pension schemes to be actuarially assessed and the actuarial profession's involvement with pension schemes has tended to be less than in the United Kingdom. Legislation is to be introduced based on the recommendations contained in the First Report of the National Pensions Board but the first actuarial valuation for a number of schemes will not take place until the beginning of the next decade. Accordingly, the provisions of paragraphs 77, 79 to 85 and 88(g) and 88(h) will not be mandatory for non-quoted companies registered in the Republic of Ireland in respect of the financial statements of periods commencing before 1 January 1993. Such companies are, however, encouraged to comply with the full requirements of this Statement as soon as possible. 54

The full requirements of this Statement will apply to companies registered in the Republic of Ireland and quoted on the International Stock Exchange of the United Kingdom and the Republic of Ireland Limited from the same date as it applies to companies registered in the United Kingdom. 55

Part 2 – Definitions

Accrued benefits are the benefits for service up to a given point in time, whether the rights to the benefits are vested or not. They may be calculated in relation to current earnings or projected final earnings. 56

An *accrued benefits method* of actuarial valuation is a valuation method in which the actuarial value of liabilities relates at a given date to: 57
  (a) the benefits, including future increases promised by the rules, for the current and deferred pensioners and their dependants; and
  (b) the benefits which the members assumed to be in service on the given date will receive for service up to that date only.

417

Allowance may be made for expected increases in earnings after the given date, and/or for additional pension increases not promised by the rules. The given date may be a current or future date. The further into the future the adopted date lies, the closer the results will be to those of a prospective benefits valuation method.

58 The *average remaining service life* is a weighted average of the expected future service of the current members of the scheme up to their normal retirement dates or expected dates of earlier withdrawal or death in service. The weightings can have regard to periods of service, salary levels of scheme members and future anticipated salary growth in a manner which the actuary considers appropriate having regard to the actuarial method and assumptions used.

59 A *current funding level valuation* considers whether the assets would have been sufficient at the valuation date to cover liabilities arising in respect of pensions in payment, preserved benefits for members whose pensionable service has ceased and accrued benefits for members in pensionable service, based on pensionable service to and pensionable earnings at, the date of valuation including revaluation on the statutory basis or such higher basis as has been promised.

60 An *ex gratia pension* or *discretionary or ex gratia increase* in a pension is one which the employer has no legal, contractual or implied commitment to provide.

61 A *defined benefit scheme* is a pension scheme in which the rules specify the benefits to be paid and the scheme is financed accordingly.

62 A *defined contribution scheme* is a pension scheme in which the benefits are directly determined by the value of contributions paid in respect of each member. Normally the rate of contribution is specified in the rules of the scheme.

63 An *experience surplus or deficiency* is that part of the excess or deficiency of the actuarial value of assets over the actuarial value of liabilities, on the basis of the valuation method used, which arises because events have not coincided with the actuarial assumptions made for the last valuation.

64 A *funding plan* is the timing of payments in an orderly fashion to meet the future cost of a given set of benefits.

65 A *funded scheme* is a pension scheme where the future liabilities for benefits are provided for by the accumulation of assets held externally to the employing company's business.

66 The *level of funding* is the proportion at a given date of the actuarial value of liabilities for pensioners' and deferred pensioners' benefits and for members' accrued benefits that is covered by the actuarial value of assets. For this purpose the actuarial value of future contributions is excluded from the value of assets.

67 An *ongoing actuarial valuation* is a valuation in which it is assumed that the pension scheme will continue in existence and (where appropriate) that new members will be admitted. The liabilities allow for expected increases in earnings.

Past service is used in this Statement to denote service before a given date. It is often used, however, to denote service before entry into the pension scheme. 68

Pensionable payroll/earnings are the earnings on which benefits and/or contributions are calculated. One or more elements of earnings (eg overtime) may be excluded, and/or there may be a reduction to take account of all or part of the state scheme benefits which the member is deemed to receive. 69

A *pension scheme* is an arrangement (other than accident insurance) to provide pension and/or other benefits for members on leaving service or retiring and, after a member's death, for his/her dependants. 70

A *prospective benefits method* of valuation is a valuation method in which the actuarial value of liabilities relates to: 71
  (a) the benefits for current and deferred pensioners and their dependants, allowing where appropriate for future pension increases; and
  (b) the benefits that active members will receive in respect of both past and future service, allowing for future increases in earnings up to their assumed exit dates, and where appropriate for pension increases thereafter.

Regular cost is the consistent ongoing cost recognised under the actuarial method used. 72

Part 3 – Standard accounting practice

Scope
This Statement applies where the employer has a legal or contractual commitment under a pension scheme or one implicit in the employer's actions, to provide, or contribute to, pensions for his employees. It also addresses discretionary and *ex gratia* increases in pensions and *ex gratia* pensions. The same principles apply irrespective of whether the scheme is funded or unfunded. 73

This Statement applies to defined contribution schemes and defined benefit schemes. 74

Although this Statement primarily addresses pensions, its principles may be equally applicable to the cost of providing other post-retirement benefits. 75

This Statement does not apply to either state social security contributions or redundancy payments. 76

Pension cost
The accounting objective is that the employer should recognise the expected cost of providing pensions on a systematic and rational basis over the period during which he derives benefit from the employees' services. The ways in which this is to be achieved are detailed in paragraphs 78 to 92. 77

419

Defined contribution schemes

78 For defined contribution schemes the charge against profits should be the amount of contributions payable to the pension scheme in respect of the accounting period.

Defined benefit schemes

79 For defined benefit schemes the pension cost should be calulated using actuarial valuation methods which are consistent with the requirements of this Statement. The actuarial assumptions and method, taken as a whole, should be compatible and should lead to the actuary's best estimate of the cost of providing the pension benefits promised. The method of providing for expected pension costs over the service lives of employees in the scheme should be such that the regular pension cost is a substantially level percentage of the current and expected future pensionable payroll in the light of the current actuarial assumptions.

80 Subject to the provisions of paragraphs 81 to 83, variations from the regular cost should be allocated over the expected remaining service lives of current employees in the scheme. A period representing the average remaining service lives may be used if desired.

81 The provisions of paragraph 80 should not be applied where, and to the extent that, a significant change in the normal level of contributions occurs because contributions are adjusted to eliminate a surplus or deficiency resulting from a significant reduction in the number of employees covered by the enterprise's pension arrangements. Except where such treatment would be inconsistent with SSAP 6 in relation to an extraordinary item, any reduction in contributions arising in these circumstances should be recognised as it occurs. Amounts receivable may not be anticipated; for example, the full effect of a contribution holiday should not be recognised at the outset of the holiday, but rather spread over its duration.

82 In strictly limited circumstances prudence may require that a material deficit be recognised over a period shorter than the expected remaining service lives of current employees in the scheme. Such circumstances are limited to those where a major event or transaction has occurred which has not been allowed for in the actuarial assumptions, is outside the normal scope of those assumptions and has necessitated the payment of significant additional contributions to the pension scheme.

83 Where a refund that is subject to deduction of tax in accordance with the provisions of the UK Finance Act 1986, or equivalent legislation, is made to the employer, the enterprise may depart from the requirements of paragraph 80 and account for the surplus or deficiency in the period in which the refund occurs.

Ex gratia pensions and discretionary and *ex gratia* pension increases

84 Where *ex gratia* pensions are granted the capital cost, to the extent not covered by a surplus, should be recognised in the profit and loss account in the accounting period in which they are granted.

85 Where allowance for discretionary or *ex gratia* increases in pensions is not made in the actuarial assumptions, the capital cost of such increases should, to the extent not covered by a surplus, be recognised in the profit and loss account in the accounting period in which they are initially granted.

Balance sheet
If the cumulative pension cost recognised in the profit and loss account has not been completely discharged by payment of contributions or directly paid pensions, the excess should be shown as a net pension provision. Similarly, any excess of contributions paid or directly paid pensions over the cumulative pension cost should be shown as a prepayment.

86

Disclosures
The following disclosures should be made in respect of a defined contribution scheme:

87

(a) the nature of the scheme (ie defined contribution);

(b) the accounting policy;

(c) the pension cost charge for the period;

(d) any outstanding or prepaid contributions at the balance sheet date.

The following disclosures should be made in respect of a defined benefit scheme:

88

(a) the nature of the scheme (ie defined benefit);

(b) whether it is funded or unfunded;

(c) the accounting policy and, if different, the funding policy;

(d) whether the pension cost and provision (or asset) are assessed in accordance with the advice of a professionally qualified actuary and, if so, the date of the most recent formal actuarial valuation or later formal review used for this purpose. If the actuary is an employee or officer of the reporting company, or of the group of which it is a member, this fact should be disclosed;

(e) the pension cost charge for the period together with explanations of significant changes in the charge compared to that in the previous accounting period;

(f) any provisions or prepayments in the balance sheet resulting from a difference between the amounts recognised as cost and the amounts funded or paid directly;

(g) the amount of any deficiency on a current funding level basis, indicating the action, if any, being taken to deal with it in the current and future accounting periods;

(h) an outline of the results of the most recent formal actuarial valuation or later formal review of the scheme on an ongoing basis.

This should include disclosure of:

(i) the actuarial method used and a brief description of the main actuarial assumptions;

(ii) the market value of scheme assets at the date of their valuation or review;

(iii) the level of funding expressed in percentage terms;

(iv) comments on any material actuarial surplus or deficiency indicated by (iii) above;

(i) any commitment to make additional payments over a limited number of years;

(j) the accounting treatment adopted in respect of a refund made in accordance with the provisions of paragraph 83 where a credit appears in the financial statements in relation to it;

(k) details of the expected effects on future costs of any material changes in the group's and/or company's pension arrangements.

89 Where a company or group has more than one pension scheme disclosure should be made on a combined basis, unless disclosure of information about individual schemes is necessary for a proper understanding of the accounts. For the purposes of paragraph 88(g) above, however, a current funding level basis deficiency in one scheme should not be set off against a surplus in another.

Group schemes
90 A subsidiary company which is a member of a group scheme should disclose this fact in its financial statements and disclose the nature of the group scheme indicating, where appropriate, that the contributions are based on pension costs across the group as a whole. Such a company is exempt from the disclosure requirements of paragraph 88(g) and (h) and should instead state the name of the holding company in whose financial statements particulars of the actuarial valuation of the group scheme are contained. This exemption only applies if the holding company is registered in the United Kingdom or the Republic of Ireland.

Foreign schemes
91 Where, in respect of foreign operations, the employer has an obligation to provide pensions, the pension charge should reflect that obligation and, therefore, be dealt with in accordance with the requirements of this Statement. An adjustment on consolidation will be necessary where the charge is not already calculated in accordance with the basis set out in this Statement, unless the nature of the employer's commitment is very different from that which is customary in the United Kingdom and Ireland. It is recognised, however, that in some cases it may be impractical to make the adjustment because of the difficulties and cost of obtaining the necessary actuarial information. In such cases, the amount charged to the profit and loss account and the basis of the charge should, as a minimum, be disclosed in the consolidated financial statements.

Transitional provisions
92 When, on implementing this Statement for the first time, a cumulative adjustment arises in respect of prior years this may either be dealt with in accordance with the other provisions of this Statement or accounted for in accordance with the provisions of SSAP 6 (Revised) 'Extraordinary items and prior year adjustments'. The way in which the transitional provisions have been applied should be disclosed in the financial statements for the period in which this Statement is first implemented.

Date from which effective
93 The accounting and disclosure requirements set out in this Statement should be adopted as soon as possible and, except in the case of certain companies registered in the Republic of Ireland as provided in paragraph 94, regarded as standard in respect of financial statements relating to accounting periods beginning on or after 1 July 1988.

94 In the case of companies that are registered in the Republic of Ireland and not quoted on the International Stock Exchange of the United Kingdom and Ireland paragraphs 77, 79 to 85 and 88(g) and 88(h) should be adopted as soon as possible and regarded as

standard in respect of financial statements relating to accounting periods beginning on or after 1 January 1993. The remainder of the required accounting practices and disclosures should be regarded as standard in respect of financial statements relating to accounting periods beginning on or after 1 July 1988. A cumulative adjustment that arises in respect of paragraph 84 on *ex gratia* pensions may either be dealt with in accordance with SSAP 6 (Revised) or allocated over the expected remaining service lives of current employees in the scheme.

Part 4 – Legal requirements in Great Britain and Northern Ireland

References are to the Companies Act 1985 and the Companies (Northern Ireland) Order 1986.

Paragraph 50(4) of Schedule 4 requires a company to give details of any pension commitments provided for in the company's balance sheet and also of any such commitments for which no provision has been made. Particulars of pension commitments to past directors of the company must be disclosed separately.   95

Paragraph 50(6) of Schedule 4 requires that disclosure under paragraph 50(4) should separately include details of commitments undertaken on behalf of, or for the benefit of, any holding company or fellow subsidiary of the company and any subsidiary of the company.   96

Paragraph 56(4) of Schedule 4 requires companies to disclose the total pension costs incurred in the year on behalf of all employees of the company, together with separate disclosure of social security costs incurred on their behalf.   97

By virtue of paragraphs 61 and 68 of Schedule 4, the above requirements also apply to group accounts.   98

Banking, insurance and shipping companies are exempt from the above requirements of Schedule 4.   99

Paragraph 28 of Schedule 5 requires companies to disclose the total amount of pension paid to directors or past directors, other than pensions funded substantially through a pension scheme. If they are so funded, the amount disclosed as emoluments has to include contributions to the scheme (paragraph 22).   100

Part 5 – Legal requirements in the Republic of Ireland

In this part references to companies legislation have been abbreviated as follows: 101
Companies Act 1963 — The 1963 Act
The Schedule to the Companies (Amendment) Act 1963 — The Schedule

102 Section 191 of the 1963 Act requires disclosure of the aggregate amount of directors' and past-directors' pensions, other than pensions under a scheme where contributions are substantially adequate for the maintenance of the scheme. The Section also requires disclosure of the aggregate amount of directors' emoluments; for the purpose of the Section emoluments include contributions paid in respect of directors to any pension scheme.

103 Paragraph 36(4) of the Schedule requires disclosure of any pension commitments included in the company's balance sheet and any such commitments for which no provision has been made. Where any such commitment relates wholly or partly to pensions payable to past directors of the company, separate particulars shall be given of that commitment so far as it relates to such pensions.

104 Information required to be disclosed under paragraph 36(5) of the Schedule is as follows:
   (a) the nature of every pension scheme operated by or on behalf of the company including information as to whether or not each scheme is a defined benefit scheme or a defined contribution scheme;
   (b) whether each such scheme is externally funded or internally financed;
   (c) whether any pension costs and liabilities are assessed in accordance with the advice of a professionally qualified actuary and, if so, the date of the most recent relevant actuarial valuation;
   (d) whether, and if so where, any such actuarial valuation is available for public inspection.

Part 6 – Compliance with International Accounting Standard No 19 'Accounting for Retirement Benefits in the Financial Statements of Employers'

105 Compliance with the requirements of this Statement will automatically ensure compliance with International Accounting Standard No 19 'Accounting for Retirement Benefits in the Financial Statements of Employers'.

Appendix 1

This appendix is for general guidance and does not form part of the statement of standard accounting practice.

Examples of disclosures

(a) *Defined contribution scheme*
The company operates a defined contribution pension scheme. The assets of the scheme are held separately from those of the company in an independently administered fund. The pension cost charge represents contributions payable by the company to the fund and amounted to £500,000 (1986 £450,000). Contributions totalling £25,000 (1986 £15,000) were payable to the fund at the year-end and are included in creditors.

(b) *Defined benefit scheme*
(i) Small company
The company operates a pension scheme providing benefits based on final pensionable pay. The assets of the scheme are held separately from those of the company, being invested with insurance companies. Contributions to the scheme are charged to the profit and loss account so as to spread the cost of pensions over employees' working lives with the company. The contributions are determined by a qualified actuary on the basis of triennial valuations using the projected unit method*. The most recent valuation was as at 31 December 1987. The assumptions which have the most significant effect on the results of the valuation are those relating to the rate of return on investments and the rates of increase in salaries and pensions. It was assumed that the investment returns would be 9% per annum, that salary increases would average 7% per annum and that present and future pensions would increase at the rate of 4% per annum.

The pension charge for the period was £50,000 (1986 £48,000). This included £5,200 (1986 £5,000) in respect of the amortisation of experience surpluses that are being recognised over 10 years, the average remaining service lives of employees.

The most recent actuarial valuation showed that the market value of the scheme's assets was £1,200,000 and that the actuarial value of those assets represented 104% of the benefits that had accrued to members, after allowing for expected future increases in earnings. The contributions of the company and employees will remain at 11% and 5% of earnings respectively.

(ii) Large group
The group operates a number of pension schemes throughout the world. The major schemes, which cover 85% of scheme members, are of the defined benefit type. With the exception of the main scheme in Germany, the assets of the schemes are held in separate trustee administered funds.

The total pension cost for the group was £2,050,000 (1986 £1,585,000) of which £300,000 (1986 £285,000) relates to the overseas schemes. The pension cost relating to the UK schemes is assessed in accordance with the advice of a qualified actuary using the attained age method*. The latest actuarial assessment of those schemes was as at 31 December 1985. The assumptions which have the most significant effect on the results of the valuation are those relating to the rate of return on investments and the rates of increase in salaries and pensions. It was assumed that the investment return would be 9% per annum, that salary increases would average 7% per annum and that present and future pensions would increase at the rate of 4% per annum. The cost has risen significantly as a result of the acquisition of ABC Limited at the beginning of the period and the resultant increase in group scheme members. Of the total cost, £350,000 (1986 £300,000) is attributable to amortisation of past service liabilities that are being written off over a ten-year period ending in 1988.

At the date of the latest actuarial valuation, the market value of the assets of the UK scheme was £32.1m and the actuarial value of the assets was sufficient to cover 85% of the benefits that had accrued to members, after allowing for expected future increases in earnings. This deficiency should be eliminated by 1991 at the current employer's contribution rate of 12% of pensionable earnings.

The element of the total pension cost relating to foreign schemes includes £280,000 (1986 £250,000) where the charge has been determined in accordance with local best practice and regulations in the Federal Republic of Germany.

A provision of £5,500,000 (1984, £5,000,000) is included in creditors, this being the excess of the accumulated pension cost over the amount funded. The major part of this provision relates to the unfunded German scheme.

---

* These and other actuarial funding methods are described in 'Pension Fund Terminology: specimen descriptions of commonly used valuation methods' issued by the Institute and Faculty of Actuaries.

Index

Note – References are to **paragraph numbers**

Accounting adjustments,
 SSAP14 **10.33**
Accounting for contingencies *See*
 Contingencies; SSAP 18
Accounting period **2.30**
 consolidated financial
 statements **10.31**
Accounting policy **5.28**
 change of **4.42**
 consolidated financial
 statements **10.28–10.30**
 deferred taxation **8.33–8.35**
 disposals **10.47**
 investment accounting **9.45**
Accounting practice, description
 of **1.38**
Accounting principles **Ch 2**
Accounting profit **2.73**
Accounting standards
 alternative pronouncement **1.45**
 arguments for and against
 mandatory **1.70**
 arguments for and against
 universal application of **1.71**
 characteristics and scope of **1.44**
 finalisation and issue of **1.59**
 future developments **1.39**
 guidance notes and
 appendices **1.39, 1.60**
 international **1.39**
 interpretations of **1.46**
 objectives of **1.35–1.39**
 obligation to justify departures
 from **1.39**
 obligation to observe **1.39**
 regulatory basis of **Ch 1**
 review and revision of **1.61**
 scope and application **1.39**
 significant departures from **1.39**
 standard setting process flowchart
 of **1.62**
 status of **1.1–1.30**
 see also SSAPs
Accounting Standards Committee
 (ASC) **1.1, 1.37, 1.39**
 present structure of **1.42**
 terms of reference **1.41**
 work programme **1.69**
Accruals **2.78, 5.39**
Acquisitions **10.36–10.44, 12.2–12.8**
 SSAP23 **12.17–12.67**
Actuarial method **14.58**
Adjusted selling price **5.21**
Adjusting events **2.47, 2.52, 2.56**
Advance corporation tax (ACT) **7.6,
 8.12**
 deferred taxation **8.28**
 due dates for **7.7**
 irrecoverable **7.14**
 on dividends **7.15**
 rules regarding set off against
 corporation tax **7.8**
 unrelieved **7.11**
Aggregation **2.38**
All-Inclusive concept **3.3, 3.4, 3.27, 3.30**
Amortisation **6.15–6.17, 11.2, 11.25–
 11.27, 11.37**
 on basis of sales **6.24**
 on basis of time **6.25**
Annuity tables **14.25**
Asset life **4.31–4.36**
 commentary on **4.37–4.40**

427

Asset valuation 1.38
Assets 2.83
  permanent diminution in value of 4.41
  revaluation of 8.22
  understated 12.16
Associated companies 9.18–9.19
  bases of accounting for 9.28–9.43
  closing rate/net investment method 13.36
  deficiency of net assets in 9.44
  definition 9.18
  disclosure of particulars of 9.52
  equity method 9.53–9.61
  extraordinary items 9.34
  investment accounting 9.49–9.61
  loss of status as 9.50
  see also SSAP1
Attributable profit 5.34–5.35, 5.39
Auditing Guideline 2.51
Auditing Practices Committee 1.18, 2.66
Average cost 5.10
Average price 5.11

Balance sheet 7.17, 14.49, 16.15
  deferred taxation 8.30
  investment accounting 9.2, 9.4, 9.6, 9.30, 9.36–9.39
Base stock 5.16–5.17
Buildings 4.56–4.60
Burton Group plc 4.70
Business combinations Ch 12
  disclosures 12.56–12.58
Business entity 2.28

Called-up share capital 16.29
Canadian Institute of Chartered Accountants 1.5, 1.11
Canadian legislation 1.5
Capital allowances in tax computations 8.21
Capital losses, deferred taxation 8.26
Carry-forward as deduction from reserves 11.5
CCAB 1.56

Claims against contractor 5.36
Communication procedure 1.43
Companies Act 1.6
Companies Act 1947 1.22
Companies Act 1948 1.22, 2.77, 4.14
Companies Act 1980 2.95
Companies Act 1981 2.1, 2.91, 2.108, 4.14, 4.64, 12.27–12.28
Companies Act 1985 1.12, 1.20, 1.21, 1.71, 2.1, 2.38, 2.78, 2.96, 4.28, 4.29, 4.48, 5.39, 6.26, 8.9, 9.64–9.66, 10.2, 10.7, 11.7
Completed contract method 5.30
Conceptual framework of accounting 2.90
Consignment stocks 2.78
Consistency 2.78
Consolidated accounts 10.5, 12.4–12.8, 12.13–12.16
Consolidated financial statements 2.40, 10.4, 13.14–13.24, 13.32
  accounting periods 10.31
  accounting policies 10.28–10.30
  arguments against 10.6
Consolidation
  exclusion from 10.7–10.26
  mechanics of 10.27
Consultation plan 1.54
Consultation procedure 1.43
Context, precision v latitude 2.36
Contingencies
  accounting for 8.9
  see also SSAP18
Contingent liability 2.63–2.70
Contracts, expected to make losses 5.37
Corporation tax 7.1–7.3
Cost
  definition 5.4, 5.9
  of conversion 5.6
  of purchase 5.5
  of stocks 5.12, 5.13, 5.16, 5.20
Cost/benefit test 1.44
Costs, methods of determining 5.10–5.21
Court Line 2.72, 2.76

INDEX

Cover concept, financial statements **13.44**
Creditors, amounts falling due within one year **8.36**
Cumulative turnover **5.44**
Current Operating Performance concept **3.2**

Davy Corporation **4.50**
Debt factoring **2.83**
Deferred taxation **7.12, Ch 8, 14.36–14.37**
    accelerated capital allowances **8.21**
        accounting policy **8.33–8.35**
        advance corporation tax (ACT) **8.28**
        alternative approaches **8.3**
        balance sheet **8.30**
        capital losses **8.26**
    combined effect of timing differences **8.38**
    criteria for assessing whether liabilities or assets will or will not crystallise **8.10, 7.13**
        debit balances **8.24**
        deferral method **8.7**
        definition **8.2**
        detailed example **8.38**
    differences between original SSAP15 and revised SSAP15 **8.14, 8.18**
    disclosure in financial statements **8.29**
    flow through (on nil provision) basis **8.3**
        full provision basis **8.3**
        groups **8.31–8.32**
    illustration of presentation in accounts **8.32**
        liability method **8.6**
    methods of computation **8.6–8.9, 8.13**
    on profit on ordinary activities **8.36–8.37**
        partial provision basis **8.3**
        principles of **8.3, 8.5**
    profit and loss account **8.29**
    provisions for liabilities and charges **8.36**
    short-term timing differences **8.19–8.20, 8.27**
    SSAP15 (revised 1985) approach **8.8–8.9**
        timing differences **8.19–8.22**
        trading losses **8.25**
Degree of approximation **2.38**
Department of Trade and Industry (DTI) **1.21, 2.100, 4.51, 11.23**
Depreciable assets
    revalued downwards **8.22**
    revalued upwards **8.22**
Depreciation **1.38, Ch 4, 14.35**
    assessment of **4.7**
    definition **4.4, 4.16–4.19, 4.65–4.70**
    methods of **4.12–4.13**
    provision for **4.20–4.22**
    split **4.28–4.29, 4.50**
    standard accounting practice **4.15–4.71**
    supplementary **4.21, 4.23–4.25**
    see also SSAP12
Development
    costs **6.15**
    definition **6.1**
    expenditure **6.6–6.14**
        annual review **6.18**
        deferred **6.15–6.20, 6.26**
Dimbula Valley (Ceylon) Tea Co. Ltd v Laurie **2.93, 2.94, 2.96**
Direct material **5.8**
Disclosures **5.28–5.29, 5.38**
    accounting policies *See* SSAP2
    business combinations **12.56–12.58**
    foreign currency translations **13.46–13.47**
    principal subsidiaries, SSAP14 **10.58**
    requirements **1.38, 3.11, 4.2, 4.71**
    research and development **6.23**
    SSAP14 **10.33, 10.43**
Disposals **10.45**

429

accounting policy **10.47**
    subsidiary company **10.52–10.57**
Disproportionate significance **2.38**
Distributable profits, SSAP20 **13.38–13.47**
Dividends **7.4**
    ACT on **7.15**

Earnings per share **3.14, Ch 15**
    basis of calculating **15.7**
    definition **15.1**
    fully diluted **15.19–15.22**
    interpretation problems **15.28–15.33**
        methods of computing **15.3**
        SSAP3 requirement **15.6**
        usefulness of figures **15.23–15.27**
ED3 **12.23–12.25**
ED16 **3.26, 3.28, 3.30**
ED31 **12.32–12.37**
ED36 **3.14, 3.27, 3.28, 3.29, 3.30**
ED37 **4.33, 4.34, 4.36, 4.46, 4.59**
ED40 **2.101, Ch 5**
ED41 **6.26–6.27**
ED42 **2.76**
Equity method **2.41–2.42**
Equity share capital **15.9–15.18**
Equity shares **15.1**
Exceptional items **3.17–3.18**
Expenses **5.8**
Exposure drafts (EDs) **1.52**
Extraordinary items **1.38, Ch 3, 16.17**
    associated companies **9.34**
    presentation of **3.11–3.14**

Fair value
    ascription to separable net assets **11.12**
    definition **11.12, 14.26**
Fair value of consideration given **11.9**
Favourable and unfavourable events **2.48**
Finance Act 1984 **3.13**
Finance lease **2.43–2.45, 14.3–14.46**
    as fixed asset in lessee's books **14.43–14.46**
        definition **14.6**

    in lessor's books **14.49–14.54**
    interest payments **14.55**
    interest rate implicit in **14.29**
    minimum lease payments **14.27–14.28**
    present value of minimum lease payments **14.17**
    substance over form argument **14.38–14.40**
Financial Accounting Standards Board (FASB) **1.9**
Financial ratios **14.41**
Financial statements **1.15, 1.22, 1.39, 5.45, 5.47, Ch 16**
    cover concept **13.44**
    special **10.32**
Financial strength **5.47**
First in, first out (FIFO) **5.12, 5.17**
Fixed assets **16.21**
    cost or revaluation of **4.8–4.9**
    research and development accounting **6.21–6.22**
    revaluation and realisation of **3.26–3.34**
    subject to amortisation **11.2**
    substance over form argument **14.38–14.40**
    without amortisation **11.2**
Fixtures and fittings **16.26**
Foreign branches **13.37**
Foreign currency translations **Ch 13**
    accounting procedures **13.1**
    choice of method **13.18–13.24**
    closing rate method **13.14–13.16, 13.19, 13.36**
    disclosures **13.46–13.47**
    individual company stage **13.2–13.13**
    net investment method **13.14–13.16, 13.19, 13.36**
    temporal method **13.17, 13.21–13.24**
Foreign equity investments **13.25–13.35**
    consolidation stage **13.32–13.35**

INDEX

individual company stage 13.25–13.31
Foreign exchange gains
    arising on long-term monetary items 13.43
    arising on settled transactions 13.41
    arising on short-term monetary items 13.42
Forward contracts 13.10–13.13
Foster v *New Trinidad Lake Asphalte Co. Ltd* 2.92
Franked investment income 7.5
    tax credit on 7.15
Freehold land 4.56–4.60
Freehold properties 4.64
Fundamental errors 3.20, 3.21

Gain on sale of shares 10.49
Going concern 2.78
Goodwill 10.51
    accounting Ch 11
    definition 11.6, 11.8
    different names for 11.36
    measurement of 11.8
    negative 9.41–9.43, 11.28–11.31
    purchased 11.13–11.24, 11.32–11.37
    purchased positive 9.40
Goodwill write-off
    creating negative reserve by 11.33
    to reserves 11.37
    use of share premium account for 11.34
Government grants App 1
Group
    changes in composition 10.36
    definition 10.3
    investment accounting Ch 10

Hedging 2.61
Hire purchase 14.56
Holding company 12.2–12.3, 12.10–12.12
    definition 10.3
    profitability 12.16

SSAP14 10.1
SSAP23 12.59–12.60

IAS11 5.30, 5.36
Immediate write-off 11.16–11.24
Income measurement 1.38
Inflation 4.25
Intangible assets 16.22
Investment accounting 2.41–2.42, Ch 9, Ch 10, Ch 11, Ch 12, Ch 13, 16.27
    absence of consolidated accounts 9.62–9.63
    accounting policies 9.45
    associated companies 9.11, 9.28–9.43, 9.49–9.61
    balance sheet 9.2, 9.4, 9.6, 9.30, 9.36–9.39
    circumstances under which each method is appropriate 9.10–9.17
    consolidated accounts 9.31–9.43
    consolidation methods 9.8–9.9
    cost method 9.2–9.3
    coterminous dates 9.45
    deficiency of assets in associated company 9.44
    effective date of acquisition or disposal 9.51
    equity method 9.6–9.7, 9.53–9.61, 9.64–9.66
    group accounts Ch 10
    individual company 9.29–9.30
    joint ventures 9.20
    long-term requirement 9.22–9.23
    methods of recognising investments 9.1
    minority interests 9.48
    profit and loss account 9.3, 9.5, 9.6, 9.29, 9.31–9.35
    restrictions on distributions 9.47
    'significant' influence factor 9.25–9.27
    size of holding 9.24
    subsidiary company 9.13–9.15
    trade investment 9.11
    unrealised profits 9.46
    valuation method 9.4–9.5
Investment income, franked 7.5

431

Investment properties 4.63, 4.72–4.76

Joint ventures, investment accounting 9.20

Labour 5.8
Land and buildings 16.23
Last in, first out 5.13–5.15
Leasehold properties 4.64
Leases Ch 14
Leesee, books of 2.43–2.45
Lessee's accounts 2.43–2.45
Liabilities 2.83
Lloyd Cheyham & Co. Ltd v *Littlejohn & Co.* 1.18, 1.32
Long-term contracts Ch 5
    SSAP9 5.31–5.33
Loss-making contracts 5.37, 5.38
Loss-making subsidiaries 10.60
Losses 2.38, 2.60, 5.37
Low profits 2.38

Material additions 10.48
Materiality
    as relative factor 2.38
    concept of 2.31–2.38
MEPC plc 4.64
Mergers 12.9–12.16
    relief conditions 12.29–12.31, 12.51–12.54
    relief provisions exploitation 12.67
    SSAP23 12.17–12.67
Minority (outside) interests 10.59
Modified accounts 1.21
Movement of funds, adjustments for items not involving 16.18

Net realisable value 5.22–5.27
Non-adjusting events 2.47, 2.53, 2.56, 2.58, 2.59, 2.60
Non-coterminous dates 10.35
Non-depreciable assets 2.107
    revalued downwards 8.22
    revalued upwards 8.22

Non-subsidiary dependent companies 2.78

Objectivity 1.24
Off-balance sheet finance 2.71–2.89, 14.42
Offset 2.38
Operating lease 14.30
    actuarial method 14.35
    in lessee's books 14.47–14.48
    in lessor's books 14.61
    sum of digits method 14.35
Organisation for Economic Co-operation and Development (OECD) 6.1
Overheads 5.7, 5.8
    allocation of 5.9

Penalties 5.36
Pension costs App 3
Percentage completion method 5.30
Planning sub-committee 1.49
Plant and machinery 16.26
Post balance sheet events, *See* SSAP17
Preference dividends 15.4–15.5
Prior year adjustments Ch 3, 3.19–3.23
Probable future economic benefits 2.83
Probable future sacrifices 2.83
Production overheads 5.7, 5.8
Profit 2.75
    concept of 3.1–3.10
Profit and loss account 3.2, 3.3, 3.11, 3.16, 3.23, 3.28, 3.29, 4.21, 4.36, 4.43, 4.48, 4.76, 5.39, 7.16, 11.37, 12.16, 12.20–12.22, 13.7, 14.34, 14.50, 15.2, 16.15
    deferred taxation 8.29
    immediate write-off to 11.3
    investment accounting 9.3, 9.5, 9.6, 9.29, 9.31–9.35
Profit before tax 16.16
Profits available for distribution 2.91–2.110
Property assets 4.61–4.64
Provisions, disclosure of 5.37
Prudence 2.47, 2.78, 2.108, 13.7

INDEX

Public sector **1.39, 1.64**

Realised loss **2.106**
Realised profits **2.108, 2.109**
Reorganisations **3.24**
Replacement cost **5.18–5.19**
Research
    applied **6.1, 6.3–6.5**
    definition **6.1**
    pure **6.1, 6.3–6.5**
Research and development
    accounting **Ch 6**
    annual review **6.26**
    comments on **6.27**
    disclosures **6.23**
    exclusions **6.26**
    fixed assets **6.21–6.22**
    see also ED41; SSAP13
Reserve movements **3.32–3.34**
Reserves **10.50**
    carry-forward as deduction from **11.5**
    goodwill write-off to **11.37**
    immediate write-off to **11.4**
Residual value **4.10, 4.19, 4.20**
Restrictions on distributions **10.63–10.64**
Retained profits **3.23, 10.50**
Return on capital employed (ROCE) **12.8, 14.41**
Revaluation, commentary on **4.48–4.53**
Revaluation deficits **2.105, 2.106, 2.107**
Revaluation of assets **8.22**
Revaluation reserves, write-off against **11.32**
Revaluations **4.43–4.55**
    in historical cost accounts **4.26–4.27**
    not incorporated in accounts **8.23**
Revalued assets, disposals of **4.54–4.55**

Sale and repurchase **2.78, 2.86**
Sears Holdings **4.55**

Separable net assets **11.10**
Share premium account **11.34, 16.29**
Shearer v *Bercain Ltd* **1.21, 12.26**
Size test **12.16**
Small companies **1.71**
Solvent subsidiaries **10.60**
Special purpose transactions **2.76**
SSAP1 **1.38, 9.18–9.19**
SSAP2 **1.12, 1.18, 1.19, 1.38, 2.1–2.45**
SSAP3 **1.71, Ch 15**
SSAP6 **1.20, 1.38, 3.4, 3.10, 3.11, 3.17, 3.21, 3.27, 3.31, 4.31, 4.33**
SSAP6 (revised) **3.10, 3.11, 3.14**
SSAP7 **2.90**
SSAP8 **Ch 7**
SSAP9 **1.20, Ch 5**
SSAP10 **Ch 16**
SSAP12 **1.20, 1.38, 3.21, Ch 4, 4.74**
    reasons for revision **4.14**
SSAP12 (revised), commentary on **4.61–4.64**
SSAP13 **1.21, 3.17, 6.1–6.25, 15.33**
SSAP14 **Ch 10**
    accounting adjustments **10.33**
    comment on requirement **10.51–10.62**
    disclosure of principal subsidiaries **10.58**
    disclosures **10.33, 10.43**
    disclosures under **10.24**
    restrictions on distributions **10.63–10.64**
SSAP15 **1.71, Ch 8, 15.33**
    comparison with revised SSAP15 **8.14–8.18**
    see also Deferred taxation
SSAP16 **1.70, 2.90**
SSAP17 **2.46–2.62**
SSAP18 **1.18, 2.63–2.70, 8.9**
SSAP19 **4.63, 4.64, 4.72, 4.73, 4.74, 4.75**
SSAP20 **Ch 13, 15.33**
    distributable profits **13.38–13.47**
SSAP21 **1.38, 14.6**
SSAP22 **1.21, Ch 11, 15.33**
SSAP23 **12.17–12.67, 15.33**

433

SSAPs
    drafting and consultation   1.55
    standard-setting process   1.47–1.62
    see also Accounting standards
Standard cost   5.20
Standard-setting process   1.40–1.69
Statements of Intent (SOI)   1.35, 1.52, 1.68, 12.38
Statements of recommended practice (SORPs)   1.39, 1.45, 1.63–1.67, 1.68, 4.13
    franked   1.67
    need for and status of   1.63
    prepared by ASC   1.66
Statements of source and application of funds   Ch 16
Statements of standard accounting practice, *See* SSAP
Stocks   Ch 5
Subsidiary company   12.2–12.3
    definition   10.3, 10.4
    disposals   10.52–10.57
    excluded from consolidation   10.10–10.23
Substance over form   2.39–2.45

Tangible assets   16.23
Tate & Lyle   5.17
Tax avoidance   2.85
Tax calculation   3.12–3.13
Tax credit on franked investment income   7.15
Tax on sale of shares   10.46

Taxation   Ch 7
    detailed example   7.20
    see also Deferred taxation
Taxation charge   15.2
Technical Release (TR 603)   2.78
Technically insolvent subsidiaries   10.61
Terminated activities   3.24–3.25
Thorn EMI   11.35
Trading losses, deferred taxation   8.25
Transfer of risks and rewards   14.15
True and correct formula   2.77
True and fair view requirement   1.2, 1.22, 1.37, 2.75, 2.100
Trusthouse Forte plc   4.70
20 per cent rule   12.65

Unfranked income and payments   7.18–7.19
Unit cost   5.10
Unit-of-measure   2.29
Useful life   4.11, 4.18, 4.69

Value added tax   App 2
Vendor placing   12.62
Vendor rights   12.63

Watts Report   1.40
Westburn Sugar Refineries Ltd v IRC   2.94
Woolworth Holdings   4.50, 4.53
Work in progress   Ch 5
Working capital, changes in   16.14